Teachers and Teacher Education in the Post-Soviet Context of Kazakhstan

Advances in Teaching and Teacher Education

Series Editor

Yeping Li (*Texas A&M University, College Station, USA*)

International Advisory Board

Miriam Ben-Peretz (*University of Haifa, Israel*)
Cheryl J. Craig (*Texas A&M University, USA*)
Jennifer Gore (*University of Newcastle, Australia*)
Stephanie L. Knight (*Southern Methodist University, USA*)
Allen Yuk Lun Leung (*Hong Kong Baptist University, Hong Kong*)
Ian Menter (*University of Oxford, UK*)
Yolanda N. Padrón (*Texas A&M University, USA*)
Hersh C. Waxman (*Texas A&M University, USA*)

VOLUME 6

The titles published in this series are listed at *brill.com/atte*

Teachers and Teacher Education in the Post-Soviet Context of Kazakhstan

Scoping Teacher Education Reforms and Realities

Edited by

Tsediso Michael Makoelle and Kairat Kurakbayev

BRILL

LEIDEN | BOSTON

All chapters in this book have undergone peer review.

The Library of Congress Cataloging-in-Publication Data is available online at https://catalog.loc.gov

Typeface for the Latin, Greek, and Cyrillic scripts: "Brill". See and download: brill.com/brill-typeface.

ISSN 2542-9574
ISBN 978-90-04-72632-1 (paperback)
ISBN 978-90-04-72633-8 (hardback)
ISBN 978-90-04-72634-5 (e-book)
DOI 10.1163/9789004726345

Copyright 2025 by Tsediso Michael Makoelle and Kairat Kurakbayev. Published by Koninklijke Brill BV, Plantijnstraat 2, 2321 JC Leiden, The Netherlands.
Koninklijke Brill BV incorporates the imprints Brill, Brill Nijhoff, Brill Schöningh, Brill Fink, Brill mentis, Brill Wageningen Academic, Vandenhoeck & Ruprecht, Böhlau and V&R unipress.
Koninklijke Brill BV reserves the right to protect this publication against unauthorized use. Requests for re-use and/or translations must be addressed to Koninklijke Brill BV via brill.com or copyright.com.
For more information: info@brill.com.

This book is printed on acid-free paper and produced in a sustainable manner.

Advance Praise for

Teachers and Teacher Education in the Post-Soviet Context of Kazakhstan: Scoping Teacher Education Reforms and Realities in Kazakhstan

"Teachers and Teacher Education in a Post-Soviet Context: A Case of Kazakhstan is a meticulously crafted and deeply insightful work that explores the transformative journey of teacher education in Kazakhstan's unique post-Soviet context. Written by a distinguished team of faculty, doctoral and master students, and postdoctoral researchers from NUGSE, along with esteemed local experts, this book offers a reflective yet critical analysis of the significant changes and ongoing reforms in Kazakhstan's educational sector since its independence in 1991.

The book comprehensively documents Kazakhstan's educational reforms, emphasizing the internationalization of education and its profound impact on teacher education. It covers crucial areas such as curriculum reforms, teacher recruitment, training, and retention, providing a thorough overview of initiatives designed to equip teachers with 21st-century skills. The nuanced discussions on ideology, identity, and professional development illuminate the complexities and challenges in the evolving educational landscape."
– **Dr. Aida Sagintayeva, Dean, Nazarbayev University Graduate School of Education**

"Current educational transformations demand innovative approaches to initial teacher education and professional teacher development. This edited volume, with its unique perspective from the authors, provides a holistic understanding of the complexities and dynamics inherent in the current context of teacher education in Kazakhstan. The book examines critical topics, including curriculum reforms, teacher recruitment and retention, professional development, the influence of internationalization on educational practices, gender equity challenges in teacher education, and the pivotal role of teacher leadership in fostering innovation and change. The authors, with their distinct insights and recommendations, aim to enhance teacher education practices locally and globally."
– **Dr. Sharkul Taubayeva, Doctor of Educational Sciences, Professor of the Department of Pedagogy and Educational Management of Al-Farabi Kazakh National University**

Contents

Foreword IX
Daniel Muijs
Preface X
Ian Menter
List of Figures and Tables XIII
Notes on Contributors XV

Introduction 1
Tsediso Makoelle

1 Teacher Education in Soviet and Post-Soviet Times: Historical and Policy Perspectives 8
Aigerim Mynbayeva and Nazgul Anarbek

2 Teacher Recruitment, Preparation, Induction, Retention, and Attrition in Kazakhstan 55
Tsediso Michael Makoelle

3 From Global Ideas to Local Classrooms: Teachers Enacting Curriculum Reforms in Kazakhstan 67
Kairat Kurakbayev

4 Kazakhstani Novice Teachers' Understanding of Teacher Professionalism: Strong Knowledge Base, Limited Autonomy, and Grand Responsibilities 98
Gulnara Namyssova, Daniel Hernández-Torrano and Elaine Sharplin

5 Access, Equity, and Inclusion in Kazakhstani Teacher Education 122
Arman Assanbayev and Tsediso Michael Makoelle

6 Trends and Challenges in STEM Education in Kazakhstan 137
Ainur Almukhambetova

7 Teacher Professional Learning: The Role of Social Media in Promoting Professional Networks 153
Assel Sharimova and Elaine Wilson

8   Teachers and Action Research in Kazakhstan: A Collaborative Action Research Case at a Technical Vocational Education and Training Institution   173
Arman Assanbayev and Tsediso Michael Makoelle

9   Teacher Leadership in Kazakhstan   191
Tsediso Michael Makoelle

10   Gender Equity and Equality in Teacher Education   203
Tsediso Michael Makoelle

11   Running on Fumes in the Steppe: An In-Depth Exploration of Teacher Burnout in Kazakhstan   215
Dana Nygmetzhanova and Daniel Hernández-Torrano

12   Mentoring in ITE Practicum Programs in Kazakhstan   238
Lyazat Turmukhambetova

13   Navigating Transformations: Early Childhood Education and Care in Kazakhstan   270
Aiida Kulsary, Laura Ibrayeva and Daniel Hernández-Torrano

14   Exploring Opportunities and Challenges of Rural Teachers in Kazakhstan   295
Gulnara Namyssova and Mir Afzal Tajik

15   Exploring Assessment in Kazakhstani Pre-Service Teacher Education: Insights and Experiences   314
Zhadyra Makhmetova

16   Teachers and Teaching during the Times of Crisis: Reflections of the COVID-19 Pandemic   338
Tsediso Makoelle

Conclusion: Teacher Education in Kazakhstan—Past, Present and Future   350
Tsediso Michael Makoelle and Kairat Kurakbayev

Index   361

Foreword

Research in education has shown that the quality of an education system cannot exceed the quality of its teachers. Teaching quality is the strongest predictor of student learning, other than the student's background, prior attainment, and motivation. The difference between being taught by a strong or weak teacher can be considerable, in some studies estimated at up to six months of learning, and the impact of teachers is particularly great on students from the least advantaged backgrounds (Muijs & Reynolds, 2017).

But of course, teachers are only as good as the education they themselves receive. Teachers are made, not born; in the first instance, they are made in our teacher training and education institutions. The quality of education is, therefore, key to improving the quality of education as a whole, and it is not surprising that many countries have chosen to reform teacher education to improve its quality and relevance. There is, however, in some cases, a certain inertia that stops policymakers from grabbing the bull by the horns, and it frequently takes an external shock to push policy forward.

Such a shock may result from unexpectedly poor performance in international comparative tests such as PISA (as was the case in Germany), from a perception that one is falling behind political and economic rivals (as in the case of the US), or from major political upheavals.

The latter is the case in Kazakhstan, where the dissolution of the Soviet Union and the formation of the independent Kazakh state provided the impetus for reform. This process is described in this book, in which a range of authors have come together to provide a critical perspective on post-Soviet reforms in teacher education, going right up to the impact of that other great upheaval of recent times, the COVID pandemic. As such, this work provides us with a fascinating and insightful overview of educational change in Kazakhstan and a lens through which we can interrogate reform to teacher education more generally and thus contribute to a higher quality of education for all.

Daniel Muijs
Professor of Education and Head of the School of Social Sciences, Education and Social Work, Queen's University Belfast

Reference

Muijs, D., & Reynolds, D. (2017). *Effective teaching: Evidence and practice.* Sage Publications.

Preface

There can be little argument with the proposition that in every nation the condition of the profession of teaching and the approach taken to teacher education are clear indicators of the social and cultural features of the country. As I have argued elsewhere (Menter, 2023), from an anthropological perspective, the dominant values within a society may be teased out and identified through a close examination of the ways in which teaching and teacher education are defined. Furthermore, increasingly in the late twentieth and early twenty-first centuries, all around the world, we have seen how politicians and policymakers have paid more careful attention to education and the quality of schools. This has led directly to a more intense focus on matters such as the preparation and ongoing support of teachers, the recruitment and supply of well-qualified education professionals and the creation of systems for the improvement of the quality of teaching.

We may observe all of these change processes most dramatically in societies that are in a period of transition, whether political, economic, cultural or social. The transitions that have characterised the fifteen nations that were re-established following the demise of the Soviet Union from the last decade of the twentieth century onwards offer a particular case in point. While all fifteen may have shared the experience of a reduction in direct control from Moscow and the Russian heartland of the USSR, each country has developed its own set of geopolitical relationships. These include new relationships with Russia itself, with the other post-Soviet nations, as well as with other nations around the world, including major power blocs such as China, the USA and the European Union.

An overview of the changes across the post-Soviet space shows a number of common themes, such as democratisation, decentralisation and diversification (Isaacs & Polesi, 2016). However, each of these terms has many distinctive connotations that are particular to each nation. For example, the nature of 'democratisation' may be experienced very differently between the Baltic States in the west of the region compared to the central Asian states further east. We may see that the term 'decentralisation' may be applied to both the new relationship with Moscow and Russia and the internal distribution of power and decision-making within each nation. Furthermore, we cannot necessarily see the twenty-first-century dispositions of the nation as being 'settlements', as continuing conflicts continue to cause destruction and disruption in some parts of the region, including Ukraine.

However, in relation to the central focus of the present book, all of these matters do have particular implications for teaching and teacher education. There is a great need for systematic analyses of the processes of reform and development that have been associated with these wider changes. Indeed it was an interest in developments across all fifteen nations that led to the creation of a collection of case studies across the whole post-Soviet space, with a comparative or transversal review of what has been happening (Menter, 2025). However, such a comprehensive collection can only offer a 'snapshot' of what has happened in each country. We need a much more detailed analysis of teaching and teacher education in each nation to gain a deep understanding of each context. This is where the present volume offers a superb model of the kind of study that is required and could be undertaken in all of the nations – very few yet exist, at least few written in English. The creation of this book in the language of English makes the insights available to a broad readership of scholars as well as policy makers and politicians. Within each nation, it will also be crucial for investigations to be reported in the nations' home languages. But a book such as this will ensure that comparative analysis can be undertaken and the international community can benefit from the insights provided.

In order to compile this book, the editors have assembled a powerful team of experts with a wide range of methodological expertise and a broad geographical background. There are scholars with experience in many parts of the world as well as a strong contingent with roots in Kazakhstan itself, many based at Nazarbayev University. Between them, they deal with numerous important topics, for example, considering pre-service as well as in-service teacher education, the links to curriculum reform, questions of supply, recruitment and retention, as well as the impact and implications of the COVID pandemic, and several other themes. Throughout the book, reference is made to international perspectives, including those of the OECD, including drawing on the influential TALIS studies. Indeed, overall, the book provides fascinating insights into a distinctive case of 'vernacular globalisation'. That is, we can detect how Kazakhstan's historical and cultural legacies, including its time as part of the Soviet Union, are now interacting with the wider processes of globalisation that are influencing education around the world.

It is hoped that this book may inspire many who are working in teacher education in other parts of the post-Soviet space so that they might carry out similarly detailed studies of how teacher education is being reshaped in the light of the new policies and economies of these fascinating societies. Each of these countries is going through distinctive processes of rebirth and regeneration as independent nations, each with their educational priorities relating to their distinctive histories, language/s and cultures. Tsediso Michael Makoelle and Kairat Kurakbayev are congratulated, along with all of their colleagues, for creating this invaluable resource for scholars and policymakers alike, providing a detailed examination of current developments in teaching and teacher education in Kazakhstan.

Ian Menter
Emeritus Professor of Teacher Education, University of Oxford, UK

References

Isaacs, R., & Polesi, A. (Eds.). (2016). *Nation-building and identity in the post-soviet space*. Routledge.

Menter, I. (2023). Teacher education research in the twenty-first century. In I. Menter (Ed.), *The palgrave handbook of teacher education research* (pp. 3–32). Palgrave-Macmillan.

Menter, I. (Ed.). (2025). *The reform of teacher education in the post-soviet space*. Routledge.

Figures and Tables

Figures

1.1 The walls of the first madrasah (the first Kazakh higher education institution) (Kopzhasarova, 2015). 16

1.2 STEP analysis of higher pedagogical education in Soviet times. 18

1.3 Professor Sanjar Asfendiyarov, Head of Teacher Education Faculty of Kazakh State University (https://iie.kz/?p=25632&lang=ru, photo 1914). 22

1.4 Personalities of Educationalists. 23

1.5 STEP analysis of factors that influenced the development of teacher education in the era of independence. 32

1.6a Gender and age pyramid of the population of the Republic of Kazakhstan (2022, p. 64). 33

1.6b Gender and age pyramid of children (2023, p. 8). 33

1.7 Development of the system of higher pedagogical education (2 periods and 6 stages). 40

2.1 Conceptual framework for teacher recruitment, preparation, induction, retention, and attrition. 62

4.1 Kazakhstani novice teachers' conceptualization of teacher professionalism and factors which affect the formation of such conceptualization. 115

5.1 Pre-service and in-service teachers agency. 125

5.2 Teacher education and inclusion framework. 131

8.1 Collaborative action research cycle. 179

9.1 Components of school leadership. 193

9.2 Conceptual framework for teacher leadership. 195

10.1 Gender policy and practice framework (Lamptey et al., 2015). 207

11.1 The conceptualization of teacher burnout, its causes, and consequences. 220

11.2 The path analysis of hypothesized causes and consequences of teacher burnout. 229

13.1 Evolution of preschool enrollees and preschool institutions in Kazakhstan (1911–2021). 274

15.1 Flowchart of the basic procedures implementing the exploratory sequential mixed methods design in this study (after Creswell & Plano Clark, 2018, p. 88). 321

16.1 Five cardinal pillars for sustainable teaching and learning (Adapted from Makoelle & Burmistrova, 2023). 340

Tables

1.1 Comparison of the periodization of the development of teacher education by Kazakhstani researchers.   14

1.2 Pedagogical institutes and student population (Khrapchenkov, 1998).   29

1.3 Combination of learning theories of local and foreign (Western) traditions (Mynbayeva, 2021, p. 247).   38

1.4 The trends in the development of higher pedagogical education.   41

1.5 Trends in the development of teacher education based on state programs, concepts for the development of education and science (1999–2029).   44

3.1 State Programs for Education Development in Kazakhstan in 2000–2025.   71

3.2 Factors Perceived to Constrain Curriculum Implementation.   81

3.3 Teacher autonomy and curricular change.   86

4.1 Demographic information about the participants.   105

9.1 Cultural dimensions for teacher leadership (Adapted from Cansoy & Parlar, 2017).   197

11.1 Demographic characteristics of participants.   222

11.2 Reliability and confirmatory factor analysis fit measures for the models tested.   223

11.3 Descriptive, reliability, and correlation coefficients for the key variables.   225

11.4 Distribution of teacher burnout across the diagnosis categories.   226

11.5 Group comparisons on teacher burnout scores across socio-demographic variables.   227

11.6 Group comparisons on teacher burnout scores across socio-demographic variables.   228

12.1 Phases of implementation framework for maximising the potential of mentoring (Ambrosetti et al., 2014).   244

14.1 Summary of participants.   301

15.1 Joint display of qualitative phase 1 and quantitative phase 3 findings on Kazakhstani primary pre-service teachers' experiences of assessment.   323

15.2 Joint display of qualitative phase 1 and quantitative phase 3 findings on Kazakhstani primary pre-service teachers' understanding of assessment.   326

15.3 Dominant trends in Kazakhstani primary pre-service teachers understanding of assessment identified from joint themes.   329

Notes on Contributors

Dr. Ainur Almukhambetova, PhD

is an associate professor at Kazakh National Women's Teacher Training University. Much of her research concerns understanding equity issues in STEM higher education. She also researches students' experiences in higher education, critical transitions, and international student mobility. Dr. Almukhambetova has published 20 papers in international peer-reviewed journals and edited volumes.

Dr. Nazgul Anarbek

Candidate of Pedagogical Sciences, Associate Professor. Her research is related to comparative education, pedagogy of higher education, forecasting educational systems, spiritual values, pedagogical conflict management, etc. She actively participates in scientific research, including about ten major scientific projects funded by the Ministry of Education of Kazakhstan. She is the author of more than 150 publications, including textbooks such as "Comparative Education", "Pedagogy of Communication", "Penitentiary Pedagogy", etc.

Dr. Arman Asssanbayev, PhD

is a PhD in Education from the Graduate School of Education at Nazarbayev University, Astana, Kazakhstan. His expertise and research focus on inclusive, special education, and Action Research Design. He is a recipient of the scholarship of the Eurasian Research Institute named after "Akhmet Yassawi", Almaty, Kazakhstan. He is an alumnus of the Anniversary Inclusive Education Fellowship Program on Inclusive Education Americans with Disabilities Act (ADA) under the Department of State, USA scholarship, 2017. As an agent of change, he translated the experience gained from the Lionsgate Academy and the University of Minnesota into the Kazakhstani TVET education system. Arman is also a volunteer promoting accessible education to high school children with disabilities, children from orphan houses and low socio-economic backgrounds. He was awarded as a volunteer in 2020 at an international competition announced by the President of Kazakhstan, K. Tokayev.

Dr. Laura Ibrayeva, PhD

is a post-doctoral research fellow at the Central Asian Research Centre for Educational Innovation and Transformation (CARCEIT), Nazarbayev University Graduate School of Education (NUGSE). She holds a PhD in Education, NUGSE, in partnership with Cambridge University, UK. She is a Bolashak scholar and completed a one-year research internship at the University of Reading, UK.

She is involved in a CARCEIT International Collaborative Education Project on the impact of positive early childhood education and care on the health and well-being of young children in Kazakhstan.

Aiida Kulsary, MSc

is a dedicated researcher and educator. She holds a Master of Arts in Multilingual Education from Nazarbayev University and a Bachelor of Arts in Translation Studies from Suleyman Demirel University. Starting as an English language teacher, she developed curriculum design and exam preparation expertise. Her commitment to quality education led her to become the CIS international accreditation coordinator at the No. 54 school lyceum, where she played a crucial role in improving academic offerings. Driven by her passion for research, Aiida joined Nazarbayev University as a Research Assistant at the Central Asian Research Centre for Educational Innovation and Transformation (CARCEIT), contributing to a project focusing on well-being and early childhood education and care.

Dr. Kairat Kurakbayev

is an assistant professor at Nazarbayev University Graduate School of Education. Kairat holds PhD in Comparative and International Education from Columbia University Graduate School of Arts and Sciences. Kairat's research interests focus on comparative education, transnational policy transfer and internationalization of curriculum. Before joining the Graduate School of Education, Dr. Kurakbayev served as an Acting Director of the Department for Strategic Planning and Deputy Director of the Department for International Cooperation at Gumilyov Eurasian National University. His professional experience includes working as an English school teacher and a teacher educator in the initial teacher education programs. Kairat was a co-principal investigator of the International Project "Development of Secondary Education Curriculum of Kazakhstan in the Context of Contemporary Reforms" in collaboration with the University of Cambridge Faculty of Education. Kairat's extensive experience includes visiting scholar positions at the University of Cambridge Faculty of Education and Seton Hall University College of Education and Human Services.

Prof. Tsediso Michael Makoelle

is a full professor at Nazarbayev University Graduate School of Education. He is a distinguished scholar, having been awarded the prestigious Nelson Mandela Scholarship to the United Kingdom (UK). He holds the degrees of Doctor of Philosophy (PhD) in Inclusive Education from the University of

Manchester, UK, and a Doctor of Education (D Ed) in Education Management and Leadership from the University of South Africa (UNISA).

Prof Makoelle's teaching and research experience spans over 30 years, with the focus being on secondary and higher education. At the beginning of his career, Prof. Makoelle started his pedagogical work as a high school teacher and then head of department, vice principal and principal in several secondary schools in the Education Department of the Republic of South Africa. He has notably worked as lecturer, Senior Lecturer and Centre Coordinator at the Cape Peninsula University of Technology, Cape Town, the University of Johannesburg and the University of Free State, South Africa.

Prof Makoelle started working at Nazarbayev University over nine years ago as an associate professor, then Director of Doctoral Studies, General Director for Research, and lately Vice Dean for Research at the Graduate School of Education. He is a visiting fellow at the International Laboratory of the Social Integration Research of National Research University Higher School of Economics, Moscow, Russia.

He has written and published extensively on inclusive education, educational leadership, management, governance, and administration for national and international audiences and readership. Prof Makoelle has supervised many Master's and PhD students. He is a member of several international research bodies. He reviews grants and funding applications for the South African National Research Foundation (NRF), reviewed papers for several international Scopus and Web of Science journals and evaluated research theses for several universities in South Africa and abroad. He has also reviewed postgraduate courses and programmes for many universities and served on several international journals' editorial boards. He has collaborated with universities from Russia, the US, the UK, Europe, and Africa. He is passionate about educational leadership and inclusive education with research interests in school leadership, school effectiveness and improvement and inclusive pedagogy in countries of the South and beyond. He has devoted his research work to the framework of Participatory Action Research, which is informed by notions of critical, reflective practitioner, and transformative epistemologies.

Dr. Zhadyra Makhmetova, PhD
is a postdoctoral research fellow working on the "Strengthening Regional Universities in Kazakhstan" project at CARCEIT, Nazarbayev University. Before her post-doctorate, she was the Head of the Academic Quality Enhancement team at Aktobe Regional University. Her PhD dissertation was on Kazakhstani primary pre-service teachers' understanding of assessment. During her PhD at Nazarbayev University, she worked as Research Assistant on several different

projects, including the collaborative research project of the Graduate School of Education of Nazarbayev University, Cambridge University, and Nazarbayev Intellectual Schools on "The Reform of Key Elements of Schools in Kazakhstan – Curriculum, Assessment, and Pedagogy," and other projects as "Gender and Schooling in Kazakhstan," "Equitable access to education in the period of COVID-19 in Kazakhstan: experience, results, challenges, and opportunities." Her research interests include teacher education, initial assessment education, education policy, mixed-methods research methodologies, and studies in Central Asian and post-Soviet contexts.

Prof. Aigerim Mynbayeva
Doctor of Pedagogical Sciences, Professor. Coordinator of the PhD program "Pedagogy and Psychology" at Al-Farabi Kazakh National University. Her research is related to the pedagogy of higher education, the digitalisation of education, the history of education, comparative education, etc. She led and implemented more than 15 scientific projects of the Ministry of Education of Kazakhstan and international foundations. Author of more than 300 publications, including manuals "Fundamentals of Higher Education Pedagogy", "Fundamentals of Scientific and Pedagogical Research", "Fundamentals of Pedagogical Teaching", etc.

Dr. Gulnara Namyssova, PhD
received her undergraduate degree in English as a Foreign Language at the Kazakh University of International Relations and World Languages (Almaty, Kazakhstan) in 2004. After getting awarded the prestigious Bolashak scholarship, she continued her studies at the Peabody College of Vanderbilt University (Nashville, Tennessee, United States) and obtained her Master of Education degree in International Education Policy and Management in 2008. She joined the Graduate School of Education of Nazarbayev University (Astana, Kazakhstan) for her doctoral studies in 2017 and completed her doctoral studies in 2021. She is currently a postdoctoral researcher at the Graduate School of Education of Nazarbayev University (Astana, Kazakhstan). Her research interests include teacher professionalism, initial teacher education, STEM education, and blended learning. She has authored over ten papers on these topics in reputable conferences and journals.

Dana Nygmetzhanova, MSc
is an educator at BINOM SCHOOL, named after Y. Altynsarin in Astana, Kazakhstan. She holds a degree in Educational Leadership: School Education from Nazarbayev University. Her academic pursuits have explored various

topics, including the efficacy of formative assessment in secondary education and the impact of the English language on the linguistic environment among Kazakhstani youth. Presently, her research interests lie in investigating teacher burnout and workload intensification, improving assessment practices, and enhancing the quality of education in rural regions.

Prof. Elaine Sharplin, PhD
is the general director of the Center for Innovation in Learning and Teaching and a Professor at Nazarbayev University. She is a passionate educator who has worked for 40 years in secondary and higher education in Australia, South-East Asia, and Central Asia. Elaine has diverse research interests within the qualitative paradigm. Her major research and teaching fields are Teacher Education and Continuing Teacher Development, Teacher Professionalism and Standards, Research Ethics and Professional Ethics, Educational Leadership, and Rural Education. Many of these topics intersect with equity, diversity and the internationalisation of education.

Dr. Assel Sharimova, PhD
is a postdoctoral scholar at Nazarbayev University Graduate School of Education. She obtained her teacher's qualification from Kazakh Humanities and Law University in Kazakhstan, an MA in Educational Leadership and Management from the University of Nottingham (UK) and a PhD in Education from the University of Cambridge (UK). Her doctoral research focused on informal learning in virtual professional communities of teachers in Kazakhstan. Before her doctoral study, she worked at the Center of Excellence under the auspices of AEO Nazarbayev Intellectual Schools. Her research interests focus on teachers' professional learning.

Dr. Mir Afzal Tajik, PhD
is an associate professor and director of the Doctoral Program at the Nazarbayev University Graduate School of Education (NUGSE) in Astana, Kazakhstan. He obtained his PhD from the Ontario Institute for Studies in Education, University of Toronto, Canada and his Master of Education from the Aga Khan University Institute for Educational Development (AKU-IED) in Karachi, Pakistan. Before joining NUGSE in September 2016, Dr Tajik worked as an Associate Professor and held leadership positions, including Interim Dean, Associate Dean, Head of Graduate Programs, and Director of Outreach Centres and education development programs at AKU-IED. He has also led AKU-IED's capacity-building programs in Afghanistan and Tajikistan.

Dr Tajik brings over 35 years of experience in school and higher education. His teaching and research interests include educational leadership and management, school improvement, English-medium instruction (EMI), teacher education, qualitative research, and community-based education. He has co-edited two books and published chapters and articles with well-reputed international publishers. He received the Nazarbayev University Award for Academic Integrity (The Kehinde Award, 2023) and the AKU's Award for Sustained Excellence in Scholarship of Application, 2009.

Dr. Daniel Hernández-Torrano, PhD

works as a professor in Educational Psychology at the Graduate School of Education at Nazarbayev University. Earlier in his career, he held research positions at the University College London (UK), Universidade do Minho (Portugal), and the University of Connecticut (USA). He teaches graduate courses in quantitative research methodology, educational psychology, and inclusive education. His current research focuses on young populations; mental health and psychological well-being, the role of affect and emotions in learning, and the personal and contextual factors that promote excellence and equity in education contexts.

Dr. Lyazat Turmukhambetova, PhD

is a researcher with a focus on mentoring and initial teacher education (ITE) programs. In her doctoral thesis, while studying at Nazarbayev University, she explored mentoring practices within Kazakhstani ITE practicum programs, shedding light on school-university partnerships, mentoring triads and examining how the university-based advisors impact the mentoring practices and mentoring culture in the secondary schools. Along with mentoring and ITE programmes, Lyazat is interested in researching equal access to education. In 2018, she participated in the SOROS Kazakhstan research fellowship and explored ungraded schools in rural areas of Kazakhstan and their access to resource centres. In 2023 and 2024, Lyazat was selected as a UN Women UK Commission delegate due to her interest in gender equality and equal access to education.

Dr. Elaine Wilson, PhD

was an associate professor at the Faculty of Education until September 2022 and is now an Emeritus Fellow of Homerton College at the University of Cambridge. Elaine was a secondary school chemistry teacher in Bath and Cambridge and was awarded a Salters' Medal for chemistry teaching. She has also received two career awards for teaching in Higher Education: The

University of Cambridge Pilkington Teaching Prize in recognition of excellence in university teaching and a National Teaching Fellowship in recognition of excellence in teacher education leadership. Elaine led the professional EdD doctorate programme at the Faculty of Education and continues supervising international doctoral students. Her research interests are Education Reform, Teacher Education and Wellbeing, and Digital Technology.

Introduction

Tsediso Makoelle

This book gives a comprehensive account of the transformation of teacher education in the post-soviet education context. Kazakhstan, as one of the countries that became independent from the Soviet Union in 1991, has embarked on educational reforms. These reforms include, among others, the internationalisation of education, including critical reforms to the role of teachers and teacher education in general. Due to the internationalisation process, Kazakhstan embarked on curriculum reforms that would see teachers apply new approaches to teaching and learning to ensure students acquire 21st-century skills. Therefore, this book problematizes teachers' education by giving a reflective but critical account of teacher education's developments and evolution since the dissolution of the USSR. The book highlights reforms' critical role in policy, curriculum, and teacher recruitment, training and retention changes. Furthermore, hotly contested teacher educational aspects such as ideology, identity and philosophy are discussed in relation to the emerging discourse of teachers and teacher education in a post-soviet space. The notion of teacher professional development is also foregrounded. It is interesting to note that STEM teacher education is undergoing massive change, and this, together with notions of teacher leadership, teacher discipline, teacher well-being and early childhood teacher preparation, have become significant in the Kazakhstani teacher education sector.

Therefore, this book makes a valuable contribution to scientific knowledge about teacher education in the post-Soviet context, Central Asia, and internationally. It will also contribute to policy and practice regarding teacher education and thus be a valuable resource for teacher educators, policymakers, teacher education scholars, and students in the discipline.

This book is an exciting read for universities, departments, colleges, and schools of education and teacher education. It is, therefore, a valuable resource for teacher educators, policymakers, teacher educators, and students in the discipline of teacher education.

1 Executive Summary

1.1 *Chapter 1: Teacher Education in Soviet and Pot-Soviet Times: Historical and Policy Perspectives*

This chapter provides an overview of the development of teacher education during the Soviet and post-soviet periods. As a result of changes in educational

© TSEDISO MAKOELLE, 2025 | DOI:10.1163/9789004726345_001

approach and changes in post-soviet countries, a detailed analysis of the transitional process from Soviet to post-soviet is important. According to Yakavets (2014), although there have been efforts to transform the education of Kazakhstan, it still bears the hallmarks of soviet education. This chapter analysis the developments in relation to teacher education policies, principles, values and practices. The chapter draws some lessons from the transition period and identifies some challenges and opportunities in the changing and transforming teacher education. Recommendations regarding the way forward are presented.

1.2   *Chapter 2: Teacher Recruitment, Preparation, Induction, Retention, and Attrition in Kazakhstan*

The recruitment, pre-service/in-service training, and retention of teachers have become important topics in most countries. According to the OECD Teaching and Learning International Survey (TALIS) (2018), teaching was the first career choice for 75% of teachers in Kazakhstan compared to 67% in OECD countries. The conditions of service for teachers, as well as workload, are issues that are debated in the field of teacher education. According to the OECD (2018), there are still inequalities with regard to teacher distribution in urban and rural schools. Furthermore, although efforts have been made to retain teachers in rural schools, the incentives provided do not seem attractive enough to entice the most qualified teachers. This chapter analyses the process of teacher recruitment, training, and teacher retention in Kazakhstan. The challenges and threats of these processes are highlighted. This chapter provides recommendations regarding how those processes (if necessary) could be enhanced.

1.3   *Chapter 3: From Global Ideas to Local Classrooms: Teachers Enacting Curriculum Reforms in Kazakshtan*

The role of teachers in curriculum development, design and delivery has changed over time. Teachers' involvement in these processes has increased significantly internationally. As a result of the internationalisation of Kazakhstani education, Kazakhstan's government embarked on secondary education curriculum reforms that have seen the established Nazarbayev Intellectual Schools (NIS) as incubators of the modern curriculum reforms. This chapter gives a comprehensive account of the changing curriculum role of teachers and the impact of curriculum reforms on teachers and their teaching practices.

1.4   *Chapter 4: Kazakhstani Novice Teachers' Understanding of Teacher Professionalism: Strong Knowledge Base, Limited Autonomy, and Grand Responsibilities*

Teacher status, identity and professionalism have become a bone of contention for many countries as they attempt to improve and professionalize teaching as

INTRODUCTION

a career. There is a belief that the teaching profession is not recognized as it should be and is riddled with many challenges. Kazakhstan is experiencing many challenges regarding teachers' status, identity and professional role. According to the OECD (2018), Kazakhstan introduced professional standards for teachers in 2017. Therefore, this chapter provides a detailed but critical discussion about the current status of teachers and how teachers transitioned from soviet to soviet in terms of professional identity and professionalism.

1.5   Chapter 5: Access, Equity and Inclusion in Kazakhstani Teacher Education

Many countries' implementation of inclusive education was inspired by the adoption of the Salamanca Statement in 1994. As a result, the role of teachers in ensuring access, equity and inclusion in school has become central and expectations for teachers to be ready for inclusive teaching are high (Makoelle & Burmistrova, 2021). In Kazakhstan, inclusive education was adopted by the Ministry of Education and Science through State Programs (2011–2019; 2016–2020; 2022–2025). This process aimed to make 70% of schools inclusive by 2020 and 100% by 2025. This chapter reviews the impact and role of teachers since the dawn of inclusive education in Kazakhstan.

1.6   Chapter 6: Trends and Challenges in STEM Education in Kazakhstan

Teaching STEM subjects has become a focus of teacher education in many countries. STEM subjects require a particular set of teaching and learning facilitation skills from the teachers. According to Japashov et al. (2022), there is an increased enrollment of students in STEM subjects in Kazakhstan. This chapter discusses the current status of STEM teaching in Kazakhstan and the preparation of STEM teachers; the chapter, therefore, highlights some successes and challenges of STEM education in the post-soviet context of Kazakhstan.

1.7   Chapter 7: Teacher Professional Learning: The Role of Social Media in Promoting Professional Networks

Due to the modern technological and pedagogical changes in education, it has become important for education departments to embark on the professional development of teachers. The Kazakhstan 2011–2020 education strategy aimed at developing a professional teacher development system in Kazakhstan. As a result, the Centre of Excellence (CoE) program was established under the Autonomous Education Organisation (AEO) 'Nazarbayev Intellectual Schools' (NIS) in partnership with the University of Cambridge to professionally the learning and expertise of teachers in the public school system. On the other hand, Kazakhstan ensures the professional development of teachers through the teacher professional development agency ORLEU. This chapter comprehensively reviews current teacher professional development processes in Kazakhstan. The chapter gives an account of the role of action research in the development of teachers.

1.8 Chapter 8: Teachers and Action Research in Kazakhstan: A Collaborative Action Research Case at a Technical Vocational Education and Training Institution

Castro Garcés and Martínez (2016) postulate that action research ensures that teachers work collaboratively to explore how to improve their teaching. However, Nagibova (2019) posit that in Kazakhstan, teachers are not yet well-vested in action research and thus still need guidance from experienced teachers. As a result, action research becomes one of the critical tools for pre-service and in-service teacher professional development. In partnership with the University of Cambridge, the Autonomous Education Organisation (AEO) 'Nazarbayev Intellectual Schools (NIS) have developed teachers' collaborative action research skills. This chapter, therefore, analyses the role of action research as a tool for teacher development within the Kazakhstani context. Teachers in Kazakhstani education are becoming more involved in decision-making about curriculum and education matters.

1.9 Chapter 9: Teacher Leadership in Kazakhstan

The curriculum reforms in Kazakhstan have seen an increase in the involvement of teachers in many education and school-related processes. However, teachers are still subjected to too much administrative and managerialism from the Ministry of Education, and as a result, they play less role in decision-making. According to Kanayeva (2019), confirmed by Qanay et al. (2021), to improve schools' teachers need to lead learning and innovation within and outside their schools. This chapter analyses the role of teachers as leaders in a Kazakhstani schooling context, how teachers conceptualize and enact teacher leadership, as well as the challenges they experience in this regard. Some lessons are drawn from the review on enhancing teacher leadership in Kazakhstan.

1.10 Chapter 10: Gender Equity and Equality in Teacher Education

Gender equity has become a hotly debated topic in teacher education globally. In Kazakhstan, the proportionate number of women in secondary school is significantly higher than their male counterparts, i.e. 81.3%. According to OECD (TALIS) (2018, p. 2) "In Kazakhstan, only 53% of principals are women, compared to 76% of teachers. This can be benchmarked against the OECD averages of 47% of women among school leaders and 68% among teachers". This chapter analyses the role of gender in the Kazakhstani teacher education context and highlights gender imbalances, their impact, and the mechanisms that are put in place to address them.

1.11 Chapter 11: Running on Fumes in the Steppe: An In-Depth Exploration of Teacher Burnout in Kazakhstan

Teacher well-being and job satisfaction have become important in teacher education worldwide. Teacher attrition and retention have become a severe challenge. It is also believed that the aspect of teacher well-being has taken a central stage due to children's unruly behaviour in schools. Kazakhstan has adopted the Law on Teachers Status since 2020. This will see the conditions of employment for teachers improve, including but not limited to a salary increase of up to 25% and a reduction of load from 16% to 18%. According to OECD TALIS (2018), about 91% of teachers reported that they are satisfied with their teaching job (OECD average 90%), while 51% of teachers are satisfied with the terms of their teaching contract (apart from salary). About 3% (18% in OECD countries) of Kazakhstani teachers reported experiencing severe stress at work. This chapter conceptualizes the notions of teacher well-being regarding teacher burnout within the context of Kazakhstani schooling. Some opportunities and challenges are highlighted. The chapter recommends enhancing teacher well-being.

1.12 Chapter 12: Mentoring in ITE Practicum Programs in Kazakhstan

The role of the practicum as an approach to pre-service teacher mentoring is very important. This chapter reviews the processes of pre-service teachers mentoring in schools. The role, skills and competencies of mentors and the impact of the mentoring process on pre-service teacher preparation for the teaching career. According to OECD (TALIS) (2018), 59% of novice teachers (with up to 5 years of experience) have an assigned mentor. The chapter highlights some of the challenges and makes recommendations towards the improvement of pre-service teacher mentoring in Kazakhstan.

1.13 Chapter 13: Navigating Transformations: Early Childhood Education and Care in Kazakhstan

Early childhood education is regarded as a significant level of education as it lays the foundation for further education of students in later stages. Kazakhstan has seen an increase in the number of kindergartens lately, so the preparation of teachers for early childhood education has become a priority. The participation of children 3–6 years old in early childhood education is 73% lower than 88% in OECD countries. According to the OECD (2016), while teachers are sufficiently qualified to teach in ECEC schools, the salaries are significantly lower. This chapter conceptualises early childhood education and how it is understood and implemented within the Kazakhstani schooling process. In this analysis, the policy context is provided, and early childhood education challenges are presented.

1.14 Chapter 14: Exploring Opportunities and Challenges of Rural Teachers in Kazakhstan

According to Tajik et al. (2022), there is a wide inequality gap between teachers in rural and urban schools in Kazakhstan. This is echoed by Nurbaev (2019), who contends that the gap between rural and urban schools in Kazakhstan is in equipment and material procurement, quality and quantity of the teaching staff, as well as academic achievements of students. This chapter conceptualizes rural education and analyses the inequalities in education from the perspective of teacher recruitment, teacher preparation, and teacher skills as aspects that influence the quality of education in rural schools.

1.15 Chapter 15: Exploring Assessment in Kazakhstani Pre-Service Teacher Education: Insights and Experiences

Research on Kazakhstani teacher education reveals a persistent influence of Soviet education, which emphasises control, correction, memorisation, and surface learning and lacks reflective and critical thinking skills. There is a notable gap in research on pre-service teachers' assessment skills, with no studies specifically focusing on assessment education. This chapter addresses this gap by exploring pre-service teachers' experiences of assessment and their understanding of assessment.

1.16 Chapter 16: Teachers and Teaching during the Times of Crisis: Reflections of Covid 19 Pandemic

The advent of the COVID-19 Pandemic has seen a transformation in how teachers deal with teaching and learning during this time of crisis. The introduction of technology and distance learning has impacted how well teachers go about their duties. This chapter reflects on how teachers' role was transformed due to the period of the pandemic. The chapter discusses the opportunities and challenges brought by this process and makes some recommendations about the way forward regarding teachers' skills and competencies during times of crisis.

References

Castro Garcés, A. Y., & Martínez Granada, L. (2016). The role of collaborative action research in teachers' professional development. *PROFILE Issues in Teachers' Professional Development, 18*(1), 39–54. http://dx.doi.org/10.15446/profile.v18n1.49148

Japashov, N., Naushabekov, Z., Ongarbayev, S., Postiglione, A., & Balta, N. (2022). STEM career interest of Kazakhstani middle and high school students. *Education Sciences*, *12*, 397. https://doi.org/10.3390/educsci12060397

Kanayeva, G. (2019). *Facilitating teacher leadership in Kazakhstan*. PhD Thesis. University of Cambridge.

Makoelle, T. M., & Burmistrova, V. (2021). Teacher education and inclusive education in Kazakhstan. *International Journal of Inclusive Education*. https://doi.org/10.1080/13603116.2021.1889048

Nagibova, G. (2019). Professional development: The challenges of action research implementation in Kazakhstan. *International Academy Journal Web of Scholar*, *2*(9(39)), 17–24. https://doi.org/10.31435/rsglobal_wos/30092019/6691

Nurbayev, Z. (2019). *Kazakhstan: Unequal Struggle for Equality in School*. https://cabar.asia/en/kazakhstan-unequal-struggle-for-equality-in-school

OECD. (2016). *Early Childhood Education and Care: Kazakhstan*. https://www.oecd.org/education/school/ECECDCN-Kazakhstan.pdf

OECD. (2018). *Education policy outlook: Kazakhstan*. https://www.oecd.org/education/Education-Policy-Outlook-Country-Profile-Kazakhstan-2018.pdf

OECD. (2018). *Kazakhstan – Country Note – TALIS 2018 Results*. https://www.oecd.org/countries/kazakhstan/TALIS2018_CN_KAZ.pdf

Qanay, G., Courtney, C., & Nam, A (2021): Building teacher leadership capacity in schools in Kazakhstan: a mixed method study. *International Journal of Leadership in Education*. https://doi.org/10.1080/13603124.2020.1869314

Yakavets, N. (2014). Educational reforms in Kazakhstan: First decade of independence. In D. Bridges (Eds.), *Educational reforms and internationalization: The case of school reforms in Kazakhstan* (pp 1–27).

CHAPTER 1

Teacher Education in Soviet and Post-Soviet Times
Historical and Policy Perspectives

Aigerim Mynbayeva and Nazgul Anarbek

Being a teacher is not a job but a God-given vocation. To do this, you must have a high soul, capable of giving your flame to other people, without demanding anything in return.

IBRAY ALTYNSARIN (1841–1889)

•••

A passionate teacher awakens the curiosity of his pupils, quenches their thirst for knowledge, and accustoms them to independent search and concentration.

ZHUSSUPBEK AIMAUTOV (1889–1931)

•••

Culture and education are, ultimately, human creativity, and this is their main purpose.The teacher needs creative abilities, skills in bringing the learning process closer to scientific research, involving students in active learning and increasing their scientific potential.

SHARKUL TAUBAYEVA (born in 1947)

∵

Abstract

This introductory review chapter examines the evolution of Kazakhstani teacher education, also known as higher pedagogical education, from the pre-Soviet era through the Soviet period and into the post-Soviet era, culminating in modern Kazakhstan's independence. A systematic review of literature, scholarly papers, historical artefacts, and policy documents was done to provide a comprehensive account and understanding

© AIGERIM MYNBAYEVA AND NAZGUL ANARBEK, 2025 | DOI:10.1163/9789004726345_002 of the development of teacher education in Kazakhstan. Among the lessons drawn from the review is the inherent tension between the hallmarks of Soviet education and the newly introduced Western ideals of teacher education. The two major periods are highlighted: the Soviet period and the period of independence, each of which consists of 3 stages. For each period, social, technological, economic and political factors (STEP-analyses), strengths and weaknesses, and trends are analyzed. Importantly, this chapter explores the key contributions of Kazakh educationalists and scholars who played pivotal roles in shaping pedagogy and education in Kazakhstan, offering a brief overview of their achievements and influence.

Keywords

teacher – teacher education – higher pedagogical education – pedagogy

1 Introduction

Since Kazakhstan gained national independence from the former Soviet Union, a range of reforms has been carried out in secondary and higher education, as well as in the field of professional teacher learning and professional teacher development. The history of higher pedagogical education in Kazakhstan dates back only a century. However, it played an important role in the formation and development of the country as an economically and socially stable state. In this chapter, we attempt to pursue and answer the following research questions:

- What factors have influenced the development of higher pedagogical education in Soviet and post-Soviet times, and how have they changed?
- What are the current trends, and how do domestic and foreign scholars view the history of Kazakhstani teacher education? How have they changed?
- What are the strengths (if any) and weaknesses (if any) of development and trends in improving higher teacher education?

Since the collapse of the ideological base of Soviet education, reforms of higher pedagogical education have been complex and associated with the combination of different approaches, resulting in deeper transformation with new paradigms and new pedagogical theories and teaching methodologies. There has been a transition from the traditions of classical education to a model characterized by digital learning innovations. This shift is externally reflected in the content of education and teaching approaches, while internally influencing teachers' and students' values, skills, attitudes, and beliefs.

This chapter's analysis is based on the following cardinal factors: social, technological, economic, and political influences. The analysis of these factors aims to achieve the purpose of this review, which is to provide a systematic review of the historical development of higher pedagogical education in Kazakhstan from the twentieth century to the present. This review aims to learn from Kazakhstani's past and current trends and experiences and chart the way forward regarding teacher education.

2   Method of Review

In this chapter, we adopted several review methods, namely historical-retrospective, historical-systemic, periodization, and historical and comparative analysis, content-analysis, to understand teacher education's historical and current trends. The historical-retrospective method, as an analytical method, is aimed at identifying the cause-and-effect relationships of historical events from the present to the past. According to Parfenov (2001), going back in time, the stages of pedagogical education formation are clarified, i.e. we see the development prospects of phenomena and processes in the past, knowing its current result. The historical-systemic method, according to Khrapchenkov (1998), helps to consider facts and phenomena in a complex hierarchy of socio-economic, political, educational systems, interrelationships and interdependence. The chronological method is associated with the study of historical events sequence over time. Together with periodization, chronology makes it possible to build an integral time-stadium structure (Tumak, 2016). According to Khrapchenkov (1998) and Tumak (2016), structural periodization can be represented as follows: epoch, period and stage. According to Igibayeva (2009), the issue of periodizing the history of Kazakhstan's educational system is a methodological problem. Scholars have proposed various periods with different time frames, principles, and criteria. However, they have not been able to reach a consensus on the periodization of the educational system. Therefore, in our work, having analyzed the periodization studies of Kaidarova (2007) and Nurkabekova (2010), we identified two large periods and three stages in each period. In this article, content analysis is used as an auxiliary research method that enhances other approaches. It is primarily qualitative, focusing on identifying trends in the development of pedagogical education as outlined in government documents.

The use of content analysis is based on the following steps:

a. The objective: to record and transform trends in the development of pedagogical education (the concept of document content analysis can be summarized as "study to know, to state");

b. The sampling frame for collecting primary information: legal acts of the Republic of Kazakhstan in the field of education from 1991 to 2023;

c. The unit of analysis: individual text fragments mentioning trends such as Humanization, Inclusion; Status enhancement; Openness, diversification, academic freedoms; Multilingualism; Development of the research environment; Practical training, practice orientation; allowing for the formalization and transformation of fragments into simple sentences;

d. The method of recording their appearance in the text: the presence of mentions in the content of each word of the text fragment;

e. The method of substantive interpretation: a summary table indicating the mentions of the studied trends (words, text fragments) with a "+" sign (Fedotova, 1988; Anarbek, 2014).

We consulted the following scholarly literature about the history of education and higher pedagogical education in Kazakhstan, the former-USSR countries, the CIS (to get internal views) and international scholars (to get external views), this included among others, e.g. Al-Farabi University Library, government websites, Google Scholar, Scopus database etc:

– Scientific literature by Kazakh authors, teachers and historians;
– Literature of research by foreign scholars (outside view), as well as joint works of researchers;
– State educational documents, legal acts, laws, programs and development concepts, etc.;
– Statistical data on demography and education;
– National reports and reviews of UNESCO and other organizations;
– Textbooks and manuals on the history of education in Kazakhstan, didactics, pedagogy, and others.

The review focuses on the Soviet and post-Soviet periods. In this review, we analyze how teacher education was built and the strengths and weaknesses of development; development trends are identified; and STEP and SWOT analyses of education development for both periods.

3 Teacher Education during the Soviet Up to the Period of Independence

There are many significant studies by Kazakh scholars during the Soviet period up to the period of independence, which were prepared in the Kazakh and Russian languages (not translated into English, and therefore not available to international readership). These are the fundamental works by teachers namely,

- Tazhibaev (1958) and Sembaev (1958) which are focused on the pedagogical thought and the formation of the education system in the 18th–19th century and the first half of the 20th century (both were people's commissars of education of the Kazakh SSR, i.e. ministers of education of Kazakhstan in the periods from 1939 to 1955);
- Scholars of the T.T. Tazhibayev Scientific School including Khrapchenkov (1998) and Zharikbaev (1995) in the 90s of the twentieth century;
- Studies by the historians in the 70s-90s of the twentieth century including those by Zhamanbaev (1972), Zhulamanov (1981), Meshitbaev (1973), Kozmenko (1999) and Zuyeva (2013) focusing on the early 2000s;
- Pedagogues – historians of education that include Ilyasova (1997), Igibayeva (2007); the history of women's education of Kunantaeva (2001), Sadvokasova (1969); the history of the educational policy of Nurtazina (2005);
- Studies on the history of education management and advanced training of teaching staff by Kolesnichenko (1984), Almukhanbetov (2002) and Akhmetova (2016).
- Modern studies of the periodization of the development of education in Kazakhstan (in English) are presented in the articles by Yakavets (2014), Mynbayeva and Pogosyan (2012), the transformation of Education analyzed by Kissane (2005) and Sievers (2013).

Five development stages characterize the development of higher pedagogical education and its content. According to Kaidarova (2007) these are:
- Creation of a system of teacher education (1928–1931);
- Formation of the content of higher pedagogical education in the conditions of unification of curricula (1932–1958);
- Development of the content of higher pedagogical education in conditions of qualitative transformation of schools (1959–1990);
- Reforming the content of higher pedagogical education in the conditions of independence of the Republic of Kazakhstan (1991–2001);
- Modernization of the content of higher pedagogical education (2002–2005).

Other researchers such as Nurkabekova (2010) in their article entitled *"Historical prerequisites for the modern reform of pedagogical education in Kazakhstan and China"* propose six stages of development of the content of higher pedagogical education which are identified as the:
- The beginning of the 19th century – 1917 – prerequisites for the formation of teacher education in Kazakhstan;
- The 1917 – mid-1930s – building a system of teacher education and the role of faculties of education;

- Mid-1930s – mid-1960s – intensive development of pedagogical education: teacher training colleges, technical schools, universities, postgraduate studies;
- Mid-1960s – late 1980s – Reforming the teacher education system by improving the structure, content, and teaching methods. Improving the material and technical base;
- The 1991–mid-2000s – building a system of continuous pedagogical diversification of education in the Republic of Kazakhstan;
- The mid-2000s – to the present – reforming the structure and content of teacher education based on a competency-based approach. Return to the system of specialized teacher education – separation of pedagogical universities from universities.

The Table 1.1 below shows the differences and similarities in terms of the periodization of the development of teacher education, as purported by Kaidarova (2007) and Nurkabekova (2010).

A comparative analysis of both periodization shows that the milestone years of teacher education development were the 30s and the end of the 50s, the mid-60s, the 90s of the twentieth century, and the 2000s. It is clear from the comparison that the earlier stages of periodization are associated with the formation of higher pedagogical education. The period from the '60s to the '90s of the twentieth century seemed to have been characterized by reforms and qualitative transformation of the system, and later, other reforms and modernization followed.

However, the differences between Kaidarova (2007) and Nurkabekova (2010) is that their periodization are characterized by different content focus for the development of teacher education, with the former focused on updating curricula, the dependence of changes in content on school reforms and the latter on connections with secondary specialized pedagogical education (working faculties) and postgraduate education (postgraduate studies), identifying trends in the construction of continuous pedagogical education, the use of a competency-based approach, etc

Based on the above analysis it would be important now to discuss in details the emergence of higher and teacher education in Kazakhstan.

4 Historical Emergence of Higher and Pedagogical Education Kazakhstan

It is important to note that during Soviet times, up to the era of Independence, several studies were conducted in search of appropriate models of higher educational institutions for Kazakhstan. Traditionally, research has

TABLE 1.1   Comparison of the periodization of the development of teacher education by Kazakhstani researchers

Comparison criteria	Periodization of Kaidarova (2007)		Periodization of Nurkabekova (2010)	
Periods of development	1.	Creation of a system of teacher education (1928–1931);	1.	The beginning of the 19th century–1917 – prerequisites for the formation of teacher education in Kazakhstan;
	2.	development of the content of higher pedagogical education in the conditions of unification of curricula (1932–1958);	2.	1917–mid-1930s – building a system of teacher education and the role of workers' faculties;
	3.	development of the content of higher pedagogical education in conditions of qualitative transformation of schools (1959–1990);	3.	mid-1930s–mid-1960s. – intensive development of pedagogical education: teacher training colleges, technical schools, universities, postgraduate studies;
	4.	reforming the content of higher pedagogical education in the conditions of independence of the Republic of Kazakhstan (1991–2001);	4.	mid-1960s–late 1980s. – reforming the teacher education system: improving the structure, content and methods of teaching. Improving the material and technical base;
	5.	modernization of the content of higher pedagogical education (2002–2005).	5.	1991–mid-2000s – building a system of continuous teacher education and diversification of education in the Republic of Kazakhstan;
			6.	mid-2000s–to the present – reforming the structure and content of teacher education based on a competency-based approach. Return to the system of specialized pedagogical education – separation of pedagogical universities from universities

focused on the Soviet and post-Soviet periods of pedagogical education or the broader education system. However, in studying post-Soviet reforms, we recognized the need to explore the pre-Soviet period of educational development. This stems from the fact that after Kazakhstan gained independence, reforms were geared toward developing an open system and adopting features influenced by the globalization of education (Spring, 2008). At the same time, the question arose: 'What are the national elements necessary for building our own education system?' This search for national traits, characteristics, and features led us to investigate the historical heritage of Kazakh education in the pre-Soviet era.

Since gaining independence, Kazakhstan has seen a surge in research by historians and archaeologists to uncover "blank spots," including the history of higher education in the country. In this subsection we would like to show modern research in the seeking out of prototypes of higher education in the pre-Russian and pre-Soviet periods. That is, from today (the present) we look back into the past, and then look into the future. In fact, the rooting of the history of Kazakhstani higher and pedagogical education occurs.

The period of the 1970's during the Soviet education academics such as Mashanov (1970) proposed an idea that on the territory of Otrar there was a *madrasah* as a prototype for a higher educational institution. This is a prototype where Abu Nasir al-Farabi, great philosopher received his education. He was brought to the madrasah by his grandfather after graduating from the *aul school* (mektep). The *madrasah* was composed of seven (7) large and twenty-four (24) small halls. In one large hall there was a library, in another was a meeting room, and in the rest were study rooms. The novices lived in small halls (Mashanov, 1970).

However, in the last 33 years of Independence, there has been a renaissance of Kazakh culture and language. During this period, archaeological research was intensified, and excavations of the Sauran settlement were carried out (Figure 1.1). Smagulov claims that in the ancient city, there was a madrasah – the prototype of a higher educational institution (Kopzhasarova, 2011; Kopzhasarova, 2015).

According to Kopzhasarova (2011), "...the central main street, which is up to 10 meters long, leads from the Northern Middle Gate inside the medieval city of Sauran. From it, the city street network arose. Two hundred meters from the Northern Gate, it opens onto the vast central city square of approximately 120 by 50 meters. On the left are the ruins of a *madrasah* from the early 16th century – the first university of modern Kazakhstan. On the right is the city Friday Mosque (Zhuma mosque). Regarding its parameters, this is the largest of the famous medieval mosques in Kazakhstan" (p. 3).

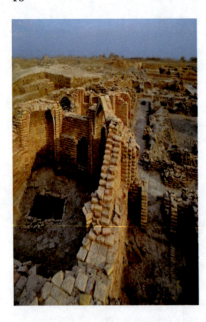

FIGURE 1.1
The walls of the first madrasah (the first Kazakh higher education institution) (Kopzhasarova, 2015)

It has now been established that the building of the *madrasah* went through two main stages: at the initial stage, there was already a *madrasah* which dates back to the 14th century, but apparently, it was built at least a century earlier. When it fell into disrepair, and a new building was opened in 1514, the old one was inhabited by all kinds of artisans. As a result, the history of the *madrasah* in Sauran falls into two distinct cultural layers with their specific content. The old *madrasah*, then the subsequent one, which Vasifi, who was present at its "opening" in 1514, wrote about.

In the uncovered *madrasah* several dozen multifunctional rooms were discovered which may represent an analogue of modern dormitories, the rooms in which students lived as explained archaeologist Smagulov (Kopzhasarova, 2015). The picture below shows the *madrasah*.

The rediscovered history of education, as well as the reinterpreted teachings of philosophers, for example, Abu Nasir Al-Farabi "On the Virtuous City", is reflected in the dissertations for students of pedagogical departments on the history of education and pedagogical theories.

The madrasahs of Otyrar and Sauran were the model prototypes of higher educational institutions in the earlier and later Middle Ages, and then teacher seminaries and institutions opened in the 19th century. At the beginning of the 20th century, the Russian Empire became the harbinger of professional pedagogical education in Kazakhstan. As is known, the system of state pedagogical education in Russia was formed only in the 1870s based on secondary educational institutions: teacher seminaries and teacher training institutions (Voitekhovskaya, 2011).

Before the revolution of 1917, there were teachers' seminaries that trained teachers for schools and colleges, for example, the Omsk Teachers' Seminary since 1872 (teachers were trained for the Akmola, Semipalatinsk and Semirechensk and other regions), the Orsk (Orenburg) teachers' school since 1883, the teachers' seminary in Semipalatinsk since 1903, teachers' seminaries in the cities of Verny, Aktyubinsk, Uralsk since 1913, teacher's institute in Tashkent since 1915. According to Sadykova (2022), the majority of seminary students were Russian Orthodox students; at the same time, among the Kazakh, Uzbek, Kyrgyz, Turkmen, and Tatar students who graduated from seminaries, Kazakh students predominated.

In teaching, emphasis was placed on religious subjects, moral and ethical instruction, labor and aesthetic education, as well as practical skills such as first aid, weather observation, and gardening (Sadykova, 2022). Kazakh historian Sadvakasova (2008), based on her study of Russian archives, notes that attempts were made to establish a university at the end of the 19th century. However, due to the national policy of the Russian Empire, the weak economic development of the Kazakh territories, and the fragmented administrative-territorial division, it was not possible to create a university before the revolution. Only after the revolution was the first university successfully established in 1928.

Based on the preceding discussions, we shall now analyze government programs, legislation, educational documents, and the scientific literature of two periods, i.e. the Soviet period and the period of independence, regarding the content of higher pedagogical education in Kazakhstan.

5 Soviet Period: From the Beginning of the Twentieth Century until 1991

5.1 Factors That Influenced on the Development of Education in the Soviet Period

Before characterizing the stages, we present a summary of factors influencing the development of higher pedagogical education in Soviet times using STEP analysis in Figure 1.2.

According to the table above the social, technological, economic and political analysis represents the following:

The social factor: the strategy for eliminating illiteracy as a result of the growth of Kazakhstan's population of Kazakhstan required the training of

Social Factor

Demographic changes influence the need to increase teacher training, change the proportion of types of schools with different languages of instruction, and the growth of female education;

-population growth of the republic, Famine, population decline during wartime, resettlement of peoples to Kazakhstan (deportations and development of virgin lands), urbanization, etc.

Technological factor

Industrialization of the country, the transition from an agricultural country (nomadic way of life) to industrial development (settled population), the development of the mining industry, agricultural industry of Kazakhstan, requires a more literate population, paying attention to the development of natural science education and the training of such teachers;
scientific and technological progress, increasing complexity of technics...
The emergence of specialized language schools (with in -depth study of the English language) and physics and mathematics schools, as well as the training of teaching staff for them

STEP-analysis (1928–1991)

Economic factor

Industrialization and collectivization of the country; planned development of the country (five-year plan); cultural revolution; Development of virgin and fallow lands, ...
Basically there was (predominated) free compulsory school and higher education.
In the 80s, 7% of GDP was allocated for education in the USSR

Political factor

Ideological foundations of education, Marxism-Leninism in teaching the humanities, the elimination of illiteracy and the cultural revolution as slogans of the Soviet Union; centralization of education management, content of teacher education...

FIGURE 1.2   STEP analysis of higher pedagogical education in Soviet times

teachers for different types of schools: primary schools, seven-year schools, commune schools, schools for peasant youth, gymnasiums, workers' faculties, technical schools, etc. The outflow of the population during the years of the famine led to changes in the number of national schools and, consequently, affected the demand for training Kazakh teachers. National Uyghur schools were also created in Kazakhstan.

The technological factor is associated with the country's industrialization; that is, it became necessary not only for a literate population in the field of natural sciences and for the training of teachers as mathematicians, physicists, and chemists but also for the training of engineers and teacher-engineers. After wartime, specialized physics, mathematics, and language schools began to be created, which also required increasing and deepening the subject training of mathematics, physics, chemistry, and English and other language teachers.

The economic factor as a driving force is aimed at the targeted allocation of financial resources and planning the gradual development of a network of higher educational institutions in the republic, the mobilization of personnel in the country, and their redeployment to and from Kazakhstan.

The political factor manifests itself through the formation of the ideal of the new Soviet man, the unity of citizens thanks to a single ideology introduced into the education system. The main translator and support in such work is the teacher. Teachers were supposed to form the "new person" – the "Soviet person".

Using these four-factor analysis framework, we now discuss the first stage the 20th century up to the year 1931.

5.2 The First Stage: The Emergence of a System of Higher Pedagogical Education

After the revolution, the state policy of the Soviet government in the field of education was followed, aimed at eliminating illiteracy in the population and providing mass professional training for the country's economic development. The industrialization of the USSR expanded the network of schools and trained teachers. In 1919, the Practical Institute of Public Education was organized in Orenburg (PIPE) and the Eastern (Tatar) Institute of Public Education (EIPE) (Zhamanbayev, 1972; Lukyanets, 1959). In 1920, several other institutes were created: Bukeev Kazakh Institute of Public Education in Urda and Semipalatinsk Institute of Public Education (based on the former seminary). Only 22 students and 11 teachers were admitted to the Bukeev Institute; 6 of them had higher education, so it was reorganized in the same year into teacher courses (Sembayeva, 1958). In 1918, the Oriental Institute was created in Tashkent (Turkestan region), and in 1920, it was transformed into a public institute that taught the Kazakh language. This educational institution was an advanced pedagogical institution and was transformed into Turkestan State University.

The Institute of Public Education in Orenburg and the Semipalatinsk Institute of Public Education were planned to become higher educational institutions. However, there were difficulties both with recruiting students and teaching staff. The first intake to the Orenburg Institute was 50 students, but by the end of the academic year, only 20 students had remained. Only one teacher had a higher education. As noted by Lukyanets (1959), the institutes of public education and enlightenment, established in the early years of Soviet rule to train teachers, did not evolve into higher educational institutions. They were reorganized into educational institutes and developed as institutions of the transitional period. Therefore, it is necessary to distinguish between *teacher* institutes and *pedagogical* institutes as institutes of pre-higher education and higher education.

A key characteristic of the 1920s was that, due to the absence of universities in Kazakhstan, Kazakhstani youth were actively sent to study at Russian universities, the Central Asian University, and other institutions. For example, in the 1923–1924 academic year, approximately 450 students from Kazakhstan were sent to universities in the Russian Soviet Federative Socialist Republic (RSFSR) and Tashkent. In the same academic year, along with those previously admitted to universities and workers' faculties, at least a thousand students studied outside Kazakhstan, of which about 100 were Kazakhs (not counting students who studied at communist universities) (Lukyanets, 1959).

In line with the organization of the *first wave of universities* after the revolution in the early 20s, the first attempt was made to create a state university in the Kazakh Republic. Since the centre of the Kazakh Autonomous Soviet Socialist Republic in the 20s was in Orenburg, in September 1921, an attempt was made to organize the Kazakh University with the faculties of biology, agriculture, economics, mining, technics, pedagogy, and social sciences. As Zhamanbaev (1972) notes:

> Universities were established without taking into account real opportunities; they did not have educational facilities, equipment, teaching staff, or sufficiently trained youth. The question of opening a university was postponed indefinitely.... Life has shown that in order to get things right, it is first necessary to expand the network of secondary schools, open preparatory courses and workers' faculties. (p. 26)

Lukyanets (1959), highlighting the challenges of establishing a university, states:

> When carrying out the preparatory work for organizing the university, the Chief Professional Education Department encountered several difficulties. In Orenburg, there was a shortage of qualified personnel needed to staff the university's main faculties. An attempt to attract scientific personnel from large cultural centres of the country did not produce the necessary results. At that time, the republic did not have the necessary contingent of Kazakh youth prepared to study at the university. There was no necessary educational and production base to organize a university in Orenburg. All these difficulties that arose during

the organization of the university confronted the republic's organizations with the need to limit themselves to opening a workers' faculty and to postpone the question of opening a university for an indefinite period. (p. 7)

Having that said, it was clear that local organizations approached this issue without taking into account the actual situation that existed in the republic. In Kazakhstan, there was not only a lack of scientific and teaching personnel and an educational and production base but, more importantly, an absence of a local youth contingent prepared for university study. Before creating an academic institution, it was necessary to strengthen and grow the network of *aul schools*, create workers' faculties and prepare the necessary conditions for the creation of a higher educational institution (Zhamanbayev, 1972, p. 7).

The second attempt to create the Kazakh University was made in 1928. According to Lukyanets (1959), the creation of the first university in Kazakhstan came at the request of republican organizations to establish the Kazakh State University in the spring of 1928 as decided by the Council of Public Commissars of the RSFSR, which instructed the Public Commissariat of Education and the State Planning Committee of the RSFSR to develop a university deployment plan and its organizational order. On June 10, 1928, the Council of Public Commissars of the Kazakh Autonomous Soviet Socialist Republic adopted a detailed resolution on the organization of the university.

"To establish in Alma-Ata," the resolution said, "a Kazakh State University consisted of faculties: a) pedagogical, b) agricultural and c) medical." From October 1, 1928, it was planned to open a pedagogical faculty of the university with the departments: a) physical and mathematical, b) natural and c) literary and linguistic, as well as a working faculty (Kiyasova, 2008). The organization of other faculties was planned to be carried out in the period 1929–1933. The Pedagogical Faculty of the Kazakh State University was opened in Almaty in October 1928 in the building of a former gymnasium, where laboratories and classrooms were equipped. Moscow, Leningrad and Kiev universities provided significant assistance in equipment and literature. Twelve scholars came from Moscow, Leningrad and Tashkent.

57 students were enrolled in the first year of the university, of which 32 were Kazakhs. 50 students were admitted to the first year of the workers' faculty and students were admitted to the preparatory department. Already in the first year of operation, the Faculty of Education showed itself to be a viable educational institution (Lukyanets, 1959, p. 10).

FIGURE 1.3 Professor Sanjar Asfendiyarov, Head of Teacher Education Faculty of Kazakh State University (https://iie.kz/?p=25632&lang=ru, photo 1914)

Sanjar Asfendiyarov (1889–1938) – a prominent statesman and public figure, historian, teacher. In 1928–1931 – director of the pedagogical department of Kazakh State University, head of the history department of University

Professor Sanzhar Dzhafarovich Asfendiyarov, (pictured in Figure 1.3) a prominent scholar and statesman who had previously worked as a professor at Moscow University, as well as the rector of the Moscow Institute of Oriental Studies, became the director of the pedagogical faculty of Kazakh State University.

Among the university's faculty were the renowned Kazakh writer Mukhtar Auezov, writer Saken Seifullin, and others (Zhamanbayev, 1972; Kunantaeva, 2001; Kiyasova, 2008). The faculty of pedagogy was considered the first university-level institution in the republic. In 1930 it was renamed *the Kazakh Pedagogical Institute (KazPI)*. The state needed an education system whose main goal was to prepare politically committed youth with solid general educational preparation for subsequent vocational education.

During this period, pedagogical vocational schools (secondary specialized educational institutions) have actively been opened, for example, the Semipalatinsk Pedagogical College (based on the Semipalatinsk Pedagogical Seminary founded in 1903, in 1920–1922 – the Semipalatinsk Institute, in 1922–1937 – the Pedagogical College, in 1937–1992 – pedagogical school, from 1992 to the present time – pedagogical college), Chimkent pedagogical school (founded in 1920, the first director was Zhusupbek Aymautov, who graduated from the Semipalatinsk Teachers' Seminary in 1918), etc., which helped in the further qualitative development of higher pedagogical education, both by preparing applicants for universities and by creating social elevators for teaching and management personnel in Kazakhstan.

As a result of the development of pedagogical courses and public institutes, the first Kazakh textbooks on pedagogy and psychology appeared. These are M. Zhumabaev's textbook "Pedagogy" (Orenburg, 1922; graduate of the Omsk

Teachers' Seminary /studied in 1913–1916/), "Teaching literacy" (1926), Zh. Aymautov "Tarbiege zhetekshi" («Pedagogical guidance», Orenburg, 1924), "Psychology" (1926), "Didactics" (1927), "Sabaktyn kompleksti zhuesinin adisteri" (Comprehensive system of methods for conducting lessons, Kyzyl-Orda, 1929) (Zharikbayev, 1995). Nazipa Kulzhanova (1887–1934) contributed to the development of pedagogy for preschool education. After graduating from the Russian-Kazakh gymnasium in 1902, in 1903–1904 she was a teacher at the Torgai Women's College, in 1905–1920 she taught at the Semipalatinsk Teachers' Seminary. After the revolution in 1920, she was a member of the Commission of the People's Commissariat of Education of the Kazakh Autonomous Republic for the development of textbooks and books (Nurlanuly, 2015). She is the author of books in the Kazakh language "Preschool education" (1923), "Mother and Child" (1927). Figure 1.4 highlights educators who made scholarly contributions to the field of teacher education in Kazakhstan.

The first universities attracted a significant number of highly qualified scholars to Kazakhstan, who devoted themselves to creating a national higher school, national scientific and teaching personnel, and studying Kazakhstan's enormous natural resources. However, this period was characterized by a mismatch between pedagogical theory and the practice of school teaching, resulting in the evidence of democracy and pluralism of secondary and higher pedagogical education at that stage (Nurkabekova, 2010).

Magzhan Zhumabaev (1893-1938). Author of the first textbook "Pedagogy" 1922 (in Kazakh) Poet. Was repressed

Zhusupbek Aimautov (1889-1931). Director of the Pedagogical College Author of the first textbook "Psychology" (1926), "Didactics" (1927) (in Kazakh) Writer. Was repressed

Nazipa Kulzhanova (1887-1934). Teacher. Author of the book "Preschool Education" 1923, "Mother and Child" 1927 (in Kazakh) Founder of preschool education pedagogy. Journalist, representative of the women's movement in Kazakhstan

Tulegen Tazhibaev (1910-1964). People's Commissar education, foreign affairs, culture (1940, 1944-1948). Doctor of Pedagogy sciences, professor. Research author on the history of Kazakhstan Zh. Aymautov's scholar. Founder of a scientific school on pedagogy, psychology, history of education

Abdikhamit Sembaev (1905-1989). People's Commissar education, minister of education KazSSR (1941-1955). Director of the Research Institute of Pedagogical Sciences named after Y.Altynsarin (1963-1974). Doctor of Pedagogical Sciences, Professor. Research author on the history of education of Kazakhstan. Founder of a scientific school on pedagogy, history of education

Sultan-Bek Kozhakhmetov (1912-1945). Candidate of Pedagogical Sciences "Main didactic principles in the Soviet school« (November 4, 1939, KazSU). Author of the textbook "Scientists of Classics of Pedagogy» (1940)

Personalities of scientists-pedagogues

FIGURE 1.4   Personalities of Educationalists

5.3   *The Second Stage: The Formation of Higher Pedagogical Education (1932–1960s)*

On July 9, 1932, the Kazakh Regional Committee of the All-Union Communist Party of Bolsheviks adopted a resolution on opening a pedagogical institute in Uralsk. On October 1, 1932, the Institute of Public Education, with the faculties of physical and mathematical, chemical and biological, Kazakh language and literature, and historical and economic, opened a pedagogical institute in Uralsk. 233 students were studying there.

In 1934, the Kazakh State University was named after Kirov, and currently, the Al-Farabi Kazakh National University, which also actively trains teachers, was opened. In 1934, there were nine (9) universities in Kazakhstan, three (3) of which were trained teachers – the Kazakh State University (KazSU) and pedagogical institutes in Alma-Ata and Uralsk. A system of higher pedagogical education emerged in Kazakhstan, including a university and two pedagogical institutes. Subsequently, the opening of pedagogical institutes in all regions of Kazakhstan was systematically carried out. In 1937, the Semipalatinsk[1] and the Kyzyl-Orda Pedagogical Institutes[2] were opened.

The first Republican Scientific and Pedagogical Cabinet was founded in 1932, and in 1933, it was reorganized into the Research Institute of Pedagogical Sciences (now the Altynsarin National Academy of Education). At the end of the 1930s, the first scientific journals began to be published – in 1937, "Scientific Notes of KazSU" was published, and in 1939, the collection "Scientific Notes of KazPI" was published.

As Eseeva and Nurkabylova (2010) note, the transformation of secondary and higher pedagogical education during the period under study was very contradictory. On the one hand, curricula gradually unified during this period; on the other hand, higher pedagogical education became more diverse (diversifying): elective disciplines were introduced.

This pre-war period was not only for creating a system of higher pedagogical education but also for postgraduate education. Postgraduate courses appeared at the Abai KazPI (since 1932) and Kazakh State University, Ural and Semipalatinsk Pedagogical Institutes (all since 1938).

At Kazakh State University, named after S. Kirov, the first defense of the dissertation on pedagogy in the Kazakh language by S. Kozhakhmetov "Sovet mektebindegi negyzgi didaktikalyk principle" (November 4, 1939, Basic didactic principles of the Soviet school) was held. The author identified five didactic principles: connections between learning and life, awareness of learning, systematic and consistent learning, scientific nature and clarity (Elbaeva, 2011). According to M. Miskaryan (1984), from the mid-30s of the twentieth century, future teachers studied pedagogy (130 hours), the history of pedagogy and psychology (more than 100 hours each), private methods – from 100 to 200 hours, as well as teaching practice – 600 hours.

The Great Patriotic War presented challenges during this period. For instance, while on the one hand, there was a significant outflow of teaching staff and students mobilised for the war, a reduction of departments in conditions of saving financial material and technical resources during wartime, on the other hand, the higher school of Kazakhstan received a powerful cultural and intellectual impulse as a result of evacuated scholars and the material and technical base relocated universities. On the territory of the Kazakh SSR, 22 universities were admitted, over 8 thousand students and 545 teachers, including 98 doctors of science and professors, 210 candidates of science and associate professors (Kunantayeva, 2001; Kruglyanskiy, 1970). In particular, the united universities of Ukraine were evacuated to Kazakhstan. The United Ukrainian University (Kyiv and Kharkiv Universities) worked in Kyzyl-Orda based on the Kyzyl-Orda Pedagogical Institute. New educational institutions are opening, the development of the main challenges of teacher education continues, and textbooks and teaching aids are being created, including for pedagogical universities (Ilyasova, 1997, pp. 447–452). At that time, Kazakhstan received not only the adult evacuated population but also many children; 149 child care centres were organised in the republic, i.e. one-hundred and nine (109) orphanages and 40 children's institutions and educational institutions with a contingent of 19 thousand people (Kruglyanskiy, 1970; Sembayev, 1958).

By the 40s of the twentieth century, the higher education sector in Kazakhstan consisted of 12 universities. Despite wartime hardships, during the Great Patriotic War, the following were opened in Kazakhstan: in 1944, a state conservatory and a women's pedagogical institute were opened in Alma-Ata. In the same year, the Almaty Teachers' Institute was transformed into a pedagogical institute of foreign languages, and in 1945, the Institute of Physical Culture was opened (Lukyanets, 1959, pp. 28–29). It is important to emphasize that the Kazakh State Women's Pedagogical Institute, which later was the *only one* for a long time, trained teachers for rural *Kazakh schools* in their *native language*. During the war years, the Research Institute of Pedagogical Sciences, named after Altynsarin, was restored in 1943. It continued to work on developing curricula for the Kazakh language and literature at school, Russian language and literature at the Kazakh school, creating textbooks for these subjects, and translating textbooks of other subjects into Kazakh.

After the war, in 1952, the Karaganda Pedagogical Institute was opened in 1955 – the Petropavlovsk and Guryev Pedagogical Institutes (they were transformed from teachers' institutes). The structures of the faculties were approximately the same: faculties of physics and mathematics, philology and natural geography. In 1957, a university and 13 pedagogical institutes operated in Kazakhstan.

As a result, the intensive work that aimed to eliminate illiteracy that began in the 20s and 30s began to yield results. According to the study by Asylbekov and Asylbekova (2016) based on the analysis of the population census, in 1926, Kazakhstan ranked 7th in terms of literacy in the USSR (51.1%) with 22.8% (among 11 union republics), ahead of Kyrgyzstan (15.1%). Turkmenistan (12.5%), Uzbekistan (10.6%) and Tajikistan (3.7%). According to the 1939 census, it came in fifth place (76.3%), ahead of Armenia and Azerbaijan. In the USSR, 81.2% were literate. Among urban residents, 82.4% of the population was literate, and in rural areas – 73.8%. The leaders were the Karaganda region (83.3), Almaty (79.3%) and North Kazakhstan (79.2%) regions. In terms of gender, literacy for men was 85.2%, and for women – 66.3% (Asylbekov, 2016). By the end of the 50s, Kazakhstan had eliminated illiteracy, carried out basic education, and transitioned to seven-year compulsory education. Regarding literacy level, the republic joined the ranks of states such as the USA, England, France, Italy, etc. (Khrapchenkov, 1998, p. 110). According to UNESCO, in terms of quantitative and qualitative education indicators, by the end of the 50s, the USSR was in second place in the world (Khrapchenkov, 1998, p. 110).

Thus, during this period, the country experienced a rise in improving people's lives and increased population literacy, training teachers despite tragic times of famine, repression, and war. The 30s of the twentieth century are associated with a change in the way of life of the Kazakh population – the transition from a nomadic to a sedentary lifestyle, collectivization, i.e. the creation of collective farms in the villages, which led in the 1930s to famine, high mortality and the outflow of the Kazakh population to Russia, China and other countries. According to various estimates, out of 4 million Kazakh people, about 2 million either died or migrated to other regions of the USSR and neighbouring countries.

The 30s became a turning point in implementing a more stringent educational policy "from above", the unification of primary schools, unity and uniformity in education on the territory of the USSR. In fact, from then on, the so-called "rigid" system of education management began to take shape. On the one hand, all this contributed to the elimination of illiteracy in the population, the formation of a new workforce, and the further industrial breakthrough of the USSR and Kazakhstan. On the other hand, the education system, including pedagogical training, played a crucial role in consolidating Soviet power and disseminating communist ideology to the masses. Alongside collectivization, it contributed to shifts in the national structure of the Kazakh population, facilitating the transition to a sedentary lifestyle and promoting the homogenization of social needs (Mynbayeva & Pogosyan, 2011). The educator-teacher had to bring the ideas of the Communist Party of the Soviet Union to the masses and introduce the principles and advantages of the socialist system of state development (Akhmetova, 2016).

Therefore, the first Soviet curriculum for the discipline of "Pedagogy" in 1933 included the following topics: "1. The essence and goals of Soviet pedagogy", "8. Children's communist movement" (developed with the participation of Krupskaya) (Savin, 1987, p.28–29). During the 1920s–1940s, the teaching profession was among the most vulnerable and life-threatening, particularly in rural areas. During this period, teachers assumed a significant social and propaganda role in safeguarding Soviet power, which, as noted by Akhmetova (2020), also resulted in widespread political repression, including imprisonment, physical violence, and executions (p. 22).

By 1956, the curriculum and textbook "Pedagogy" began to contain 4 sections: "General Fundamentals of Pedagogy", "Didactics", "Theory of Communist Education", "School Studies" (Savin, 1987, p. 31; Mynbayeva, 2021, p. 51). According to E. Vasilkovskaya (2006), from the 30s to the mid-50s, the state actively intervened, harshly ideologised and uncompromisingly eliminated other concepts and ideas for the development of education. (Vasilkovskaya, 2006)

5.4 The Third Stage: The Development of the System of Higher Pedagogical Education (1960s–Late 1980s)

The urbanization of the population of Kazakhstan characterized the 50s–60s. In the 50s, mass development of virgin and fallow lands began. According to experts, about a million new residents from Russia, Ukraine and Belarus were resettled in Kazakhstan. In 1955, 146 primary and 109 seven-year schools were created on new state farms on virgin lands (Sembayev, 1958). In some regions and villages, Russian classes appeared in Kazakh schools. At this time, about 700 Kazakh schools were closed in Kazakhstan.

The structure of the school system was changed: primary school – grades 1–4; eight-year-old – grades 1–8; middle – grades 1–10. The introduction of eight-year compulsory education was filled with qualitative changes: strengthening of labor and polytechnic education, and more attention was paid to schoolchildren's practical and psychological preparation for work. In addition, the number of hours for the Kazakh language and literature, mathematics, physics, chemistry, music, and physical education increased, and the time for studying the Russian language, geography and biology decreased (Sembayev, 1958).

In the second half of the 50s, the following important changes took place: Since 1956, a new type of educational institution appeared – a boarding school; from the mid-50s, industrial training was introduced in combination with practical training; in 1958, eight-year compulsory education was introduced, and secondary school became eleven years old (Satrikova, 2008, p. 224). Moreover, worldwide requirements began to be imposed on teacher training – a teacher must have qualified skills in teaching and education, deep knowledge of the subject and specialty, a broad outlook and scientific erudition (Mei Hancheng, 2005).

In the '60s–70s, the main priority of the educational policy of the USSR was the transition to universal secondary education. Resolutions were issued "On measures further to improve the secondary school" (1966), "On completing the transition to universal secondary education and on the further development of the secondary school" (1972), "On measures to further improve the work of the rural secondary school" (1973), "Fundamentals of legislation of the USSR and union republics on public education" (1973), "On further improvement of teaching, education of students in secondary schools and preparing them for work" (Khrapchenkov, 1998, p. 113). These decisions were duplicated in the Union republics.

By 1976, the transition to universal secondary education in the USSR was completed. The primary school moved to three years of study. In the context of education for subjects at the middle and senior levels of school, demands were made to bring the educational material of the basic sciences of the school closer to the real development of sciences in the USSR and the world. The scientific principle was actively used in secondary school didactics. Optional courses were introduced, etc. The material and technical laboratory equipment of natural science disciplines were strengthened. By the end of 1969 in Kazakhstan, for example, the number of physics classrooms had increased by 750 compared to 1967, and by 750 in chemistry-730, in biology – by 316 (Oku-agartu isi, 1980, p. 397).

By 1975, there were 49 universities in the Kazakh SSR, including two universities and 20 pedagogical institutes (in the USSR, there were 63 universities and 199 pedagogical institutes) (Table 1.2).

Analysis of the data in Table 1.2 shows the stability of the structure of the higher pedagogical education system, with an increase in the total number of students, which corresponds to the needs of the republic's population growth.

TABLE 1.2 Pedagogical institutes and student population (Khrapchenkov, 1998)

	1970	1980	1989
Pedagogical institutes	20	20	20
Students	65,4	70,2 (growth of 7%)	85,6 (growth of 21,9%)
Admission	13,8	15,3	19
Graduation	10,8	12,2	13,4

In 1985 and until the independence of Kazakhstan, the number of universities and the structure of higher education virtually did not change – 55 universities. Note that the system of higher pedagogical education was more evenly distributed throughout Kazakhstan (unlike, for example, higher polytechnic education), which later, under conditions of independence, was used by the state to create universities in each region of the republic. This stage is characterized by qualitative transformations of the school. It is associated with strengthening the theoretical component of teachers' psychological and pedagogical training and the practical orientation of higher pedagogical education (fundamentalization and pragmatization of teaching). The development of pedagogical science at this time is determined by the emergence of new concepts of the content of secondary education (Lerner, Krayevsky and Lednev), which are taught at teacher education institutions (Kaidarova, 2007).

According to Akhmetova (2002), "the educational ideal of the Soviet school was the comprehensive and harmonious development of the individual" (pp. 16–17). This ideal was "sublimed," both in the sense of recognizing the high social mission of education and in that it was shaped by the ideology of a future ideal society – one abstracted from real-world contradictions. As Akhmetova (2002) goes on to note,

> on the one hand, this ideal distanced people from real life, setting lofty goals for teachers and students. On the other hand, these high standards were aligned with the strategy of cultivating an 'omniscient' personality. However, insufficient attention was given to developing skills for independent work, fostering a culture of self-education and self-development, and encouraging the creative nature of mastering knowledge. (pp. 16–17)

The points made by Akhmetova resonate with the study by Fimyar and Kurakbayev (2016).

Reproductive teaching methods also prevailed in teaching methods. As Nurtazina (2005, pp. 19–20) postulates:

> The main argument of the verbal and book education of the Soviet school was based on the statement: in the era of the scientific and technological revolution, the importance of scientific knowledge increases, the intellectual development of the younger generation becomes a necessary condition for their effective labor and social activity in all spheres of life. (Nurtazina, 2005, pp. 19–20)

Similarly, Pogosyan (2020) posit that "Soviet school curricula reflected a state of monopoly in education and were absolutely "reader's" texts (according to Barth's 1974 concept, "reader's" and "writer's" texts are distinguished) – they were not a place for making any changes in the subjects of study, their sequence and content, as well as textbooks and books for teachers strictly prescribed what and how to teach. The centralised programs for each subject/course had lists of "didactic units" defining the content to be taught and learned. Teachers were required to use selected textbooks at the national level, which also implies that the same educational content and teaching methods were used in all schools throughout the USSR (Pogosyan, 2020, p. 124). The era of "reader's" texts was associated with a discourse not of different interpretations but with the correct understanding and implementation of state educational policy (communist ideology and approaches). These aspects can be considered a weak link in school education of this period.

In the 1980s, the development of the secondary education system stagnated, and a crisis in education, including teacher education, began. Conventionally, during Soviet times, two traditions of higher pedagogical education were developed: (1) university education with a priority on teaching the subject of study on a high scientific basis; (2) education in pedagogical institutes, where much attention was paid to the pedagogical and methodological component of training. For example, the following disciplines were included in the teacher training curricula at the university: history of the CPSU, philosophy, political economy, scientific communism, pedagogy, history of pedagogy, psychology, methods of teaching the subject, school hygiene, physical education (Zykin, 2013). Curricula in the USSR were uniform for different types of universities; that is, Kazakh universities and pedagogical institutes were studied according to uniform curricula developed in Moscow (Zajda, 1984; Kerr, 1991). University pedagogical education had a broader scientific and theoretical training of students and less pedagogical and methodological training (Zykin, 2013, p. 251).

It was assumed that teachers with a university education could work in specialized advanced schools (language, physics, and mathematics schools) and senior secondary schools, where the content of scientific education became more complex (physics, astronomy, chemistry, algebra and geometry, biology, languages, etc.). With such baggage, the republic approached the moment of acquiring independence.

6 Strengths and Weaknesses of Higher Pedagogical Education of the Soviet Period in the Kazakh SSR

6.1 *Strengths*
– an extensive infrastructure of higher pedagogical education in Kazakhstan has been created. It is represented by 2 universities, 20 pedagogical institutes, including those for the training of teachers for foreign languages, physical culture, and art;
– the established system of postgraduate education (postgraduate studies), the defense of PhD theses in the field of pedagogy;
– extensive training of female teachers, including training at the Kazakh State Women's Pedagogical Institute since 1944. In KazGoszhenPI, training was conducted in Kazakh for the further work of teachers in their native language, including in villages;
– research activities of the Institute of Education Problems (now the National Academy of Education named after Y.Altynsarina), the established scientific and pedagogical schools of T.Tazhibaeva, R. Lemberg, A.I. Sembayeva, J. Seiteshova, N.D. Khmel, etc.;
– publication of scientific and methodological journals on education and pedagogy;
– fundamental teacher training, the use of didactic foundations and the theory of education, the theory of the holistic pedagogical process in teaching "Pedagogy", teaching the basics of psychology, pedagogical skills, methods of teaching subjects for future teachers; etc.

6.2 *Weaknesses*
– the ideological content in the teaching of socio-humanitarian disciplines at educational programs for teacher training; the unified content of curricula for teacher training in all republics of the USSR (was sent from Moscow), which actually did not take into account regional, ethnic characteristics of teacher training; in the Kazakh SSR, for a long time, higher education was conducted in Russian mostly; the use of reproductive methods in teacher training, and accordingly in teaching at school, the weak use of independent work methods, creative search for methods of schoolchildren teaching, etc.

7 Period of Independence, the Development of Higher Pedagogical Education: Factors That Influenced on the Development of Education in the Post-Soviet Period

This period of independence is important as it represents the development of the country's human capital and the quest to ensure the sustainability of its society.

Since 1991, a new historical period in education development in Kazakhstan has begun. It is characterized by national self-determination, the search for optimal development paths, the dynamics of constant reforms, integration processes, etc.

We again use the STEP analysis to summarize new factors influencing the development of higher pedagogical education in post-Soviet times (Figure 1.5).

The social factor is again associated with the demographic situation, an increase in the number of children in the 90s of the twentieth century, then a sharp decline, and an increase again in the 2010s (Figure 1.6a,b). Within the framework of the social factor, we will also define the *cultural factor* – the renaissance

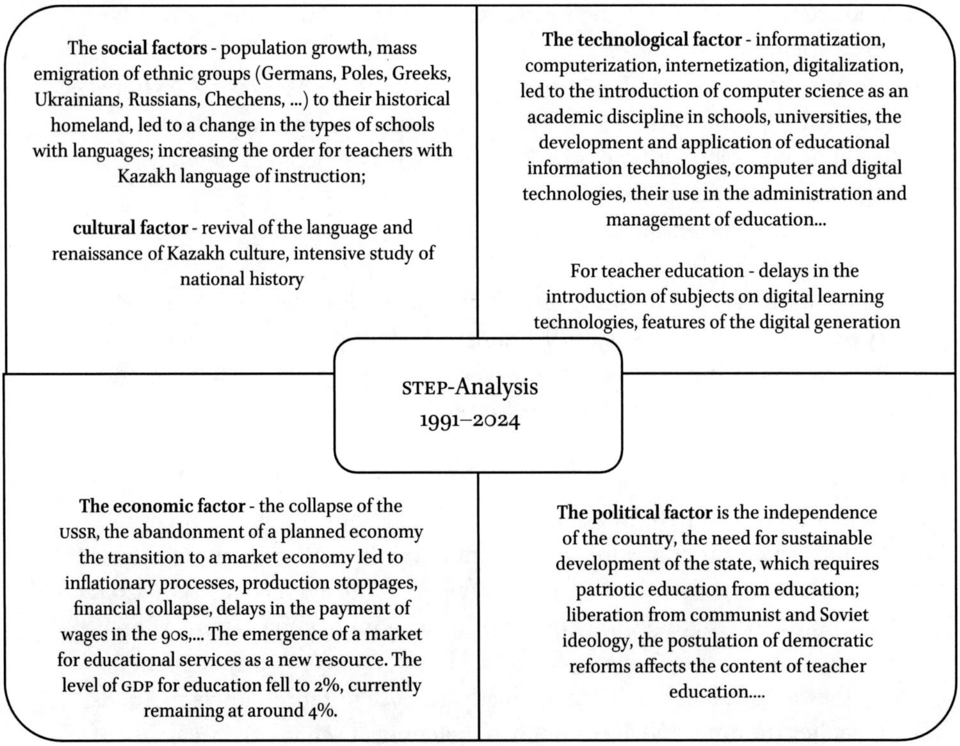

The **social factors** - population growth, mass emigration of ethnic groups (Germans, Poles, Greeks, Ukrainians, Russians, Chechens, ...) to their historical homeland, led to a change in the types of schools with languages; increasing the order for teachers with Kazakh language of instruction;

cultural factor - revival of the language and renaissance of Kazakh culture, intensive study of national history

The **technological factor** - informatization, computerization, internetization, digitalization, led to the introduction of computer science as an academic discipline in schools, universities, the development and application of educational information technologies, computer and digital technologies, their use in the administration and management of education...

For teacher education - delays in the introduction of subjects on digital learning technologies, features of the digital generation

STEP-Analysis
1991–2024

The **economic factor** - the collapse of the USSR, the abandonment of a planned economy the transition to a market economy led to inflationary processes, production stoppages, financial collapse, delays in the payment of wages in the 90s,... The emergence of a market for educational services as a new resource. The level of GDP for education fell to 2%, currently remaining at around 4%.

The **political factor** is the independence of the country, the need for sustainable development of the state, which requires patriotic education from education; liberation from communist and Soviet ideology, the postulation of democratic reforms affects the content of teacher education....

FIGURE 1.5   STEP analysis of factors that influenced the development of teacher education in the era of independence

of national culture and language, the revival of the national school, and therefore the transition of teacher training in universities to the Kazakh language.

The technological factor currently plays a key role, deeply transforming education and higher education, on the one hand, becoming a new resource for the development of teachers, and on the other hand, presenting challenges for

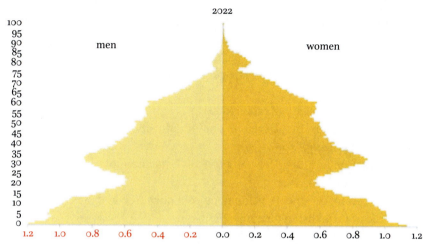

FIGURE 1.6A   Gender and age pyramid of the population of the Republic of Kazakhstan (2022, p. 64) (*Source:* Kazakhstan demographics zhylnamalygy / Demographic Yearbook of Kazakhstan (2022). Astana, Bureau of National Statistics. p. 276)

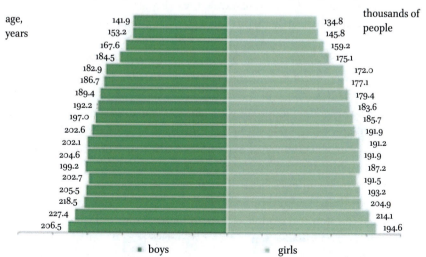

FIGURE 1.6B   Gender and age pyramid of children (2023, p. 8) (*Source:* Children of Kazakhstan / Statistical collection. 2018–2023. (2023, p. 126) Astana, Agency for Strategic Planning and Reforms of the Republic of Kazakhstan Bureau of National Statistics.)

teachers as a result of the need for information, computer and digital literacy and competence.

The economic factor has created conditions for new opportunities to attract financial resources from students themselves to study at universities, including pedagogical universities, and the emergence of a market for educational services.

The political factor is associated with a change in focus from the ideological base to the educational function of patriotic citizens for the stability of the state and confrontation with external challenges. State policy in the development of education, including pedagogical, can be traced through 6 programs adopted sequentially:

– State Program "Education" (2000–2004),
– State Program for the Development of Education in the Republic of Kazakhstan for 2005–2010,
– State Program for the Development of Education of the Republic of Kazakhstan for 2011–2020,
– State Program for the Development of Education and Science of the Republic of Kazakhstan for 2016–2019;
– State Program for the Development of Education and Science for 2020–2025;
– Concepts for the Development of Higher Education and Science in the Republic of Kazakhstan for 2023–2029 (2023).

It is interesting to note that in each program, the questions about teacher education and teacher status (from almost the latest tasks in the programs 2000, 200–2010 to 2 and then 1 in State programs 2011, 2016, 2020, 2023) are raised.

7.1 The Fourth Stage: Reforming the Content of Initial Teacher Education Amid Kazakhstan's Democratization and Development (1991–Mid-2000s)

Based on the programs adopted by the state, one can assert that *the fourth stage* is characterized by reforming the content of higher pedagogical education as set out in the conditions of democratization and development of the sovereign Republic of Kazakhstan (1991–mid-2000s)

The era of independence began with a deep socio-economic and political crisis when ties between enterprises of the newly independent states collapsed, which led to the stop and gradual closure of many plants and factories, powerful inflation, and criminalization of society (Silova, 2002). There was a powerful outflow of teaching staff from universities and schools, especially teachers of the young and middle generation, and a reduction in the number of schools and students to the minimum population levels in 2002 (Figure 1.6a – pyramid).

In the 90s of the twentieth century, teachers began to receive salaries unstably and with delays. At the same time, the market economy led to the emergence of the private sector of higher education, which, along with the state sector, began to train teachers. Kazakhstan's most famous private universities are the "Kainar" and "Turan".

Legally, to preserve the educational potential infrastructure and maintain the sustainability of the education system, the first generation of laws on education was adopted: the Law "On Education" (1992), the Law "On Higher Education" (1993), second generation – Law "On Education" of 1999 (replaced both laws); third generation – 2007. In 2019, the Law of the Republic of Kazakhstan "On the Status of a Teacher" was adopted. The first generation of laws of the early 90s duplicated Soviet legislation. A qualitative change is observed in the 1999 law concerning transforming the infrastructure and content of schools and higher education, including teacher education.

The higher education system was characterized by the most dynamic changes during this period; it was the first to be significantly transformed in Kazakhstan (infrastructure, introduction of specialty standards, transition to a credit education system), which also led to the transformation of secondary education. In the mid-90s (1994), Kazakhstan experienced the enlargement and consolidation of regional universities and their transfer to the status of state universities. Thus, in each regional centre of Kazakhstan (administrative unit of Kazakhstan), a *state university at the regional level* was created based on the existing pedagogical institute. The accumulated potential of the Soviet higher education infrastructure was strategically used to create a stable system for training professional personnel in all regions, creating a uniform territorial system of university education on a state scale. Accordingly, the training of teachers continued in these universities.

In 1994, the state standard for the higher education of the Republic of Kazakhstan (basic provisions) was approved, and for the first time, the regulation determined the introduction of the structure of a multi-level system of higher education in the country, academic bachelor's and master's degrees. The first Kazakhstani educational standards for higher pedagogical education were adopted (Kaydarova, 2007).

The beginning of 2001 was marked by developments and scientific research in creating a Kazakhstani model of higher pedagogical education (multi-level and multi-stage) for the 21st century. These were the years of searching to create a single educational space for the CIS countries and the Council of Europe. A new approach, along with those already developed, was standardization. In higher pedagogical education, the competency-based approach was adopted. This period was marked by the development of innovative technologies and the introduction of a credit education system in universities. The transition process meant knowledge-centric to competency-based approaches, subject-oriented and person-centred learning. At this stage, the trend of universityization of higher education with a characteristic of universities is visible as the fundamentalization of pedagogical education (Kaydarova, 2007).

7.2 Fifth Stage: Modernization of the System of Higher Pedagogical Education (from 2004 to 2015)

In 2004, the Government decided to create five pedagogical universities in the Republic. Thus, again, from April 1, 2004, pedagogical institutes were revived. The institutes again acquired the status of pedagogical ones, separated from universities, and got a second wind. Accordingly, higher pedagogical education is modernizing- a departure from general university training to specialized pedagogical training.

Conventionally, a new strategic stage in the development of the higher education system began in 2010, aimed at strengthening Kazakhstan's position in the global educational space. Kazakhstan joined the Bologna process, which affected higher pedagogical education. A new State Program for the Development of Education until 2011–2020 has been adopted.

In 2010, there was a complete transition to three cycles of education: bachelor's – master's – PhD. Defenses of doctoral and master's theses under the Soviet system have been stopped. The system of training scientific and scientific-pedagogical personnel has been completely transformed.

In 2012, KazNPU, named after Abay, developed new educational programs for higher pedagogical education with the involvement of foreign experts and regional teachers and stakeholders. The program structures included not only the purpose, objectives and list of subjects but also the expected results according to Bloom's taxonomy, assessment and teaching methods. These programs were aimed at incorporating updated 12-year education content.

In 2013, the Professional Standard "Teacher" was adopted. Interestingly, the first state standards of higher education were developed by specialities; they regulated the discipline of CD (compulsory disciplines – History of Kazakhstan, Kazakh and foreign languages, political science, sociology, cultural studies), basic and specialized disciplines (BD and SD) (UNESCO, 2015). For teacher training, the basic ones were "Introduction to Teaching," "Pedagogy," "Psychology," "History of Pedagogy", "Ethnopedagogy", "Physiology and human anatomy" and other special subjects; the specialized ones were – "Methods of teaching the subject", "Pedagogical skills", "Pedagogical technologies", etc. From 2014 to 2015, unification took place, and a new state standard of higher education was introduced in the appendix, in which the standard curriculum regulates only the cycle of compulsory disciplines and pedagogical practices, as well as final works. Universities are given greater didactic autonomy in the design of educational programs. A separate recommendation is the introduction of the subjects "Inclusive education" and "Criteria-based assessment".

7.3 Sixth Stage: Reforms of Educational Programs of Higher Pedagogical Education

Since 2015, a new stage of development has conventionally begun, associated with reforms of educational programs of higher pedagogical education, the introduction of standards for preparing for a 12-year school, as well as elements of international approaches to teacher professional development (tested at NIS, the NIS Center for Pedagogical Excellence, the country's advanced training system) for training teachers. According to Utyupova (2017), there was an imbalance during the period of reforms in the school education system and training of teachers (p. 133).

If at first this updated content was introduced through continuing professional development programs, then since 2015 the ministry has persistently recommended that universities integrate best practices to teacher professional development established at the NIS Center for Teaching Excellence into initial teacher education programs.

On the one hand, this was done by promoting cooperation with the Center for Teaching Excellence of NIS, the National Academy of Education named after Y. Altynsarin. On the other hand, through the introduction of a new system of certification of teachers – the National Qualification Testing of Pedagogical Workers (i.e. testing of teachers), gradually, instead of simple categories for the career growth of teachers in schools, certification along the following trajectories was proposed: "teacher" → "teacher- moderator" → "teacher-expert" → "teacher-researcher" → "teacher-master". This career trajectory was developed in Nazarbayev Intellectual Schools. Then, along with the translation of secondary education curricular content from NIS to schools throughout the republic, a system of teacher career growth was also promoted to motivate teachers.

In 2015, the Kazakh National Pedagogical University, named after Abai, began introducing innovative educational programs (Güngör, 2016), in which the mandatory component was reduced, future teachers developed a focus on developing students' functional literacy, and practice was increased. According to Akhmetova (2016), a teacher is an educator capable of not only transferring knowledge, skills and abilities, but also called upon to help students implement their life plans and strategies, which involve the formation of functional literacy and the development of the abilities of each student (Akhmetova, 2016).

Active reforms of the secondary and higher education system in Kazakhstan since 2010 have led to the expansion of Western traditions of learning theory. This is due to the opening of foreign private schools in Kazakhstan, globalization processes, and the increasing internationalization of secondary education reforms. This trend is also manifested in the transition to Pedagogy 2.0 and constructivist theories of education and discoveries in the neurophysiology of the brain. Table 1.3 compares didactic theories of local and foreign traditions.

According to Yakavets et al. (2017), teacher training in Kazakhstan has been predominantly shaped by domestic traditions, supplemented by the integration of Western theories. For instance, teachers' professional knowledge and professional training in institutes are built within the framework of Kazakh and Soviet pedagogical traditions, with some references to foreign scholars. Teachers' professional knowledge is formed based on pedagogical theories mediated by educational scholars who participate in educational reform in Kazakhstan. At the same time, the didactic style of teaching continues to limit critical engagement, and research into the consequences of this practice remains lacking (Yakavets et al., 2017).

TABLE 1.3   Combination of learning theories of local and foreign (Western) traditions (Mynbayeva, 2021, p. 247)

Theories of teaching/learning. Local tradition	Foreign (Western) tradition
The theory of the holistic pedagogical process (broader than the theory of learning) Construction of a lesson according to R. Lemberg Theory of educational activity Elkonin-Davydov's theory L.V. Zankova's theory P.Ya. Galperin's theory of the gradual development of mental actions Z.I. Kalmykova's theory Pospelov's theory, etc. Association theory Behaviorism Theory of assessment V. Bespalko Ethnopedagogical education	Theory of learning styles by D. Kolb Fleming and Mills VARK model (learning styles by representational systems) G. Gardner's theory of multiple intelligences Scaffolding theory, etc. Association theory Behaviorism Constructivism Connectivism Assessment theory (B. Bloom's taxonomy)

8 Critical Trends in Teacher Education

Summarising the results of the transition, we see that the traditions of Soviet and new pedagogical education are intertwined, or, in other words, layered on top of each other (Figure 1.7). According to Yakavets (2014), although attempts have been made to transform education in Kazakhstan, it still bears the features of Soviet education. Recent studies on the implementation of updated 12-year education in pilot schools also indicate that there are barriers and contradictions among teachers. As Yakavets et al. (2023) note, there is a contradiction between educational reform, updated educational content and new approaches to teaching that encourage creative, critical thinking and problem solving, on the one hand, and social values that encourage submission to authority, on the other. Perhaps this is natural as the Soviet tradition of teacher education has deeper roots, developed over more than 60 years (1928–1991), while the new tradition has only evolved in the recent period of not more than 30 years of flow (1991–2024). Moreover, the directions and strategies of new traditions have changed more over time. According to Kissane (2006), since the 90s of the twentieth century, education in Kazakhstan has been pursuing implementation of a new national narrative aimed at developing a de-Sovietized-re-Kazakhified national identity (Kissane, 2006).

According to post Soviet education scholars, there are some commonalities between countries in terms of the 'post-socialist education reform package' (Silova, 2011; Silova & Steiner-Khamsi, 2008). These scholars mention a set of policy reforms symbolizing the adoption of Western educational values including such "travelling policies" as student-centred learning, the introduction of curriculum standards, decentralization of educational finance and governance, privatization of higher education, standardization of student assessment, and liberalization of textbook publishing' (Silova, 2011, p. 3). This interpretation coincides with the assessment of the Russian researcher Romanenchuk (2006) who avers "in the 2004 concept of education development, the forced "Westernization" of education (transfer of the Western model of education to Kazakh soil) is embodied in its entirety" (p. 12). On the one hand, we can partially agree with such assessments; on the other hand, it is necessary to take into account the powerful trend of revival of Kazakh schools and the ethno-pedagogical foundations of education.

In conclusion, it is crucial to summarize the essence of trends in the development of higher pedagogical education over almost a century (from 1928 to 2024). We highlight this process in the Table 1.4.

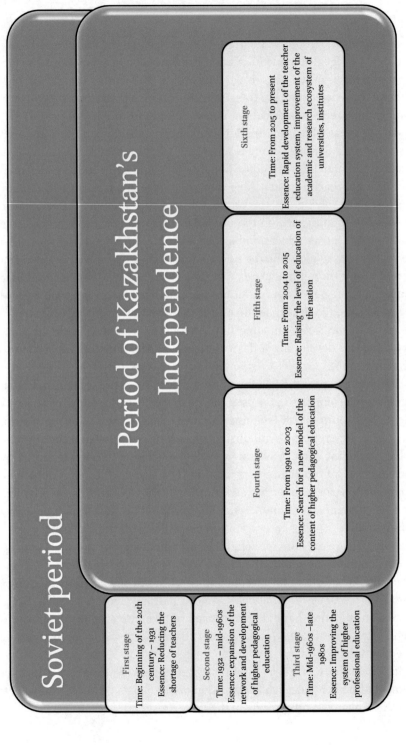

FIGURE 1.7 Development of the system of higher pedagogical education (2 periods and 6 stages)

TEACHER EDUCATION IN SOVIET AND POST-SOVIET TIMES 41

TABLE 1.4   The trends in the development of higher pedagogical education

Period	№	Stage	General characteristics: time, essence and trends
Sovet period	1	First stage	*Stage*: Beginning of the 20th century–1931. *Essence*: Reducing the shortage of teachers *Trends*: 1. Emergence of universities, ideologization of higher professional education; intensification of teacher training for Kazakh schools; democracy and pluralism of teacher education
	2	Second stage	*Stage*: 1932–mid-1960s *Essence*: Expansion of the network and development of higher pedagogical education *Trends*: 1. Unification of educational programs of pedagogical higher institutions 2. Polytechnization and politicization of the content of personnel training 3. Construction of a system of continuous pedagogical education 4. During the war years, a cultural and intellectual impulse arises, diversification occurs and contradiction is observed
	3	Third stage	*Stage*: Mid-1960s–late 1980s. *Essence*: Improving the system of higher professional education. *Trends*: 1. Fundamentalization and pragmatization of higher pedagogical education 2. The emergence of new didactic concepts in the system of higher professional education 3. Improving the structure, content and methods of teaching

(cont.)

TABLE 1.4   The trends in the development of higher pedagogical education (*cont.*)

Period	№	Stage	General characteristics: time, essence and trends
Period of independence	4	Fourth stage	*Stage*: From 1991 to 2003 *Essence*: Search for a new model of the content of higher pedagogical education *Trends*: 1. Construction of a system of continuous pedagogical education 2. Humanization of higher pedagogical education 3. Universityization of the system of higher professional education 4. Search for a national model of the system of higher pedagogical education
	5	Fifth stage	*Stage*: From 2004 to 2015 *Essence*: Raising the level of education of the nation *Trends*: 1. Humanization of higher professional pedagogical education 2. Return to the system of specialized pedagogical education – separation of pedagogical higher institutions from universities; 3. Modernization of higher professional pedagogical education; 4. Changing the structure of higher pedagogical education, intensive development of the postgraduate level and the system of retraining and advanced training of teachers.
	6	Sixth stage	*Stage*: From 2015 to present *Essence*: Rapid development of the teacher education system, improvement of the academic and research ecosystem of universities, institutes *Trends*: 1. Expanding the autonomy of universities 2. Openness of educational programs 3. Increasing the prestige of the teaching profession 4. Practice-oriented content of teacher education, strengthening the connection between school and university 5. Development of multilingualism 6. Development of scientific and pedagogical schools

To understand the trends in the development of teacher education in post-Soviet times, we have provided a content analysis of state program documents in the table below. In this analysis, we attempted to show the depth of transformation processes in the transition from Soviet traditions of teacher training to the Kazakh traditions of Kazakhstan as an independent republic. We show the focus of each strategic document developed for teacher education (Table 1.5).

An analysis of policy documents on the development of teacher education in the post-Soviet period reveals that some trends were more relevant in the early decades, while others emerged later.

The first documents indicate the humanization of teacher education since without it, it is impossible to move away from the polytechnicization of education, thus the introduction of a block of humanities and inclusive education for students with special needs.

This is followed by the prioritization of increasing the role of social protection and increasing the prestige of teachers through increasing teachers' salaries. From program to program, a mechanism for increasing the status of the teaching profession was developed and refined through the emphasis on depth and systematic reforms. Thus, a new certification system for teachers and a results-oriented remuneration mechanism has been introduced, the requirements for the training of future teachers have also been strengthened, and conditions have been created for students of pedagogical specialities – the state educational order for pedagogical specialities have been increased, first at the bachelor's degree (2005), then at the master's degree (2023), the admission rules have been changed by analogy with leading foreign universities (2015), scholarship of the students is 62% more than that of the other students (except for medical specialities).

The construction of a national teacher education system implied a move from a unified, standardized content of education to a multivariate one since the need to meet the needs of independent Kazakhstan, local, and regional educational institutions, and each student became a priority. The first steps in this direction were made through the adoption of standards in teacher training, recognized in the world (1999), the creation of variable training models, the involvement of international partners in additional training programs, the introduction of double specialties (educator-psychologist and others) (2005). Then, in connection with the final transition of the country's pedagogical education to a three-stage training system, curricular autonomy was strengthened, that is, the share of elective disciplines taught ranges from 70% at undergraduate level to 90–95% at the doctoral level (2011); training conducted by domestic and foreign specialists in accordance with international standards (2016), which gave rise to a surge in the development of dual-degree programs in pedagogical universities, the unification of formal and informal education, that

TABLE 1.5 Trends in the development of teacher education based on state programs, concepts for the development of education and science (1999–2029)

	Humanisation, inclusion	Status upgrade	Openness, diversification, academic freedom	Multilingualism	Development of the research environment	Practical training, practice orientation
State Program 1999–2000	+	+	+			
State Program 2005–2010	+	+	+	+		+
State Program 2011–2020	+	+	+	+		+
State Program 2016–2019		+	+	+		+
State Program 2020–2025		+	+	+	+	+
Concept for the development of higher education and science of the Republic of Kazakhstan 2023–2029			+		+	+

is, certificates and credits obtained through short-term courses will be transferred in "Stackable degree" (2023).

The trend called "multilingualism" in program documents appeared in connection with a deep reform of the content of school education and the need to transition from the stable trend of Soviet education – ideologization and the priority of the Russian language and the Russian pedagogical scientific school. In 2005, the goal was set to train a multilingual teacher proficient in innovative pedagogical technologies, search, research and creative skills, information and distance learning technologies (2005). By 2020, a mechanism for such training has been developed and implemented, especially for future teachers of physics, chemistry, biology and computer science (2020).

Strengthening practical training, increasing practice orientation in the content of educational programs, and expanding the "school-university" connection imply a departure from the fundamentalization of education. It is in the system of pedagogical education that this issue was raised acutely in 2011, and practice in schools for students of pedagogical specialities was expanded then with the introduction of the reforms aimed at the rewened content of secondary education since 2016 onwards; it was planned to update the content of education based on increasing practice orientation, from 2023 – the formation of a modern academic and research ecosystem universities, integrated into the national and regional context through expanding connections between schools and pedagogical universities. The task has also been set to develop digital competencies as a mandatory element of the professional standard of a teacher.

The development of the research environment as a top-down reform trend is one of the most recent. However, despite this, it has gone from close research-to-practice interaction between and preschool organizations and schools to developing scientific and pedagogical schools based on teacher education universities.

The rapid growth of the infrastructure of higher education, the expansion of the Kazakh department in universities, including pedagogical ones, and the increase in the number of students and teachers also personify the renaissance, the revival of the nation, the tradition of the Kazakh nation of "love of knowledge and wisdom" is manifested. Kazakhs have many proverbs and sayings about the importance of knowledge in life: «Жер — ырыстың кіндігі, білім — ырыстың тізгіні», «Жердің сәні — егін, ердің сәні — білім», «Білімді бесіктен тесікке дейін ізден». In English the meaning of these proverbs are as follows: "The earth is the basis of happiness, knowledge is the reins of happiness", "The beauty of the Earth is the harvest, the beauty of the human being is knowledge" and "Seek knowledge from the cradle to the end of life".

Therefore, the strategy of accelerated development of the teacher education system, focusing on the quality of training of teachers and creating an academic and research ecosystem in the preparation of teachers, is expected to lead to a robust growth of the country's human capital and will contribute to the sustainable development of Kazakhstan. This vision of the periodization of the development of teacher education in the Soviet and post-Soviet eras is only one view of the course of history and can be supplemented by other studies. We tried to record the main directions and trends of development for further discussion and comprehension and to search for ways of development.

9 Contemporary International Context

Analyzing the international context, Robertson (2012) draws conclusion that the current era of new public management in the last 30 years has turned anew to the problem of the quality of teacher training and activity. Building a knowledge society requires a high-quality education system and more contribution to the development of human capital. In this respect, Barber and Mourshed (2007) emphasize that "the quality of the education system cannot exceed the quality of its teachers" (p. 7).

Looking ahead to 2050, UNESCO's Reimagining Our Futures Together: A New Social Contract for Education (2021) underscores the need to rethink pedagogical approaches and recognize the transformative role of teachers. The report emphasizes that "teaching should be further professionalized as a collaborative endeavour where teachers are recognized for their work as knowledge producers and key figures in educational and social transformation" (UNESCO, 2021, p. 4). Additionally, it calls for "pedagogies that foster cooperation and solidarity" (UNESCO, 2021, p. 50), highlighting the necessity of reimagining education to support collective learning and societal progress. The Internet, the knowledge economy, the development of neurocognitive sciences (neuroplasticity of the human brain) creates a new essence and learning environment. Robertson (2012), having studied historical, managerial and international changes since the 1960s, speaks about the transition from the concept of training a knowledgeable teacher to a teacher who constructs knowledge together with a student. Thus, as Robertson (2012) points out, "in relation to teacher beliefs, there are two opposing indexes: direct transmission (bad teacher) or constructivism (good teacher)"; ... the competent teacher "facilitates" the learning of the pupil (making knowledge), rather than "direct transmission" to the learning (taking knowledge) (Robertson, 2012, p. 594).

According to the OECD International Study on Teaching and Learning TALIS-2018 in OECD countries, pedagogical training in universities includes:

> Other than subject content, pedagogy and classroom practice, teachers' formal education and training tends to include instruction on student

behaviour and classroom management (for 72% of all teachers across OECD countries and economies in TALIS), monitoring students' development and learning (70%), teaching cross-curricular skills (65%), teaching in a mixed-ability setting (62%) and use of information and communication technology (ICT) for teaching (56%). In comparison, teaching in a multicultural or multilingual setting (35%) is more rarely included as an element of teachers' formal education or training» (OECD, 2020, TALIS 2018 Results (Volume II), 2020).

In general, this is comparable with Kazakhstan practice: in addition to pedagogy, the content of the discipline, pedagogical universities teach age psychology and education management, criteria assessment, inclusive education, information and communication technologies for learning.

What motivates the new generation to enter pedagogical universities? The Kazakhstan research shows, that factors of intrinsic motivation (such as love of the subject) along with a tendency to altruism, have a much more significant impact on the motivation of future teachers in Kazakhstan than "mercantile" considerations. At the same time, more than half of the students in the 2019 study reported, that they consider the teaching profession as a short-term career (Analytical Report, 2019). The low status of a teacher, a large outflow of strong teachers, and low wages stimulated the adoption of the law "On the Status of a Teacher" in Kazakhstan (2019). Now, school teachers, who have passed the qualification certification procedure, have a salary comparable to the average salary in Kazakhstan. Similar results were obtained in the TALIS-2018 OECD study: «participate in the Teaching and Learning International Survey (TALIS), around 90% of teachers consider the opportunity to influence children's development and contribute to society to be a major motivation for joining the profession. Only 60% to 70% of teachers report that the financial package and working conditions of the teaching profession were important to them, but this share is higher in countries where teachers are highly valued in society and their economic status is better than that of other professions» (OECD, 2020, TALIS 2018 Results (Volume II), 2020, chapter 4).

A comparison with the countries of Central Asia and the CIS shows the leading positions of Kazakhstan higher education in internationalization and reforms in Central Asia. However, according to UNESCO, in Kazakhstan, "traditional teaching methods still prevail in higher education, with a great emphasis on memorization, which leads to ignoring other important socio-economic skills (UNESCO (2021b, pp. 4–5)). In general, expenditures on higher education in proportion to GDP amounted to only 0.25% in Kazakhstan, 0.18% in Kyrgyzstan, 0.52% in Tajikistan, and there are no data for Uzbekistan (UNESCO (2021b, p. 7); Mynbayeva, 2024).

Analyzing the strengths and weaknesses of higher pedagogical education in modern Kazakhstan, one notable advantage is its resilience following periods of crisis, as evidenced by the development and expansion of an extensive system of higher and postgraduate pedagogical education. Additionally, its integration into the global educational and research community, particularly through participation in the Bologna Process, has facilitated alignment with international standards and practices.

On the one hand, the strengths of higher pedagogical education in Kazakhstan include the preservation of traditional fundamental pedagogical training and the revival of national pedagogical higher education. On the other hand, a key weakness is the slow transformation of pedagogical education content, particularly in integrating new theories and teaching methodologies for future educators. However, a gradual shift is occurring, moving from a predominantly theoretical foundation to a more practice-oriented approach. This transition includes an increased emphasis on practical training in pedagogical universities and the expansion of digital and creative competencies among teachers.

10 Conclusion

Our research builds on existing scientific findings on the development of pedagogical education and aims to systematize ideas about the transformation of the Kazakh education system from the Soviet era to an independent national framework. The main trends in the current stage of pedagogical education development are – Humanisation, Inclusion, Status Enhancement, Openness, Diversification, Academic Freedom, Multilingualism, Development of the Research Environment, Practical Training, and Practice Orientation – they all have different origins and foundations. For instance, Inclusion is a trend in leading Western countries, while Humanisation not only characterises open education systems, but was also inherent in the education of Kazakhs in the pre-Soviet era. Furthermore, multilingualism and practical training, emphasizing the application of knowledge, were prevalent in the education of Kazakh children during the pre-Soviet period of Kazakh pedagogical development. Our research shows that among the various trends in pedagogical education development during the Soviet era, essentially only one remains – centralisation and limited progress in school educational policy. We argue that over the course of 30 years, Kazakhstan's pedagogical education has become independent, open, and has acquired its own national identity.

While higher pedagogical education in Kazakhstan continues to develop, it simultaneously preserves its distinct characteristics and values while undergoing increasing internationalization as a result of regionalization. The evolution and historicity of higher pedagogical education show the connections between the past and the present and may be used to predict the future of Kazakhstan teacher education. However, the educational traditions of the past – "the love of knowledge" and human curiosity, the development of a "perfect person", the education of a virtuous personality striving to achieve happiness, the traditions of public education – to modern times – improving the quality of professional training, continuity of the education system, personality-oriented and student-centered learning, liberalization and humanization of education, are transmitted into the future. It is also evident that "education long and wide throughout life" (Lifelong learning + Lifewide Learning – LLL + LWL), equal access to education, digitalization of education, harmony of ethnic, national and global societies, universal values, education leadership, the competitiveness of the nation, and other principles and traditions are yet to be achieved.

Notes

1　October 31, 1937, the Resolution of the Council of People's Commissars of the Kazakh SSR "On the Semipalatinsk Pedagogical Institute" /Eskendirov, 2011/.
2　Based on the Far Eastern Korean Institute.

References

Akhmetova, G. (2020). *Repressed teachers*. Kazakh University, 250–245.

Akhmetova, G. K. (2016). *System for advanced training of teaching staff in the Republic of Kazakhstan; renewal strategy*. Kazak University, 212.

Akhmetova, G. K. (2002). Teacher training in pedagogical HEIs of Kazakhstan (1958 – 2000). *A review of doctoral dissertation*. Karaganda.

Almukhanbetov, B. A. (2002). History of the formation and development trends of the system for advanced training of teaching staff in the Republic of Kazakhstan. *A review of doctoral dissertation*. KazNPU.

Anarbek, N. (2014). Контент-талдаудың салыстырмалы-педагогикалық зерттеу әдісіретіндегі ерекшеліктері [Features of content analysis as a comparative-pedagogical research method]. *Vestnik Al-Farabi KazNU. Pedagogical Series, 1.* 127–134.

Asylbekov, M.-A. H., & Asylbekova, Zh. M.-A. (2016). *Socio-demographic development of the population of Kazakhstan in 1926–1939.* Almaty: Kazak University.

Baypakov, K. M., & Akylbek, S. Sh. (2012). Second Sauran madrasah. News of the academy of sciences of the republic of Kazakhstan. *Social Sciences and Humanities Series, 3*(283), May–June 2012. Almaty, 84–93

Barber, M., & Mourshed, M. (2007, September 1). *How the world's best performing systems come out on top.* McKinsey. https://www.mckinsey.com/industries/education/our-insights/how-the-worlds-best-performing-school-systems-come-out-on-top

Children of Kazakhstan / Statistical collection. 2018–2023. (2023). Astana, Agency for Strategic Planning and Reforms of the Republic of Kazakhstan Bureau of National Statistics, 126.

Government of the Republic of Kazakhstan. (2023). *Concepts for the development of higher education and science in the Republic of Kazakhstan for 2023–2029.* Astana. https://adilet.zan.kz/rus/docs/P2300000248

Elbaeva, Z. U., & Muhangalieva, R. A. (2012). S. Kozhakhmetov is a pedagogical teacher. Sultan Kozhakhmetov and the development of didactics in his pedagogical heritage. Bulletin of KazNU. *Pedagogical Series, 37*(3).

Fetodova, L. N. (1988). *Контент-аналитические исследования средств массовой информации и пропаганды: Учебно-методическое пособие* [Content-analytical studies of the media and propaganda: Educational and methodological manual]. Moscow University Publishing House.

Fimyar, O., & Kurakbayev, K. (2016). 'Soviet' in teachers' memories and professional beliefs in Kazakhstan: points for reflection for reformers, international consultants and practitioners. *International Journal of Qualitative Studies in Education, 29*(1), 86–103.

Güngör, D. S. (2016). К вопросу о подготовке учителей в Республике Казахстан. [On the issue of teacher training in the Republic of Kazakhstan]. *Eurasian Union of Scientists, 7*–1 (28), 50–58.

Igibayeva, A. K. (2007). The genesis and development trends of the education system in Kazakhstan (the end of the XIX century – the middle of the XX century.). *A review of doctoral dissertation.* Almaty

Игибаева А. К. (2009). Проблемы периодизации, этапы становления и развития образовательной системы Казахстана [Problems of periodization, stages of formation and development of the educational system of Kazakhstan]. *Conference Proceedings "Contribution of young researchers to industrial and innovative development".* Ust-Kamenogors. https://articlekz.com/article/6779

Ilyasova, A. N. (1997). Problems of Development of Pedagogical Theory of Kazakhstan (1900–1960). *A review of doctoral dissertation.* Almaty.

Irsaliev, S. A., Kamzoldaev, M. B., Tashibaeva, D. N., & Kopeeva, A. T. (2019). *Analytical report "Teachers of Kazakhstan: why do young people choose this profession and what motivates them to stay in it?"* Astana: Public Association "Center analysis and strategy 'Beles'"p. 126.

Kaydarova, A.D. (2007). Formation and development of the content of higher pedagogical education in the Republic of Kazakhstan (1928–2005): Abstract. Doctoral dissertation. Almaty.

Kazakhstan demographics zhylnamalygy / Demographic Yearbook of Kazakhstan (2022). Bureau of National Statistics, p. 276.

Kerr, S. T. (1991). Beyond dogma: Teacher education in the USSR. *Journal of Teacher Education, 42*(5), 332–349.

Khrapchenkov, G. M., & Khrapchenkov, V. G. (1998). *The History of School and Pedagogical Thinking of Kazakhstan.* Almaty.

Kissane, C. (2005). History education in transit: where to for Kazakhstan?. *Comparative Education, 41*(1), 45–69.

Kiyasova, B. (2008). Kazakstandagy zhogary mektep pedagogikasyn kalyptasu zhane damu tarikha. Almaty, 104. [Kiyasova, B. (2008). *History of the formation and development of pedagogy of the Kazakh higher school.* Almaty, 104 (In Kazakh)]

Kolesnichenko, L. I. (1984). *History of the creation and development trends of the system for improving teaching staff in Kazakhstan.* Alma-Ata.

Kopzhasarova, L. (2011). *From Kazakh Troy only a citadel can remain. Komsomolskaya Pravda- Kazakhstan.* October 6–13, 14–15. https://online.zakon.kz/Document/ ?doc_id=31063443&pos=3;-80#pos=3;-80

Kopzhasarova, L. (2015, November 15). *Treasures of Sauran.* Komsomolskaya Pravda – Kazakhstan. http://old.kp.kz/incidents/10978-sokrovishcha-saurana

Kozmenko, O. P. (1999). *Training of teaching staff in Kazakhstan in the post-war years, 1946–1958* (Abstract of candidate of historical sciences,.07.00.02). Moscow.

Kruglyansky, M. R. (1970). *Higher school of the USSR during the Great Patriotic War.* Moscow, Higher School, p. 314.

Kunantaeva, K. K. (2001). Development of education in Kazakhstan. 1917–2000.

Law of the Republic of Kazakhstan. (1992). "On Education". In *Collection of legislative and normative documents on higher education (1996).* Lawyer.

Law of the Republic of Kazakhstan. (2007). "On Education" Retrieved from http://nkaoko.kz/documents/law_of_education/

Law of the Republic of Legislation on Education in the Republic of Kazakhstan "On Education" (1999). *The legislation on education in the republic of Kazakhstan (2002).* Lawyer.

Lukyanets I. K.(1959). The emergence and development of higher education in Kazakhstan. *Notes of Kazakh State University named after Kirov, 42*(11), 3–36.

Mashanov, A. (1970). *Al-Farabi.* Alma-Ata.

Mei, H. (2005). Reform of teacher education in China and Russia (comparative analysis): A review of cand. ped. Sci. dissertation. Moscow, 26.

Meshitbaev, T. (1973). Activities of the Communist Party of Kazakhstan in the preparation and education of teaching staff during the pre-war five-year plans (1928–1941): *A review of* Dis. ...cand. ist. Sci. Alma-Ata.

Mynbayeva, A. (2021). *Methods of teaching pedagogy*. Kazak University, 322.

Mynbayeva, A., & Pogosian, V. (2014). Kazakhstani school education development from the 1930s: History and current trends. *Italian Journal of Sociology of Education, 6*(2), 144–172.

Mynbayeva, A., Minazheva, G., Sadyrova, M., & Zholdassova, M. (2024). Examining leadership styles in higher education management: Evidence from Kazakhstan. *International Journal of Leadership in Education*, 1–22.

Nurkabekova, G. (2010). *Historical prerequisites for the modern reform of teacher education in Kazakhstan and China*. Almaty.

Nurlanuly M. (2015) *The first Kazakh woman journalist – Nazipa Kulzhanova*. https://e-history.kz/ru/news/show/6667

Nurtazina, R. A. (2005). The educational policy of the Republic of Kazakhstan in the context of globalization. *A review of doctoral dissertation*. Almaty

OECD (Organization for Economic Cooperation and Development). (2009). *Creating Effective Teaching and Learning Environments: First Results from TALIS*. OECD.

OECD. (2020). *TALIS 2018 Results (Volume II): Teachers and School Leaders as Valued Professionals*, TALIS, OECD Publishing. https://doi.org/10.1787/19cf08df-en

Oku-agartu isi. (1980). Educational and methodological activities. In *Kazakh Soviet Socialist Republic: Encyclopedia* (pp. 394–396). Almaty. (In Kazakh)

Parfenov, I. D. (2001). *Методология исторической науки: курс лекций*. [Methodology of historical science: a course of lectures]. Publishing house of Saratov University.

Pogosian V. (2020) Participatory Decision Making in Russian Schools. *Italian Journal of Sociology of Education, 12*(1), 122–139. https://doi.org/10.14658/PUPJ-IJSE-2020-1-8

Romanenchuk, K. V. (2006). Reforming Russian educational institutions in the system of education of Kazakhstan in 1991–2004. *A review of doctoral dissertation*. Saint Petersburg.

Robertson, S. L. (2012). Placing teachers in global governance agendas. *Comparative Education Review, 56*(4), 584–607.

Sadvokasova, K. (1969). *Development of women's education in Kazakhstan*. Alma-Ata, Kazakhstan.

Sadvokasova, Z. T. (2008). *The policy of tsarism in the field of education in Kazakhstan (II half of the 19th – early 20th centuries)*. Kazakh University.

Sadykova, A. K. (2022). *History of educational institutions of vocational pedagogical education (using the example of Semirechensk and Syrdarya regions in the second half of the 19th century – 1917)*. [Doctoral dissertation, Kazakh National Pedagogical University named after Abay]. https://www.kaznpu.kz/docs/doctoranti/sadykova/1/ann_rus.pdf

Savin, N. V. (1987). *Methods of teaching pedagogy*. Education.

Sembayev, A. (1958). *Essays on the history of the Kazakh Soviet school*. KazUchPedGIZ.

Sievers, E. W. (2013). *The post-Soviet decline of Central Asia: sustainable development and comprehensive capital*. Routledge.

Silova, I. (Ed.). (2002). *Right for quality education; constructing schools of kind attitude to the child in Central Asia*. UNICEF.

Silova, I., & Steiner-Khamsi, G. (Eds.). (2008). *How NGOs react: Globalization and education reform in the Caucasus, Central Asia and Mongolia*. Kumarian Press.

Silova, I. (2011). *Globalization on the margins: education and postsocialist transformations in Central Asia*. IAP – Information Age Publishing, Inc.

Spring, J. (2008). *Globalization of education: An introduction*. Routledge.

Starikova, L. D. (2008). *History of pedagogy and philosophy of education*. Phoenix.

State Program "Education" (2000–2004). (2002). *The legislation on education in the republic of Kazakhstan*. Lawyer.

State Program for the Development of Education and Science for 2020–2025. (2019). *Astana, MES RK*. https://adilet.zan.kz/rus/docs/P1900000988

State Program for the Development of Education and Science of the Republic of Kazakhstan for 2016–2019. (2015). *Astana*. https://adilet.zan.kz/rus/docs/U1600000205

State Program for the Development of Education in the Republic of Kazakhstan for 2005–2010 (2004). Astana. https://adilet.zan.kz/rus/docs/U040001459_

State Program for the Development of Education of the Republic of Kazakhstan for 2011–2020 (2010). Astana. https://adilet.zan.kz/rus/docs/U1000001118

Tazhibayev, T. T. (1958). *The development of education and educational thought in Kazakhstan in the 2nd part of the XIX century*. Part 1. Academy of Sciences of Kazakh SSR.

Tumak, O. (2016). Критерії визначення етапів розвитку методики навчання англійської мови в закладах освіти Буковини (кінець XIX–початок XX століть). [Criteria for determining the stages of development of English language teaching methods in educational institutions of Bukovyna (late 19th–early 20th centuries)]. *Scientific notes of Ternopil National Pedagogical University named after Volodymyr Hnatyuk. Series: pedagogy, (4)*, 233–239]

UNESCO. (n.d.). *National report on the development of the higher education system of the Republic of Kazakhstan*. http://www.unesco.kz/education/he/kazakh/kazakh_ru.htm Accessed on September, 9, 2015.

UNESCO. (2021a). *Reimagining our futures together: A new social contract for education*. Paris, France: Educational and Cultural Organization of the United Nations.

UNESCO. (2021b). *Policy brief: Higher education in Central Asia* (ATA- 2021/PI/2). https://unesdoc.unesco.org/ark:/48223/pf0000377911

Utyupova, G. E. (2017). *Development of the teaching staff training system in Kazakhstan and Germany (using the example of primary school teachers)* [Doctoral dissertation, Doctor of Phil. (PhD)].

Vasilkovskaya, E. I. (2006). *Power and the formation of the Soviet model of the school system: early 30s – mid 50s: author's abstract.* Saratov, 26. https://www.dissercat.com/content/vlast-i-formirovanie-sovetskoi-modeli-shkolnoi-sistemy-nachalo-1930-kh-nachalo-1950-kh-gg

Voitekhovskaya, M. P., Kochurina, S. A., & Perova, O. V. (2011). *Teachers' seminaries and teacher's institutes of the West Siberian educational district. Collection of documents and materials.* Publishing house of Tomsk State Pedagogical University.

Yakavets, N. (2014). Educational reforms in Kazakhstan: First decade of independence. In D. Bridges (Ed.), *Educational Reforms and Internationalization: the case of school reforms in Kazakhstan,* (pp 1–27). Cambridge University Press.

Yakavets, N., Bridges, D., & Shamatov, D. (2017). On constructs and the construction of teachers' professional knowledge in a post-Soviet context. *Journal of Education for Teaching, 43*(5), 594–615.

Yakavets, N., Winter, L., Malone, K., Zhontayeva, Z., Khamidulina, Z. (2023). Educational reform and teachers' agency in reconstructing pedagogical practices in Kazakhstan. *Journal of Educational Change, 24*(4), 727–757.

Zajda, J. (1984). Recent educational reforms in the USSR: their significance for policy development. *Comparative Education, 20*(3), 405–420.

Zhamanbaev, K. J. (1972). *Higher school in Kazakhstan.* Alma-Ata, Kazakhstan.

Zharikbaev, K. B., & Kaliev, S. K. (1995). *Anthology of pedagogical thought of Kazakhstan.* Rauan.

Zhulamanov, K. D. (1981). *Higher education in Central Asia and Kazakhstan.* Alma-Ata.

Zuyeva, L. I. (2013). Этапы развития школьной системы образования Республики Казахстан: анализ моделей обучения и проблемные области в методологии дидактики. [Stages of development of the school education system of the Republic of Kazakhstan: analysis of models of instruction and problem areas in the methodology of didactics]. *Journal of Karaganda State University, 8,* 8–15.

Zykin, A. V. (2013). On the formation and development of the teacher education system in Russia. *Tsarskoye Selo Readings, 2*(XVII), 249–254.

CHAPTER 2

Teacher Recruitment, Preparation, Induction, Retention, and Attrition in Kazakhstan

Tsediso Michael Makoelle

Abstract

The recruitment, pre-service/in-service training, and retention of teachers have become an important topic in most countries. According to the OECD Teaching and Learning International Survey (TALIS) (2018), teaching was the first-choice career for 75% of teachers in Kazakhstan compared to 67% in OECD countries. The conditions of service for teachers as well as workload are issues that are debated in the teacher education field. According to the OECD (2018), there are still inequalities in teacher distribution in urban and rural schools. Furthermore, although efforts have been made to retain teachers in rural schools, the incentives provided seem not attractive enough to entice the most qualified teachers. This chapter analyses the process of teacher recruitment, preparation, and retention of teachers in Kazakhstan then presents a conceptual framework for recruitment, preparation, induction, retention, and attrition (TRPIRA). The challenges and threats of these processes are highlighted. In this chapter, recommendations regarding how those processes (if necessary) could be enhanced are provided.

Keywords

teacher recruitment – teacher education – teacher preparation – teacher attrition – teacher retention

1 Introduction

Teacher recruitment, teacher preparation (pre-service and in-service) as well as teacher induction and retention have become hotly debated issues in the field of teacher education in recent years. Questions about how to recruit suitable candidates for the teaching profession, and retain highly effective teachers in the profession have been raised. The models of pre-service teacher preparation and professional development of in-service teachers have recently been

© TSEDISO MICHAEL MAKOELLE, 2025 | DOI:10.1163/9789004726345_003

a focal point. This chapter, therefore, problematizes the notions of teacher recruitment, preparation, induction, and retention within the Kazakhstani post-soviet teacher education context. Provides a historical context of teacher education in Kazakhstan and discusses the current teacher education system, the chapter further explores factors contributing to teacher recruitment, preparation, induction, and retention globally. A comparative analysis is made with the Kazakhstani context and lessons are drawn from the review to synthesis recommendations going forward.

2 Method of Review

This review investigated the notions of teacher recruitment, preparation, and retention within the teacher education of Kazakhstan. The review was mapped to achieving the following objectives:

- To conceptualize notions of teacher recruitment, preparation, induction and retention within the Kazakhstani and global context;
- To determine factors influencing these notions both internationally and locally;
- To make recommendations about teacher recruitment, preparation, induction and retention in Kazakhstani teacher education going forward.

The criteria used to select the literature were guided by the availability of supportive empirical evidence. Speculative literatures were deliberately excluded. While the literature was reviewed for a study focused on teacher recruitment, preparation, and retention, some of the reviewed work had inclined towards teacher education in general as closely related disciplines such as teacher leadership and educational policy were considered.

I consulted several databases such as Eric, Scopus, and Google Scholar. Further sources of relevant information were internationally accredited journals among others the International Journal of Inclusive Education. The Nazarbayev University library was consulted and books, articles, theses, and electronic sources were perused for relevant, up-to-date literature on the topic.

3 The Notions of Teacher Recruitment, Preparation, Induction, Retention, and Attrition

The process by which new teachers are accepted into the teaching profession is called *"teacher recruitment"*. While it may seem straightforward this process may be fraught with many challenges. The recruitment process follows the supply and demand. According to Sutcher, Darling-Hammond and Carver-Thomas (2019) the demand for teachers is determined by what they call *"teacher shortage"* which they describe as the production of teachers against the enrolled number of students and the retirement of teachers. They also mention that teachers may not be enough as a result of other factors such as teacher "turnover, changes in educational programs and pupil-teacher ratios, and the attractiveness of teaching generally and in specific locations" (p, 4). The process of getting teachers to fully qualify to be teachers is often referred to as *"teacher preparation".* Teacher preparation is regarded as the application of theoretical knowledge about teaching and learning as well as practical exposure of pre-service teachers to the real teaching and learning world through the practicum. There are debates about whether theory or practice should be the focal point. In this regard, Deng (2004) postulates that while theory and practice are important in teacher preparation, pre-service teachers need to be made aware of the complexities, and intellectual and moral nature of classroom practice. On the contrary Feiman-Nemser (1989) through learning to teach must involve going through the process of teaching itself referring to this as "experience is a good teacher"

Once teachers have gone through a teacher preparation program, they are taken through a process referred to as *"teacher induction".* Teacher induction is a period from which the new teacher develops to become a fully professional teacher. The inductions may range from a year to five years. According to Howe (2006), the induction process involves the process through which the novice teacher learns together with experienced teachers in a supportive environment that promotes collaborative learning, reflection, and acculturation into the profession of teaching that fosters professional growth. While some teachers are inclined to stay in the profession till they retire, some teachers do not. This process whereby teachers decide to stay in the profession is often referred to as *"teacher retention"* According to Geiger and Pivovarova, (2018) teacher retention is normally associated with the conditions under which teachers work, and favorable conditions may influence the retention of teachers positively. When teachers decide to leave the teaching profession the process is often referred to as "teacher attrition" In the literature it is indicated that teacher attrition is a common global problem (den Brok et al., 2017).

4 Factors Influencing Teacher Recruitment, Preparation, Induction, Retention, and Attrition Globally

Klassen et al. (2020) postulate that teacher recruitment has become a global crisis, quoting UNESCO (2016) Klassen et al. (2020) aver that there was a need to recruit 69 million teachers translating into 24.4 million primary-level teachers and 44.4 million secondary-level teachers to ensure the sustainability of developing countries. There are various reasons why people may decide to take up the teaching profession. Lee, Akin and Goodwin (2019) postulate that the choice of the teaching profession depends much on the beliefs of those being recruited about the profession. For instance, potential candidates who have convictions about social justice, change, and community well-being could opt for teaching to pursue their personal and political ambitions to contribute to the social upliftment of those communities through education. Various approaches are applied in teacher recruitment. This depends much on the goal of recruitment in various contexts. For instance, Klassen et al. (2020) states that in England a two-step approach is followed i.e. identifying areas and subjects of acute shortage then the provision of incentives for potential recruits. The recruitment process could be stifled by inaccessible potential candidates several mechanisms are applied such as public adverts but Lim and O'Halloran (2012) think televised adverts which use the principle of commodification with consumerist culture might be appealing to potential candidates. Wilson et al. (2004) posit that in some cases consultants and marketing strategies are involved in teacher recruitment.

The preparation of teachers is very crucial and it could determine if teachers are of good quality or not. According to Zhang and Zeller (2016) when teachers have been well prepared for their duties they are likely to enjoy their work and stay much longer in the teaching profession. Boyd et al. (2009) believe that there is a debate about whether getting quality teacher candidates depends on the quality of recruits or the quality of the preparation. They argue that a good program with a good quality practical component is significant for preparing good teachers. According to Allen (2003:1) drawing from the work in the US context argues that effective teacher preparation should be aimed at answering eight key questions i.e.

(1) the extent to which subject knowledge contributes to teacher effectiveness; (2) the extent to which pedagogical coursework contributes to teacher effectiveness; (3) the extent to which high quality field experience prior to certification contributes to teacher effectiveness; (4) alternative route programs that graduate high percentages of effective new teachers with average or above average rates of teacher retention; (5) teacher preparation strategies that are likely to increase new teacher effectiveness in hard-to-staff and low-performing schools; (6) whether setting more stringent teacher preparation program entrance requirements, or conducting more selective screening program candidates, can ensure that prospective teachers will be more effective; (7) whether

accreditation of teacher preparation programs contributes significantly to the likelihood that graduates will be effective and remain in the classroom; and (8) whether institutional warranties for new teachers contribute to the likelihood that recent graduates will be effective.

It is believed that a good teacher preparation program impacts the general attitudes of pre-service teachers toward their work. According to Kim (2011), the attitudes of teachers toward new teaching aspects such as inclusive education are even impacted positively.

Most teacher education scholars believe that a good induction program can affect how beginner teachers will see and think about the teaching profession. For instance, Wilson et al. (2004) posit that when pre-service teachers are subjected to a well-organized mentoring program, it is likely to provide much-needed support for novice teachers. While school mentors could play a role in teacher mentoring, Zhang et al. (2019) contends that such mentoring should encompass the role of the school principal and co-leaders. It is believed that leadership that gets involved is likely to inspire confidence among the novice teachers. In recommending an effective induction program for novice teachers, Arends & Rigazio-DiGilio (2000, p. 1) have identified the following aspects as significant: "clear program goals and purpose; a research-based, ethically sound definition of effective teaching; and develop and implement an effective evaluation component for the induction program itself". According to Wise (1987) placement of teacher in the right setting through a comprehensive induction plan with a good evaluation system for early career teachers is important for their long teaching career.

While effective teacher recruitment, preparation and induction are thought to influence teacher retention in many ways, teacher retention is a complex phenomenon that is impacted upon by various factors. For instance, Brown and Wynn (2009) found that teacher retention was influenced by the school leadership. In a school where the principal is aware of the issues affecting the novice teachers and take a proactive role in supporting the beginner teachers, and was committed to professional growth and excellence for themselves, students and teachers (new and experienced) schools experience high rates of teacher retention. This fact is echoed by Boyd et al. (2011). While teacher working conditions such as salary could be a factor in teacher retention (See et al. 2020), studies such that of Hughes (2012) found that combined with a conducive collaborative culture from students and parents, it can influence the decision of teachers to stay longer. Factors related to teacher well-being could have far reaching influence on teacher retention. For instance, Sass et al. (2011) found that students experiencing stress could be depressing for teachers and as such likely to impact on the decision of teachers to stay or leave. This compounded with teachers health related issues could have a profound impact on teacher well-being and thus consequently impact on teacher retention (Casey-Hayford et al. 2022).

Non teacher retention results in teacher attrition. According to Minarik, Thornton and Peppeault (2003) inadequate induction, lack of support from school leadership, isolation, lack of professional growth and development, low levels of reward and ill-discipline of students' are motivating factors for teacher attrition. Teacher attrition can even be higher if teachers' characteristics, personal qualities, qualifications and work environment are not compatible to the profession (Billingsley, 2004). It is also believed that the working conditions such as performativity and accountability may put such a lot of pressure on teachers that they decide to quit (Perryman & Calvert, 2019). In rural context, Seelig and McCabe (2021) postulate that teacher only stay on when they show commitment to students, see the opportunities for leadership and collaboration, community connection and professional ties. According to Frahm and Cianca (2021) the rural school leadership that is supportive could decrease rural teacher attrition. Similarly, Geiger and Pivovarova (2018) think teacher are not likely to leave if the working conditions are favourable.

5 Teacher Recruitment, Preparation, Induction, Retention, and Attrition in Kazakhstan

Teacher education in Kazakhstan is undergoing rapid changes. According to Sharplin et al. (2020) Kazakhstan is at the stage where to sustain effective and sustainable teacher education several aspects need to be taken into consideration. There needs to be a connection between quality teachers and current educational reforms. This according to Sharplin et al. (2020) would impact on quality of curriculum and professional practice in schools. As a result, the national policy has to address this through initial teacher education's regulatory framework, curriculum content, teacher education qualification pathways and accountability measures. These views are echoed by Tastanbekova (2018) who postulates that the successful implementation of new curriculum reform depends very much on the quality of teachers in the Kazakhstani education system.

The number of teachers in Kazakhstan in 2014 was 297 200 (TIMSS, 2015). Teachers are prepared in pedagogical colleges and universities. There are current efforts to strengthen and modernize teacher education in Kazakhstan. According to Susimetsa, Porkkonen and Laurikainen (2023) Kazakhstan through the International Bank for Reconstruction and Development (World Bank) and Hame University of Applied Sciences (HAMK) through the Education Mordenisation Project are developing 30 new initial teacher education curriculum. Despite these reforms and changes in teacher education several factors influences teachers' recruitment, preparation, induction, retention, and attrition.

According to Courtney et al. (2023) teachers who enter the teaching profession with altruistic intentions are likely to stay on. It is further stated that of teaching is the first career choice for potential teacher recruits in Kazakhstan, this is likely to translate into long commitment to the profession. On the other hand, Polovnikova and Qanay (2023) aver that well-constructed teacher identity is a prerequisite for sustainable teacher career in Kazakhstan. There are other motivating factors for teachers to choose the teaching career and stay in it for long. However, more women are inclined to choose teaching as a profession. According to Bakayev (2022) men do not choose teaching as a career as it is projected as a career for females. It is recommended that career counselling is needed to advocate and encourage men to enter the teaching profession.

The preparation of teachers in Kazakhstan plays a pivotal role in how the profession is seen. There are issues of preparation that need to be taken care of, for instance, Karimova believe that the mentoring of pre-service teachers does not well achieve the goal of professional sustainability, it is suggested that rather than focus on only on teaching feedback other factors relating to the profession in general needs to be looked at carefully. In support of this aspect, Yussupova, Zhussipbek and Dwyer (2023) state that shortage of teachers could also be affected by specialisation. For instance they indicate that teachers who can teaching in inclusive schools are not enough as the teacher education institutions have not yet made this aspect a priority.

According to Mir, Shamatov and Fillipova (2022) motivating factors such as reward, recognition and professional development go a long way in ensuring a sustainability and reduced teacher attrition. Conversely, Nurymbetov (2022) postulate that reforms and efforts that are been made to improve and modernize teacher education have yielded positive results as students who got good results from the Unified National Testing (UNT) are beginning to have teaching and a career of choice. Teacher retention is a multifaceted notion, albeit conducted in TVET context, Sultangaliyeva (2019) found that salary, workload, administrative support, collegiality, professional opportunities influenced the retention of teachers. Regarding teacher well-being and safety, Dosmurzina (2021) found that teachers in Kazakhstan sometimes experience intimidation or verbal abuse by students which could impact on teacher stress and consequently their well-being and safety. Tajik and Makoelle (2024) lament the top down leadership structure in Kazakhstani School that creates fear in teachers rather than creativity and innovation. Such leadership may impact on teacher well-being and thus encourage some teacher to seek alternative forms of employment.

Although there are suggestions to improve salaries of teachers in Kazakhstan and Tastanbekova (2020) believes that a total overhaul of teacher benefits should be initiated in order to enhance prestige, status and esteem of the teaching profession. This view is echoed by Baishemirov (2024) who contends that improving the prestige of the teaching profession would ensure sustainable teacher retention.

6 Lesson from the Review

The lesson learned from the review is that recruitment, preparation, induction, retention, and attrition are better understood in Kazakhstan using a developed conceptual framework: (TRPIRA) Teacher Recruitment, Preparation, Induction, Retention, and Attrition:

According to this conceptual framework teacher education policy is at the heart of recruitment, preparation, induction, retention and attrition. The policy must provide sufficient and clear regulatory framework and accountability measures for the teaching profession. The need to transform curriculum from the traditional (teacher centered approach) to modern (student centered). Therefore, the review of current teacher education policy with a view of enhancing the status of teachers is important.

To enhance quality, it is evident that the selection of potential recruit should base on suitability based on the number of criteria. Candidate must

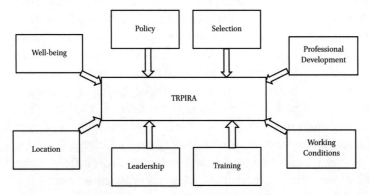

FIGURE 2.1 Conceptual framework for teacher recruitment, preparation, induction, retention, and attrition

be of the right personality, have altruistic intentions and show passion and interest for the profession. The fact that more women enter the profession that their male counterpart, is an indication that advocacy and encouragement for male teachers to join the teaching profession is necessary.

While teachers are been trained, more collaborative approaches to teacher development seem needed. The need for teacher professional learning, establishment of teacher professional learning groups could enhance teacher support for both novice and experienced teachers and thus lower the burden of individual work. The whole process of novice teacher mentoring could be re-imagined and organized in such a way that it provides sustained support which could impact positively to teacher retention.

While there are indications that the salaries of teachers in Kazakhstan may contribute to attrition, the findings of the review show that other working conditions such as opportunities for professional growth and discipline in the school are equally important. It is evident that the preparation and training program should be characterized a progressive curriculum which recognize teachers as partners rather than as mere curriculum implementers. This indicates a need to empower teachers to make curriculum decisions. The top down curriculum development process does not instill confidence in teachers and as a result some could opt out. It became evident that qualifications pathways could provide aspirant teachers with a variety of choices within the profession (Sharplin et al., 2020).

The review has shown that there are also challenges with regard to teacher well-being and safety. Practical measures are needed to deal with teacher well-being as this contribute to less teacher job satisfaction and consequently may encourage teacher attrition. It is evident that the top down leadership styles in schools could impact on teacher well-being and thus on the decision to continue or not to continue with the teaching profession. While teacher recruitment and retention could be a challenge to all schools, the location of the school impact greatly on this. For instance, the rural ungraded schools in Kazakhstan could have limited resources and conditions that could influence teachers to work at them or not. It became evident that more needed to be done to improve the conditions of schools in the rural parts of Kazakhstan.

7 Conclusion

The chapter has based in both the international and local literature synthesized a conceptual framework for teacher recruitment, preparation, induction, retention and attrition in Kazakhstan. The authors is mindful that although conclusions from this chapter offer some insights into the processes,

Kazakhstan's education is rapidly changing. However, this chapter contributes to the debate about teacher recruitment and retention in Kazakhstan and could be a valuable resource for teacher education policy makers, teacher education administrators, teacher educators and school leaders.

References

Allen, M. (2003). *Eight questions on teacher preparation: What does the research say? A summary of the findings.*

Arends, R. I., & Rigazio-DiGilio, A. J. (2000). *Beginning teacher induction: Research and examples of contemporary practice.*

Baishemirov, Z. (2024). Issues and perspectives on teacher education for education for sustainable development in Kazakhstan. In *Science education for sustainable development in Asia* (pp. 325–338). Springer Nature Singapore.

Bakayev, D. (2022). *Reasons men in Kazakhstan choose a teaching career: A replication study using the fit choice scale* (Master's thesis, Nazarbayev University Graduate School of Education).

Boyd, D., Grossman, P., Ing, M., Lankford, H., Loeb, S., & Wyckoff, J. (2011). The influence of school administrators on teacher retention decisions. *American Educational Research Journal, 48*(2), 303–333.

Boyd, D. J., Grossman, P. L., Lankford, H., Loeb, S., & Wyckoff, J. (2009). Teacher preparation and student achievement. *Educational Evaluation and Policy Analysis, 31*(4), 416–440.

Billingsley, B. S. (2004). Special education teacher retention and attrition: A critical analysis of the research literature. *The Journal of Special Education, 38*(1), 39–55.

Brown, M. K., & Wynn, R. S. (2009). Finding, supporting, and keeping: The role of the principal in teacher retention issues. *Leadership and Policy in Schools, 8*(1), 37–63.

Casely-Hayford, J., Björklund, C., Bergström, G., Lindqvist, P., & Kwak, L. (2022). What makes teachers stay? A cross-sectional exploration of the individual and contextual factors associated with teacher retention in Sweden. *Teaching and Teacher Education, 113*, 103664.

Courtney, M., Karakus, M., Sharplin, E., Hernández-Torrano, D., Helmer, J., & Jumakulov, Z. (2023). The role of teacher selection criteria and preparation on teacher self-efficacy, satisfaction, and commitment: An analysis of Kazakhstani TALIS data. *Teacher Development, 27*(3), 394–414.

den Brok, P., Wubbels, T., & Van Tartwijk, J. (2017). Exploring beginning teachers' attrition in the Netherlands. *Teachers and Teaching, 23*(8), 881–895.

Deng, Z. (2004). The role of theory in teacher preparation: An analysis of the concept of theory application. *Asia-Pacific Journal of Teacher Education, 32*(2), 143–157.

Dosmurzina, D. (2021). *Understanding teacher safety in schools in Kazakhstan* (Master's thesis, Nazarbayev University Graduate School of Education).

Feiman-Nemser, S. (1989). *Teacher preparation: Structural and conceptual alternatives.* National Center for Research on Teacher Education.

Frahm, M. T., & Cianca, M. (2021). Will they stay or will they go? Leadership behaviors that increase teacher retention in rural schools. *The Rural Educator, 42*(3), 1.

Geiger, T., & Pivovarova, M. (2018). The effects of working conditions on teacher retention. *Teachers and Teaching, 24*(6), 604–625.

Howe, E. R. (2006). Exemplary teacher induction: An international review. *Educational Philosophy and Theory, 38*(3), 287–297.

Hughes, G. D. (2012). Teacher retention: Teacher characteristics, school characteristics, organizational characteristics, and teacher efficacy. *The Journal of Educational Research, 105*(4), 245–255.

Karimova, N. (2020). *Mentoring programs for novice teachers in Kazakhstani mainstream schools: Experiences and attitudes of main stakeholders* (Master's thesis, Nazarbayev University Graduate School of Education).

Kim, J. R. (2011). Influence of teacher preparation programmes on preservice teachers' attitudes toward inclusion. *International Journal of Inclusive Education, 15*(3), 355–377.

Klassen, R. M., Rushby, J. V., Durksen, T. L., & Bardach, L. (2021). Examining teacher recruitment strategies in England. *Journal of Education for Teaching, 47*(2), 163–185.

Lee, C. C., Akin, S., & Goodwin, A. L. (2019). Teacher candidates' intentions to teach: Implications for recruiting and retaining teachers in urban schools. *Journal of Education for Teaching, 45*(5), 525–539.

Lim, V., & O'Halloran, K. L. (2012). The ideal teacher: An analysis of a teacher-recruitment advertisement. *Semiotica, 2012*(189), 229–253.

Minarik, M. M., Thornton, B., & Perreault, G. (2003). Systems thinking can improve teacher retention. *The Clearing House, 76*(5), 230–234.

Nurymbetov, Y. (2022). Recruiting the high-achieving graduates to the teaching profession. The case of Kazakhstan. *Pedagogical Quarterly/Kwartalnik Pedagogiczny, 68*(2).

Perryman, J., & Calvert, G. (2020). What motivates people to teach, and why do they leave? Accountability, performativity and teacher retention. *British Journal of Educational Studies, 68*(1), 3–23.

Polovnikova, X. V., & Qanay, G. A. (2023). Pre-service teachers' professional identity in Kazakhstan. *Bulletin of the Kazakh National Women's Pedagogical University,* (1), 9–21.

Sass, D. A., Seal, A. K., & Martin, N. K. (2011). Predicting teacher retention using stress and support variables. *Journal of Educational Administration, 49*(2), 200–215.

See, B. H., Morris, R., Gorard, S., Kokotsaki, D., & Abdi, S. (2020). Teacher recruitment and retention: A critical review of international evidence of most promising interventions. *Education Sciences, 10*(10), 262.

Seelig, J. L., & McCabe, K. M. (2021). Why teachers stay: Shaping a new narrative on rural teacher retention. *Journal of Research in Rural Education, 37*(8).

Sharplin, E., Ibrasheva, A., Shamatov, D., & Rakisheva, A. (2020). Анализ педагогического образования Казахстана в контексте современной международной практики [Analysis of teacher education in Kazakhstan in the context of modern international practice]. *Vestnik KazNU. Pedagogical Series, 64*(3), 12–27.

Sultangaliyeva, A. (2019). *Factors Influencing Instructors' Retention in TVET* (Master's thesis, Nazarbayev University Graduate School of Education).

Sutcher, L., Darling-Hammond, L., & Carver-Thomas, D. (2019). Understanding teacher shortages: An analysis of teacher supply and demand in the United States. *Education Policy Analysis Archives, 27*(35).

Tajik, M. A., & Makoelle, T. M. (2024). Leadership lessons from the great steppes of central Asia: Opportunities, obstacles, and the way forward. In *Redefining educational leadership in central Asia* (pp. 221–234). Emerald Publishing Limited.

Tajik, M. A., Shamatov, D. A., & Fillipova, L. N. (2022). Teachers'quality in Kazakhstani rural schools. *Bulletin of the Kazakh National Women's Pedagogical University,* (3), 6–16.

Tastanbekova, K. (2020). Professional prestige, status, and esteem of educational occupation in Kazakhstan: Temporal, regional and gender analysis of payroll data. *Journal of Eastern European and Central Asian Research (JEECAR), 7*(2), 175–190.

Tastanbekova, K. (2018). Teacher education reforms in Kazakhstan: Trends and issues. 筑波大学教育学系論集= *Bulletin of Institute of Education, University of Tsukuba, 42*(2), 87–97.

Wilson, S. M., Bell, C., Galosy, J. A., & Shouse, A. W. (2004). "Them that's got shall get": Understanding teacher recruitment, induction, and retention. *Yearbook of the National Society for the Study of Education, 103*(1), 145–179.

Wise, A. E. (1987). *Effective teacher selection: From recruitment to retention.* The Rand Corporation.

Yussupova, D. S., Zhussipbek, T. Z., & Dwyer, H. (2023). Analysis of specialists' shortages in schools with inclusive education in Kazakhstan. *Bulletin of the Karaganda University Economy Series, 110*(2), 123–135.

Zhang, G., & Zeller, N. (2016). A longitudinal investigation of the relationship between teacher preparation and teacher retention. *Teacher Education Quarterly, 43*(2), 73–92.

Zhang, S., Nishimoto, M., & Liu, K. (2019). Preservice Teacher Expectations of the Principal's Role in Teacher Induction. *New Waves-Educational Research and Development Journal, 22*(1), 72–89.

CHAPTER 3

From Global Ideas to Local Classrooms
Teachers Enacting Curriculum Reforms in Kazakhstan

Kairat Kurakbayev

Abstract

In the context of globalization of education, teachers have become key agents in adapting transnational curriculum policies to fit local school environments. This study explores how public school teachers in Kazakhstan engaged with and enacted nationally driven curriculum reforms influenced by transnational policy transfers. Drawing on the interpretive framework of transnational policy borrowing research and the concepts of policy enactment and teacher agency, this research investigates the enablers and constraints teachers face when implementing top-down curriculum reforms based on the local adaptation of global education policies. Additionally, it examines how teachers, working within national educational systems that encounter global education policies and best practices, translate these into their own logic to address the unique needs of their schools. Using a mixed-methods approach, data were collected through individual interviews with 14 teachers, six school leaders and an online survey of 215 educators across four mainstream schools, both urban and rural. The findings highlight the complexities of scaling international reforms across diverse educational contexts, underscoring the critical role of teachers in contextualizing global education policy ideas within local realities.

1   Introduction

National curriculum reforms have traditionally been viewed as the domain of national expertise. However, there is a growing body of research providing evidence that national curriculum reforms are increasingly characterized by the adoption of global education policies and transnational policy expertise (Sivesind et al., 2016; Baek et al., 2018). National policymakers tend to engage in selective borrowing of global policy discourses and practices for various economic, cultural, and political reasons (Steiner-Khamsi, 2014). More recently, scaling and spreading international standards from a cluster of innovative schools to the entire public school system became an attractive reform modality for policymakers in various countries (Bridges, 2014; Looi & Teh, 2015; Looi

© KAIRAT KURAKBAYEV, 2025 | DOI:10.1163/9789004726345_004

et al., 2015; McLaughlin et al., 2023; Sargsyan, 2018). I use the notion of international standards as broadly defined international best practices and global education policies (e.g., competence-based education, outcomes-based education, 21st-century skills, and English as a medium of instruction) that national governments endeavor to adopt in their public school systems (Waldow, 2012; Steiner-Khamsi, 2016; Steiner-Khamsi & Dugonjić-Rodwin, 2018).

On the one hand, scaling transnational policy ideas – usually deemed as 'best practices' – is an attractive reform modality for national governments as the scale up is typically a prescriptive and standardized process. Standardized practices are easier and more efficient to implement compared to change efforts that require local development (Datnow et al., 2002). On the other hand, scaling-based reform models imply that an innovation was not developed within a local school context but was externally initiated. In this respect, Datnow et al. (2002) note that 'scaling' involves "external partners" and is thus considered "an externally developed reform model" (pp. 2–3).

The dissemination of externally developed reforms is increasingly characterized by challenges for schools embedded in their own local policy contexts (Braun et al., 2011). Scaling international standards as a school reform modality requires teacher's professional buy-in and policy stability (Sabelli & Harris, 2015). Centrally directed and nationwide transfer of foreign ideas further complicates the 'scale-up' process across various school contexts. This study stems from a larger study that focused on the scale-up reform wherein national policy actors involved international education service providers in order to adapt and disseminate international standards from the autonomous system of Nazarbayev Intellectual Schools (NIS) to the system of mainstream public schools (Kurakbayev, 2023). Being implemented during the period of 2015–2021, this reform was based on the scale-up of transnational curricular innovations from a local network of highly selective public schools for gifted children "Autonomous Educational Organization 'Nazarbayev Intellectual Schools'" to the entire national system of more than 7000 mainstream public schools. This curriculum reform is widely referred to as the 'national curriculum renewal' reform (National Academy of Education, 2015).

The purpose of this study is to examine how the innovation policy transfer was translated into actual practice at mainstream public schools. I specifically examined the role of teachers in national curriculum reform based on transnational policy transfer. The study pursued the following research questions: (1) How do teachers perceive and navigate the challenges posed by centrally driven curriculum renewal policies during the process of policy enactment? and (2) In what ways do teachers adapt centrally driven curriculum renewal policies to fit their specific school contexts during the process of policy enactment?

This study, conducted between November 2021 and April 2022, explored a mature phase of the curriculum renewal reform. By capturing the final stage in the curriculum implementation process, it contributes to a deeper understanding of how teacher agency and practices have evolved over time, offering insights into the sustainability and depth of the reforms as teachers gain further experience with the renewed curriculum.

2 Context and Background

Like other countries of the former Soviet Union, Kazakhstan's national school curriculum inherited the Soviet system's structure, principles, and ideological views on content, pedagogy, and assessment (Fimyar & Kurakbayev, 2016). The Soviet system was known for its "fundamentality, consistency, and access to free education" (Bekishev, 2011, p. 89). Following the USSR's collapse, post-socialist reforms aimed at dismantling Soviet structures sparked debates among policymakers, teachers, parents, and various actors (Chankseliani & Silova, 2018). Even after 30 years of independence, the Soviet legacy in curriculum remains divisive. Advocates of international ('Western') curriculum standards tend to criticize the Soviet system, while opponents of these standards still hold the Soviet school system in high regard.

After the USSR collapsed in 1991, post-socialist states, including Kazakhstan, had to develop national policies for rebuilding. In Central Asia, all five post-socialist republics created their own national school curricula while dismantling Soviet ideology. Kazakhstan's curriculum reforms sought to restore national identity while searching for effective ways to reform the school system. During the early post-Soviet period, reforms largely retained the tradition of rote learning, with limited room for student autonomy or creativity (Mynbayeva et al., 2014). Revisions prioritized academic subject knowledge over practical and functional skills, adhering to a subject-based structure (Working Group of the Ministry of Education and Science and the Soros Foundation, 2003).

2.1 Alignment of National School Curriculum Reforms with International Large-Scale Assessments

Since gaining national independence from the former Soviet Union, Kazakhstan aimed to align its education system with international standards and "integrate into the world's educational space" (Government of Kazakhstan, 2004, p. 20). This approach reflected the broader goals of the "Kazakhstan 2050" national strategy, linking education with the government's ambition to become internationally competitive (Government of Kazakhstan, 2015).

Global benchmarks, particularly from the OECD, shaped Kazakhstan's education policies (Government of Kazakhstan, 2015).

By the end of its first decade of national independence, Kazakhstan's Ministry of Education and Science[1] (MoES) began developing long-term strategies for educational reforms. From 2000 onwards, the government started to introduce program-based reforms – so-called 'state programs for education development'. For instance, the State Program 'Education' for 2000–2005 states that "the goal of the reforms carried out in the education system of our state is to ensure its qualitative transformation in the conditions of a market economy, taking into account globalization" (Government of Kazakhstan, 2004, para. 6). Table 3.1 lists state programs for education development from 2000 to 2025, highlighting the national education policy goals that impacted curriculum reforms in public schools. The table also shows the government's introduction of the OECD's Program for International Student Assessment (PISA) and other international large-scale assessments (ILSA) in national curriculum documents and policies.

This sequence of state programs highlights how Kazakhstan's government has increasingly accepted ILSAs and comparative educational data as essential tools for policy-making, benchmarking progress, setting standards, and fostering policy learning (Addey & Sellar, 2020). The alignment with global benchmarks and the scaling-up of curriculum reforms have become central strategies for advancing the national education agenda.

2.1.1 Translating International Standards to State Standards of Education

As part of the state's ecology (Abbott, 2005), the national curriculum is based on the "State Mandatory Standards of Education" (henceforth, Standards), a government-issued policy document that regulates national curriculum policies in the public school sector. The Standards outline the core components of national curricula, specifying the mandatory content, required learning outcomes, number of contact hours, and assessment processes for each subject that all mainstream public schools must follow.

Before the initiation of the centralized reform through the transfer of curriculum reforms from the NIS to mainstream public schools in 2016, the national school curriculum was developed by the community of post-Soviet scholars that represented a special branch of education 'didactics' that deals with issues, principle and theories of curriculum design and development (Mynbayeva, et al., 2014). On the institutional level, scholars of didactics were based in the National Research Institute of Pedagogical Sciences[4] that was later transformed into the current National Academy of Education (henceforth,

FROM GLOBAL IDEAS TO LOCAL CLASSROOMS

TABLE 3.1   State programs for education development in Kazakhstan in 2000–2025

#	Title of the state program	Key national education policy objectives related to school curriculum reforms
1	State Program "Education" for 2000–2005	Improving the content and methods of teaching in order to raise the quality of education at schools.
2	State Program of Education Development of the Republic of Kazakhstan for 2005–2010	Transforming the content of school curriculum from a knowledge-centered one to a competence-based and outcomes-based curriculum. Getting the public school system participate in international large scale assessments (PISA[2], TIMMS[3]).
3	State Program of Education Development of the Republic of Kazakhstan for 2011–2020	Transition to the 12-year schooling model with the renewed content of curriculum. International benchmarking with OECD countries and setting desired scores in prospective PISA, TIMMS, PIRLS tests. Building 22 Nazarbayev Intellectual Schools with one school per each region with the attraction of international providers of educational services and products.
4	State Program of Education and Science Development of the Republic of Kazakhstan for 2016–2019	Scaling renewed content of curriculum from Nazarbayev Intellectual Schools (NIS) to mainstream public schools. International benchmarking of the national school system with OECD countries based on the PISA and TIMMS results. Updating the State Standards of Primary and Secondary Education with the emphasis on developing students' functional literacy and novel ways of assessment.
5	State Program of Education and Science Development of the Republic of Kazakhstan for 2020–2025	Completing the transition of secondary education to the renewed curriculum based on the NIS curriculum. International benchmarking of the national school system with other countries based on international-large scale assessments (PISA, TIMMS). Planning a phased transition to the 12-year education.

NAE). Prior to the revision of the national curriculum in 2016, the NAE was the sole policy actor with the mandate over national curriculum design.

The NAE developed the first Standards in 1998 and revised them in 2002. Those Standards did not propose something different from the post-Soviet curriculum (Working Group of the Ministry of Education and Science and the

Soros Foundation, 2003). The Standards amplified the post-Soviet tradition of the subject-based principle of curriculum design. In 2003, the Soros Foundation, in partnership with the MoES and with the support of international consultants, including former OECD associates, proposed the idea of "the school model oriented towards outcomes" (Working Group of the Ministry of Education and Science and the Soros Foundation, 2003, p. 3). This conceptual school model reflected principles of curriculum design based on outcomes-based education and competence-based education viewed as 'international standards' in this study (Waldow, 2012). By making external references to national educational systems of the Global North – including Australia, England, New Zealand, and Scotland – that had adopted this global school model (Waldow, 2012), the working group argued for the relevance and necessity of curriculum reform through outcomes-based education (Working Group of the Ministry of Education and Science and the Soros Foundation, 2003).

Despite its revisions in 2002 and 2010, the national curriculum was mainly characterized by the traditional "'knowledge-centered' orientation of school subjects" (Shuinshina et al., 2019, p. 3). Though the national educational policy managed to distance itself from "the communist monopoly of the party in ideology and education" of the Soviet period (Mynbayeva et al., 2014, p. 133), a knowledge-centered paradigm of education has still been entrenched in teachers' beliefs, values and attitudes. Kazakhstan's post-Soviet traditions of curriculum design was strictly centered on the inputs, that is, curriculum objectives rather than the outputs of expected academic performance and learning outcomes.

In 2012, the NAE developed the new Standards. These standards introduced the concept of "functional literacy" which was framed as an international standard (Government of Kazakhstan, 2012). Despite the reference to functional literacy, the Standard of 2012 remained focused on the subject matter knowledge-centered paradigm. In 2016, the work on the adaptation of the NIS curriculum administered by the NIS in partnership with the NAE led to the revision of the Standards of 2012. Amendments in the Standards of 2012 led to the development of the Standards of 2016. The Standards revised in 2016 put more emphasis on the importance of functional skills, introduction of criterion-referenced assessment, formative assessment (assessment for learning) and learning outcomes rather than a subject matter knowledge-centered paradigm.

2.1.2   Autonomous Educational Organization "Nazarbayev Intellectual Schools" and Its Role in the National Curriculum Reform

The Autonomous Educational Organization "Nazarbayev Intellectual Schools" is part of a broader educational network that includes Nazarbayev University and the Nazarbayev Fund. This network was created to implement "parallel reforms" in both school and higher education sectors (Hartley & Ruby, 2017). According to its mission, NIS strives to "increase Kazakhstan's intellectual capacity by integrating the best national and international practices and significant scientific achievements in the field of school education" (NIS, 2018, p. 12). Intellectual schools focus on providing education in natural sciences and mathematics, contributing to the nation's intellectual growth (NIS, 2018). As a cluster of selective schools, NIS aims to cultivate an intellectual elite and to become "a successful experience *dissemination model* for managing and introducing innovation to the national education system" (NIS, 2018, p. 8, emphasis added).

NIS was established as part of the national project "Intellectual Nation – 2020," initiated in 2009 by Kazakhstan's first president, Nursultan Nazarbayev (Nazarbayev, 2009). Its goal was to develop competitive human capital by 2020. Nazarbayev described NIS as essential for creating a "core of national intellect" (Nazarbayev, 2009, para. 141). NIS schools enjoy institutional autonomy and substantial government funding. In 2011, a special law granted NIS and its partners autonomy, self-governance, and academic freedom, allowing the schools "to implement their independently developed special academic programs as well as academic programs of international partners" (Government of Kazakhstan, 2011, p. 7).

As an innovation hub for mainstream schools, NIS has formed strategic partnerships with prestigious international institutions, including Cambridge University and Cambridge Assessment International Education in particular, International Baccalaureate Organization, Cito (educational assessment organization in the Netherlands) and the Johns Hopkins Center for Talented Youth. NIS operates 22 schools in major cities across Kazakhstan.[5] Most of these schools follow the "NIS Program," developed in partnership with Cambridge Assessment International Education, while one school offers the International Baccalaureate Program (NIS, 2018). NIS can be conceptualized as 'international-standard schools' (Coleman, 2009; Steiner-Khamsi & Dugonjić-Rodwin, 2018). These schools, typically national projects, borrow long-standing educational innovations from the private sector and adapt them to public education. Characterized by their dual mission of serving gifted students and disseminating best practices to regular public schools, international-standard schools are an emerging policy trend in the Global South.

3   Conceptual Framework of the Study

3.1   *Transnational Policy Borrowing Research*
This study draws on the theoretical framework of policy borrowing and lending, as outlined by Steiner-Khamsi (2014). Originating from a sociological systems perspective (Luhmann, 1997; King & Thornhill, 2003), this framework is

instrumental in examining the cultural and political dynamics that shape the adaptation of international standards within a specific local context. According to Steiner-Khamsi (2014), the local context is essential for understanding social, cultural and political reasons behind borrowing policies (externalization), the ways in which they are adapted and applied within the local settings (recontextualization), and the effects they have on existing structures, policies, and practices (internalization).

3.2 Policy Enactment and Teacher Agency in Curriculum Reforms

There is little explicit research on issues and challenges that teachers as recipients of 'travelling reforms' encounter as they attempt to make meaning of new educational practices and, more importantly, international ideas and concepts which accompany these practices. Spillane et al. (2002) point out that "the content of a policy – its ideas about changing extant behavior – depends crucially on the implementing agents – their ideas, their expertise, and their experiences" (pp. 393–394). In this regard, the conceptualization of policy by Ball et al. (2012) and their point on the role of teachers in policy enactment are relevant. Ball et al. (2012) argue that schools have their own 'take' on policies and reforms. Policy is a continuously contested process that is "subject to 'interpretation'" as it gets enacted "rather than implemented" within schools (Braun et al., 2011, p. 586). The meaning of educational policymaking is usually taken for granted as policymakers tend to neglect school-specific factors including "constraints, pressures and enablers of policy enactments" (Braun et al., 2011, p. 585).

Addressing the question of 'how schools do policy', Ball et al. (2012) draw conceptual differences between the notion of 'policy implementation' and 'policy enactment'. According to Ball et al. (2012), education policy enactment is characterized by creative processes of interpreting, translating and recontextualizing abstractions of policy ideas into contextualized practices. Policy enactments occur within interpretation, that is, "a making sense of policy" and translation of policy texts into action characterized by creativity (Ball et al., 2012, pp. 43 & 45). Policy intentions to scale international best practices have implications for various local school contexts. Schools, operating in multiple contexts, come up with their own particular tactics to enact policies and to respond to policy demands of national reforms.

The instability of the original concepts of different international standards and innovations – especially when taken out of their social and geographical contexts – is highly likely to have a different meaning for local actors as they take the cascaded policy further down their own locale (Datnow et al., 2002). Thus, while utilizing the tenets of international policy transfer, this study applied the concept of teacher agency. Ketelaar et al. (2012) note that "teachers who experience agency within their work feel in control of the work-related choices they make, which they base upon their own goals, interests, and motivations" (p. 994). The concept of agency can be viewed from an ecological approach (Biesta & Tedder, 2006). With an ecological view, "actors always act *by means* of their environment rather than simply *in* their environment" (Priestley et al., 2013, p. 189, emphasis in original). Priestley et al. (2013) offer an analytical model for understanding teacher agency in the context of curriculum reforms based on the three dimensions as follows: (1) Iterative dimension (life histories, professional histories), (2) Practical-evaluative dimension that includes cultural aspects (ideas, values and beliefs, discourses and language), structural aspects (social structures, relationships, roles, power and trust) and material aspects (resources and physical environment) and (3) Projective dimension (short-term and long-term) incorporates the imaginative exploration of potential future courses of action, where established ways of thinking and acting "may be creatively reconfigured in relation to actors' hopes, fears, and desires for the future" (Priestley et al., 2013, p. 189).

Importantly, teacher agency reflects the quality of how actors interact with the temporal and relational contexts surrounding their actions, rather than a characteristic of the individuals themselves. This perspective allows for a deeper understanding of how people can exercise reflexivity and creativity, sometimes pushing against societal constraints, while also being shaped and restricted by their social and material environments (Priestley et al., 2013).

Priestley et al. (2016) observe a tendency in national curriculum policies "to construct teachers explicitly as agents of change" (p. 134). Yet, in various public school systems, national governments tend to rely on prescriptive and top-down curricula. Teacher agency gets paramount importance when the government's intention is to provide the spread and sustainability of curricular innovations at mainstream public schools as the final stage of transnational policy transfer. Thus, as a nationally driven policy, the scale-up of curricular innovations can be viewed as a case of policy enactment in mainstream public schools. Policy enactment implies schools' creative responses to multiple policy demands. Contextual dimensions and institutional factors are likely to affect "how policies are interpreted and enacted" in multiple school contexts (Braun et al., 2011, p. 586).

4   Methods

4.1   *Mixed Methods Research Design*
Drawing on a mixed methods research approach, this study employed an exploratory sequential mixed methods research design (Creswell & Plano Clark, 2018). The rationale behind this sequential design is that the outcomes of the initial qualitative method can assist in shaping or guiding the subsequent

quantitative method. This design is often used when variables are unknown, measures or instruments are not yet available, and the goal is to explore a phenomenon in depth (Creswell & Plano Clark, 2018). The research participants from the same sample were involved in both phases of the study.

4.2 Research Sites and Participants

To examine how mainstream public schools responded to the scale-up of international standards as part of the curriculum renewal reform, four secondary public schools in the north-east of Kazakhstan were purposefully selected. Using a criterion sampling strategy (Patton, 1990), the schools included two urban and two rural sites, each representing typical mainstream schools in Kazakhstan. These schools are neither special schools for the gifted and talented nor academically selective institutions like gymnasia or lycées. Importantly, this study goes beyond the 30 public schools ('pilot schools') that tested the renewed curriculum during the 2015–2016 academic year (NAE, 2015).[6] The four selected schools introduced the curriculum reform without the benefit of piloting the renewal in their local contexts. The focus on secondary schools was intentional, as these schools are more likely than elementary schools to have students participate in national and international large-scale assessments, particularly PISA. Consequently, secondary teachers are more exposed to political pressures from the MoES to adopt certain international standards and practices, many of which have been transnationally borrowed and disseminated by the NIS school network.

Alongside one-to-one interviews with 14 teachers and six school leaders (two principals and four vice principals) from four mainstream public schools, I held an online teacher survey in those four schools (n = 215). Some responses were incomplete and excluded from specific analyses, resulting in varying sample sizes for different variables. The sampling frame included teachers working in secondary classes (Grades 5–11). The survey response rate was 79%, with responses from 134 urban-school teachers and 81 rural-school teachers. Thus far, the findings in this study are mainly based on the integration of qualitative interview data and descriptive statistics derived from the teacher survey at the four mainstream schools.

The demographic profile of the survey participants revealed a diverse group of teachers characterized by varying gender, age, academic qualifications, teaching experience, and school settings. Predominantly female (80.2%), the respondents also included a notable concentration of individuals aged 30–39 (32.4%) and 40–49 (29.7%). Most held a Bachelor's degree (45.5%) or a specialist's degree[7] (39.2%). The teaching experience ranged widely, with the largest group having 11–15 years of experience (22.1%). A majority taught in urban schools (62.3%), with a significant portion from rural settings (37.7%).

4.3 Data Collection Instruments

To collect 'rich data' and adequately capture the process of local adaptation and consequent transportation of international standards from NIS to the public school system (Maxwell, 2013; Seidman, 2019), semi-structured interviews were conducted with the teachers. These interviews, lasting approximately 60 minutes each, followed open-ended questions with probing to explore the specifics of the scale-up reform (Merriam & Tisdell, 2016)

In addition to the qualitative data gathered through interviews, a quantitative approach was employed to further investigate the teachers' experiences and perceptions by administering a survey to teachers from the same four public schools. The survey instrument, which was divided into eight sections, consisted of 42 closed-ended questions and one open-ended question focused on teachers' perceptions regarding the scale-up.[8] The survey's eight sections were as follows: (1) Survey participants' background information; (2) Teachers' policy knowledge about the NIS curriculum, the role of NIS in the scale-up of curricular innovations as well as teachers' self-reported knowledge about the key concepts of the curriculum reform based on the adaptation of the NIS curriculum in regular public schools; (3) Teachers' professional development and training regarding curriculum renewal reform; (4) Teachers' perceptions about the impact of the curriculum renewal reform on teaching and learning at regular public schools; (5) Teachers' attitudes towards the implementation of curriculum renewal reform; (6) Teacher's professional autonomy in the curriculum renewal reform; (7) Factors constraining teacher's work according to the renewed curriculum and (8) Teachers' support for the curriculum renewal reform. As part of the survey development and the design of some scales (teachers' attitudes toward the reform implementation, teachers' perceived impact of the reform, and teachers' support for the curriculum renewal reform in particular), I drew on the study and the survey instrument developed by Pizmony-Levy and Woolsey (2017).

4.4 Data Analysis Strategies

Using an exploratory sequential mixed methods research design, the qualitative interview data were analyzed first, followed by the analysis of the quantitative survey data. Also, the study employed thematic analysis of policy documents (n = 29), media accounts (n = 38), and interview data (Braun & Clarke, 2006; Clarke et al., 2015). Qualitative data were analyzed in two stages:

1. *First Cycle (Structural Coding)*: Data were coded according to key themes and categories relevant to the research questions (Saldaña, 2016). Structural coding was applied to align the data with the study's focus.
2. *Second Cycle (Pattern Coding)*: Pattern coding was then used to identify emergent themes and inferential patterns in the data (Saldaña, 2016).

All qualitative data were organized using ATLAS.ti software to maintain a structured analysis approach. I employed a theory-driven approach to thematic analysis (Braun and Clarke, 2006), drawing on the analytical model for defining and theorizing teacher agency in the context of curriculum change developed by Priestley et al. (2013). This model was used "to guide data-collection and assist data-analysis" (Priestley et al., 2013, p. 190), which facilitated the categorization and coding process, allowing for a structured interpretation of the data within the study's conceptual framework.

For the quantitative data, descriptive statistics were performed using SPSS (Version 29), highlighting teachers' beliefs, attitudes, and perceptions about the reform's impact. To ensure the reliability of the scale measuring the factors that teachers perceived as constraining curriculum implementation (Table 3.2), Cronbach's alpha was calculated for all 10 variables included in the scale. The overall reliability coefficient (Cronbach's alpha) was 0.84, indicating a high level of internal consistency among the items. This suggests that the scale is a reliable measure for assessing teachers' perceived factors impacting curriculum implementation in the study.

4.5 Ethical Considerations

This study did not involve more than minimal risk and was approved by Teachers College Columbia University Institutional Review Board (IRB). During the negotiation of access to schools, I conducted online meetings with each school's principal and faculty, where I introduced my study and provided brief informational flyers. Participation was entirely voluntary, and non-participation did not affect teachers' status at the school. This information was also outlined in the written consent forms, in compliance with the IRB process at Teachers College, Columbia University. To ensure confidentiality and mitigate any potential risks, all data were stored on a secure, password-protected network server. Additionally, the online teacher survey did not request any direct or indirect identifiers, maintaining participant anonymity.

5 Findings

While school responses to the centrally driven curriculum renewal policies varied, I categorized the qualitative interview and survey data based on the analytical model for understanding teacher agency in curriculum change developed by Priestley et al. (2013). The first theme, "Teachers' Ideologies and Curriculum Change", combines the iterative and cultural dimensions of teacher agency, highlighting how teachers' life histories, professional experiences, values, and beliefs shape their responses to curriculum reform. The second theme "Material Contexts and Organizational Constraints", and the third theme "Social Structures and Teacher Agency" are both grounded in the practical-evaluative dimension of teacher agency as described by Priestley et al. (2013). This dimension reflects the capacity of actors to make practical and normative judgments among various possible courses of action, responding to the immediate demands, dilemmas, and uncertainties of evolving situations.

5.1   Teachers' Ideologies and Curriculum Change

Teachers' ideologies, based on their life histories, professional histories, values and beliefs, play a crucial role in teacher buy-in to curricular changes (Datnow & Castellano, 2000; Priestley et al., 2013). As teachers are not a homogenous mass, teachers participating in the interviews expressed mixed reactions towards the curriculum reform. I found that some teachers were supportive of the reform, while others were resistant. The support or resistance to the reform was based on teachers' ideologies as they kept referring to their past pedagogical practices, values and beliefs about the curriculum.

Based on the thematic analysis of interview data and open-ended survey responses, I found that most teachers referred to the official discourse surrounding the scale-up reform, making statements such as "it is time for change," "curriculum renewal is the imperative of modern times," and "the reform meets modern standards". Conversely, some veteran teachers, who resisted the reform, wrote in their open-ended survey responses "to bring back Soviet education" (*vernite sovetskoye obrazovaniye*) as they believed that the curriculum renewal had a negative impact on the education quality. Newspaper articles of the critical accounts of the national curriculum renewal confirm these data. Such titles from news accounts as "It's a harsh and unsuccessful experiment", teachers report on the renewed program of education" (Brzhanova, 2019), "Are we breeding dropouts?" (Akulova, 2020), "Teach" – "I Don't Want!" (Tikhonova, 2018), "Educator Galina Klypa on the school reform: children will be illiterate" (Nurseitova, 2019) reinforce the criticisms of the scale-up reform. Some veteran teachers challenged the reform making positive references to Soviet education in the media as follows:

> The Soviet education system provided a strong foundation in many subjects, enabling graduates to become highly skilled specialists. When people today claim that the old system failed to connect learning with real life and that students struggled to adapt or apply their knowledge in practice, I believe this is a misconception. (Tatilya, 2021, para. 4)

Other teachers lamented the fact that the scale-up reform increased teacher accountability as the specification of learning aims and learning outcomes per each curriculum subject demanded much paperwork related to the development of assessment tasks and feedback provision to each student in overcrowded classes.

While adopting the state's modernization reform rhetoric, most interviewed teachers acknowledged NIS as a key developer of curricular innovations. One rural-school vice principal, during an interview, noted that the scale-up reform was "based on international curricula" adopted by NIS experts (Rural School #2, Vice Principal for Academic Affairs). However, less than half of the respondents (47.9%; n = 102) reported having heard "a fair amount" about NIS. A majority of teachers (combining those who were "not at all informed" and "not very well informed") indicated that they did not feel well-informed about the NIS curriculum (53.1%; n = 118). This finding can be explained by the fact that NIS-led curricular innovations were translated into the public school system through centralized curriculum reform, which was based on mandatory state standards rather than the voluntary adaptation of innovations by schools. While mainstream schools appreciated the access to teaching and learning materials provided on the NIS websites, some teachers expressed a desire to visit these schools to observe lessons firsthand.

5.2 Material Contexts and Organizational Constraints

During my fieldwork in both urban and rural schools, I often heard teachers describe their institutions as 'ordinary schools' with 'ordinary teachers' and 'ordinary students'. The conditions in which mainstream schoolteachers have historically worked became one of the key themes emerging from both interviews and survey data. Given that a central aim of the curriculum renewal reform was to "disseminate the NIS experience" (NIS, 2018, p. 3), teachers in both urban and rural settings frequently compared their local circumstances to those of NIS teachers. While some teachers recognized NIS as national flagships that embody best practices, others bluntly remarked that "NIS schools and ordinary schools are like heaven and earth" (Rural School #2, History Teacher).

Most teachers agreed that the curriculum reform would have a positive impact on both teaching and learning. For instance, 63.1% (n = 215) agreed that "the renewed curriculum will improve teaching" and 58.1% of teachers agreed that "the renewed curriculum will improve learning". Using a rating scale, a majority of teachers agreed (combination of "agree" and "strongly agree") with the statement "The designers of the dissemination of renewed curriculum considered local circumstances of public schools". Yet 43.4% (n = 93) disagreed with that statement. At the same time, teachers indicated various factors

FROM GLOBAL IDEAS TO LOCAL CLASSROOMS

that constrained their work according to the curriculum reform demands (Section 7 of the survey). Table 3.2 presents descriptive statistics for Likert scale opinion questions based on those factors.

TABLE 3.2   Factors perceived to constrain curriculum implementation (Survey question: "Is your teaching according to the renewed curriculum affected by any of the following factors?")

#	Description of item	N	Mean	SD	Not at all	Very little	To some extent	A lot	Missing system
1	Extreme complexity of the renewed curriculum for my students	199	2.90	0.78	5.4%	15.8%	50.5%	18%	10.4%
2	Lack of clarity about changes in the curriculum	200	2.79	0.83	8.6%	17.1%	49.5%	14.9%	9.9%
3	Inadequate or poor-quality educational materials	195	2.86	0.89	9.0%	14.9%	43.2%	20.7%	12.2%
4	Mixed ability classes	202	2.95	0.78	5.0%	15.8%	49.5%	20.7%	9%
5	Overloaded teaching	200	2.54	0.96	16.2%	23.0%	36.9%	14.0%	9.9%
6	Overloaded curriculum	196	2.82	0.96	9.0%	16.7%	44.1%	18.5%	11.7%
7	Overcrowded school and a large number of students in my classroom	196	2.95	0.91	6.8%	18.5%	35.1%	27.9%	11.7%
8	Absence of the position of a homeroom teacher similar to this role at NIS	197	2.89	1.02	13.1%	12.6%	34.2%	28.8%	11.3%
9	Poor access to the Internet	202	2.87	0.94	11.7%	11.7%	44.1%	23.4%	9.0%
10	Absence of opportunities to divide a grade cohort into two subgroups while teaching	202	2.97	0.98	10.4%	14.9%	33.3%	32.4%	9.0%

Given that most teachers, especially those of STEM disciplines, found the renewed curricular content intellectually challenging for their students, I tried to probe if most teachers working at those four mainstream schools perceived this factor as a hindrance in the enactment of the curriculum reform. One teacher highlighted that the extensive list of topics within the new curriculum "does not provide the opportunity to study the material effectively. Children do not have time to perceive the information at the proper level" (Urban School #1, Biology Teacher). This factor is interrelated with that of mixed-ability classes. The qualitative interview data revealed that teachers highlighted challenges in delivering the renewed curriculum, especially since most classes in mainstream schools are of mixed ability. An urban school vice principal explained, "Since we have students with special needs, we must adapt the curriculum to meet their needs, allowing them to learn and acquire knowledge on par with their peers" (Urban School #1, Vice Principal for Academic Affairs).

These challenges are further compounded by the selective nature of gifted education schools, which, according to mainstream schoolteachers, exacerbate the difficulties of implementing the renewed curriculum by drawing away high-achieving students and experienced teachers. Interestingly, mainstream schoolteachers associated NIS with 'cream skimming', as many gifted students leave to attend a local NIS school. An urban school principal expressed frustration, noting that gifted education schools accept students from Grade 7 onwards, taking "our best students as well as best teachers" (Urban School #1, Principal). Meanwhile, mainstream schools are required to accept students with a range of abilities. Half of the teachers (50.5%, n = 112) reported that the "extreme complexity of the renewed curriculum" impacted curriculum implementation to some extent. Similarly, 49.5% (n = 110) indicated that "mixed ability classes" also posed challenges to implementing the curriculum.

The lack of clarity about changes in the curriculum emerged as another important factor related to curriculum implementation. Understandably, as policymakers experimented with the introduction of novel curricular ideas and practices in the public school system, teachers tried to cope with the uncertainty of the reform. 49.5% (n = 110) of teachers indicated that the lack of clarity about curricular changes affected curriculum implementation to some extent. In this respect, formative assessment (assessment for learning) was a distinctive feature of the curriculum renewal reform that caused much uncertainty among interviewed teachers. As a feature of international curricula, formative assessment implies that teachers provide feedback on student performance including elements of peer and self-assessment (Black & Wiliam, 2009). As introduced by NIS in 2016, the initial idea of using formative assessment in mainstream public schools was provision of teacher feedback without grading and marking student performance. Most teachers at mainstream schools, from my interviews, indicated that it was imperative to hold students accountable for their learning and therefore it was important to grade and mark student performance per lesson. Influenced by the Soviet holdover, teachers fell into the old habit of grading students in each class. One of the rural school-teachers candidly noted that "there is no way to teach a class without daily grading of student work. We need to motivate students with grades" (Rural School #1, Kazakh Teacher). This sentiment aligns with similar concerns expressed by other teachers in media accounts, such as one who stated, "We work for a salary, and children work for a grade. When a child gets a mark of 5 (Excellent), it is pleasant and good for both them and their parents" (Mustafayeva, 2019, para. 6).

Interviewed teachers expressed concerns about demands of learner-centered pedagogy in overcrowded classrooms that they had to work in. One of the vice principals for academic affairs noted "for example, in the past, we were able to divide high-school classes – such as the tenth and eleventh grades – when students specialized in certain subjects, like in physics and mathematics tracks. However, with the growing number of students, we no longer have this opportunity. We have even had to switch to a shortened academic program" (Urban School #2, Vice Principal for Academic Affairs). Based on the rating scale, a majority of teachers (a combination of "some to extent" and "a lot") indicated overcrowded schools and a large number of students in their classrooms as a significant factor that affected curriculum implementation. The issue of overcrowded mainstream public schools has been a significant negative factor in the national school reforms. In 2021, the Information-Analytic Center (MoES Data Analytics Center) noted that "the shortage of student places remains an acute problem that the education system will continue to face in the coming years. According to forecasts, by 2025 the shortage of student places could reach 670 000" (IAC, 2021, p. 163).

During interviews in both urban and rural schools, most teachers referred to the lack of resources including the number of printers, smartboards, paper, and other supplies. Other teachers shared that they found it challenging to combine the duties of a content teacher and a homeroom teacher when implementing the curriculum. NIS schools have homeroom teachers who are responsible of social upbringing of students whereas mainstream schoolteachers have to combine the roles of content teacher and homeroom teacher responsible for housekeeping, being assigned to a grade cohort. With the combination of "to some extent" and "a lot", 63.9% (n = 142), surveyed teachers believed that the absence of the position of a homeroom teacher at mainstream schools, similar to this role at NIS, had a negative effect on the curriculum implementation in mainstream schools.

Schoolteachers of both urban and rural schools indicated the shortage of learning materials as a barrier to the effective delivery of curricular innovations.

Given that competence-based and outcomes-based approaches to secondary education are associated with learner-centered education, teachers found it challenging to attend to every student's needs given the lack of learning resources. This finding is consistent with the point made by Schweisfurth (2013) that "resources are clearly an issue in implementation that cannot realistically be alleviated purely through management and innovative teaching" (p. 144). Thus, teachers working at mainstream public schools noted the issue of classroom resources as a mundane aspect of curriculum reform in their local school settings.

A Spearman's rank-order correlation analysis was performed to analyze the relationship between teachers' perceptions about the adequate provision of resources to their schools for the implementation of the educational reform (item 30) and their attitudes towards the renewed curriculum (item 40). The results demonstrate a positive, moderate, statistically significant correlation between the two variables (ρ = .56, N = 216, p < .001). This means that teachers who perceive that their schools have adequate resources for implementing the educational reform also tend to have more positive attitudes toward the renewed curriculum.

Research in international contexts supports this finding, as studies indicate that resource availability significantly shapes teacher perceptions of educational reforms. Adequate resources, including teaching materials, classroom infrastructure, and professional development opportunities, enhance teacher engagement and instructional effectiveness (Fullan, 2016; Darling-Hammond et al., 2017). In contrast, when teachers face persistent resource shortages – particularly in their efforts to implement learner-centered education – they may view reforms as burdensome and unfeasible, leading to resistance or only superficial implementation (Schweisfurth, 2013). Global research confirms that well-supported teachers are more likely to sustain curricular innovations (OECD, 2019). In Kazakhstan, equitable resource distribution – particularly between urban and rural schools – remains crucial for the successful enactment of educational reforms.

To explore potential differences between urban and rural schoolteachers' perspectives on curriculum reforms, I examined whether they believed that the dissemination of the renewed curriculum adequately considered local contexts. The Independent Samples Mann-Whitney U Test was employed to compare the responses of urban (n = 134, Mdn = 3) and rural (n = 80, Mdn = 2) schoolteachers (N = 214) to the statement: "The designers of dissemination of the renewed curriculum considered local circumstances of public schools" (Survey Item 31). This comparison was necessary because material contexts and organizational constraints are linked to specific local conditions found in both urban and rural mainstream public schools. Since the outcome variable was ordinal [1 = strongly disagree, 2 = disagree, 3 = agree, 4 = strongly agree], the Mann-Whitney U Test was chosen. The obtained results, U = 4,390, p = .016, indicate a significant difference between the groups. These results suggest that urban and rural schoolteachers differed in their perceptions of whether the renewed curriculum considered local circumstances. This difference may be attributed to the fact that rural-school teachers, who often face challenges such as limited resources, facilities, and infrastructure, may feel that the renewed curriculum does not adequately consider the unique local circumstances of rural schools. Research has shown that rural schools frequently struggle with such constraints (Tajik et al., 2022), which might explain why rural-school teachers were less likely to agree with the statement.

5.2.1   Social Structures and Teacher Agency

Teachers operate within a broader institutional and policy context that impacts their ability to enact curriculum reforms (Priestley et al., 2013). Most teachers referred to the fact that the scale-up reform (based on the dissemination of NIS practices to mainstream schools) came to their classrooms via mandatory state standards and national curriculum guidelines issued by the MoES and NAE. By discussing the nature of the imposed curricular changes in their schools, teachers raised the issue of power and limited teacher engagement with curriculum development (Priestley et al., 2013). Some schoolteachers reported that they were doing something of their own initiatives before the scale-up reform entered their schools. One group of modern foreign language teachers in one of the urban schools shared that they had to dismantle their German language program as the scale-up reform aggressively advocated the increase of English classes given the trilingual education policy. In this respect, Hatch (2002) notes that "ironically, the true measure of whether a school has the capacity to take advantage of an improvement program may be whether the school community has the power to say "no" and the knowledge, flexibility, and theories to pursue another approach" (p. 634).

Teacher autonomy emerged as an important issue in experimenting with curricular changes. Viewing teacher autonomy as part of teacher agency (Biesta & Tedder, 2006), I specifically asked teachers about their professional freedom to test and experiment with new ideas despite the constraints of the centralized reform. The descriptive statistics from the survey data, shown in Table 3.3, indicate that almost half of the surveyed teachers (a combination of "strongly disagree" and "disagree") do not believe that they have total freedom in making changes to curricular content in their subject areas.

Similarly, 43.3% of the teachers (combination of "strongly disagree" and "disagree") assumed that they did not have total freedom in choosing textbooks and other teaching materials for their classes. It is important to bear in mind that the scale-up reform has been conducted in a centralized fashion and teachers were held accountable for the reform implementation.

TABLE 3.3   Teacher autonomy and curricular change

| | | | | Would you agree or disagree with the following statements: | | | | |
#	Description of item	N	Mean	SD	Strongly disagree	Disagree	Agree	Strongly agree	Missing system
1	"I have total freedom in making changes to curriculum content in my school subject"	213	2.52	0.64	3.2%	44.1%	44.1%	4.5%	4.1%
2	"I have total freedom in choosing textbooks and other teaching materials for my classes"	213	2.57	0.68	4.1%	39.2%	46.4%	6.3%	4.1%

5.3   *Internalization of International Standards in Mainstream Public Schools*

This final subsection attempts to examine emergent patterns of internalization of borrowed international standards (Steiner-Khamsi, 2002). This study found that despite constraints and external pressures, mainstream schools still tried to adapt and adopt international standards, even though, these were watered-down versions of imported international standards. While NIS-based policymakers projected their own version of "integration of best national and international educational models" (NIS, 2011, p. 14), mainstream schools pursued their own context-specific strategies for "'coping' with policy and assembling school-based policy responses" (Braun et al., 2011, p. 586). I briefly provide examples of how mainstream schools coped with policy and tried to incorporate international standards in their local circumstances. First, given the policy discourse of trilingual education wherein the use of English is a marker of international competitiveness, one of the rural schools tried to introduce English-medium classes in their science curriculum. The vice principal of that rural school explained:

> We have trilingual education in our school. Our teacher of computing teaches his class 50% in English and 50% in the mother tongue. Just that teacher is able to use English as a medium of instruction. We cannot insist that every teacher uses English in their classes. (Rural School #1, Vice Principal for Academic Affairs)

FROM GLOBAL IDEAS TO LOCAL CLASSROOMS

Thus, rural schools came up with creative approaches to coping with policy demands and most importantly exercised their agency to enact international standards in their local circumstances.

Another example of internalizing international standards in the local public school system is the case of formative assessment (Assessment for Learning). As noted by Cambridge Assessment International Education (2019), the original purpose of formative assessment is to provide "formative feedback without marks and/or grades as appropriate" (p. 3). Teachers in mainstream public schools, regardless of their personal values, attitudes, and beliefs about teaching and learning, were expected to adopt the 'common sense' idea that giving formative feedback tied to clear success criteria helps students focus on improving their work without "the distraction of marks or grades" (Cambridge Assessment International Education, 2019, p. 3). Reform designers incorporated this innovative assessment practice as a requirement in the national curriculum standards. However, mainstream schools resisted the direct replication of this practice. Instead, mainstream schools came up with the hybridization of formative assessment with Soviet-styled norm-referenced assessment wherein teachers provide feedback and at the same time give grades, interpreting this practice as 'formative assessment'. Developing such hybridization of formative assessment allowed teachers to apply their subjective assessment. In effect, the MoES had to accommodate the teaching community's insistence on using grades and marks as part of formative assessment in their school practices.

To established teachers who were accustomed to using their judgment over marking and grading students' academic performance without externally developed criteria, the Western idea of competence-based assessment encroached on this area of their expertise. One veteran math teacher from an urban school expressed their frustration:

> It was very bad when we were not allowed to give marks for students' work. Students saw no point in studying if they didn't receive marks. With this curriculum renewal reform, the main thing for students was not to understand the learning material but to pass the tests at the end of the course unit and at the end of each quarter of the academic year. (Urban School #2, Math Teacher)

In the context of teacher's expertise in assessing and grading students' academic performance, it is tensions between subjectivity and objectivity that came forth in the struggle over the curriculum reform. The MoES, in their argument for implementing the reform, states that "the new system of student assessment will provide an *objective assessment of student progress*" (Kaukenova,

2014, para. 15, emphasis added). The incorporation of formative assessment as a novel international standard aimed to challenge teachers' established beliefs and assessment practices in the post-Soviet school education context. Reform designers, guided by an outcomes-focused curriculum policy orientation, sought to adopt Western conceptions of educational quality. In this regard, Minina (2017) points out that in the post-Soviet context, educational quality was "traditionally seen as an inherent element of [the] educational system, indivisible into proxies and measured by subjective assessment by the educator" (p. 177). In contrast, a neoliberal understanding of quality, as reflected in criteria-based assessment, emphasized measurable learning outcomes and clearly defined competencies.

6   Discussion

Addressing the research questions (1) "How do teachers perceive and navigate the challenges posed by centrally driven curriculum renewal policies during the process of policy enactment?" and (2) "In what ways do teachers adapt centrally driven curriculum renewal policies to fit their specific school contexts during the process of policy enactment?", this study attempted to understand the impact of borrowed international standards, formulated as a standardized reform package, on mainstream schools as constituents of the school system intended for the masses. This study underscores the importance of recognizing teacher agency as influenced by multiple external factors, echoing Priestley et al. (2013), who caution against placing the full responsibility for agency on individual teachers alone. Promoting meaningful curriculum reform in Kazakhstan requires engaging with material, organizational, and structural dimensions, ensuring that teachers have the necessary support rather than bearing the burden of agency in isolation.

The challenge of the scale-up reform was that the innovations that were adapted in a flexible and well-resourced environment of the NIS school network had to be transported to the system of more than 7000 public schools. Importantly, the educational innovations that were institutionalized in an autonomous school system (NIS) were formulated as centralized requirements in the mandatory state standards of education in the system of mainstream schools. Thus, the innovation policy discourse was recontextualized for the purpose of holding mainstream schools accountable for the quality of school education based on international standards. While the scale-up was intended to innovate the national curriculum, the reform designers had to make sure that mainstream public schools had "substantial capacity" to carry out curricular changes as an essential condition for the scale-up (Hatch, 2000, p. 347).

The conceptualization of the scale-up of educational innovations as a mandatory state standard reveals a certain conception of scale. The fact that policymakers tried to incorporate innovative features of the NIS curriculum into the national curriculum signaled their belief in the "replicated use of an innovation to reproduce particular outcomes" (Coburn et al., 2020, p. 2509). Replication as a conception of scale is characterized by the assumption that if an innovation is implemented with fidelity, it "will reproduce reliable results in different settings" (Coburn et al., 2020, p. 2509). With their firm belief that the NIS curriculum is aligned with PISA-like competencies, the reform designers assumed that the replication logic would help the public school system to increase students' functional literacies and thus gain higher places in PISA. However, as Peck and Theodore (2015) argue in their concept of 'fast policy', the mobility of policy models often encounters friction when transplanted into new policy contexts, as there is 'much that cannot be so easily bottled for export' (p. XVII). Thus, while the replication logic aimed to reproduce the NIS curriculum's success, it had to contend with the diverse local contexts of public schools, underscoring the need to adapt "what is spread" to the "existing local context" (Coburn et al., 2020, p. 2510).

However, various school factors were overlooked at the start of the scale-up reform. At the time, it was suggested that implementing the curriculum reform would not require special conditions across schools at the national level. Existing facilities and resources at mainstream schools were deemed sufficient to support the educational process as required by the new standards (Mozhayeva, 2015). The main concern identified by the reform designers was "the readiness of teaching staff to work according to new teaching approaches and methods" (Mozhayeva, 2015, para. 5). As this study showed, local school contexts do matter. Public school teachers, in their turn, played a critical role in adapting externally imposed curricular innovations towards their school contexts.

The transnational policy transfer as part of globalization processes "disturbed practical and theoretical boundaries that once anchored understandings of teacher professionalism" (Seddon et al., 2013, p. 7). This disruption contributed to policy enthusiasm for the transnational policy transfer being stalled in the system of mainstream schools. Teachers' beliefs and values about education, shaped by their professional experiences and local contexts, often influenced their perceptions of NIS as an innovative model yet distanced from the realities of mainstream schools. These teachers had to operate within their local circumstances, characterized by a host of hindrances to implementing educational innovations during the scale-up reform. These hindrances were typical barriers that still characterize the public school system, e.g., overcrowded classes, lack of qualified content teachers to use English as a medium of instruction in teaching STEM disciplines, poor classroom equipment, and a lack of learning resources per student. Since competence-based education and outcomes-based education, as key features of the renewed curriculum, implied learner-centered pedagogies, attending to each student's needs has been very challenging in mainstream schools during the reform implementation.

7 Conclusion

This study has examined how Kazakhstan's national school system engaged in the process of selecting, adapting, and implementing international standards, particularly through the scale-up curriculum reform based on the NIS Program. While the reform aimed to introduce innovative practices into mainstream schools, the study highlighted numerous challenges posed by the transfer of these international standards in the local (non-Western) context. From an analytical perspective, it is important to recognize that transnational policy borrowing and lending are not neutral processes. As Steiner-Khamsi (2014) emphasizes, analyzing transnational policy borrowing goes beyond simply identifying 'best practices'. It requires examining why and how certain travelling reforms are borrowed and how these reforms interact with the local educational, political, and social contexts. In this case, the reform designers' emphasis on replicating NIS's successes in mainstream schools through international standards reveals a prescriptive and standardized approach to transnational policy transfer. However, the local adaptation of these standards was mediated by teachers' agency, resource constraints, and organizational factors in public schools.

In considering the question of "who benefits, who loses" in the act of transnational policy transfer (Steiner-Khamsi, 2014, p. 154), the study underscores the uneven distribution of advantages and challenges across different types of schools. NIS as a school reform modality attempts to respond to multiple policy agendas wherein externalization to international standards enables reform designers to gain credibility in their policy solutions (Waldow, 2012; Waldow, 2019). Special schools for the gifted and talented, which enjoy greater autonomy and resources, stand as the primary beneficiaries of the reform, gaining further credibility as national flagships of innovation. In contrast, mainstream public schools, particularly those in rural and under-resourced areas, faced significant barriers in implementing the reform. Teachers in mainstream schools struggled with overcrowded classrooms, inadequate materials, and limited professional development, leading to the conclusion that the reform disproportionately favored well-resourced schools while imposing additional burdens on those with fewer resources.

Ultimately, this study aimed to contribute to the growing body of research that adopts an analytical approach to transnational policy transfer. The study sought to challenge the dominant normative perspective in transnational policy borrowing research, which, as Gong et al. (2023) argue, often reflects a Western-centric worldview characterized by a "blind faith in universality" and "the belief in "best practice" as an ideal education norm" (p. 298). While the reform's goal was to improve education quality nationwide, it is crucial to continue examining why and how international standards are selectively borrowed, translated, and implemented in ways that may benefit some while disadvantaging others.

Notes

1 This study refers to the Ministry of Education and Science as it existed before being divided into the Ministry of Education and the Ministry of Science and Higher Education on June 11, 2022.
2 The Program for International Student Assessment (PISA) is a global study conducted by the Organization for Economic Co-operation and Development (OECD).
3 The International Association for the Evaluation of Educational Achievement's Trends in International Mathematics and Science Study (TIMSS) is a series of international assessments measuring students' mathematics and science knowledge worldwide.
4 The National Institute of Pedagogical Sciences succeeded the National Research Institute of Content and Methods of Education of the Kazakh Soviet Socialist Republic.
5 NIS schools are not located in rural areas. However, rural-school graduates who receive scholarships to study at NIS are provided with free boarding and dormitory facilities.
6 The 30 pilot public schools were located across 14 regions of Kazakhstan, as well as in Astana and Almaty. These schools were situated in both urban and rural areas, with some being ungraded rural schools. The medium of instruction in these schools was either Kazakh, Russian, or both, as they operated as so-called 'mixed schools.
7 Specialist's degree means a Soviet-styled five-year higher-education diploma that is formally recognized as the equivalent of holding a master's degree.
8 The full survey instrument can be found in Kurakbayev (2023, pp. 247–256).

References

Abbott, A. (2005). Linked ecologies: States and universities as environments for professions. *Sociological Theory, 23*(3), 245–274.

Addey, C. and Sellar, S. (2020). The rise of international large-scale assessments and rationales for participation. In B. Lingard (Ed.), *Globalisation and education* (pp. 160–178). Routledge.

Akulova, O. (2020). *Плодим недоучек?* [*Are we breeding dropouts?*]. Time.kz. https://time.kz/articles/territory/2020/06/10/plodim-nedouchek

Baek, C., Hörmann, B., Karseth, B., Pizmony-Levy, O., Sivesind, K., & Steiner-Khamsi, G. (2018). Policy learning in Norwegian school reform: A social network analysis of the 2020 incremental reform. *Nordic Journal of Studies in Educational Policy, 4*(1), 24–37.

Ball, S. J., Maguire, M., & Braun, A. (2012). *How schools do policy: Policy enactments in secondary schools*. Routledge.

Bekbassova, A. (2019, December 23). *Реформы образования идут мимо села [Education reforms go past the village]*. Ratel.kz. https://ratel.kz/raw/reformy_obrazovanija_idut_mimo_sela

Bekishev, K. (2011). Тенденции развития системы образования в Республике Казахстан [Trends in the development of the education system in the Republic of Kazakhstan]. *Russian Journal of Chemistry, 55*(4), 89–96.

Biesta, G., & Tedder, M. (2006). How is agency possible? Towards an ecological understanding of agency-as-achievement [Working Paper 5]. *Learning lives: Learning, identity, and agency in the life course*. https://www.researchgate.net/profile/Michael-Tedder/publication/228644383_How_is_agency_possible_Towards_an_ecological_understanding_of_agency-as-achievement/links/00b4952cadd9bd2b6a000000/How-is-agency-possible-Towards-an-ecological-understanding-of-agency-as-achievement.pdf

Black, P., & Wiliam, D. (2009). Developing the theory of formative assessment. *Educational Assessment, Evaluation and Accountability, 21*, 5–31.

Braun, A., Ball, S. J., Maguire, M., & Hoskins, K. (2011). Taking context seriously: Towards explaining policy enactments in the secondary school. *Discourse: Studies in the Cultural Politics Of Education, 32*(4), 585–596.

Braun, V., & Clarke, V. (2006). Using thematic analysis in psychology. *Qualitative Research in Psychology, 3*(2), 77–101.

Bridges, D. (Ed.). (2014). *Educational reform and internationalization: The case of school reform in Kazakhstan*. Cambridge University Press.

Brzhanova, A. (2019, October 21). "Это жестокий неудачный эксперимент", - учителя об обновленной программе образования ["It's a harsh and unsuccessful experiment", teachers report on the renewed program of education]. *Astana TV*. https://astanatv.kz/ru/news/51649/

Cambridge Assessment International Education. (2019). *Assessment for learning*. UCLES. https://www.cambridgeinternational.org/Images/271179-assessment-for-learning.pdf

Chankseliani, M., & Silova, I. (2018). Reconfiguring education purposes, policies and practices during post-socialist transformations: Setting the stage. In M. Chankseliani & I. Silova (Eds.), *Comparing post-socialist transformations: Purposes, policies, and practices in education* (pp. 7–25). Symposium Books.

Clarke, V., Braun, V., & Hayfield, N. (2015). Thematic analysis. *Qualitative psychology: A practical guide to research methods, 3*, 222–248.

Coburn, C., Higgs, J., Morel, R. P., & Catterson, A. (2020). Spread and scale in the digital age: A conceptual framework. In M. Gresalfi & I. S. Horn (Eds.), *The interdisciplinarity of the learning sciences, 14th International Conference of the Learning Sciences*

(*ICLS*) *2020, Volume 5* (pp. 2507–2514). International Society of the Learning Sciences.

Coleman, H. (2009, May 19). Are 'International Standard Schools' really a response to globalisation? [Seminar paper]. *International Seminar 'Responding to Global Education Challenges'*, Universitas Negeri Yogyakarta. Yogyakarta, Indonesia.

Creswell, J. W., & Plano Clark, V. L. (2018). *Designing and conducting mixed methods research*. Sage publications.

Darling-Hammond, L., Hyler, M. E., & Gardner, M. (2017). *Effective teacher professional development*. Learning Policy Institute.

Datnow, A., Hubbard, L., & Mehan, H. (2002). *Extending educational reform: From one school to many*. Routledge.

Datnow, A., & Castellano, M. (2000). Teachers' responses to Success for All: How beliefs, experiences, and adaptations shape implementation. *American Educational Research Journal, 37*(3), 775–799.

Fimyar, O., & Kurakbayev, K. (2016). 'Soviet'in teachers' memories and professional beliefs in Kazakhstan: points for reflection for reformers, international consultants and practitioners. *International Journal of Qualitative Studies in Education, 29*(1), 86–103.

Fullan, M. (2016). The elusive nature of whole system improvement in education. *Journal of Educational Change, 17*(4), 539–544.

Gong, B., Jiang, J., & Silova, I. (2023). Redefining educational transfer and borrowing in the pluriverse. In *International encyclopedia of education* (4th ed., pp. 290–301). Elsevier.

Government of the Republic of Kazakhstan. (2004). *О Государственной программе развития образования в Республике Казахстан на 2005–2010 годы* [On the State Program for the Development of Education in the Republic of Kazakhstan for 2005–2010]. https://adilet.zan.kz/rus/archive/docs/U040001459_/11.10.2004

Government of the Republic of Kazakhstan. (2011). Закон Республики Казахстан от 19 января 2011 года № 394-IV. О статусе "Назарбаев Университет", "Назарбаев Интеллектуальные школы" и "Назарбаев Фонд" [Law of the Republic of Kazakhstan dated January 19, 2011 No. 394-IV. About the status of "Nazarbayev University", "Nazarbayev Intellectual Schools" and "Nazarbayev Foundation"]. Adilet.zan.kz. https://adilet.zan.kz/rus/docs/Z1100000394

Government of the Republic of Kazakhstan. (2012). *Об утверждении государственных общеобязательных стандартов образования соответствующих уровней образования. Постановление Правительства Республики Казахстан от 23 августа 2012 года № 1080* [On the approval of state compulsory education standards for the corresponding levels of education. Decree of the Government of the Republic of Kazakhstan dated August 23, 2012, No. 1080]. Ministry of Justice.

Government of the Republic of Kazakhstan. (2015). *План нации: 100 конкретных шагов. Программа Президента Республики Казахстан от 20 мая 2015 года* [National Plan: 100 Concrete Steps. Program of the President of the Republic of Kazakhstan as of 20th May 2015]. Adilet.zan.kz. https://adilet.zan.kz/rus/docs/K1500000100

Hatch, T. (2000). What does it take to "go to scale"? Reflections on the promise and the perils of comprehensive school reform. *Journal of Education for Students Placed at Risk, 5*(4), 339–354.

Hatch, T. (2002). When improvement programs collide. *Phi Delta Kappan, 83*(8), 626–639.

Hartley, M. and Ruby, A. (2017). Parallel Reforms: Nazarbayev Intellectual Schools and Nazarbayev University. *Pedagogical Dialogue, 3*(21), 31–33.

Information-Analytic Center, Ministry of Education and Science. (2021). *О состоянии и развитии системы образования Республики Казахстан (по итогам 2020 года)* [On the state and development of the education system of the Republic of Kazakhstan (based on the results of 2020)]. Information-Analytic Center.

Kaukenova, A. (2014, August 15). *В МОН РК рассказали о тонкостях введения 12-летнего образования в школах* [The Ministry of Education and Science of the Republic of Kazakhstan spoke about the intricacies of the introduction of 12-year education in schools]. Zakon.kz. https://www.zakon.kz/4646591-v-mon-rk-rasskazali-o-tonkostjakh.html

Ketelaar, E., Beijaard, D., Boshuizen, H. P., & Den Brok, P. J. (2012). Teachers' positioning towards an educational innovation in the light of ownership, sense-making and agency. *Teaching and Teacher Education, 28*(2), 273–282.

King, M., & Thornhill, C. (2003). *Niklas Luhmann's theory of politics and law.* Palgrave Macmillan.

Kurakbayev, K. (2023). *International-standard schools as a school reform modality: A study of policy transfer from Nazarbayev Intellectual Schools to regular public schools in Kazakhstan* [unpublished doctoral dissertation]. Columbia University. https://doi.org/10.7916/dnx4-5k82

Looi, C. K., Sun, D., Wu, L., & Ye, X. (2015). Seeding a curricular innovation from one school to five schools: A case study from Singapore. In C. K. Looi & L.W. The (Eds.), *Scaling educational innovations* (pp. 151–178). Springer.

Looi, C. K., & Teh, L. W. (Eds.). (2015). *Scaling educational innovations.* Springer.

Luhmann, N. (1997). Globalization or world society: How to conceive of modern society? *International Review of Sociology, 7*(1), 67–79.

Maxwell, J. A. (2013). *Qualitative research design: An interactive approach.* Sage.

McLaughlin, C., Winter, L., & Yakavets, N. (Eds.). (2023). *Mapping educational change in Kazakhstan.* Cambridge University Press.

Merriam, S. B., & Tisdell, E. J. (2016). *Qualitative research: A guide to design and implementation.* Jossey Bass.

Minina, E. (2017). 'Quality revolution' in post-Soviet education in Russia: From control to assurance? *Journal of Education Policy, 32*(2), 176–197.

Mozhayeva, O. (2015). *О трансляции опыта Назарбаев Интеллектуальных школ в рамках обновления содержания общего среднего образования* [On the translation of the experience of Nazarbayev Intellectual Schools as part of updating the curricular content of general secondary education]. *Open School, 1*(142), 1–5.

Mustafayeva, S. (2019, June 11). Известный педагог Галина Клыпа предлагает изменить школьную программу с учетом старой [Well-known educator Galina Klypa advises to change the school program with the consideration of the old one]. *Zakon.kz.* https://www.zakon.kz/stati/4973140-izvestnyy-pedagog-galina-klypa.html

Mynbayeva, A. K., Taubayeva, Sh.T., Bulatbayeva, A.A. & Anarbek, N. A. (2014). Образовательная Политика [Education Policy]. Almaty: Kazakh National University named after Al-Farabi.

National Academy of Education, Ministry of Education and Science of the Republic of Kazakhstan. (2015). *Об особенностях преподавания основ наук в общеобразовательных организациях Республики Казахстан в 2015-2016 учебном году.* [Guidelines for Instruction and Teaching Methodology "About the features of teaching the basics of sciences in general education organizations of the Republic of Kazakhstan in the 2015-2016 academic year"]. Astana: National Academy of Education.

Nazarbayev, N. (2009, October 13). *Казахстан в пост-кризисном мире: интеллектуальный прорыв в будущее* [Kazakhstan in the Post-crisis World: Intellectual Breakthrough into the Future]. Lecture by the President of the Republic of Kazakhstan N.A. Nazarbayev at Al-Farabi Kazakh National University. https://online.zakon.kz/Document/?doc_id=30486542&pos=6;-109#pos=6;-109

Nazarbayev Intellectual Schools. (2012). *Annual report of the autonomous educational organization "Nazarbayev Intellectual Schools" in 2012.* Nazarbayev Intellectual Schools. https://www.nis.edu.kz/ru/about/reports/?id=2098

Nazarbayev Intellectual Schools. (2018). *2030 Development Strategy: "Nazarbayev Intellectual Schools", Autonomous Educational Organization.* https://www.nis.edu.kz/en/about/str-doc/

Nurseitova, T. (2019, May 31). Педагог Галина Клыпа о реформе в школе: Дети будут неграмотные [Educator Galina Klypa on the school reform: children will be illiterate]. *Zakon.kz.* https://www.zakon.kz/redaktsiia-zakonkz/4971722-izvestnyy-pedagog-galina-klypa-o.html

Organisation for Economic Co-operation and Development. (2019). *TALIS 2018 results (Volume I): Teachers and School Leaders as Lifelong Learners.* OECD Publishing. https://www.oecd.org/en/publications/2019/06/talis-2018-results-volume-i_03d63387.html

Patton, M. Q. (1990). *Qualitative evaluation and research methods.* Sage.

Peck, J., & Theodore, N. (2015). *Fast policy: Experimental statecraft at the thresholds of neoliberalism*. University of Minnesota Press.

Pizmony-Levy, O., & Woolsey, A. (2017). Politics of education and teachers' support for high-stakes teacher accountability policies. *Education Policy Analysis Archives, 25*(87).

Priestley, M., Biesta, G., & Robinson, S. (2013). Teachers as agents of change: Teacher agency and emerging models of curriculum. In M. Priestley & G. Biesta (Eds.), *Reinventing the curriculum: New trends in curriculum policy and practice* (pp. 187–206). Bloomsbury Publishing.

Priestley, M., Biesta, G., & Robinson, S. (2016). Teacher agency: What is it and why does it matter? In J. Evers & R. Kneyber (Eds.), *Flip the system: Changing education from the ground up* (pp. 134–148). Routledge.

Ruby, A., & Hartley, M. (2017). Parallel reforms: Nazarbayev intellectual schools and Nazarbayev university. *Pedagogical Dialogue, 3*(21), 31–33.

Sabelli, N. H., & Harris, C. J. (2015). The role of innovation in scaling up educational innovations. In C-K. Looi & L.W. Teh (Eds.), *Scaling educational innovations* (pp. 13–30). Springer.

Sargsyan, L. (2018). *Araratian Baccalaureate: Transforming the future or creating selective education?* EVN Report. https://www.evnreport.com/raw-unfiltered/araratian-baccalaureate-transforming-the-future-or-creating-selective-education

Schweisfurth, M. (2013). *Learner-centred education in international perspective: Whose pedagogy for whose development?* Routledge.

Seidman, I. (2019). *Interviewing as qualitative research: A guide for researchers in education and the social sciences*. Teachers College.

Seddon, T., Ozga, J., & Levin, J. S. (2013). Global transitions and teacher professionalism. In T. Seddon & J. S. Levin (Eds.), *World yearbook of education 2013* (pp. 3–24). Routledge.

Shuinshina, Sh. M., Alpeisov, E. A., Akhmetova, B. S., Tuyakov, E. A., & Adamova, M. E. (2019). Некоторые вопросы модернизации системы образования Казахстана. [Some issues of modernization of the education system of Kazakhstan]. *Sovremennye problemy nauki i obrazovaniya [Modern problems of science and education], (2),* 48–48. https://science-education.ru/ru/article/view?id=28692

Sivesind, K., Afsar, A., & Bachmann, K. E. (2016). Transnational policy transfer over three curriculum reforms in Finland: The constructions of conditional and purposive programs (1994–2016). *European Educational Research Journal, 15*(3), 345–365.

Spillane, J. P., Reiser, B. J., & Reimer, T. (2002). Policy implementation and cognition: Reframing and refocusing implementation research. *Review of Educational Research, 72*(3), 387–431.

Steiner-Khamsi, G. (2002). Reterritorializing educational import: Explorations into the politics of educational borrowing. In A. Nóvoa & M. Lawn (Eds.), *Fabricating Europe.* (pp. 69–86). Kluwer Academic Publishers.

Steiner-Khamsi, G. (2014). Cross-national policy borrowing: Understanding reception and translation. *Asia Pacific Journal of Education, 34*(2), 153–167.

Steiner-Khamsi, G. (2016). Standards are good (for) business: standardised comparison and the private sector in education. *Globalisation, Societies and Education, 14* (2), 161–182.

Steiner-Khamsi, G., & Dugonjić-Rodwin, L. (2018). Transnational accreditation for public schools: IB, PISA and other public–private partnerships. *Journal of Curriculum Studies, 50*(5), 595–607.

Tajik, M.A., Shamatov, D., & Fillipova, L. (2022). Stakeholders' perceptions of the quality of education in rural schools in Kazakhstan. *Improving Schools, 25*(2), 187–204.

Tatilya, K. Какая школа была лучше – старая советская или новая казахстанская? [Which school was better – the old Soviet one or the new Kazakhstani one?]. *QMonitor.* https://qmonitor.kz/society/1540

Tikhonova, E. (2018, April 11). Учи – не хочу! [Teach – I Don't Want]. Time.kz. https://time.kz/articles/ugol/2018/04/11/uchi-ne-hochu

Waldow, F. (2012). Standardisation and legitimacy: Two central concepts in research on educational borrowing and lending. In G. Steiner-Khamsi & F. Waldow (Eds.), *World yearbook of education 2012*: *Policy borrowing and lending in education* (pp. 431–447). Routledge.

Waldow, F. (2019). Introduction: Projection in education policy-making. In F. Waldow & G. Steiner-Khamsi (Eds.), *Understanding PISA attractiveness: Critical analyses in comparative policy studies* (pp. 1–21). Bloomsbury Publishing.

Weiss, R. (1994). *Learning from strangers: The art and method of qualitative interview studies.* The Free Press.

Working Group of the Ministry of Education and Science and the Soros Foundation. (2003). *Образовательные стандарты общего среднего образования Республики Казахстан: состояние, поиск и перспективы. Рабочий документ для обсуждения* [General education standards in the Republic of Kazakhstan: current situation, exploration and alternatives. Working paper for discussion]. Ministry of Education and Science of the Republic of Kazakhstan.

CHAPTER 4

Kazakhstani Novice Teachers' Understanding of Teacher Professionalism

Strong Knowledge Base, Limited Autonomy, and Grand Responsibilities

Gulnara Namyssova, Daniel Hernández-Torrano and Elaine Sharplin

Abstract

The development of teachers' roles and status have been key reform agenda items in Kazakhstan since its independence. The evolving conceptualizations of teaching and teachers in Kazakhstan necessitate a deeper understanding of teachers' perceptions of teacher professionalism. This is particularly important for novice teachers in the process of forming their professional identity. Therefore, this study explores novice teachers' understanding of teacher professionalism by identifying their perceptions of the attributes of teacher professionalism. The study employed a qualitative phenomenological approach. Semi-structured interviews were conducted with 19 novice teachers of public schools in Astana city. An analytical inductive approach was utilized to analyze the collected data. The study revealed that novice teachers of public schools in Astana city understand professionalism as a phenomenon that implies a strong knowledge base, limited decision-making power, and grand responsibilities for human betterment. These findings contribute alternative perspectives to the dominant Western discourse and may inform future teacher reform in Central Asia and other post-Soviet contexts.

Keywords

teacher professionalism – novice teachers – teacher knowledge – teacher autonomy – teacher responsibility – Kazakhstan

1 Introduction

Since its independence in 1991, Kazakhstan has aimed to improve teacher quality and elevate the status of the teaching profession. Diverse policies and regulations have focused on new conceptual approaches to the professional development of teachers (Autonomous Education Organization

© GULNARA NAMYSSOVA, DANIEL HERNÁNDEZ-TORRANO AND ELAINE SHARPLIN, 2025
DOI:10.1163/9789004726345_005

Nazarbayev Intellectual Schools, 2018), the development of professional standards (Atameken, 2017), a new teacher attestation (certification) system (MoES, 2018), and a recent law on 'Teacher Status' (MoES, 2019).

These policies and reforms represent prescribed professionalism, envisioned by policymakers, but are remote from experienced reality (Evans, 2008). In other words, they represent teachers' professionalism as envisioned by the government, not by the teachers who enact it. According to Evans (2008, p. 13), the 'only meaningful conception of professionalism' comes from the depiction of teachers' daily practice.

In light of all the policy developments taking place in Kazakhstan, and given the vulnerability of novice teachers, there is a need to hear the voice of novice teachers and explore their understanding of teacher professionalism at the start of their professional path. Therefore, this study explored novice teachers' understanding of teacher professionalism, by identifying their perceptions of the attributes of teacher professionalism. The gap in the empirical literature on teacher professionalism through teacher self-reflection (e.g., Bair, 2014; Swann et al., 2010; Tichenor & Tichenor, 2005), especially in the Kazakhstani, Central Asian, and post-Soviet contexts, makes this study timely and relevant.

2 Background and Context

Currently, there are 7,687 schools in Kazakhstan with more than 3.7 million students (Bureau of National Statistics, 2024) and around 340,000 teachers. The teaching profession in Kazakhstan is feminized, with women comprising 81% of the workforce. The majority of teachers (around 60%) work in rural schools.

One of the challenges of the teaching profession in Kazakhstan is the workload. According to a report by the Faculty of Education at Cambridge University (2016), teachers' excessive workload is a critical issue, primarily due to class planning and extensive reporting duties. Similarly, a study conducted by Irsaliyev et al. (2019) found that one of the leading causes of attrition among student teachers who participated in their study was excessive workload.

Another commonly discussed challenge in the teaching profession in Kazakhstan is teacher salaries (Sharplin et al., 2020). According to Kulakhmetova et al. (2014), low salaries are usually associated with the low status of the profession and make it less attractive to top graduates. Irsaliyev et al. (2019) studied the salary levels of teachers in Kazakhstan and found that teachers' salaries are only 68% of the average salary in the country. Similarly, the OECD (2018) identified low salaries as one of the critical issues that need to be addressed in Kazakhstan, arguing that low salaries force teachers to seek additional work, such as teaching extra hours either in or outside of school.

Furthermore, attracting and retaining teachers is a significant challenge in Kazakhstan. With over 27% of teachers aged 50 and above, and 12% nearing retirement age (OECD, 2018), there is a pressing need to renew the teaching workforce. The OECD further predicts that Kazakhstan will need to replace a quarter of its teachers in the next decade. Adding to this challenge is the continuous rise in the number of school-age children, which has significantly increased from around 2.5 million in 2010 to nearly 3.7 million in 2023 (Bureau of National Statistics, 2024). Novice teachers, in particular, face a higher risk of leaving the profession early, with 25% expressing intentions to do so within five years (Irsaliyev et al., 2019).

Until there is a deep understanding of the issues novice teachers face as they begin their teaching profession and necessary efforts are made to support them, novice teachers are likely to continue struggling and leaving the teaching profession. Hence, this study is set to explore Kazakhstani novice teachers' lived experience and understanding of teacher professionalism during the initial years of their careers.

3 Literature Review

3.1 Teacher Professionalism: Definition and Attributes

Multiple definitions of teacher professionalism are available in the literature (Creasy, 2015; Day, 2017; Demirkasımoğlu, 2010; Furlong et al., 2000; Hargreaves, 2000; Hoyle & John, 1995; Sexton, 2007; Sharplin et al., 2017; Storey & Hutchinson, 2001; Tichenor & Tichenor, 2005), however, the lack of consensus about teacher professionalism (Torres & Weiner, 2018) makes teacher professionalism a 'contested' (Sachs, 2015, p. 2) and 'problematic' (Helsby, 1996, p. 136) concept. According to Helsby (1996), the 'elusiveness and the continual reinterpretation of these concepts' (p. 136) make teacher professionalism a complex concept to be studied.

Although there is no definitional consensus, there seems widespread agreement that teacher professionalism is a multifaceted concept (Brehm et al., 2006; Chong & Lu, 2019; Creasy, 2015; Demirkasımoğlu, 2010; Hoyle & John, 1995) encompassing a wide range of characteristics (Carr, 2000; Hoyle & John, 1995; Sachs, 2015; Shulman, 1998). For example, Sexton (2007) analyzed literature extensively on attributes that scholars considered as characteristics of the teaching profession and found that these attributes could be grouped into three separate but interrelated groups: knowledge attributes (e.g., knowledge and training), autonomy attributes (e.g., autonomy, decision making, and trust), and service attributes (e.g., ethics, responsibility, and altruism). These three attributes (knowledge, autonomy, and responsibility) remain constant across diverse timeframes, backgrounds, and contexts (Sexton, 2007), regardless of the many changes and challenges imposed externally on the teaching profession (Day, 2017). The literature related to each of these attributes is reviewed.

3.1.1 Knowledge Base

Studies related to professions, or professionalism identify a knowledge base as the main criterion of any profession, including the teaching profession (Creasy, 2015; Furlong, 2020; Hoyle & John, 1995; Sexton, 2007; Shulman, 1998). According to Hoyle and John (1995), conceptualizing professional knowledge in the field of teaching is a complex task, mainly due to the 'wide variety of theoretical models that have been used to explain and describe it' (p. 44).

Teacher knowledge is commonly categorized depending on its structure and nature. In terms of structure, teacher knowledge can be divided into two main types: theoretical knowledge (codified) and practical knowledge (non-codified) (Hoyle & John, 1995; Wilson & Demetriou, 2007). The first one is described as abstract (Khora, 2011), technical knowledge (Furlong, 2020; Hoyle & John, 1995), which can be codified (Hoyle & John, 1995; Wilson & Demetriou, 2007) and acquired through professional journals, texts, or formal training. Such knowledge is 'universal, teachable, and precise' (Furlong, 2020, p. 41).

Practical knowledge, on the other hand, is acquired as a result of reflecting on one's practice (Hoyle & John, 1995) and observing more experienced teachers (Furlong, 2020). It is usually taken for 'granted' (Wilson & Demetriou, 2007, p. 215) by teachers who are not aware of how it affects their behavior. Shulman (1987) refers to such notions as 'maxims' (p. 11) that guide teachers' practices. Practical knowledge cannot be easily codified and is rather experiential and implicit (Hoyle & John, 1995), personal and contextual (Thurlings & van Diggelen, 2021), and situated (Aspfors et al., 2019). According to Wilson and Demetriou (2007), such knowledge is usually acquired informally, mainly through participation in 'social activities' (p. 215) such as professional development, conferences, and working with other more experienced teachers.

In this study, teacher knowledge is conceptualized as a set of knowledge about the subject matter and how to teach the subject matter obtained through formal education and practical experience.

3.1.2 Autonomy

Another main attribute of teacher professionalism is autonomy (John & Hoyle, 1995; OECD, 2019). Autonomy can be defined as freedom over one's work (OECD,

2016) and professional practice (Hoyle & John, 1995). Pearson and Moomaw (2005) argue that autonomy refers to 'the perception' that teachers have regarding whether they control 'themselves and their work environment' (p. 42).

Autonomy is a 'dynamic' (Helgoy & Homme, 2007, p. 233) and generally a positively perceived concept (Booth et al., 2021). However, for some teachers, increased autonomy is related to feeling unsupported and having limited development or progression opportunities (Booth et al., 2021). Some also negatively associate it with supervisors reducing their own workload by sharing the authority with teachers (Pearson & Moomaw, 2005).

According to Hoyle and John (1995), professional autonomy is a contextual concept, and the main contexts in teaching are the school and classroom. Teacher autonomy in the classroom implies autonomy over curricular choices, instructional planning, and classroom standards of conduct (OECD, 2016). In the school context, teacher autonomy can be expressed in school curricular content, pedagogical practices, and assessment techniques (OECD, 2016). Ingersoll (1997) emphasizes the importance of both school-level and classroom-level autonomy of teachers. The author (Ingersoll, 1997) states that teachers should be able to participate in decision-making regarding education issues. If they do not participate in it and if it comes from the top-down, teachers will not be interested in the implementation and success of the decisions made by others.

Based on the key ideas and discussion presented above, in this study, the second domain of teacher professionalism, autonomy, is conceptualized as teachers' freedom to make decisions based on the full range of their professional knowledge.

3.1.3   Responsibility

Responsibility is regarded by Hoyle and John (1995, p. 103) as the 'reciprocal of autonomy', i.e. when professionals have the autonomy they should act responsibly. It entails 'voluntaristic commitment to a set of principles governing good practice' (Hoyle & John, 1995, p. 103), associated with trust and commitment (Solbrekke & Englund, 2011). Sexton (2007) associates the third attribute of teacher professionalism with altruism and ethics. Similarly, Arthur (2003) argues that above all, teaching is a 'self-giving' (p. 318) profession.

In terms of the ethical attributes of teacher professionalism, Macmillan (1993) states that members of any profession, including teaching, should be responsible for adhering to the ethical norms as any other citizen, such as being honest or fair. Furthermore, professionals should follow the ethics set by their professions and know about the 'ethical dimensions of the relations among professionals and clients, the public, the employing institution, and fellow professionals' (Macmillan, 1993, p.189).

In this study, teacher professionalism is defined as the attainment of knowledge necessary for teaching; the autonomy to make decisions based on that knowledge, and the ability to act responsibly within the values and norms of the profession (Furlong et al., 2000).

3.2   *Teacher Professional Formation*

Becoming a teacher professional requires more than just 'learning to teach' (Vonk, 1995, p. 10). It is a process that consists of several developmental stages (Katz, 1972; Huberman, 1989, Caspersen & Raaen, 2014; Vonk, 1995). According to Vonk (1995), the professional path of teachers starts with the preprofessional phase, defined by the acquisition of competencies. This is followed by a threshold phase, which is characterized by 'teachers' change in perspective of the teacher role' (Vonk, 1995, p. 3). Together, they represent the transition phase from student to teacher (Vonk, 1995). In other words, novice teachers transition from the pre-service stage, during which they acquire professional education, to the in-service stage, when they are considered teacher professionals who can apply their professional skills (Schatz-Oppenheimer & Dvir, 2014).

Researchers consider this 'transition' period as the most difficult period in a teacher's career (e.g., Cherubini, 2009; Fantilli & McDougall, 2009; Nahal, 2010). Newly certified teachers must deal with practice shock (Farrell, 2016) and reality shock (Kim & Cho, 2014; McCormack & Thomas, 2003; Nahal, 2010) while fulfilling the same duties and responsibilities as veteran teachers (Schatz-Oppenheimer & Dvir, 2014). This challenging experience often leads to novice teacher stress, burnout, and attrition and negatively affects student performance (Nahal, 2010; O'Brennan et al., 2017). Indeed, this period signals for many the end rather than the start of the career in teaching (Trevethan, 2018), because the contemporary discourse of 'beginning teaching' is characterized by terms such as: 'survival, sink or swim, overwhelming, shocking and bleak' (p. 50). As an example, Ewing and Smith (2003) state that 25 to 40% of new teachers in the Western world feel burnout and quit during their first three to five years of teaching. Joiner and Edwards (2008) report that in the USA almost 50% of novice teachers leave the teaching profession within the first five years, and more than 30% within the first three years. Similar results were found in the study conducted in Kazakhstan. According to Irsaliyev et al. (2019), more than 25% of novice teachers who participated in their study planned to leave the profession within the next five years.

4 Research Design

The social constructivism philosophical perspective guided the current research. In the social constructivism approach, researchers assume that individuals try to understand the world they live in and develop the "subjective meaning of their experience" (Creswell, 2014, p. 8). But meanings are not out there "imprinted on individuals" (Creswell & Poth, 2018, p. 60), they are constructed as a result of interaction with others. In other words, social constructivism is not about discovering meanings but constructing them (Crotty, 1998). In this study, we construct meaning and knowledge by listening to what participants have to say about the phenomenon being studied.

A hermeneutical phenomenological research design was chosen to 'unveil the world as experienced by the subject through their lifeworld stories' (Kafle, 2011, p. 186), in this case, the research participants were Kazakhstani novice teachers. The phenomenological design enabled the making of the meaning of novice teachers' lived experiences (Carpenter, 2013; Creswell & Poth, 2018; van Manen, 1990). This study involved not only a description of the experiences of novice teachers but also the interpretation of their experiences to construct meaning of the phenomenon based on their experience.

4.1 *Participants*

Participants of this study were chosen purposively based on the following criteria to ensure that the selected participants have common experiences relevant to the phenomenon under study:

- One to three years of teaching experience. The transition phase is in which teachers transition from their student role to their teacher role (Huberman, 1989).
- Currently teaching grades 5–11 in public secondary schools in Astana. Narrowing the selection of teacher participants with diverse experiences (Padilla-Diaz, 2015) the study was limited to secondary school teachers (grades 5–11). Yet, to ensure heterogeneity of the group the participants were recruited from different public secondary schools of Astana city and their teacher preparation occurred at different institutions. Astana is a new city and its population has more than doubled in the last twenty years from 501,998 in 2003 to 1,451,525 in 2024. Consequently, the number of school-age children is also growing rapidly. In other words, Astana is a dynamically growing city, and it will continue to attract novice teachers due to the increasing number of school-age children. Because of this, we considered Astana as a suitable setting to study novice teachers and their experiences.
- Graduates from initial teacher education (ITE) institutions. Graduating from pedagogical universities with teacher training programs is the main

way of becoming a teacher in Kazakhstan. According to OECD (2019), more than 90% of teachers in Kazakhstan have a bachelor's degree or equivalent from ITE institutions.

After the granting of ethical approval for the study by the institutional review committee, seven public schools were contacted to seek permission to conduct the study. Three schools were visited to conduct face-to-face interviews with eight eligible teachers. Another eleven teachers from four additional schools were interviewed online. In total, there were 19 participants from seven schools in Astana city.

The profiles of the participants are summarized in Table 4.1. The participants were between 21 and 26 years of age and 17 of the 19 participants were women. This gender imbalance is consistent with the high ratio of female teachers

TABLE 4.1   Demographic information about the participants

Participant	Gender	Age	Discipline	Teaching experience (years)
Participant 1	Female	23	English	2
Participant 2	Female	22	English	1
Participant 3	Female	25	Informatics	3
Participant 4	Male	26	History	3
Participant 5	Female	N/A*	Informatics	2
Participant 6	Female	N/A*	Chemistry	2
Participant 7	Female	24	English	3
Participant 8	Female	23	Informatics	2
Participant 9	Female	22	Russian Language and Literature	1
Participant 10	Female	24	English	2
Participant 11	Female	23	Informatics	1
Participant 12	Female	22	English	1
Participant 13	Female	22	Informatics	2
Participant 14	Female	24	English	2
Participant 15	Female	21	English	1
Participant 16	Female	N/A*	Biology	2
Participant 17	Male	25	Kazakh Language and Literature	3
Participant 18	Female	25	English	2
Participant 19	Female	N/A*	Geography	2

*Participants chose not to disclose their age.

within the whole teacher population of Kazakhstan, i.e., 81% of teachers in Kazakhstan are female (Bureau of National Statistics, 2024).

A substantial number (42%) of the participants were teachers of the English language. According to the principal of one school, many English teachers find other better-paid jobs and schools have to recruit new teachers each year, as there is demand in the market for those who know English. All participants had between one and three years of experience, as per inclusion criteria.

4.2 Data Collection and Analysis Procedures

Semi-structured interviews were used in this study for data collection due to their flexibility, which enabled the building of rapport between the investigator and participant (Cohen et al., 2007; Padilla-Diaz, 2015). Face-to-face interviews were initially chosen as the data collection method. However, due to the Covid-19 pandemic, the majority of interviews (11 out of 19) were conducted online after receiving pertinent approval from IREC committee. For interviews, the preferred digital application for the participants was WhatsApp (without video). The interviews were conducted in the language of preference of the interviewees: Kazakh (15 out of 19) and Russian (4 out of 19) languages. The data collection process lasted for about three months in total. The interviews were transcribed and then translated into English.

The collected data was analyzed according to the inductive analysis approach proposed by Miles et al. (2014). Specifically, the interviews were transcribed and coded (data condensation). The codes were then analyzed with the help of matrices and networks (data display). Techniques such as noting patterns and clustering common answers were used to categorize the codes and identify the themes (drawing conclusions). NVIVO software was used for data analysis.

For this study, member checking and peer-debriefer strategies were undertaken to ensure the trustworthiness of the data analysis process. Specifically, the interview transcripts were sent to the participants to check the accuracy of their responses (Rossman & Rallis, 2012). Also, all three authors constantly reviewed the processes of data analysis of the data, which involved co-coding and questioning for the justification of findings (Merriam & Tisdell, 2016).

5 Ethical Considerations

The study was conducted in accordance with the rules and regulations of the Nazarbayev University Institutional Research Ethics Committee (IREC). The study participants were provided with printed (for face-to-face interviews) and electronic (for online interviews) versions of the consent form. The collected data was saved in password-protected files and a USB flash drive which is also password-protected. The identities of the participants and schools where the participants work was protected by using pseudonyms.

6 Findings

The findings of the study suggest that novice teachers in Kazakhstan perceive teacher professionalism to be an attainment of three attributes dominant in the international literature: knowledge base, autonomy, and responsibility. However, the interpretation of these concepts by the participants was significantly different from the conceptualizations in the international literature. The Kazakhstani novice teachers' perspective on each of these attributes will be presented below.

6.1 *Knowledge Base*

The knowledge base was the most dominant attribute of teacher professionalism that emerged in this study. The participants identified two categories of knowledge as critical to their concepts of professionalism: theoretical knowledge and practical knowledge.

6.1.1 Theoretical Knowledge

Theoretical knowledge is understood as a crucial component of the knowledge base of the teaching profession which encompasses abstract and codified knowledge of the subject and pedagogy.

Subject knowledge was identified as the most critical theoretical component of teacher knowledge by the participants. For them, subject knowledge referred to knowledge of topics, concepts, rules, and the material base (resources) of the subject they teach. There was consensus among the participants that teacher professionals need to have extensive knowledge of the subject they teach. Most of the research participants referred to it as 'the first' and 'the most important' knowledge, because according to them, one is not capable of teaching a subject without a thorough knowledge of that subject. Participant 13's response was indicative of the responses of many other participants: 'First of all, it is knowing your subject very well, I think to teach others you need to know it well yourself'. Moreover, having the ability to answer all the questions students have to ask about that subject was identified as an important factor in gaining respect among their students. This requires a depth and breadth of knowledge to go beyond the planned content knowledge of a specific lesson, as discussed by Participant 18:

> Any professional teacher should know their subject well and be able to answer all the possible subject-related questions of the students. If they [teachers] cannot answer those questions, they need to keep learning, such that students do not say 'That teacher could not answer our questions'. That is very important to me.

In other words, weak subject knowledge could hurt their confidence as professional teachers. Indeed, the participants perceived subject knowledge to be the foundation of their professional lives, gained in the first instance from their pre-service teacher education. However, the participants considered that teacher subject knowledge needs to constantly develop. The subject knowledge obtained during ITE needs to be updated as teachers' careers progress. Participant 1, a teacher of the English language, stated 'I should not stop learning, new words and new things such as TOEFL, IELTS are appearing. I want to pass them [the exams] and keep improving my English language proficiency'.

Another reason for considering subject knowledge as the most important knowledge for teachers is related to the perception that 'transmitting knowledge' is their main responsibility. As knowledge transmitters, they feel obligated to have the strong subject knowledge to pass on to students. Their responsibilities as teachers will be discussed further in the following subsections.

Besides subject knowledge, the participants perceived that teacher professionals should have extensive *pedagogical knowledge*. The participants acknowledged that professional teachers should know effective teaching methods, student capabilities, and age-related developmental differences. This was reflected in Participant 14's response that 'Professional teachers have a large repertoire of teaching methods which they can effectively use in practice'. Another participant expressed that teachers' subject knowledge becomes useless if they do not know the methods of passing that knowledge to students and if they do not know how to make their subject interesting. 'I might know the topic very well, but if I do not know how to make my lesson exciting, how to present that material interestingly, or how to keep students' attention, then they will not learn anything' (Participant 5). Participant 12 reaffirms this and elaborates on pedagogical knowledge, defining it as the 'knowledge on how to correctly present materials to the pupils considering their peculiarities and age differences'.

Most of the participants believe that being a teacher professional requires synergistic utilization of subject and pedagogical knowledge. Participant 6, a Chemistry teacher, elaborated:

> I think the main goal of teachers is to explain a certain topic to students using various methods. For that, teachers need to know different methods

and should choose a suitable one depending on the topic. They should even know how to use intonation. If they speak monotonously, students may not absorb that information.

Overall, the participants perceive both subject knowledge and pedagogy as fundamental theoretical knowledge of the teaching profession.

6.1.2   Practical Knowledge

Another component of the knowledge base of the teaching profession is practical knowledge. It encompasses the teaching knowledge and skills acquired through experience and practice.

The participants agreed that having an ITE degree was not sufficient to be a professional teacher. They believed that teachers also need practical knowledge, which is derived from their experience and is pivotal for their practice. They referred to it as the knowledge that is 'gained in practice' (Participant 16), 'over years' (Participant 15), and 'through reflection on their own and other colleagues' practice' (Participant 9). Participant 10 elaborated about knowledge gained through experience: 'For instance, my difference from experienced professional teachers is their learning on the job, their knowledge gained over the years. Whereas we as novice teachers do not know many things yet'. Participant 9 mentioned that by participating in her colleagues' classes she understood how the experience makes a difference: 'During the first year I participated in different experienced teachers' classes. Every lesson they teach, the methods they use for each lesson are unique. They teach so much better than novice teachers.'

A common belief of novice teachers in this study was that through experience, teachers acquire confidence. Teachers need to keep learning and excelling in practice until they 'do their job easily and confidently' (Participant 14). Since novice teachers do not have sufficient practical knowledge, they feel less confident than their more experienced colleagues. As a result, they feel that they are treated differently by students: 'Professionalism is an experience, a core they have worked for and, you know, students see it. Students look at novice teachers differently than they look at experienced teachers' (Participant 15).

6.2   *Teacher Autonomy*

Kazakhstani novice teachers perceive that their autonomy is limited to classroom and lesson organization-related matters such as choosing teaching methods, assessment, selecting materials, and other lesson organization matters. Classroom autonomy is important for the teachers as 'no one knows that class or those students better than teachers, therefore only teachers know how to better deliver the lesson to a particular class' (Participant 16).

Autonomy was linked back to the foundation of teacher subject knowledge. Knowledge empowers novice teachers to be able to make decisions and act independently. According to Participant 18 'autonomous teachers do not rely on anyone. They rely on their knowledge and skills to conduct their lessons'.

Even though participants believe that teachers should be given autonomy inside the classroom, they emphasized the limits of their autonomy by referring to not 'crossing the lines', 'knowing the limits', and working within the 'plan'. Participant 12 said 'As a teacher, you cannot be completely autonomous, you still need to follow the plans and work within the approved curriculum'. Participant 3 commented that 'Every teacher has his/her viewpoint or vision about the lesson, vision on how to work with children. However, they should not go out of the curriculum' (Participant 3). The prescribed curriculum, academic plan, and textbooks are perceived as 'borders' that should not be crossed while teaching.

Participants did not refer to autonomy outside of the classrooms. Only one of the participants, when asked about school-level autonomy, stated that it is the responsibility of the school administration, and she should not interfere with their decisions: 'here is a school administration that makes school-related decisions. It is not my responsibility' (Participant 16). Novice teachers do not consider themselves to be members of the school or community who can participate in the development of school policies or contribute to the wider community. They perceive their autonomy as limited to the classroom where they teach.

6.3 *Responsibility*

All participants were very confident about two main responsibilities of professional teachers: responsibilities for teaching knowledge and teaching values to students. They refer to 'transmitting knowledge' as the main responsibility of the teaching profession, which is understood as passing their subject knowledge on to students. Student outcomes are perceived as the result of the successful transmission of such knowledge: 'It is teaching children your subject. For me, a teacher of the English language, it is important that students at the end of the semester know, understood, and could talk in English,' said Participant 18. 'When you teach your subject to children and you see that they understood everything, it is such a joy for me,' said Participant 6 about students' progress.

Participants believe that by transmitting their subject knowledge to students, they are contributing to human betterment and the formation of future generations. Participant 17 said: 'I teach the Kazakh language. Some teach mathematics, some teach the Russian language and if each of them teaches their subject well, eventually those students will become educated and literate citizens' (Participant 17).

In addition to knowledge transmission, teachers view themselves as transmitters of 'values'. In this respect, they need to be responsible for their professional conduct and practice. They believe that students look up to them and learn from them. They are the people with whom students interact most after their family members. Therefore, they need to 'be fair', 'respect children', 'have good manners', 'be ethical' and even 'look like teachers'. In other words, they view themselves as 'role models' from whom the students learn morals and values. 'Besides giving them knowledge, we should be ethical and be role models for them. Since they see us daily, they also learn from us how to communicate and how to behave,' said Participant 16. Participant 17 also noted, 'Being respectful to students, having good manners. And seeing these, children will learn from us.'

Teaching seems more than just a profession for the participants. They perceive it as a 'status' (Participant 15) and a 'calling' (Participant 14); the responsibilities and obligations of which go beyond the context of the school system and profession. They do not perceive their profession as an occupation with set working hours. They feel that they always have to live up to that status inside and outside of school. Responsibilities of their profession become part of their everyday life, and any breach of those responsibilities will result in a loss of reputation. This view was illustrated by the following participants:

> Teaching is a status, and you need to behave according to that status. You should not be rude; you should look appropriate and always watch your behavior. You need to keep being a role model and ethical even outside of school. If the students see you outside of school misbehaving or being unethical, they may change their opinion about you. Therefore, you should always behave yourself accordingly. (Participant 15)

> Being a teacher is not a profession, it is a 'calling' that comes with 'frames'. 'Frames of how to talk, how to conduct, and present yourself. You should not go beyond those frames, and you must live up to this calling every day'. (Participant 14)

Some of the participants mentioned the altruistic aspect of the profession. For instance, one of the participants referred to teachers as 'the second mothers who need to teach students what is good and what is bad inside and outside the classroom' (Participant 15). Whereas Participant 14 sees her responsibility as 'helping students with the school and out of school-related issues'. And for Participant 18 it is important to motivate and support students when they need it most: 'sometimes, especially when they [students] feel down, they only need support from you. That is why I support and motivate them' (Participant 18).

7 Discussion

The main finding of this study of novice teachers' understanding of teacher professionalism in secondary schools of Astana city is that in Kazakhstan novice teachers' understanding of three attributes of professionalism is in alignment with the ones prevalent in other contexts: knowledge base, autonomy, and responsibility (Furlong et al., 2000; Hoyle & John, 1995; Sexton, 2007). However, the interpretation of those attributes significantly differed in the Kazakhstani context. Kazakhstani novice teachers attach different values to these three attributes. In particular, the knowledge base is understood as the central attribute of teacher professionalism. The other two attributes, autonomy, and responsibility, are referred to as attributes dependent on the knowledge base.

Within the knowledge base, subject knowledge was referred to as the most important knowledge of the teaching profession. Attaching such high value to subject knowledge might stem from Soviet doctrines, which tended to prioritize subject knowledge over other types of knowledge (Yakavets et al., 2017). This study indicates that such practice is still in place. Also, for novice teachers' subject knowledge is related to knowledge of topics, concepts, rules, and the material base (resources) of the subject they teach. Shulman (1987) refers to subject knowledge as the knowledge about facts and concepts of the subject and knowledge of the structures of the subject i.e., the teacher should be able not only to define and explain the subject matter to students but also be able to explain why a particular proposition is worth knowing. In other words, the participants' conceptualization of subject knowledge is limited compared to the one provided by Shulman (1987).

Regarding the second attribute of teacher professionalism, autonomy, the participants were aware of the importance of autonomy for teachers. However, autonomy in their understanding is circumscribed to decision-making related to lesson planning matters (e.g., teaching methods, student assessment, and material base) within the classroom. Even these decisions are made following the prescribed curriculum, textbooks, and lesson plans. At this point, none of the novice teachers involved in this study believe that they are expected or invited to contribute to school-level decisions. Therefore, the participants' conceptualization of autonomy is limited to classroom-level decision-making, nor do they see themselves as members of a broader professional community in which they are able to influence any form of decision-making.

Unlike autonomy, the participants believe that their responsibility goes beyond the classroom. Transmitting knowledge and moral values are seen as the main responsibility of the teaching profession by novice teachers in Kazakhstan. They also perceive altruism, ethics, and self-giving (Arthur, 2003) as part of their responsibility. They are aware that teachers need to adhere to the highest level of ethics established by their profession in order to live up to the status of being a teacher. By fulfilling their responsibility, they believe they are contributing to human betterment. The question is whether the teachers can fulfill such grand responsibility with the perception that they do not have control or autonomy over their own work, or perceive that they have any influence on the broader profession within or outside of the school, beyond their own personal actions.

This study demonstrated a sharp contrast between novice teachers' understanding of teacher professionalism and the notions of teacher professionalism promoted by the current policies such as those aimed to update professional standards of the teaching profession and improve teacher professional status (Atameken, 2017; MoES, 2019). First, novice teachers believe that subject knowledge is the most important type of knowledge to be acquired and transmitted. However, these policies promote an understanding of a strong knowledge base which does not only imply subject knowledge of teachers, but also pedagogical and psychological preparedness of teachers. Second, teachers associate autonomy with making decisions in the classroom for efficacious transmission of this knowledge. On the contrary, autonomy, is presented in the policies as a class and school-level decision making and, hence, includes not only following 'prescribed' materials but participating in the development of those. The third attribute of teacher professionalism, responsibility is perceived as transmitting knowledge and values to students. Whereas in the policies responsibility is presented as developing students and constantly enriching themselves as teachers and helping others in their community to develop. This indicates that there is a gap between the 'prescribed' understanding of teacher professionalism and the 'enacted' understanding of teacher professionalism among novice teachers.

In summary, novice teachers of Kazakhstan have a different understanding of teacher professionalism which implies a strong knowledge base, limited decision-making power, and grand responsibilities of improving human betterment. These understandings represent a significantly different interpretation to dominant notions of professionalism in other international contexts, where constructivist conceptions of the teaching profession are dominant and teachers are professionally empowered and expected to use their expertise for the improvement of education within the school and community through engagement with policy-related decision making (OECD, 2016; Salokangos et al., 2019).

8 Implications for Practice

The study finds that novice teachers consider subject knowledge as the most important knowledge of the teaching profession. This might be due to their ITE experience, which mainly emphasizes subject knowledge (Yakavets et al., 2017). Indeed, subject knowledge is often referred to as a foundation for teaching (Grossman et al., 2005; Ko et al., 2013), although it is not sufficient, in isolation, to teach students effectively (OECD, 2019). Therefore, a practical implication for ITE institutions is to provide prospective teachers with more opportunities to develop and apply their pedagogical content knowledge in various classroom contexts.

Also, the participants understand that completing the ITE programme is not sufficient to become a professional and they must continue learning after entering the profession. Therefore, schools need to support novice teachers to continue their professional learning by providing necessary continuing development and seminars (Darling-Hammond, 2017; Kearney, 2014). Reduced teaching and release from paperwork should be offered for novice teachers to give them time to regularly meet their mentors and reflect on their own practice (Darling-Hammond, 2017; Kearney, 2014; OECD, 2019).

The gap between 'prescribed' understanding of teacher professionalism and 'enacted' understanding of teacher professionalism among novice teachers needs to be addressed. One of the ways of minimizing this gap might be by integrating teacher professional standards into the curriculum of the ITE programme (Call, 2018). Course descriptions should be linked to professional standards through a list of learning outcomes. The integration of the professional standards into the programme can be assessed through the certification of novice teachers which can also 'inform initial licensure and provide leverage on improving teacher preparation' (Darling Hammond, 2017, p. 296).

9 Implications for Theory

The current study contributes to the theory by providing a conceptualization of teacher professionalism from novice teachers' perspectives in the context of Kazakhstan. Figure 4.1 illustrates Kazakhstani novice teachers' conceptualization of teacher professionalism as identified in this study. The original conceptual framework developed by Hoyle and John (1995) framed teacher professionalism as consisting of three attributes: knowledge base, autonomy, and responsibility. While this study supported the view that these three components are considered elements of teacher professionalism by Kazakhstani novice teachers, the findings demonstrated that the attributes are not considered

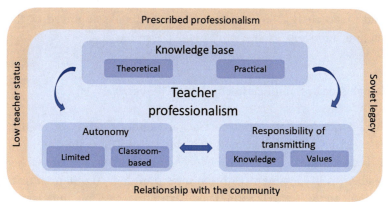

FIGURE 4.1   Kazakhstani novice teachers' conceptualization of teacher professionalism and factors which affect the formation of such conceptualization

of equal value. Novice teachers consider the knowledge base as the fundamental attribute that serves as the basis of the other two attributes. According to the participants, only teachers with a strong knowledge base can be autonomous and make decisions based on their knowledge. As for responsibility, novice teachers point out that only a knowledgeable teacher can transmit that knowledge to the students.

The orange square around three attributes of teacher professionalism illustrates the challenges which affect the participants' formation of understanding of teacher professionalism. To be specific, the Soviet-era doctrine, prescribed professionalism, low teacher status, and relationship with the community seem to affect the formation of the novice teachers' understanding of the phenomenon. For instance, data analysis indicates that subject knowledge was identified as the most important knowledge of the profession. Attaching such a high value to subject knowledge might be related to Soviet doctrine which tended to prioritize subject knowledge and transmit that knowledge to the students (Yakavets et al., 2017). This study indicates that such practices are still in place and future teachers continue being taught mainly subject knowledge during initial teacher education. Consequently, they keep perceiving subject knowledge as the most important knowledge of the teaching profession. The abovementioned challenges also shape the participants' understanding of their autonomy and responsibility. For instance, during Soviet times, teachers practiced authoritarian decision-making (Matyash, 1991). Such practice is still in place and even nowadays teachers continue strictly to follow the policies and initiatives launched by the government. Moreover, the participants do not consider themselves as school members who can participate in the development of school and government policies or contribute to the wider community. They associate their decision-making only with lesson organization matters and they strictly follow curriculum and textbooks approved by the Ministry of Education and Science while in the classroom.

10   Conclusion and Implication for Future Research

This study set out to explore novice teachers' understanding of teacher professionalism in secondary schools of Astana city. The main finding of this study is that in Kazakhstan novice teachers' understanding of teacher professionalism is in alignment with the ones prevalent in other contexts (Furlong et al., 2000; Hoyle & John, 1995; Sexton, 2007). They understand professionalism as the attainment of three attributes: knowledge base, autonomy, and responsibility. Unlike in other contexts in Kazakhstan, novice teachers attach different values to each attribute with knowledge base being the central attribute of teacher professionalism. The other two attributes, autonomy, and responsibility were regarded as secondary and dependent on knowledge base attributes.

The study results indicate that novice teachers have a very limited understanding of teacher professionalism, especially regarding two attributes of teacher professionalism: autonomy and responsibility. Considering the importance of these attributes in developing the professionalism of novice teachers, research is needed on ways to develop their understanding of these attributes and what stakeholders (initial teacher education institutions, school leaders, and the Ministry of Education) can do to achieve this objective. Since this study was concerned only with novice teachers, it would be well-suited to study experienced teachers' understanding of teacher professionalism and identify similarities and differences in their understanding.

To conclude, the present study was based on interviews with 19 novice teachers from Astana city. The findings of the study cannot be generalized, and 19 novice teachers cannot be representative of the whole novice teacher population of Kazakhstan. Therefore, it is recommended to conduct a larger-scale study with a national sample of novice teachers. The current study findings could provide insights and information to develop necessary instruments for future larger-scale studies in Kazakhstan.

References

Arthur, J. (2003). Professional value commitments. *British Journal of Educational Studies, 51*(4), 317–319.

Aspfors, J., Eklund, G., & Hansén, S. E. (2019). Early career teachers' experiences of developing professional knowledge: From research-based teacher education through five years in the profession. *Nordisk tidskrift för allmän didaktik (NoAD), 5*(1), 2–18.

Atameken. (2017). *Professional standard 'Pedagogue', Annex to the order of the Chairman of the Board of the National Chamber of Entrepreneurs of the Republic of Kazakhstan.* Retrieved October, 2018, from http://atameken.kz/uploads/content/files

Autonomous Education Organization Nazarbayev Intellectual Schools. (2018). *Godovoi otchet za 2018 god* [Annual report of 2018]. Center of Excellence.

Bair, M. A. (2014). Teacher professionalism: What educators can learn from social workers? *Mid-Western Educational Researcher, 26*(2), 28–57.

Bureau of National Statistics of Agency for Strategic planning and reforms of the Republic of Kazakhstan. (2024). *Statistics.* https://stat.gov.kz/en/

Booth, J., Coldwell, M., Müller, L. M., Perry, E., & Zuccollo, J. (2021). Mid-career teachers: A mixed methods scoping study of professional development, career progression and retention. *Education Sciences, 11*(6), 1–33.

Brehm, B., Breen, P., Brown, B., Long, L., Smith, R., Wall, A., & Warren, N. S. (2006). Instructional design and assessment: An interdisciplinary approach to introducing professionalism. *American Journal of Pharmaceutical Education, 70*(4), 1–5.

Call, K. (2018). Professional teaching standards: A comparative analysis of their history, implementation, and efficacy. *Australian Journal of Teacher Education, 43*(3), 93–108.

Carpenter, C. (2013). Phenomenology and rehabilitation research. In P. Liamputtong (Ed.) *Research methods in health: Foundations for evidence-based practice* (pp. 115–131). Oxford University Press.

Carr, D. (2000). *Professionalism and ethics in education.* Routledge.

Caspersen, J., & Raaen, F. D. (2014). Novice teachers and how they cope. *Teachers and Teaching, 20*(2), 189–211. https://doi.org/10.1080/13540602.2013.848570

Cherubini, L. (2009). Reconciling the tensions of new teachers' socialization into school culture: A review of the research. *Issues in Educational Research, 19*(2), 83–99.

Chong, S., & Lu, T. (2019). Early childhood teachers' perception of the professional self and in relation to the early childhood communities. *Australian Journal of Teacher Education, 44*(7), 53–67. http://dx.doi.org/10.14221/ajte.2019v44n7.4

Cohen, L., Manion, L., & Morrison, K. (2007). *Research methods in education* (6th ed.). Routledge Falmer.

Creasy, K. L. (2015). Defining professionalism in teacher education programs. *Journal of Education & Social Policy, 2*(2), 23–25.

Creswell, J. W. (2014). *Research design: Qualitative, quantitative and mixed methods approaches* (4th ed.). Sage.

Creswell, J. W. & Poth, C. N. (2018). *Qualitative inquiry and research design: Choosing among five approaches* (4th ed.). SAGE.

Darling-Hammond, L. (2017). Teacher education around the world: What can we learn from international practice? *European Journal of Teacher Education, 40*(3), 291–309.

Day, C. (2017). *Teachers' worlds and work: Understanding complexity, building quality.* Routledge.

Demirkasımoğlu, N. (2010). Defining teacher professionalism from different perspectives. *Procedia Social and Behavioral Sciences, 9,* 2047–2051.

Evans, L. (2008). Professionalism, professionality and the development of education professionals. *British Journal of Educational Studies, 56*(1), 20–38.

Faculty of Education Cambridge University. (2016). *Report on the introduction of the new curriculum, pedagogy and assessment in primary schools (Grade 1 in Kazakhstan).* http://www.educ.cam.ac.uk/networks/eri/casestudies/kazakhstan/researching/2016%2 oReport_short.pdf

Fantilli, R. D., & McDougall, D. E. (2009). A study of novice teachers: Challenges and supports in the first years. *Teaching and Teacher Education, 25*(6), 814–825.

Farrell, T. S. C. (2016). Surviving the transition shock in the first year of teaching through reflective practice. *System,* 61, 12–19.

Furlong, J. (2020). Re-forming initial teacher education in Wales: A personal review of the literature. *Wales Journal of Education, 22*(1), 37–58.

Furlong, J., Barton, L., Miles, S., Whiting, C., & Whitty, G. (2000). *Teacher education in transition: Re-forming professionalism?* Open University Press.

Grossman, P., Schoenfeld, A., & Lee, C. (2005). Teaching subject matter. In L. Darling-Hammond & J. Bransford (Eds.), *Preparing teachers for a changing world: What teachers should learn and be able to do* (pp. 201–231). Jossey-Bass.

Hargreaves, A. (2000). Four ages of professionalism and professional learning. *Teachers and Teaching: Theory and Practice, 6*(2), 151–182.

Helgoy, I., & Homme, A. (2007). Towards a new professionalism in school? A comparative study of teacher autonomy in Norway and Sweden. *European Educational Research Journal, 6*(3), 232–249.

Helsby, G. (1996). Defining and developing professionalism in English secondary schools. *Journal of Education for Teaching, 22*(2), 135–148.

Hoyle, E., & John, P. D. (1995). *Professional knowledge and professional practice.* Cassell.

Huberman, M. (1989). The professional life cycle of teachers. *Teacher College Records, 91,* 31–57.

Joiner, S., & Edwards, J. (2008). Novice teachers: Where are they going and why don't they stay. *Journal of Cross-Disciplinary Perspectives in Education, 1*(1), 36–43.

Kafle, N. P. (2011). Hermeneutic phenomenological research method simplified. *An Interdisciplinary Journal, 5*(1), 181–200.

Katz, L. (1972). Developmental stages of preschool teachers. *Elementary School Journal, 73*(1), 50–54.

Kearney, S. (2014). Understanding beginning teacher induction: A contextualized examination of best practice. *Cogent Education, 1*(1), 1–15.

Khora, S. (2011). *Education and teacher professionalism.* Rawat Publications.

Kim, H., & Cho, Y. (2014). Preservice teachers' motivation, teacher efficacy, and expectation of reality shock. *Asia-Pacific Journal of Teacher Education, 42*(1), 67–81.

Ko, J., Sammons, P., & Bakkum, L. (2013). *Effective teaching: A review of research and evidence.* CfBT Education Trust.

Kulakhmetova, A., McLaughlin, C. & Ayubayeva, N. (2014). *Preparing teachers: An international review of the evidence on initial teacher education.* Research project "Development of strategic directions for education reforms in Kazakhstan for 2015–2020". Nazarbayev University Graduate School of Education.

Macmillan, C. J. B. (1993). Ethics and teacher professionalization. In K. Strike & L. Ternasky (Eds.), *Ethics for professionals in education: Perspectives for preparation and practice* (pp. 202–216). Teachers College Press.

Matyash, O. (1991). Social values and aims in soviet education. *Journal of Education for Teaching, 17*(1), 5–9. https//doi.org/10.1080/0260747910170102

Merriam, S. B., & Tisdell, E. J. (2016). *Qualitative research: A guide to design and implementation* (4th ed.). Jossey Bass.

McCormack, A., & Thomas, K. (2003). Is survival enough? Induction experiences of beginning teachers within a New South Wales context. *Asia-Pacific Journal of Teacher Education, 31*(2), 125–138.

Miles, M. B., Huberman, A. M., & Saldaäna, J. (2014). *Qualitative data analysis: A methods sourcebook* (3rd ed.). Sage.

MoES (Ministry of Education and Science). (2018). *Prilojenie k prikazu Ministra obrazovaniya I nauki Respubliki Kazakhstan ot 12 aprelya 2018 goda # 152* [Annex to the order #152 of the Ministry of Education and Science of the Republic of Kazakhstan from April 12, 2018]. Retrieved April 10, 2019, from edu.gov.kz

MoES (Ministry of Education and Science). (2019). *Проект закона Республики Казахстан «О статусе педагога»* [Draft law on the 'status of a teacher' of the Republic of Kazakhstan]. Retrieved September 8, 2019, from http://edupvl.gov.kz/files/telefonogrammy/zakonproekt.pdf

Nahal, P. S. (2010). Voices from the field: Perspectives of first-year teachers on the disconnect between teacher preparation programs and the realities of the classroom. *Research in Higher Education Journal, 8,* 1–19.

O'Brennan, L., Pas, E., Bradshaw, C. & Reschly, A. (2017). Multilevel examination of burnout among high school staff: Importance of staff and school factors. *School Psychology Review, 46*(2), 165–176.

OECD. (2016). *Supporting teacher professionalism: Insights from TALIS 2013.* OECD Publishing. http://dx.doi.org/10.1787/9789264248601-en

OECD. (2018). *Education policy outlook: Kazakhstan.* http://www.oecd.org/education/Education-Policy-Outlook-Country-ProfileKazakhstan-2018.pdf

OECD. (2019). *TALIS 2018 results (Volume 1): Teachers and school leaders as lifelong learners.* OECD Publishing.

Padilla-Díaz, M. (2015). Phenomenology in educational qualitative research: Philosophy as science or philosophical science? *International Journal of Educational Excellence 1*(2), 101–110.

Pearson, L. C., & Moomaw, W. (2005). The relationship between teacher autonomy and stress, work satisfaction, empowerment and professionalism. *Educational Research Quarterly, 29*(1), 38–54.

Rossman, G. B., & Rallis, S. F. (2012). *Learning in the field: An introduction to qualitative research* (3rd ed.). Sage.

Sachs, J. (2015). Teacher professionalism: Why are we still talking about it? *Teachers and Teaching, 22*(4), 1–13. https//doi.org/10.1080/13540602.2015.1082732

Salokangas, M., Wermke, W., & Harvey, G. (2019). Teachers' autonomy deconstructed: Irish and Finnish teachers' perceptions of decision-making and control. *European Educational Research Journal, 19*(4) 329–350. https://doi.org/10.1177/1474904119868378

Schatz-Oppenheimer, O., & Dvir, N. (2014). From ugly duckling to swan: Stories of novice teachers. *Teaching and Teacher Education, 37*(1), 140–149.

Sharplin, E. D., Ibrasheva, A., Shamatov, D., & Rakisheva, A. (2020). Analiz pedagogicheskogo obrazovaniya Kazakhstana v kontekste sovremennoi mejdunarodnoi praktiki. [Analysis of Teacher Education in Kazakhstan in the Context of Modern International Practice]. *Pedagogikalyk gylymdar seriyasi, 3*(64), 12–27.

Sexton, M. (2007). Evaluating teaching as a profession implication of a research study for the work of the teaching council. *Irish Educational Studies, 26*(1), 79–105.

Sharplin, E. D., Wake, D., & Howitt, C. (2017). Becoming a teaching professional: Ethical and legal issues. In J. Allen & S. White (Eds.), *Teaching in a new era.* Cambridge Press.

Shulman, L. (1987). Knowledge and teaching: Foundations of the new reform. *Harvard Educational Review, 57*(1), 1–23.

Shulman, L. S. (1998). Theory, practice, and the education of professionals. *The Elementary School Journal, 98*(5), 511–526.

Solbrekke, T. D., & Englund, T. (2011). Bringing professional responsibility back in. *Studies in Higher Education, 36*(7), 847–886.

Storey, A., & Hutchinson, S. (2001). The meaning of teacher professionalism in a quality control era. In S. Mayes, A. Banks, & Frank. B. (Eds), *Early professional development for teachers* (pp. 41–53). David Fulton.

Swann, M., McIntyre, D., Pell, T., Hargreaves, L., & Cunningham, M. (2010). Teachers' conceptions of teacher professionalism in England in 2003 and 2006. *British Educational Research Journal, 36*(4), 549–571.

Thurlings, M., & van Diggelen, M. (2021). Perceptions of practical knowledge of learning and feedback among academic teachers. *European Journal of Engineering Education, 46*(1), 139–160.

Tichenor, M. S., & Tichenor, J. M. (2005). Understanding teachers' perspectives on professionalism. *The Professional Educator, 17*(1/2), 89–95.

Torres, A. C., & Weiner, J. M. (2018). The new professionalism? Charter teachers' experiences and qualities of the teaching profession. *Education Policy Analysis Archives, 26*(19).

Trevethan, H. (2018). Challenging the discourse of beginning teaching: Only one crying phone call. *New Zealand Journal of Educational Studies, 53*(1), 49–63.

van Manen, M. (1990). *Researching lived experience: Human science for an action sensitive pedagogy.* Althouse Press.

Vonk, J. H. C. (1995). *Conceptualizing novice teachers' professional development: A base for supervisory interventions* [paper presentation]. Annual meeting of the AERA 1995, San Francisco, CA.

Whitty, G. (2006). *Teacher professionalism in a new era* [paper presentation]. General teaching council for Northern Ireland annual lecture 2006, Belfast, Ireland.

Wilson, E., & Demetriou, H. (2007). New teacher learning: Substantive knowledge and contextual factors. *Curriculum Journal, 18*(3), 213–229.

Yakavets, N., Bridges, D., & Shamatov, D. (2017). On constructs and the construction of teachers' professional knowledge in a post-Soviet context. *Journal of Education for Teaching, 43*(5), 594–615.

CHAPTER 5

Access, Equity, and Inclusion in Kazakhstani Teacher Education

Arman Assanbayev and Tsediso Michael Makoelle

Abstract

Many countries' implementation of inclusive education was inspired by the adoption of the Salamanca Statement in 1994. As a result, the role of teachers in ensuring access, equity, and inclusion in school has become central, and expectations for teachers to be ready for inclusive teaching are high (Makoelle & Burmistrova, 2021). In Kazakhstan, inclusive education was adopted by the Ministry of Education and Science through State Programs (2011–2019; 2016–2020; 2022–2025). This process aimed to make 70% of schools inclusive by 2020 and 100% by 2025. This chapter reviews the impact and role of teacher education since the dawn of inclusive education in Kazakhstan.

Keywords

access – equity – inclusion – inclusive education – teacher education

1 Introduction

In the Kazakhstani context, students experience institutional and other educational barriers that hinder the educational process; as such, teachers' capacity to teach in an inclusive classroom is significant. Barriers and factors affecting teaching and learning in Kazakhstani schools' diverse classrooms include all children in education, their socio-economic backgrounds, abilities/disabilities, and ethnicities. The approach to inclusive education in Kazakhstan means the right to quality education, equitable access to all educational opportunities, and avoiding segregation.

Makoelle (2013) postulates that teachers are central to implementing inclusive education. Their role is to create an enabling educational environment that widens the participation of all learners regardless of background and other circumstances. According to Makoelle (2013), this enables equitable

© ARMAN ASSANBAYEV AND TSEDISO MICHAEL MAKOELLE, 2025 | DOI:10.1163/9789004726345_006 access to education through the support from the teachers, considering their abilities and educational needs as Mittler (2000) states, learning experiences and opportunities are created for learning by all. This review highlights that access to educational opportunities is fundamental to inclusive education.

Teachers in Kazakhstan need teaching strategies that play an essential role in accommodating the educational needs of all learners in inclusive and diverse classrooms. Teachers should be in a position to provide rich learning opportunities for every student in the classroom (Florian & Black-Hawkins, 2011), while responding to their needs (Ainscow and Sundil, 2010) and addressing their abilities, disabilities, strengths, and weaknesses as well as provided with appropriate support to unlock their potential to succeed academically (Makoelle, 2016). It was, therefore, crucial in this chapter to ask the question:

– How do pre-service and in-service teachers understand and operationalise notions of access, equity, and inclusion in Kazakhstani schools
– What challenges do pre-service and in-service teachers experience with these notions?
– How can teacher education enable access, equity, and inclusion in Kazakhstani education?

2   Method of Review

This review investigated the notions of access, equity, and inclusion within the teacher education of Kazakhstan;

The review was mapped to achieving the following objectives:

– To explore how pre-service and in-service teachers understand and operationalise notions of access, equity, and inclusion in Kazakhstani schools;
– To identify challenges (if any) that pre-service and in-service teachers experience with these notions;
– To suggest a conceptual framework for teacher education that may enable access, equity, and inclusion in Kazakhstani education.

The criteria used to select the literature were guided by the availability of supportive empirical evidence. Speculative literatures were deliberately excluded. While the literature was reviewed for a study focused on equity and equality in teacher education, some of the reviewed work had inclined towards equity and equality in education in general as closely related disciplines such as political science, law, and sociology were considered.

I consulted several databases such as Eric, Scopus, and Google Scholar. Further sources of relevant information were internationally accredited journals among others the International Journal of Inclusive Education. The Nazarbayev University library was consulted and books, articles, theses, and electronic sources were perused for relevant, up-to-date literature on the topic.

3 Teachers as Agents of Change

In this chapter, we assume that teachers, as agents of change, are better placed to implement inclusive education and equity and access. In this chapter, we adopt the concept of teacher agency theory by Priestly, Robinson, and Biesta (2015), who contend that teachers are agents of change. They postulate that teachers' agency theory is mainly applied as a school-based reform approach. Drawing from the work of John Dewey and Herbert Mead, they define agency as the capacity of individuals to address a problematic situation through efficacy as independent individuals. As a result, the application of agency individuals affects the environment through an interplay of resources and contextual factors. Butera et al. (2021) regard the social influence that teachers may have to ensure that change happens. The agency is an active engagement with the environment to produce desirable change. As Manan (2020) states teachers could do this through their transformative pedagogies, reflexivity, and activism. Drawing from Giddens Structuration Theory (1984), there is a dual relationship between the agent (teachers in this case), agency (what teachers do), and the social structure (education structure in this case). While agents may impact the structure and produce change, the structure may also constrain agents and, consequently, their agency, hindering the change process. It is, therefore, vital that teachers, as agents of change, are empowered to enable their agency. Datnow (2020) postulates that when the grassroots model of decision-making prevails, teachers are in a better position to act as agents of change. In these chapters, we have identified three vital processes that may enable teacher agency, i.e. practicum for pre-service teachers, professional development and learning for in-service teachers, and change in practice (pedagogical, teaching, and learning practice) which when applied judiciously may then enhance practices that may enhance the provision of education that enable access, equity, and inclusion. The figure below demonstrates the relationship between teachers' agency, the enabling factors, and access, equity, and inclusion.

The figure shows how if pre-service teacher practicum and in-service teacher professional development and learning are well configured and structured to promote teacher agency for change (in pedagogical, teaching, and learning practices) may enable educational processes that may enable access, equity, and inclusion.

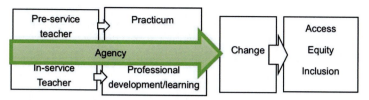

FIGURE 5.1   Pre-service and in-service teachers agency

4   The Notion of Access, Equity, and Inclusive Education (Inclusion)

Access is defined as the process through which education is made available to all students through inclusive policies and practices. On the other hand, equity or equitable education provision recognises that students come to school with unequal socio-cultural capital and the gap that exists must be addressed (Motala, 2015). Inclusion or inclusive education is the provision of education that seeks to widen the participation of all students in the educative process regardless of their backgrounds such as gender, age, disability, language, race, ethnicity, or socio-economic status (Prisiazhniuk, Makoelle & Zangieva, 2024). In Kazakhstan, access to and equitable provision of education is guaranteed by the Constitution of Kazakhstan (1995) article 30 and the Law on Education (2007). Both documents guarantee education as a basic right for all to be provided without any discrimination.

The understanding of inclusive education in Kazakhstan is evolving as part of the global movement towards education for all and the Kazakhstan rectification of the United Nations Convention on the Rights of Persons with Disabilities in 2015. In Kazakhstan, as Suleimenov (2015) argues, although there is no one universal definition of the concept, there is, however, consensus that inclusive education includes broad participation of all students regardless of age, gender, socio-economic status, ability/disability, and removing the barriers to learning, respect, equity and tolerance (Makoelle & Somerton, 2021). In Kazakhstan, the notion of inclusive education is developing, and as such, the definition may need to be more conclusive as a policy on inclusion is being developed.

The Kazakhstani view of inclusive education seems to be consistent with that of Booth and Ainscow (2016), who postulate that the main principle of inclusive education is the participation of all learners, supported by all stakeholders, including as well staff at educational institutions, families of all learners and the wider school community (p. 22). The role of stakeholders within a participatory system is to empower and provide support for students with disabilities, special needs, and other educational barriers. Therefore, removing all institutional barriers enables inclusive teaching and learning that respond to the needs of all students. As a result, adjusting the teaching strategies, pedagogical content knowledge, and assessment may ensure that students' educational needs are addressed.

5 Teacher Education and Inclusion (International)

Undoubtedly, teacher education is the core for facilitating inclusive education. Teachers need to know the basic philosophy of inclusive education and have the knowledge and skills to accommodate the diverse educational needs of learners. Internationally, educational practices have shifted to the social model of disability (SMD); more specifically, the SMD focuses on including people with disabilities in mainstream education, which has been a priority globally (Gesser & Martins, 2019). The goal of the SMD or designing the educational processes would include raising the participation of students with disabilities and others without disabilities. Therefore, in achieving this, the importance of teacher education and the preparation of both pre-service and in-service teachers for teaching in inclusive classrooms has become paramount.

Teachers' preparation is of cardinal significance for promoting the inclusion of diverse students, including those with disabilities, in education since the teachers are responsible for facilitating teaching and learning processes in the classroom. The teachers identify students with educational needs or experiencing barriers in the classroom and decide how much support is needed, then adapt their lesson plans with appropriate teaching and learning strategies (Matthews, 2009). Teachers need to be more competent and skilled in accommodating students with diverse educational needs in mainstream classrooms (Klang et al., 2020). As a result, most education systems invest in preparing teachers to deal with educational barriers whenever they emerge. This is done mainly by in-service training, professional development, and pre-service teacher practicum.

Barriers to effective teaching and learning could be institutional, pedagogical, structural, or attitudinal(Alsolami, Vaughan, 2023). Therefore, dealing with barriers would widen and enable student participation in the educative process (Makoelle,2012); Engelbrecht et al., 2017, p.684; Saloviita, 2020). Therefore, it enhances students' achievements (Adams et al., 2018).

When teachers are prepared for inclusive teaching and learning, their well-being can be positively affected. Dealing with students experiencing barriers could evoke stress for both teachers and students. This could also impact negatively on teachers' attitudes towards inclusion. Teachers who experience high levels of stress may be inclined to be less favourable towards inclusion.

When teachers are well prepared for inclusive teaching and learning, they can exhibit positive attitudes towards inclusive education and effectively address barriers towards inclusion in the classroom. They may be able to utilise their time judiciously when dealing with diverse students, including those with special educational needs and disabilities. Teachers may be able to develop individual education plans that may respond efficiently and adequately to students's educational needs. Teachers may also be able to apply an ecosystemic approach towards student support by mobilising parents, psychologists, and NGOs, which also contribute to overall student support.

Because inclusion is a relatively new phenomenon, continuous professional development of teachers is crucial. Teachers must be updated with relevant theoretical knowledge, skills, and knowledge about types of equipment and devices and inclusive teaching and learning methodologies that foster student participation and inclusive learning.

Therefore, due to a positive relationship between the teachers' preparedness and the successful realisation of inclusive education, higher education institutions are responsible for preparing teachers and other stakeholders to create inclusive educational environments. As Humaira and Rachmadtullah (2021) stress, the teacher education curriculum should prepare teachers to conceptualise inclusive education, develop an inclusive curriculum and deliver it using appropriate and relevant inclusive teaching methodologies that address the needs of all students in the classroom.

A transformed teacher education curriculum should produce inclusively inclined teachers who can make the right pedagogical choices regarding their teaching practice and student learning. Through pre-service teacher education, teachers are prepared for inclusive teaching.

6 Pre-Service Teacher Preparation the Role of Practicum (International)

The adoption of inclusive education has led pedagogic institutions to change pre-service teacher education according to the requirements of inclusive education (Alsarawi & Sukonthaman (2021). Teaching in an inclusive environment by teachers constitutes a new paradigm. A large body of literature discusses the importance of practicum for pre-service teachers aiming to teach in inclusive classrooms. This means that mastering practical teaching skills in inclusive classroom settings along with the theory has become crucial. however, several studies indicate that the existing teacher preparation programs do not always address the skills of pre-service teachers' ability to teach students with special educational needs and disabilities.

As a result, pre-service teachers' preparation will need a renewed curriculum aimed at teaching and learning in a new realm. As a response, the goal of the pre-service teacher practical component should be to allow them to teach in an inclusive classroom setting. Such a task may require universities to redesign the curriculum focused on inclusion, and incorporating the values consistent with inclusive education.

According to Makoelle & Burmistrova (2021), such a curriculum should focus on the methodological training for pre-service teachers, and enable the understanding of the policy promoting inclusion. Similarly, Humaira and Rachmadtullah (2021) argue that the gap between theory and practice in student-teacher preparation programs at universities should be addressed. In other words, while theory about teaching is important, investing more time in student-practical, inclusive teaching could be very instrumental. This according to McCracken, Chapman & Piggott (2023) has the potential to influence the attitudes of pre-service teachers positively about inclusion.

Aeshah Alsarawi and Rumpasri Sukonthaman (2021) also highlighted the role of inclusive teaching practicums in pre-service teacher preparation. They suggest combining general and special education programs in the teacher preparation curriculum of universities willing to enhance in-service teacher preparation. The practicum provides a critical platform for pre-service teachers to learn together with their mentor teachers in schools (Vandervieren & Struyf, 2021)

Waitoller and Kozleski (2010) have explored the concept of Professional Learning Schools as an option for pre-service teacher placement for inclusive teaching. Such schools would create conditions for pre-service teachers to be prepared for the inclusive teaching and learning role, albeit not only about inclusion and slightly different the notion of Professional Practice Schools was also explored in South Africa, as schools that could create conditions for pre-service teacher learning appropriate for their preparation (Robinson, 2021).

7 In-Service Teacher Preparation for Inclusive Teaching (International)

Teacher education is widely regarded as a vehicle for the transformation of education institutions to inclusive education (Florian et al., 2010). In-service teachers' Professional Development (PD) is regarded as the driver of implementing inclusion internationally. Professional Development courses usually focus on teaching teachers how to teach to meet the diverse educational needs of students. PD tackles the issues associated with the teachers' challenges in the development of curriculum, methodology, and inclusive teaching strategies. Therefore, teachers must stay tuned with their disciplines' new knowledge and skills and apply them to facilitate inclusive education. In other words, the teachers learn about inclusive teaching practices (Ackah, 2016).

Through PD, inclusive schools could be developed if the school leaders are committed to inclusion and facilitate the culture of sharing the experience of inclusive teaching among the teachers through ongoing collaboration and learning (Brennan et al., 2021). The school administrations should develop professional learning for inclusive teaching across the continuum of teacher education and practice. PD allows the in-service teachers to upgrade their teaching skills to learners' diverse needs while in the field. Such education by teachers could be facilitated by fostering PD through the collaboration of professional teachers as a Professional Learning Community (PLC) and Communities of Practice (CoP). Bahr, Newberry, and Rino (2021) found that the CoP made teachers learn from one another but also provided much-needed mutual support.

Similarly, PLC is the platform that supports such learning by the teachers for the teachers in a friendly environment. In other words, the teachers often take courses, workshops, and seminars devoted to inclusive teaching and continue their teaching career in their institutions.

PLC initiates collaboration among the teachers and allows them to design PD programs and establish goals (Admiraal et al., 2021). The teachers under PLC as learners themselves indicate the concepts and skills they lack to be professional in their classrooms. There are different core concepts covered by in-service teachers internationally, such as enabling in-service teachers to create inclusive education curriculum and material for classes, the methodology of inclusive teaching and learning and developing teaching skills in inclusive classrooms. PLC usually covers all these concepts and strengthens the teacher's capacity for inclusive teaching and learning. For instance, they learn how to design the curriculum considering the diverse educational needs of learners in the inclusive classroom. They support the inclusive curriculum with the teaching methodology and learn the teaching skills from one another during PD. The teachers bring the challenges from their teaching practices to the seminars and workshops under PD and develop solutions to the existing real-world problems in inclusive teaching.

Teacher learning for inclusive teaching across the teacher education continuum is crucial for facilitating inclusive schools. The literature has demonstrated that teachers need to get continuum education, and PD is a meaningful solution. Since PD is facilitated for the teachers and by the teachers, the PLC could take that responsibility to respond to the challenges in the context. The

PD program could hardly respond to every challenge of the selected school without the active engagement of the teachers for whom the PD programs are designed. Next, it is unlikely that one PD course will cover all the issues and challenges of inclusive teaching. Such findings of this review inform us that PD should also be on a continuum basis. The section argues that the PD program should be informed by the teachers and administration of the selected schools as a PLC. This review has shown that PLC facilitates support to novice in-service teachers by experienced and highly qualified teachers to enact inclusive teaching practices, leading to positive outcomes both for the teachers and learners. Thus, PLC enables the teachers to meet the educational needs of all learners by devising the curriculum, methodology, and teaching skills on a continuum basis.

8 Teacher Education and Inclusion in Kazakhstan

Since Kazakhstan gained independence in 1991, the Kazakhstani government prioritised inclusive education (Helmer et al., 2023). The next step towards inclusion was that the Government of Kazakhstan adopted the State Program on Education Development 2011–2020 (MoES, 2011). The program has set an ambitious and clear goal to make 100% of Kazakhstani schools inclusive by 2020. The crucial role of such changes was put on pedagogical universities to prepare teachers for implementing the program. Therefore, the schools, albeit faced with many challenges, started promoting the inclusion of all learners regardless of their backgrounds. Inclusion in Kazakhstani schools means catering to the diverse needs of all learners in the classroom, which requires appropriate teaching skills and practice.

Inclusive education in Kazakhstan still bears the hallmarks of Soviet education, which advocated segregated classes for students with special needs and disabilities. The adoption of inclusive education meant a policy shift toward inclusive education. While inclusive education policy has been adopted in the Kazakhstani education system, the preparation of teachers for inclusive education is still riddled with challenges.

First, although the understanding of inclusive education is becoming clear, there are still pockets of misunderstanding whereby the notion of inclusive education is attributed to the education of students with disabilities. Although there has been a need for training among teachers, the quality and depth of such pieces of training and their relevance have not been determined. As the initiative to facilitate inclusive education to in-service teachers' capacity building, Orleu, the National Center for Professional Development, has been established. The centre Orleu aims to retrain the in-teachers to facilitate inclusive teaching practices in an inclusive classroom environment.

Teachers are prepared in pedagogical universities for their teaching. However, there have been calls to review the pedagogical university curriculum to align it with the ideals of inclusive teaching. Sometimes, an inclusive education curriculum has just been equated to defectology (the Soviet unique education model).

Although Kazakhstan has adopted criterion-based assessment, the overemphasis on standardized assessment as a measure of student achievement is still not tailored to the students' needs. Thus, it may not respond to students' needs and thus promote exclusion.

Although pre-service teachers are subjected to the practicum, more is needed to know whether such school placements are done considering inclusive settings and whether such practical tasks prepare pre-service teachers to handle a diverse and inclusive classroom.

9   Lesson Drawn from the Review (Findings)

The international and local literature analysis suggests that teacher education's role in facilitating access, equity, and inclusion is based on the triad cardinal pillar, i.e. pre-service, in-service, and practice, which depend on teacher agency as enabled within the education structure. The figure below illustrates the relationship between the cardinal pillars of teacher preparation for access, equity, and inclusion:

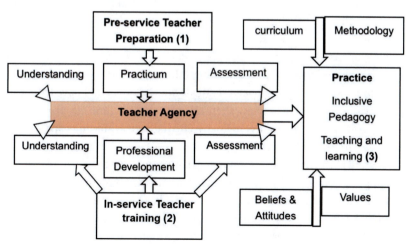

FIGURE 5.2   Teacher education and inclusion framework

10 Understanding

The findings of this review have confirmed that inclusive education could be promoted if the concept is understood and conceptualised by Kazakhstani teachers. While there is to a lesser degree that inclusion is about students with disabilities and special needs, this review seems to have confirmed that there is a shift in understanding inclusion to encompass a broader spectrum of needs and barriers. The understanding of inclusive teaching and learning must go beyond just classroom activities but transcend beliefs, attitudes, and values (Makoelle, 2022).

11 Teachers Agency

In this review, it is evident that although teacher education is better placed within the Kazakhstani education system to address issues of access, equity, and inclusion, more flexibility and autonomy are needed to empower teachers to make decisions about teaching and learning. According to Li and Ruppar (2021), the are five core aspects of teacher agency that enable them to influence change i.e. identity, professional competence, inclusive professional philosophy, autonomy, and reflexivity.

12 Pre-Service Teacher Preparation

Next, the review has indicated that both pre-service teachers and in-service, more specifically, the basic philosophy of inclusive education, knowledge, and skills are required by aspirant teachers to accommodate the diverse educational needs of learners in one classroom. It is evident that a dialogue between pre-service teachers, their teacher educators, and school mentors is necessary to re-consider pre-service practical experience on inclusive teaching and inclusive learning. This review then recommends facilitating pre-service teacher programs that encompass inclusive curricula and building capacity for inclusive teaching skills to students.

Kazakhstani pedagogic universities need to introduce a renewed curriculum, methodologic training, and practicum focused on equipping future in-service teachers with inclusive teaching and learning skills (Makoelle & Burmistrova, 2021). Such a shift in in-service teacher education requires incorporating the right values of inclusive education which may influence the right perspectives and beliefs about diversity in the classroom. On the other hand, the practicum facilitated at the schools should help the in-service teachers understand the realities of their future profession. As such, students should be able to balance theoretical knowledge and practical knowledge thus ensuring future improvement regarding the teaching of classrooms with diverse students.

The review indicates that school-teacher education institution partnerships are critical. Such partnerships between the universities and schools help to improve the methodological training of pre-service teachers.

13   In-Service Teachers' Continuous Professional Development and Learning

This review has shown that facilitating PD for in-service teachers supports teachers in meeting the challenges in their inclusive teaching classrooms. As the review has found in-service teachers face challenges in the development of curriculum, lesson design, and methodology of inclusive teaching. The review also indicates that the teachers need to be updated with the latest knowledge and inclusive teaching strategies. The significance of the PLC to foster the updating of the teachers' knowledge and teaching skills via establishing collaboration among them has been foregrounded. Through PLC, teachers as a community of learners learn from one another. The PLC, therefore becomes the platform that helps to indicate the problem, discuss the possible solutions, and implement changes in the teaching practice. Conducted continuously, PLC supports and helps socialise novice in-service teachers into inclusive pedagogies by the experienced and highly qualified teachers to research and reflect on their practice, to foster creativity for the new methods and strategies of accommodating diverse educational needs of all learners in inclusive and diverse classrooms.

14   Conclusion

The chapter explored the state in which teacher education in Kazakhstan enables access, equity, and inclusion. The analysis of the review indicates that although a lot was done policy-wise by the government of Kazakhstan, teacher education facilitators, pedagogic universities, and training institutions, there is still room for practical realisation of inclusion by the teacher education system. Balancing both theory and practice through international experience on both pre-service and in-service teacher education is necessary for the stakeholders, the government, and the pedagogic institutions to adopt best and relevant practices. A more concerted effort is needed to infuse a shift from segregation practices as a result of the legacy of Soviet education legacy to embracing diversity, equality, and equity for all learners in the classrooms.

It is evident that inclusion in Kazakhstan is not an isolated process but interwoven with developments in the Central Asian context and globally. Therefore, the findings from this review may contribute to debates about educational access, equity, and inclusion and how to promote it in Central Asia, especially in Kazakhstan.

As the concluding remark, although the review has shed light on the emergence of inclusive education and how it was further translated into Kazakhstani teacher education and consequently in school, it must be kept in mind that change and transformation are necessary by State Programs, teacher education universities, and institutions to produce the programs which build the learning and teaching capacity to both pre-service and in-service teachers benchmarked on international practice. Such programs should be able to ensure teacher readiness in pre-service teacher education and in-service teachers to practice inclusive pedagogy and ensure that the needs of diverse students in inclusive classrooms are addressed.

References

Ackah-Jnr, F. R. (2016). Implementation of inclusive early childhood education policy and change in Ghana. *Unpublished Doctoral dissertation). Griffith University*.

Admiraal, W., Schenke, W., De Jong, L., Emmelot, Y., & Sligte, H. (2021). Schools as professional learning communities: what can schools do to support professional development of their teachers?. *Professional Development in Education, 47*(4), 684–698.

Alsarawi, A., & Sukonthaman, P. (2021). Preservice teachers' attitudes, knowledge, and self-efficacy of inclusive teaching practices. *International Journal of Disability, Development and Education*. https://doi.org/10.1080/1034912X.2021.1922992

Ainscow, M., Booth, T., & Dyson, A. (2006). *Improving schools, developing inclusion*. Routledge.

Alsolami, A., & Vaughan, M. (2023). Teacher attitudes toward inclusion of students with disabilities in Jeddah elementary schools. *PloS One, 18*(1), e0279068.

Bahr, D. L., Newberry, M., & Rino, J. S. (2021). Connecting preservice and inservice teacher learning: Communities of practice. *School Science & Mathematics, 121*(2).

Berdahl, R. (1990). Academic freedom, autonomy and accountability in British universities. *Studies in Higher Education, 15*(2), 169–180.

Brennan, A., King, F., & Travers, J. (2021). Supporting the enactment of inclusive pedagogy in a primary school. *International Journal of Inclusive Education, 25*(13), 1540–1557.

Butera, F., Batruch, A., Autin, F., Mugny, G., Quiamzade, A., & Pulfrey, C. (2021). Teaching as social influence: Empowering teachers to become agents of social change. *Social Issues and Policy Review, 15*(1), 323–355.

Datnow, A. (2020). The role of teachers in educational reform: A 20-year perspective. *Journal of Educational Change, 21*(3), 431–441.

Florian, L., & Black-Hawkins, K. (2011). Exploring inclusive pedagogy. *British Educational Research Journal, 37*(5), 813–828.

Gesser, M., & Martins, R. M. (2019). Contributions of a teacher training program to inclusive education. *Paidéia (Ribeirão Preto), 29*, e2907

Helmer, J., Kasa, R., Somerton, M., Makoelle, T. M., & Hernández-Torrano, D. (2023). Planting the seeds for inclusive education: one resource centre at a time. *International Journal of Inclusive Education, 27*(5), 586–602.

Humaira, M. A., & Rachmadtullah, R. (2021). Teachers' perceptions of the role of universities in mentoring programs for inclusive elementary schools: A case study in Indonesia. *Journal of Education and e-Learning Research, 8*(3), 333–339.

Kazakhstan. (1995). *The Constitution of the Republic of Kazakhstan*. Astana.

Klang, N., Göransson, K., Lindqvist, G., Nilholm, C., Hansson, S., & Bengtsson, K. (2020). Instructional practices for pupils with an intellectual disability in mainstream and special educational settings. *International Journal of Disability, Development and Education, 67*(2), 151–166.

Makoelle, T. M., & Burmistrova, V. (2021). Teacher education and inclusive education in Kazakhstan. *International Journal of Inclusive Education,* 1–17.

Makoelle, T. M. (2022). Developing an inclusive curriculum strategy: An action research case. *Alternation, Special Edition 39*, 372–339. https://doi.org/10.29086/2519-5476/2022/sp39a17

Manan, S. A. (2020). Teachers as agents of transformative pedagogy: Critical reflexivity, activism and multilingual spaces through a continua of biliteracy lens. *Multilingua, 39*(6), 721–747.

Matthews, N. (2009). Teaching the 'invisible'disabled students in the classroom: Disclosure, inclusion and the social model of disability. *Teaching in Higher Education, 14*(3), 229–239.

McCracken, T., Chapman, S., & Piggott, B. (2023). Inclusion illusion: A mixed-methods study of preservice teachers and their preparedness for inclusive schooling in Health and Physical Education. *International Journal of Inclusive Education, 27*(4), 507–525.

Ministry of Education and Science. (2007). *Law on Education*. Astana

Motala, S. (2015). Equity, access and quality in basic education: A review. *Journal of Education,* (61), 159–175.

Organisation for Economic Co-operation and Development (OECD). (2018). *Education policy outlook: Kazakhstan*. http://www.oecd.org/education/Education-Policy-Outlook-Country- Profile-Kazakhstan2018.pdf

Prisiazhniuk, D., Makoelle, T. M., & Zangieva, I. (2024). Teachers' attitudes towards inclusive education of children with special educational needs and disabilities in central Asia. *Children and Youth Services Review, 160*, 107535.

Robinson, M. (2021). Research for policy and practice in teacher education: The case of the professional practice schools research project. *Journal of Education (University of KwaZulu-Natal)*, (82), 100–112.

United Nations. (2006). Convention on the rights of persons with disabilities. *Treaty Series, 2515*, 3.

Vandervieren, E., & Struyf, E. (2021). Facing social reality together: Investigating a pre-service teacher preparation programme on inclusive education. *International Journal of Inclusive Education, 25*(13), 1524–1539.

Waitoller, F. R., & Kozleski, E. (2010). Inclusive professional learning schools. In *Teacher education for inclusion* (pp. 91–99). Routledge.

CHAPTER 6

Trends and Challenges in STEM Education in Kazakhstan

Ainur Almukhambetova

Abstract

This chapter aims to provide a comprehensive overview of the state of STEM education and STEM teacher education in Kazakhstan, current trends and challenges through a systematic review of international and local literature as well as the available policy documents and government reports. Several key findings are drawn from this review. Although Kazakhstan strives to align its STEM education with international standards, there is a significant difference between the international and local conceptualization of STEM education, which stems from a variety of historical, economic, and cultural factors. The review identified such challenges in STEM education in Kazakhstan as educational disparities, growing educational stratification, uneven access to STEM educational resources, and the need to improve access for underrepresented populations. Some key lessons are outlined, and recommendations are provided.

Keywords

innovation – STEM education – teacher education – STEM education curriculum – STEM teaching

1 Introduction

STEM education is critical for the development of a knowledge-based economy and the preparation of students for the demands of the modern workforce. The educational context in Kazakhstan is undergoing significant changes and reforms. A certain share of these reforms is related to the development of STEM education and STEM teacher education and significant efforts have been made to reform and enhance STEM education. This chapter aims to review these initiatives, evaluate their effectiveness, identify persistent challenges,

© AINUR ALMUKHAMBETOVA, 2025 | DOI:10.1163/9789004726345_007 and suggest some recommendations. The chapter was guided by the following research question:

1. What is the current state of STEM education and STEM teacher education in Kazakhstan?
2. What challenges and barriers exist in the implementation of STEM education?
3. What successful strategies and practices have been identified in the literature?

To answer this research question, the chapter provides a comprehensive review of the context of STEM education in Kazakhstan, the current challenges in STEM education, and the history and development of STEM teacher education in Kazakhstan. The main purpose of the chapter was to explore the trends and challenges of STEM education and STEM teacher education in Kazakhstan to develop a conceptualization of STEM education in Kazakhstan, identify current challenges, and synthesize some lessons from the review to make recommendations for addressing these challenges.

1.1 Search Strategy

The following databases were used: Scopus, Web of Science, ERIC and Google Scholar.

The following keywords were used: "STEM education in Kazakhstan," "STEM education post-Soviet," "STEM education," "Kazakhstan STEM curriculum," "STEM curriculum spot-Soviet," "STEM teacher training post-Soviet," "STEM teacher training Kazakhstan," "challenges in STEM teacher education Kazakhstan," "challenges in teacher education post-Soviet"; "technology in STEM education Kazakhstan."

Inclusion Criteria: Peer-reviewed articles, conference papers, government reports, and policy documents published between 2000 and 2023. The literature with supportive empirical evidence was prioritized according to the selection criteria. Literature that provided vague, speculative, and generalized findings was avoided.

A standardized form was used to extract relevant information, including study aims, methods, findings, and conclusions. Each source was evaluated using a quality assessment tool based on criteria such as research design, sample size, and data analysis method. A narrative synthesis approach was employed to integrate findings from different studies, identifying common themes and gaps in the literature.

2 The Notion of STEM Education

The scientific literature does not agree on the definition of STEM education. Definitions vary significantly, as some scholars advocate considering STEM as an integrated group while others suggest treating each subject separately.

For instance, Shaughnessy (2013) defines STEM education as problem-solving using science and mathematics concepts and procedures and incorporating applied engineering strategies and techniques. Conversely, Merrill (2009) suggests a different perspective, viewing STEM as a meta-discipline based on learning standards with an integrated teaching and learning approach without dividing specific content. STEM is also closely connected to developing economic competitiveness in the global market and is considered as an integral component of creating human capital (Boe et al., 2011). STEM education is also seen as crucial for economic competitiveness and innovation.

The notion of STEM education encompasses several key principles and goals:

1. Interdisciplinary learning. STEM education emphasizes the integration of the four disciplines (Science, Technology, Engineering, Mathematics), encouraging the students to apply knowledge from multiple fields to solve complex problems.
2. Focus on problem-solving and critical thinking. By engaging in hands-on, inquiry-based learning activities, students learn to analyze problems, think creatively and devise innovative solutions.
3. Incorporating technology is a fundamental aspect of STEM education. This includes using digital tools, software and other technologies to enhance learning and prepare students for a technology-driven world.

3 The Context of STEM Education in Kazakhstan

Implementing STEM education can vary widely depending on the educational context, resources, and goals. However, a widespread agreement exists that STEM advancement is a critical factor for every country's economic success (UNESCO, 2019). Kazakhstan is not an exception. As Kazakhstan aims to increase the overall economic development of the country (President's message, January 10, 2018), it started to face two important issues- a need to diversify its predominantly resource-extraction-oriented economy and the need to strengthen the sectors of the economy, associated with industry, innovation and technologies. Kazakhstani government also started to pursue a very active innovation development policy. It has adopted the State Program of Industrial and Innovative Development (SPIID) for 2020–2025, focusing on the advanced development of the manufacturing industry and innovative clusters (Ministry of Industry and Infrastructure Development, 2019).

The successful outcomes of Industrialization Program implementation depend on addressing a related problem of the deficit of qualified STEM workforce. The State Program of Education (2020–2025) highlighted the importance of achieving a high quality of STEM secondary and higher education that will meet labor market demands (MES, 2019). The government of Kazakhstan considers a high-quality STEM-focused education as a driver for developing the nation's human capital and improving the country's innovative capacity (Almukhambetova & Hernandez-Torrano, 2021). The measures undertaken by the government include providing more scholarships for students willing to enter STEM majors (Almukhambetova & Kuzhabekova, 2020) and developing STEM-focused education at the secondary level.

In order to achieve the aim of developing STEM education, Kazakhstan has implemented several reform initiatives, mainly focused on support of specialized STEM-focused schools as flagships for further development of STEM education (Kuzhabekova et al., 2018), prioritizing the "developing a cadre of very high achieving students" (OECD, 2018; Winter et al., 2019). The government continued to support the development of STEM-focused schools for gifted children which existed previously (Daryn schools for gifted children and BIL lyceums) and also established another network of elite STEM-focused schools (NIS) for gifted and talented students, which was later accredited by the Council of International Schools (CIS). Another rationale behind establishing these specialized STEM-focused schools was to get a unique testing ground for new innovative approaches to education, the implementation of trilingual policy, and 12-year education (AEO NIS, 2016).

Before 2023, the NIS schools operated autonomously, were regulated by special law, were independent of the Ministry of Education and Science, and created their own curriculum, monitoring, and assessment system (Karabassova, 2021). All NIS schools have two distinct STEM specializations: Physics/Math or Chemistry/Biology. Another important characteristic of NIS is the opportunity to attract the best local STEM teachers. The students are admitted to NIS and BIL based on highly competitive examinations after grade 6, which include tests on students' mathematical and language skills. The NIS entrance examination also includes the test on spatial ability and the test on natural sciences (starting from 2021). NIS and BIL schools also have strong academic facilities, such as STEM laboratories, where the students are engaged in hands-on STEM activities, developing science projects for various national and international STEM competitions. The STEM Olympiad movement is especially intense in Daryn and BIL schools, where the most talented students are offered additional hours for Olympiad preparation.

3.1 *STEM Secondary Curriculum*

Kazakhstani science curriculum is subject-oriented. Each science subject, physics, chemistry and biology has its own curriculum. From 2015–2016, Kazakhstani secondary school students learned Natural Science from grade 3 and science subjects, such as Biology, Chemistry, and Physics, from grade 7. Technology lessons are also an essential component of STEM education in Kazakhstan and are taught from grade 3.

One of the peculiarities of teaching STEM subjects in Kazakhstan is that such subjects as biology, physics, and chemistry are not integrated into a single science subject but are taught separately (Balta et al., 2023). The teaching of STEM subjects is characterized by a more rigid and theoretical approach with a strong focus on foundational knowledge. In most Kazakhstani schools, the science curriculum (grades 7–11 or 7–12) might be described as a spiral curriculum. Each STEM subject in this curriculum is taught for several years and with the opportunity to revise the previous themes. For example, the students start to study Physics in grade 7, and continue for the next 5 years. In grade 7, the students study the physics phenomena, the structure of matter, pressure, work, power, and energy. In the following grade, the students are taught electrical, electromagnetic and thermal phenomena. This is followed by kinematics, conservation laws and waves in grade 9. In grades 10 and 11, the students are taught electrodynamics, electromagnetic waves, molecular physics, and quantum physics.

The STEM curriculum at NIS schools is different of that in mainstream schools. Although NIS schools have adopted the University of Cambridge A and AS levels for middle and high school, the NIS did not introduce the integrated Science subject. Instead, all the STEM subjects are taught separately and in small groups. In grade 12, all STEM subjects are taught in English. The students who need additional support are offered individual tutorials in STEM subjects. All the graduating NIS students have to take the final examination in two subjects they specialized in during the last two years: Physics, Chemistry, Biology, and Technology. The students who focused on technology during the last two years at school learned to create their own projects, which replaced the written examination on this subject. The Math examination is mandatory for all graduating NIS students.

3.2 Challenges in STEM Secondary Education

After the breakup of the USSR, Kazakhstan's important legacy was a well-educated population with a high literacy rate. However, in the transition period, education quality has declined at school and higher education levels, particularly in math and science subjects (Silova, 2009). At that period, there was a significant brain drain of experienced teachers. In the 1990s, a significant proportion of mid-career teachers left the country or profession for more lucrative employment within Kazakhstan or immigrated to other countries (Silova, 2009). Overall, interest in the teaching profession has declined. The education system at that period faced other challenges, such as the school closure and reduction of teacher salaries (OECD, 2018)

Another critical issue with math and science education after the breakup of the Soviet Union was the complex situation with the languages of instruction and curriculum. According to Fierman (2005, 2006), during the first year of independence, ethnic Kazakhs constituted only 40 % of the overall population, with the majority (around 78%) fluent only in the Russian language. The number of schools with Kazakh language of instruction constituted only 11.3 % of all urban schools in 1988–1989, and only 15 % of the textbooks for higher education technical institutions were published in Kazakh. During the first 13 years of independence, the share of Kazakh medium-class enrollment increased to 46.4 % in urban areas by 2013 and almost an xx increase in the subsequent 10 years (by 2023). This change in the language of instruction and the increase in the number of students has required the development of a new curriculum, the publication of textbooks in the Kazakh language, and the development of new STEM terminology (Berkaliyev, n.d).

There was an urgent need to develop a new curriculum, as the previous curriculum was dictated by the Soviet centrally-driven command economy. The main goal of math and science education at that time was to prepare many future scientists and engineers for the needs of Soviet industry. The curriculum was not focused on science and mathematics education for developing critical thinking and problem-solving skills or using knowledge to solve societal problems. Instead, the lessons in all science subjects were more oriented on rote learning of theoretical knowledge (Hofstein, 2011).

The main aim of teaching science and mathematics in Soviet times was to transfer subject matter knowledge. According to Kharlamov (1990), the science lessons were overwhelmingly teacher-centered and primarily assessed the learning of scientific theories and facts. The students had fewer opportunities to perform laboratory work as it was restricted to teacher demonstrations. The Soviet pedagogical literature was restrictive and suggested five types of lessons: (1) lessons where the teacher introduces the new knowledge; (2) lessons strengthening received knowledge; (3) lessons reviewing the knowledge (4) lessons aimed at assessing and controlling the knowledge (5) lessons combining first three types (Kharlamov, 1990).

After gaining independence, Kazakhstan faced the demands of a new market economy, and the education system in Kazakhstan, similarly to other post-Soviet countries, faced the problem of changing the subject matter and teacher-centered paradigm in line with these developments (Kapanadze et al, 2010; Zhilin, 2010; Fernandez et al., 2013). In 2007, Kazakhstan started to participate in large-scale international assessments such as PISA and TIMSS. In PISA (2009), Kazakhstan students demonstrated very low results, especially in students' abilities to apply knowledge in practice, and significantly below the OECD average in mathematical and natural science literacy (Shamshidinova et al., 2023).

In the next round of PISA (2012) and TIMSS (2011), the results of Kazakhstan students were also significantly lower than the OECD average. The international assessments identified that secondary school students in Kazakhstan have difficulties demonstrating scientific knowledge, conducting experiments, interpreting scientific phenomena and working with data (Dimitrov et al., 2020). As recommended by OECD (2014), the secondary school curriculum had to be revised to change its focus from theoretical knowledge to practical application.

The curriculum content in Mathematics and Natural Science has been changed from tasks that require memorization to more complex intellectual tasks, such as comparison, analysis, applying knowledge, and argumentation. for example, the updated curriculum in Mathematics in primary school offered an early introduction to mathematics concepts, such as percentages and ordinary fractions (Dimitrov et al., 2020). In primary school, the updated curriculum offered teaching Math and the Fundamentals of natural sciences from grade one and Technology from grade 3 (Toybazarova & Nazarova, 2018). The updated science curriculum, which previously had more materials on biology and geography, included sections on physics, astronomy, and chemistry to introduce the students to physics, chemistry, and biology (Dimitrov et al., 2020). This also ensures the continuity of school science education. Overall, the updated curriculum for all STEM subjects demands student-centered, problem-based pedagogy, including hands-on and inquiry-based learning in practical and laboratory classes to ensure the transition from a knowledge-centered paradigm to an activity-centered paradigm.

The updated curriculum and criteria-based assessment were first implemented at NIS schools which were designed as the testing ground for new approaches in teaching and updated curriculum (Shamshidinova et al., 2023) and then translated into the wider secondary school system in Kazakhstan, however, NIS is criticized for having been chosen as a platform for testing new approaches to teaching and assessment as the context of NIS schools is different from overall secondary education context. As one example, the NIS has successfully implemented the teaching of STEM subjects in the English language. However, translating this experience to mainstream schools was unsuccessful as STEM teachers were not adequately prepared to deliver instruction in the English language (Karabassova, 2020) and were forced to start teaching after relatively short training.

3.3   *Uneven School Landscape*

For a country that lacks a quality STEM workforce and experiences pressing socio-economic demands, the quality of education is crucial. The focus on excellence initiatives in education and prioritizing elite schools during the last two decades has resulted in the fact that there is a growing disparity between the schools, and educational stratification has become one of the significant problems. Access to quality STEM education is limited to more affluent families who can afford private tutoring in STEM subjects to enter prestigious STEM schools like NIS and BIL and prepare for UNT to get a scholarship for university studies (Hajar & Abenova, 2021).

According to OECD (2015), Kazakhstan has around 7450 schools of different types. However, almost 70% of these schools are located in rural areas with limited resources and are of inferior quality (Balta et al., 2023). PISA 2018 and 2022 results also confirm the existing educational inequity in Kazakhstan. According to OECD (2018), school location is a significant factor in students' performance, and the results of the PISA display that school location explains the greater share of student variance (6.7%) in reading performance than across OECD countries (4,5%). In 2018, the students from Astana, the country's capital city, scored 428 on average, compared to 344 for the students from Atyrau (a city in the West of Kazakhstan). This also confirms that there are more educational opportunities in larger cities and a lack of adequate attention to improving education in marginalized areas (OECD, 2018).

Obviously, the geographical disparities in access to quality education result in further inequity to higher education (in entrance test results and scholarship distribution) and further economic opportunities. The language of instruction also causes unequal access to education opportunities. There is also a significant gap in students' results according to the language of instruction. The results of grade 8 and 9 students in Russian medium of instruction schools differed significantly from those of Kazakh medium schools (Shamshidinova et al., 2023). As mentioned previously, one of the reasons was the lack of quality teaching resources in the Kazakh language, especially lack of textbooks in STEM subjects in earlier years (Shamshidinova et al., 2023).

The challenges of providing quality education to all students in Kazakhstan are exacerbated by the demographic trends in the country's population, high levels of urbanization and growing educational inequality. The capital cities, like Astana and Almaty, are facing the issue of school shortage. Starting from 2018, the government of Kazakhstan started to address the issue of school shortage and prioritize the quality of STEM education in mainstream schools. Due to public-private partnerships, a new network of STEM public schools has appeared. Currently, there are 6 Binom schools in Astana and 2 schools in Atyrau. These schools are characterized by fewer students per class (<30) and the implementation of a STEM-integrated model of education developed in partnership with Finland and South Korea. In contrast, other public schools in Astana are overcrowded, with the number of students per class often exceeding 35–40 students. The schools are equipped with modern STEM laboratories in physics, chemistry, nanotechnology, and biotechnology (Prime Minister portal, 2021). Another important initiative of the government in recent years to address the shortage of schools is establishing per-capita funding in secondary education. It should be noted that the number of private STEM-focused schools has increased, especially in capital cities, due to the introduction of a per capita funding scheme. Overall, while there is a push towards improving access to STEM learning opportunities, the actual implementation is uneven, with significant variations between urban and rural schools and also between specialized STEM-focused schools and mainstream schools.

3.4 *Increasing STEM Participation*

The successful implementation of the State Program of Industrial Development depends on addressing a related problem of the deficit of qualified STEM workforce. The main industrial clusters of Kazakhstan are situated in the regions, and this deficit is especially pronounced there. There is a lack of qualified engineers in the oil-extracting industry, which is addressed by attracting specialists from abroad. Around 9900 specialists are needed for the construction sector, and 7600 specialists are needed for the industrial sector (Atameken, 2019). Therefore, several measures have already been taken within this framework to improve the situation of the lacking STEM workforce.

One of the significant challenges for increasing the educated STEM workforce is the brain drain. Many talented young people choose to pursue STEM higher education and careers outside Kazakhstan. According to the National Center for the Development of HE (ENIC), the number of Kazakhstani students participating in outbound academic mobility for the last 12 years demonstrates an almost tenfold increase in outbound student numbers. Moreover, Kazakhstan takes 8th place among the top 20 countries for outbound student mobility, according to the T.I.M.E Association report (2021).

An additional factor that facilitates the brain drain is the difference in the level of preparedness provided by STEM-focused schools and the quality of STEM education at higher education level. The number of students from Kazakhstan willing to pursue education outside Kazakhstan and mostly in STEM fields, is growing each year (Akhmetzhanova, 2022). A significant proportion of students who intend to pursue STEM majors choose to study outside Kazakhstan as they perceive that the quality of STEM higher education is low (Almukhambetova & Kuzhabekova, 2022). Recent research revealed that students consider that majority of universities in Kazakhstan lack the STEM capacity and STEM infrastructure (Almukhambetova et al., in press).

Kazakhstan's government has implemented several measures in the higher education sector to address the brain drain issue, such as establishing partnerships with reputable universities to open dual degree programs, mainly in STEM specialties. In 2021–2022, the branch campuses of De Monfort University and Russian National Nuclear University in Almaty, the branch of the Gubkin Russian State University of Oil and Gas in Atyrau, and the affiliate of the University of Arizona in Kozybayev University were opened. In February of 2024, the Minister of Higher Education and Science announced that overall,

12 branches of foreign universities were opened in Kazakhstan, including the Herriot-Watt's branch campus in Aktobe.

Despite the initiatives undertaken by the government, the problem of the deficit of the STEM workforce is not fully resolved (SPIID, 2020–2025). Although the number of STEM scholarships produced in Kazakhstan has risen steadily, the number of students willing to pursue STEM majors is still very low. Moreover, the completion of a degree in STEM does not seem to guarantee STEM-related employment, and the number of STEM degree holders far exceeds the number of individuals employed in STEM (MES, 2018). According to Japashov et al. (2022), 27% of students enter STEM programs, but this number is still insufficient to satisfy the need for a qualified STEM workforce.

One of the major strategies for addressing the problem of the shortage of STEM workforce is attracting the traditionally underrepresented populations, such as women students and rural students, to STEM education and careers. Little attention from the government is still given to attracting rural and small-town students to STEM fields. Meanwhile, this demographic group of students, who account for approximately 32 % of the student population in Kazakhstan, might face unique barriers that shape their educational and occupational pathways in contrast to their urban counterparts. Rural students encounter such barriers as outdated school facilities, limited access to the Internet, lack of instructional materials and textbooks, lack of access to STEM extracurricular activities and advanced coursework, and lack of career advising support. Rural students are also less likely to apply to university than their urban counterparts (Chankseliani et al., 2020).

There are notable gender disparities in STEM education, with female students less likely to pursue STEM careers due to societal attitudes and a lack of role models. Kazakhstani female students also demonstrate low enrolment rates in STEM university majors (31.6 % of the total population of students) and are less likely to persist as they advance in their education. In some math-intensive majors, female students constitute only 13 % of overall enrollment (ADB, 2016). Therefore, more effort should be directed to recruiting and retaining traditionally underrepresented populations to STEM education and career trajectories.

4 STEM Teacher Education

The history of teacher training in post-Soviet space can be traced back to the middle of the 18th century when Moscow University was founded in 1755. The first three-year teacher training program was launched in this university in 1779-the date which might be considered the starting point of the history of teacher education programs (Kallimulin et al., 2024). In the following years, the teachers were trained by completing a two-year program at universities located in such cities as Moscow, St Petersburg, Kazan, Kyiv, and Kharkiv (Eskin, 1952). According to Nefedova (2013), these teacher training programs specialized in preparing the teachers for uyezd (district), municipal and primary schools that started appearing on the Russian Empire's territory at the end of the 19th century.

The history of teacher education programs in Kazakhstan dates back to 1883 – the year of the establishment of the first Kazakh teachers' school in the Orynbor region (Mynbayeva et al., 2014). The Semipalatinsk Pedagogical Institute, which is considered the cradle of Kazakhstani teacher education, was founded in 1903. One of the priorities of the Russian Empire at that time was to create a universal learning space for all the nations living on its territory (Kalimullin et al., 2020). At the beginning of the 20th century, almost 70% of the population of the Russian Empire was illiterate. Therefore, the growing demand for population literacy resulted in mass primary education, which required increasing the number of teachers. Therefore, Tsarist Russia implemented several reforms, such as developing a comprehensive school system (Valeeva & Kalimullin, 2019).

One of the unique features of the school system at that time was the establishment of elite schools-gymnasiums, which advantageously differed from European schools by the scope of the subjects and the in-depth study of such subjects as Maths, Physics and Chemistry. The tradition of focusing on Math and Science subjects proceeded in the Soviet era. For the Soviet government, the teacher was the primary instrument for the realization of the goals of the Communist Party (Whitelaw & Lindquist, 1963). Therefore, teacher education was considered as "the great strategic importance" and "national interest" (Whitelaw & Lindquist, 1963, p. 119). In the 1960s, the Supreme Council of the USSR initiated teacher education reform, emphasizing polytechnical education as the core of education for communism (Whitelaw & Lindquist, 1963). According to Balzer (1993), the Soviet government created "an impressive but contradictory system of education and science," allocating a significant amount of resources for scientific research and bringing science and technology education to the highest standards in the world (p. 889).

The distinguishing feature of Math and Science education in the 1960s-70s was the establishment of specialized schools that focused on Math and Science (fizmat schools). The schools offered an advanced curriculum and were able to educate several generations of well-educated individuals and laid the foundation of 'Soviet intelligentsia' (Gerovitch, 2019). The STEM programs at Soviet STEM-focused schools tended to be very detailed and required strong teacher and student capacities. It is estimated that around 80% of professional mathematicians in the Soviet Union in the 1990s were graduates of these schools (Tokar, 1999). In 1962, the Soviet government declared the urgent need for specialists in such fields as nuclear physics, cybernetics, and others and supported the expansion of special

STEM-focused schools for a partial solution to the problem, including the establishment of Physics and math boarding schools in the whole territory of Soviet Union. The first 'fizmat' boarding school in Kazakhstan -the Republican Physics and Math School in Almaty, was established in 1972 (RPHMS website).

Another significant feature of Soviet STEM education was the focus on STEM subject Olympiads. The first Math Olympiad for school children was organized in 1934 at Leningrad State University in Moscow and Kyiv in the following year (Tokar, 1999). The Olympiad movement was characterized by its informal style as opposed to the regular school curriculum and offered non-standard problems, promoting the perception of Math and science as fun activities (Gerovitch, 2019).

One of the main principles of STEM education in Soviet times was the high degree of uniformity- there was a single STEM subject curriculum "for every classroom across the nation." (Whitelaw & Lindquist, 1963). After the launch of Sputnik, US educators analyzed the contents of Soviet Mathematics textbooks trying to understand the roots of Soviet triumph in math and science (Gerovitch, 2019). The scholars highlighted the high level of specificity in Math textbooks, referring to lesson plans and home tasks that each Math teacher across the country should follow. It means that the school curriculum in all subjects, including STEM subjects, was unified across all regions of the Soviet Union. One of the important characteristics of STEM subjects teaching in Soviet times was that STEM subjects were taught by teachers who did not teach anything except the subject they specialized in.

To address the needs of the planned economy oriented to the needs of industry, the Soviet government paid significant attention to STEM teacher education. The Soviet Union offered different training tracks for future teachers, depending on targeted school levels. The primary school teachers were prepared by teacher training colleges ('pedagogicheskoye uchilische'), with different lengths of study which depended on their educational background. The students who graduated from secondary schools took a two-year program. The students who entered the teacher training college after 8th grade took a four-year program. The graduates of teacher training colleges graduated with the degree which allowed them to teach at primary school. The primary school teacher was also supposed to teach Math till grade three. The secondary school STEM subject teachers were trained in a five-year program in pedagogical institutes and graduated with a specialization as a Math or Science teacher.

4.1 STEM Teacher Education in Post-Soviet Kazakhstan

Similar to Soviet times, there are two pathways to becoming a STEM teacher in Kazakhstan: 1) entry into the teaching profession with a vocational degree and 2) entry into the teaching profession with a disciplinary Bachelor of Education degree (OECD, 2018). There are also two pathways for getting the STEM teaching vocational degree. The first pathway entails the completion of grade 9 (lower secondary school) and taking examinations in a profession-oriented STEM subject and Kazakh/Russian language to enter the teacher training college. The second pathway entails completion of grade 11 (upper-secondary school) and taking such subjects as the History of Kazakhstan and the Kazakh/Russian language as a profession-oriented STEM subject (OECD, 2018). The duration of study is four and three years, respectively. During their last year of study, the students are required to take a 6-month internship at school.

277 colleges offer teacher-training programs in Kazakhstan, and 11 are specialized pedagogical colleges (based on 2018 OECD data). The graduates with vocational degrees in STEM subjects can teach in middle school after graduation. However, most teacher-training college graduates continue their education in university teacher-training programs. Only 19 % of the teachers in Kazakhstan do not have a higher education degree (IAC, 2019).

According to the national classificatory of specialties of the postsecondary programs in Kazakhstan (2009), the training of teachers in Kazakhstan is being done in 23 specialties in teacher training universities (Makoelle & Burmistrova, 2021)., the minimum UNT score requirement for entering the teacher training program at university initially was 60 points, which includes the score for profession-specific STEM subject. Starting in 2020, the minimum score required for entering the pedagogical specialty was raised to 70 (OECD, 2018). Completing 240 credits and 15–20 weeks of pedagogical internship is mandatory for graduation. Currently, 86 universities in Kazakhstan offer teacher education programs (Makoelle & Burmistrova, 2021).

4.2 Current Challenges in STEM Teacher Education

One of the most important problems in STEM teacher education is teacher recruitment. Although the UNT score requirements have been raised, they are still relatively low compared to other specialties. Another problem is the relatively low salaries. The students who graduate with STEM pedagogical degrees prefer to pursue career opportunities not related to teaching or enter the private tutoring market as teacher salaries are very low.

Another problem in initial teacher education is the lack of knowledge of addressing the needs of special groups of students. STEM teacher educators themselves display a lack of knowledge and instructional strategies to teach future teachers how to teach different categories of students (Almukhambetova, 2024; Makoelle & Burmistrova, 2021).

The most important achievement in addressing the issue of teacher shortage was the introduction of the Law on Teacher Status, which was a major step in raising the status of the teaching profession in the country. However, much needs to be done to improve the quality of initial teacher education. More support should be provided for STEM early career teachers. There should be an emphasis on continuous professional development and training in the latest pedagogical methods and STEM advancements.

5 Conclusion and Recommendations

This chapter presented the current state of STEM Education and STEM Teacher education in Kazakhstan, along with the existing challenges. The overview presented in the chapter identified that STEM education in Kazakhstan has seen significant advancement yet faces several challenges that require ongoing attention. Addressing these issues through targeted policies and practices can further strengthen STEM education, ultimately contributing to the country's socio-economic development.

Although Kazakhstan is making strides toward aligning its STEM education with international standards, there is a significant difference between the international and local conceptualization of STEM education, which stems from a variety of historical, economic, and cultural factors. Kazakhstan's STEM education is characterized by a more rigid and theoretical approach with a strong focus on foundational knowledge. Certain efforts are being made to align with international standards, but implementation varies widely due to disparities in resource allocation, particularly between urban and rural schools, STEM-focused specialized schools and mainstream schools. Many schools still lack advanced STEM facilities, and widespread access to STEM educational resources remains challenging.

Continued investment in STEM educational resources, teacher training, and curricular reforms will be crucial for bridging these gaps. Significant effort should be made to reconsider teacher training programs to improve quality and alignment with international standards. An emphasis should be placed on inclusive teaching strategies, stressing gender equality and supporting underrepresented groups in STEM fields.

References

Akhmetzhanova, A. (2020). Outflow of Kazakhstani students to russian universities: Where to look for reasons? In *SOROS.kz*.

Almukhambetova, A. (2024). Exploring STEM teacher educators' gender awareness and understanding of gender-responsive pedagogies in Kazakhstan. In *The political economy of education in Central Asia: Evidence from the field* (pp. 97–115). Springer Nature Singapore.

Almukhambetova, A., & Hernández-Torrano, D. (2021). On being gifted at university: Academic, social, emotional, and institutional adjustment in Kazakhstan. *Journal of Advanced Academics, 32*(1), 70–91.

Almukhambetova, A., & Kuzhabekova, A. (2020). Factors affecting the decision of female students to enroll in undergraduate science, technology, engineering, and mathematics majors in Kazakhstan. *International Journal of Science Education, 42*(6), 934–954.

Balta, N., Japashov, N., Karimova, A., Agaidarova, S., Abisheva, S., & Potvin, P. (2023). Middle and high school girls' attitude to science, technology, engineering, and mathematics career interest across grade levels and school types. *Frontiers in Education, 8*, 1158041.

Balzer, H. (1993). Science, technology, and education in the former USSR. *The Former Soviet Union in Transition: Study Papers, 103*(11), 889–908.

Berkaliev, Z. (n.d.). Mathematics Education Issues in post-Soviet Kazakhstan: An international perspective. http://math.unipa.it/~grim/21_project/21_charlotte_

Bøe, M. V., Henriksen, E. K., Lyons, T., & Schreiner, C. (2011). Participation in science and technology: Young people's achievement-related choices in late-modern societies. *Studies in Science Education, 47*(1), 37–72.

Chankseliani, M., Gorgodze, S., Janashia, S., & Kurakbayev, K. (2020). Rural disadvantage in the context of centralised university admissions: A multiple case study of Georgia and Kazakhstan. *Compare: A Journal of Comparative and International Education, 50*(7), 995–1013.

Dimitrov, D. M., Mozhayeva, O. I., Shilibekova, A. S., Ziyedenova, D. B., & Rakhymbayeva, Z. K. (2020). Updated content of education in Kazakhstan: Longitudinal trajectories of learning performance in mathematics and science. *Journal of Education and Human Development, 9*(1), 88–102.

Fisher, A., & Margolis, J. (2002). Unlocking the clubhouse: the Carnegie Mellon experience. *ACM SIGCSE Bulletin, 34*(2), 79–83.

Gerovitch, S. (2013). Parallel worlds: formal structures and informal mechanisms of postwar soviet mathematics. *Historia Scientiarum, 22*(3), 181–200.

Holbrook, J. (2008). Introduction. In P. Reiska, J. Holbrook & M. Rannikmae (Eds.), *The need for a paradigm shift in science education for post-soviet societies*. P. Lang.

Japashov, N., Naushabekov, Z., Ongarbayev, S., Postiglione, A., & Balta, N. (2022). STEM career interest of Kazakhstani middle and high school students. *Education Sciences, 12*(6), 397.

Kalimullin, A. M., & Valeeva, R. A. (2022). Teacher education in post-Soviet states: Transformation trends. In *The Palgrave handbook of teacher education research* (pp. 1–20). Springer International Publishing.

Kalimullin, A., Valeeva, R., & Baklashova, T. (2024). From the Soviet Union to Russia: Fifty years of reforms in initial teacher education. *Journal of Education for Teaching, 50*(5), 801–815.

Kapanadze, M., Janashia, S., & Eilks, I. (2010). From science education in the soviet time, via national reform initiatives, towards an international network to support inquiry-based science education – The case of Georgia and the project SALiS. In I. Eilks & B. Ralle (Eds.), *Contemporary science education* (pp. 237–242). Shaker

Karabassova, L. (2022). Is top-down CLIL justified? A grounded theory exploration of secondary school science teachers' experiences. *International Journal of Bilingual Education and Bilingualism, 25*(4), 1530–1545.

Kharlamov, I. F. (1990). *Pedagigika.* Visschaia Shkola

Kuzhabekova, A., Soltanbekova, A., & Almukhambetova, A. (2018). Educational flagships as brokers in international policy transfer: Learning from the experience of Kazakhstan. *European Education, 50*(4), 353–370.

Makoelle, T. M., & Burmistrova, V. (2021). Teacher education and inclusive education in Kazakhstan. *International Journal of Inclusive Education,* 1–17.

Merrill, C. (2009, March). The future of TE masters degrees: STEM. Presentation at the 70th Annual International Technology Education Association Conference, Louisville, Kentucky.

Mynbayeva, A., & Pogosian, V. (2014). Kazakhstani school education development from the 1930s: History and current trends. *Italian Journal of Sociology of Education, 6*(2), 144–172.

Shamshidinova, K., Ispusinova, S., Zhontayeva, Z., & McLaughlin, C. (2023). Mapping educational change in Kazakhstan. In C. McLaughlin, L. Winter, & N. Yakavets (Eds.), *Mapping educational change in Kazakhstan* (pp. 13–24). Cambridge University Press.

Shaughnessy, J. M. (2013). Mathematics in a STEM context. *Mathematics Teaching in the Middle School, 18*(6), 324–324.

Silova, I. (2009). The crisis of the post-Soviet teaching profession in the Caucasus and Central Asia. *Research in Comparative and International Education, 4*(4), 366–383.

State Program of the Education and Science Development of the Republic of Kazakhstan. (2019). *State program for 2020–2025.* Approved by the Decree of the Government of the Republic of Kazakhstan dated December 27, 2019 No. 988.

Tokar, I. (1999). *Schools for the mathematically talented in the former Soviet Union.* Columbia University.

Toybazarova, N. A., & Nazarova, G. (2018). The modernization of education in Kazakhstan: Trends, perspective and problems. *Bulletin of National Academy of Sciences of the Republic of Kazakhstan, 6*(376), 104–114.

Valeeva, R. A., & Kalimullin, A. M. (2019). Learning to teach in Russia: A review of policy and empirical research. In *Knowledge, policy and practice in teacher education: A cross-national study* (pp. 193–213).

Whitelaw, J. B., & Lindquist, C. B. (1963). The continuing challenge of Soviet teacher education. *Journal of Teacher Education, 14*(2), 119–127.

Winter, L., Hernández-Torrano, D., McLellan, R., Almukhambetova, A., & Brown-Hajdukova, E. (2022). A contextually adapted model of school engagement in Kazakhstan. *Current Psychology, 41*(4), 2479–2495.

CHAPTER 7

Teacher Professional Learning

The Role of Social Media in Promoting Professional Networks

Assel Sharimova and Elaine Wilson

Abstract

Teachers' professional networks have been reinforced internationally in the context of professional learning. Recognising that social media platforms within teachers' professional networks could effectively address teachers' isolation, this chapter discusses insights into the nature of Kazakhstani teachers' professional networks within the social media space. With the overarching aim of understanding how to promote teachers' professional learning, the chapter presents one part of a larger parallel mixed-method study that captured teachers' experiences from 29 schools by collecting self-reported practices using paper-based questionnaires (n = 440) and face-to-face interviews (n = 41). The chapter provides insights into the actors and factors related to the existence of teachers' professional connections in social media space. Offering empirical evidence for the widespread use of social media in teacher professional networking, this chapter explores the role of organisational structure, teacher professional development courses, and teacher agency.

Keywords

teacher professional learning – professional networks – social media – Kazakhstan

1 Introduction

The importance of a high-quality teaching profession in shaping society's future has always been highlighted at the national and international levels. Teachers' importance is stressed in the process of achieving the Sustainable Development Goal (SDG 4), which is dedicated to providing inclusive and equitable quality education for all (UNESCO & International Task Force on Teachers for Education, 2024). The recruitment of suitable individuals into teaching roles and the provision of opportunities for professional growth have been

© ASSEL SHARIMOVA AND ELAINE WILSON, 2025 | DOI:10.1163/9789004726345_008

pivotal in propelling the world's most improved school systems to succeed and continue to improve (Mourshed et al., 2010). Therefore, research, policy and practice all over the world aim to place teachers highly on their agenda. The definitions and metrics of teaching quality vary significantly in educational research, pointing to the importance of distinguishing teaching quality from teacher quality. While teacher quality is essentially concerned with the characteristics and abilities of professional educators, including their values, capacity, and capabilities, teaching quality centres on professional practice, in other words, what teachers do in their classrooms (Gu, 2023).

Understanding effective teaching as a key component of successful education systems, countries use various strategies to improve it. In this regard, the research literature suggests that educators and policymakers have pursued three main strategies to enhance teaching such as attracting talented individuals, enhancing the qualifications of both entering or already in the profession and refining instructional methods used in classrooms (Hiebert & Morris, 2012). These strategies are not mutually exclusive. While the first two approaches operate under the premise that enhanced teaching stems from the talents and qualifications of the educators themselves, the third approach concentrates on refining teaching methods rather than solely focusing on the individuals who teach. Elevating the significance of the last approach is one of the key aspects in the process of improving the fundamental aspects of education – the interactions in classrooms between teachers and students regarding the subject matter (ibid.). In this way, the existing research literature suggests that by focusing on the third approach in educational research, policy and practice, it is possible to create a system that supports all teachers and students in their learning.

Focusing on effective teaching, there is growing acknowledgement of the vital role of teachers' professional learning in this process (Sancar et al., 2021). Although the process of entering the teaching profession and initial teacher education is crucial for ensuring new teachers' competence and readiness, these initial steps alone are insufficient to fully equip teachers for the various challenges they will face in maintaining or enhancing their perceived and evidence-based classroom effectiveness in providing opportunities for learning and accomplishment for all their students (Boeskens et al., 2020; Day, 2017). Continuing professional learning is important for teachers to update, enhance and expand their knowledge as well as to stay up-to-date with the evolving research, tools, and practices. In particular, continuing teacher professional learning is required to respond to the growing diversity of learners, their contextual learning needs and motivations. Moreover, the shifts in government policies, which prioritise particular values and human capital development in terms of employment readiness and qualifications, always influence the curriculum and its instructional approaches along with the increase in technology use (Day, 2017). Consequently, it has become imperative to integrate initial teacher preparation and continuing professional learning systems with a lifelong learning approach to teacher professional learning (UNESCO & International Task Force on Teachers for Education, 2024).

Emphasising the importance of teachers' continuing professional learning, education is envisioned as a shared societal goal aimed at achieving a common good with the collaborative teaching profession that requires strategies focused on collaboration, social dialogue, and innovation (UNESCO & International Task Force on Teachers for Education, 2024). To this end, with the increasing research on the role of teacher networks as a contributor to teachers' professional learning and the growing social media space, the use of these platforms within professional networks of teachers has become an agenda for both research and practice. Therefore, intending to understand how to promote teachers' professional learning, this chapter provides some insights from the empirical research aimed at exploring teachers' use of social media for professional networking in Kazakhstan. We begin by conceptualising teachers' professional learning, followed by a review of the literature on teacher networks and professional learning, the framework for exploring the use of social media for professional learning and the contextual background for the following discussion of the insights from an empirical study of teachers' use of social media for professional networking.

2 Literature Review

2.1 Conceptualising Teacher Professional Learning

Despite widespread agreement regarding the significance of teachers' professional learning, there are still ongoing debates on the most effective approaches to conceptualising this process. There is a wide range of terms used to characterise the learning process of teachers, where most commonly researchers and practitioners consistently and interchangeably use the concepts of professional development and professional learning. In this chapter, we use the term "professional learning" to encompass a variety of learning avenues for professional growth, where conventional professional development workshops or seminars are conceptualised as one of the elements within a broader spectrum of ongoing professional learning opportunities. The choice for the use of professional learning is in line with the conceptual changes in this field, associated with the tendency to use the term 'development' in its passive connotation, where senior leaders oversee the development of staff, rather than positioning teachers as the primary agents of professional change (Boeskens et al., 2020; O'Brien & Jones, 2014). Such an expansive and critically reflective as well as less performative approach to professional learning is notably different from the structured career advancement linked with professional development. As the developments in education do not follow a linear path, necessitating a degree of adaptability for professionals to engage in critical and constructive consideration of change, the term "professional learning" better embodies the essential qualities of critical evaluation, reflective practice and life-long learning (O'Brien & Jones, 2014).

The research literature on teachers' professional learning repeatedly categorises the process according to the level of formality (Eraut, 2004; Kyndt et al., 2016; Richter et al., 2011). Formal learning opportunities are defined as structured educational settings with a predetermined curriculum. This definition recognises that teachers enhance their knowledge and skills through participation in courses and workshops. In contrast, informal learning opportunities are not confined to specific environments or prescribed curricula; rather, they are typically initiated and organised by teachers themselves (Richter et al., 2011). Consistent with this perspective, De Laat (2012) proposes that informal learning emerges organically from within a professional culture of self-regulated professionals. Supporting teachers' continuous professional growth, informal learning provides timely support for addressing the daily challenges encountered in the workplace (Tran & Pasura, 2023). Nevertheless, it's essential not to dichotomise formal and informal professional learning, as they represent opposite ends of a continuum, spanning from entirely unstructured learning occurring incidentally during work to learning deliberately organised within an educational context. Formal and informal professional learning should be viewed as existing along a continuum (Eraut, 2004; Kyndt et al., 2016; Mansfield & Gu, 2019). Even as informal learning is commonplace in all organisations, it is never enough on its own. Depending only on informal learning does not appear sufficient since what is implicitly learnt through informal learning may not necessarily be desired. Similarly, implicit informal learning can be converted into explicit knowledge through formal learning, and both of these ways should be regarded as equally significant for workplace learning (Kyndt et al., 2016). In this regard, reviewing the literature on professional learning practices, Opfer and Pedder (2011) conceptualise teacher professional learning as a complex system, acknowledging the interconnection among different processes, elements, and actions, depending on the situation and context within three subsystems (the teacher, the school and the learning activity). In line with the complexity theory framework, highlighting social and collaborative aspects of learning, research into the role of teacher networks as a possible contributor to teacher's professional learning is increasing.

2.2 Teacher Networks and Professional Learning

The growing body of research on teacher professional networking indicates that along with increasing social support, commitment, and sense of belonging (Clandinin et al., 2015; Fox & Wilson, 2015; Le Cornu, 2013; Struyve et al., 2016), it encourages the exchange of knowledge (Caduff et al., 2023; Coburn et al., 2010) and positively associated with student performance (Leana & Pil, 2017; Ronfeldt, 2017). Acknowledging that the benefits of professional networks depend entirely on the content of interaction (Coburn & Russell, 2008), existing research literature indicates that professional networking could promote teachers' professional learning and broaden their teaching arsenal (Coppe, 2024; Lieberman & Mace, 2010). In this regard, as the result of the literature review, it is synthesised that while formal professional development programs can support teachers in acquiring new knowledge, informal social connections are instrumental in how information is processed, distributed, and placed in context (Demir, 2021).

In line with this research, the idea of professional networks has evolved to become essential in shaping the current understanding of teacher professionalism (Hargreaves & Fullan, 2012; Hargreaves & O'Connor, 2018; Shirley, 2016; Spillane et al., 2017). The conceptual framework outlined in the Teaching and Learning International Survey (OECD, 2016, 2019) underscores the significance of collaborative networks among teachers. Emphasising the crucial effect of professional capital on enhancing effective teaching, Hargreaves and Fullan (2012) stress the significance of social capital as a key element of professional capital, alongside human capital and decisional capital, as human capital, which refers to the essential knowledge and skills of individual educators, can be enhanced by promoting peer learning within and across schools and establishing networks and environments that encourage collaboration and trust among teachers. Highlighting the importance of professional networks of teachers, Shirley (2016) suggests that educators should take proactive steps in building their social capital. In this regard, within the expanding social media landscape, it will become crucial for educators, parents, and communities to understand how to recognize, differentiate, and leverage valuable opportunities and learning that technology can offer (Daly & Stoll, 2018).

The connectedness available within online social networks (Van Dijck et al., 2018) provides an opportunity for teachers to be connected, irrespective of time and location. Teachers with busy schedules have the flexibility to be connected at their convenience (Ghamrawi, 2022; Hur & Brush, 2009). The potential benefit of social media for professional networking could be suggested for teachers who are the only instructors of a particular subject with potentially fewer chances for subject-specific professional support within their schools (Wesely, 2013). Furthermore, online professional networking stands out for its accessibility, enabling participation on a global scale and fostering connections among teachers from diverse backgrounds, potentially nurturing collaboration and innovation (Grunspan et al., 2021). Recognizing the cost-effectiveness and flexibility offered in this domain, educators with limited resources find that such professional interactions foster a sense of connection and inspire positive changes in teaching (Le et al., 2022).

With the increase of research literature considering teachers' use of social media technologies, recent literature reviews (Greenhow et al., 2020; Lantz-Andersson et al., 2018; Macià & García, 2016) recognize informal online communities and networks as a potential resource for teacher professional learning. Widening networks of knowledge (Greenhow et al., 2020), it could serve as a platform for exchanging and refining new ideas and providing emotional and professional support (Lantz-Andersson et al., 2018) as well as assisting teachers in reflection on their teaching methods and exchanging resources and experiences (Macià & García, 2016). The recent pandemic has reinforced the use of social media for the professional learning of teachers (Alwafi, 2021; Ghamrawi, 2022).

The existing research indicates that social media's role in professional learning is examined through various lenses, mostly within the frameworks of either a community (Davis, 2015) or a network (Fancera, 2020). Drawing on Wenger's (1999) theory of learning, this chapter discusses the virtual professional community of teachers following the definitions of networks and communities outlined by Wenger et al. (2011). Wenger (1999) characterises communities of practice through mutual engagement, a joint enterprise and a shared repertoire. The practice is sustained because individuals participate in activities that are mutually agreed upon; therefore, membership in a community of practice is predicated on mutual engagement. Communities of practice necessitate a collective endeavour shaped by members, fostering relationships of shared responsibility, and within the communities of practice, members develop shared resources. The establishment of mutual accountability through a joint enterprise and the cultivation of interpersonal relationships facilitate the necessary and pertinent exchange of information (Wenger, 1999). The establishment of a community enables participants to create and maintain learning partnerships centred around a shared domain. A community's learning value stems from its combined endeavours to foster learning within a specific domain. The shared commitment to both the domain and the community members serves as a learning asset, facilitating the flow of information (Wenger et al., 2011). Therefore, while the community is linked to the establishment of a learning partnership centred on a shared agenda, the network is related to the connectivity between individuals (Wenger et al., 2011). The network can construct one interconnected community or establish interconnected communities, facilitating the exchange of information. Thus, communities and networks represent two social aspects of learning (ibid.). Advancements in technology have broadened the opportunities for communities, enabling online and asynchronous communication, implying the potential adoption of the term virtual professional communities.

2.3   *Teacher Networks in Kazakhstan*
The educational system comprises a complex network of different types of schools, reflecting influences from the Soviet era, the establishment of a national education system since independence, the transition to a market economy, and aspirations for international integration. The expansion of the school network mirrors the country's vast geographical area and its policy of ensuring universal and mandatory access to education. The public school network consists of 7631 schools with 367,823 teachers 57 per cent of whom work in rural schools (Taldau, 2023). Identifying professional networks as an effective form of professional learning that provides an opportunity for the co-construction of knowledge and support tailored to teachers' actual needs, the report of TALIS 2018 suggests that Kazakhstan is one of the countries where at least 65 per cent of teachers are involved in networks "formed specifically for the professional development of teachers" (OECD, 2019, p. 160). Considering professional collaboration with direct links to classroom instruction, the report indicates that a significant number of teachers in Kazakhstan (61%) are engaged in "observing other teachers' classes and providing feedback" at least once a month (OECD, 2020, p. 151). Pointing to the variance of teachers' collaborative practices due to cultural and country-specific contextual factors, this report highlights the existing subject methodological association in Kazakhstan as a school-based structure for teacher collaboration (OECD, 2020). This subject Methodological Units (SMUs), groups of teachers who teach the same subject, function as a space for organizing and enhancing educational processes within schools and facilitating the professional development of teachers.

Along with the existing school-based structure for collaboration, the reported professional networking could be a reflection of the current education reform movement, where the frequent availability of "school-based professional development opportunities for teachers" was identified as a strength in Kazakhstan's school improvement process (OECD, 2018, p. 13). One part of the education reform movement was the establishment of the Centre of Excellence (CoE) in 2011 under the auspices of Nazarbayev Intellectual Schools with its network of branches in all the regions of the country with the aim of building capacity within the national in-service teacher training system. The CoE was tasked with creating a multi-level in-service teacher training program in collaboration with the University of Cambridge's Faculty of Education, which was delivered in close partnership with the National Centre for Professional Development «Orleu» with branches in all regions of Kazakhstan (Turner et al., 2014). The programme aimed to extend teachers' pedagogical knowledge and skills and provide new ways of working to improve teaching and learning within the schools in line with '21st-century skills', promoting teacher learning and reflection by increasing collaboration within and beyond the schools through working in collaborative coaching and mentoring teams to enhance pedagogical practice and by leading teacher Action Research and Lesson Study inquiries (Wilson, 2017; Wilson & Sharimova, 2019). In this way, supporting the reforming agenda these organizations increased attention in Kazakhstan to teacher collaboration for professional learning (Chernobay & Tashibaeva, 2020).

Advocating for the importance of capitalizing on the momentum of recent reform initiatives, Ayubayeva (2018) contends that teachers' personal beliefs and values regarding collaboration depend on micro-political dynamics, school organizational culture, and socio-political factors, largely stemming from the legacy of the Soviet education system, as well as uncertainties in the interpretation and implementation of top-down reform initiatives. At the same time, the blend of cultural context and performance pressure, which fosters competition among teachers to be perceived as top performers, could result in a notable reluctance to share their best practices (McLaughlin et al., 2014; Kanayeva, 2019). In this regard, Chankselliani and Silova (2018) note that, as a result of marketization, individualization and competition have become prominent features in post-socialist transformations. Finally, with the distribution of the school network in Kazakhstan, where half of the teachers work in rural areas, teachers may experience isolation as they might be the only instructors of a particular subject, leading to limited opportunities for subject-specific professional collaboration within their schools. Considering the opportunities for teachers' continuing professional learning within virtual professional communities, this chapter will discuss some insights from the empirical research aimed at understanding informal learning in virtual professional communities of teachers in Kazakhstan.

TEACHER PROFESSIONAL LEARNING

3 Methodology

Aiming to discuss teachers' use of social media for professional networking in Kazakhstan, this chapter presents one part of a larger parallel mixed-method study that captured the experiences of teachers from 29 schools in one of the regions of Kazakhstan in 2017–2018. The study collected teachers' self-reported practice using paper-based questionnaires and face-to-face interviews. Questionnaire and interview respondents were recruited using a volunteer-convenience sampling approach. Paper-based questionnaires (440) were collected with different response rates within each school; the average response rate across the whole sample was fifty per cent, where 84.5 per cent of respondents were from schools located in rural areas. 41 teachers were interviewed, where thirty-one interview participants were recruited from twenty-three rural schools, five teachers were recruited from two district centres and five teachers were recruited from the regional centre. The diversity among survey and interview participants, including their teaching experience and subject areas, results in a wide spectrum of perspectives. The number of female participants accounted for 83.6 and 85 per cent of the survey and interview samples respectively, which mirrored the demographic composition of teachers across the country, with females comprising 80.3 per cent of the teaching population in 2017 (IAC, 2018). All the data for the study was collected in Kazakh and Russian languages after obtaining official written permission and recruitment of the participants on a voluntary basis. In line with this study's mixed-methods parallel research design to achieve complementarity, the findings presented in this chapter are based on both qualitative and quantitative approaches to analysis. While presented insights from the paper-based questionnaire are based on descriptive statistical analysis, the insights from the interview are based on thematic analysis (Braun & Clarke 2006). Transcribed interviews and questionnaires were analysed in original languages, with only codes, themes, and selected quotes translated into English.

4 Findings and Discussion

4.1 *Leveraging Social Media for Virtual Professional Communities*

Most of the survey respondents (89.3 per cent) used social media for virtual professional communities. In this way, the study findings contributed to the increasing body of literature examining the widespread use of social media platforms for teachers' professional networking. This could be explained by the rapid expansion of social media platforms along with the general increase in digital platforms. In 2018, Van Dijck et al. described this phenomenon as the emergence of a "platform society," indicating that platforms have deeply influenced societies, impacting institutions, economic activities, and social and cultural norms. Despite the potential availability of multiple social media platforms for personal and professional purposes, WhatsApp emerged as the preferred teacher's choice for virtual professional communities among both survey participants and interviewees: WhatsApp (n = 346/40), Facebook (n = 44/2), Vkontakte (n = 44/3), Telegram (n = 21/5) and Mail.ru (n = 27/4). The leverage of social media for professional learning, particularly the use of WhatsApp groups has also been recently pointed out by school principals in Kazakhstan (Sarmurzin, Menlibekova & Orynbekova, 2023). The platform selection mirrors the dominance of an interconnected network of platforms controlled by five major technology companies (Alphabet-Google, Facebook, Apple, Amazon, and Microsoft), as described by Van Dijck et al. (2018). WhatsApp is readily available on smartphones and widely utilised across the country. Like other messaging platforms, it is simple to use and enables discussions within closed groups. However, unlike other social media platforms, it does not necessitate users to maintain profiles on social networking sites: "Some teachers don't have a profile on Facebook or Vkontakte, but everyone has a mobile phone". Additionally, the widespread adoption of WhatsApp messenger could be attributed to practical factors like Internet accessibility. Teachers may prefer to use WhatsApp due to Internet coverage, which still has been noted as a persistent challenge in rural areas (Durrani et al., 2023).

The examination of both qualitative and quantitative data reveals a growing tendency among teachers in Kazakhstan to utilise social media within professional communities to acquire professional knowledge, which was manifested in an overlapping mix of news, information, opinions, experience and resources: "For instance, I am a biology teacher, and I asked for anatomy related videos"; "Sometimes news, what is going on in our district, sometimes in different districts, because in my course group, we are from different districts of our region"; "In this group, we are all deputy heads of the schools within our region, and we discuss various issues". The type of knowledge sharing among teachers on social media aligns with findings from existing research. In exploring teachers' involvement in social media, Hu et al. (2018) discovered that social media served as a platform for accessing instructional materials, local and global educational news, and virtual discussions.

4.2 *Organisational Structure and Professional Development Courses*
Our work has found that social media facilitates connections among teachers horizontally, spanning across different levels, and vertically, extending to

district, regional, and national levels. The involvement in virtual professional communities reflected the formal organisational structure and processes within schools. For example, teachers indicated their membership in the subject methodologic units [*adistimilik birlestikter (Kaz) metodicheckie ob'edineniya (Rus)*] at the school and district level: "My first working group is the one with teachers of English language at our school"; "When something is not clear to me, I ask my school MU group". They noted their involvement in virtual professional communities by virtue of their positions as deputy school principals: "My second group is the one with deputy heads of our region"; "If I tell you about our deputy heads' group, we discussed a lot about the moderation process, mostly shared our opinions, how everyone is doing". Participation in virtual professional communities mirrored the central school management, where the Local Executive Authorities at regional and district levels are responsible for educational provision in schools and Subject Methodological Units (SMUs) serve as platforms for organising and enhancing educational processes within the schools and facilitating the professional development of teachers. Recognising that without active facilitation, there is a decrease in member participation (Nelimarkka et al., 2021), those virtual professional communities established by formal leaders highlight the importance of facilitators. Particularly the need for centring interactions within virtual professional communities on instructional matters with the understanding that changes in teachers' instructional practices could be more influenced by on-the-job professional learning than by formal professional development opportunities (Shirrell et al., 2019).

In our study, fifty-eight per cent of the questionnaire responses and seventy-eight per cent of interviewed teachers mentioned that they have groups within the virtual professional networks that originated from attending a face-to-face teacher training course or seminar. In this way, our work suggests that in-service teacher training courses can catalyze teachers from various schools to interact in virtual professional communities. The interview participants mentioned their membership in virtual professional communities mostly with the recent initiatives implemented within the country's in-service teacher training system: "This is the group from the updated curriculum course that I took last year in May...in this group, we find answers only to our questions related to the updated curriculum. It is helpful. I and the others, we all share our thoughts there... I ask and always find answers to my questions"; "As teachers, who have completed the highest level within the multi-level programme, we have our group". Teachers mentioned the Center of Excellence's multi-level professional development program (Wilson, 2017), which was acknowledged by teachers as an opportunity to update their teaching methods (Yakavets et al., 2023) as well as the professional development courses organised within the curriculum renewal for secondary education (Shamshidinova et al., 2023). Thus, the results of this study align with the increasing recognition that effective learning for teachers consists of a combination and interconnection of formal and informal professional learning opportunities (Greenhow et al., 2023; Kyndt et al., 2016; Mansfield & Gu, 2019). In this regard, based on the underlying premise that professional networking facilitates the professional growth of teachers, one of the implications of social network research for the design of the professional development programme is that the latter should also be aimed at strengthening teacher networks (Baker-Doyle & Yoon, 2020).

4.3 Teacher Agency and Virtual Professional Communities

The study discussed in this chapter indicates that virtual professional communities were initiated and led not only by school formal leaders, local educational authorities at district and regional levels, as well as in-service teacher training organisations but also by teachers themselves: "Once we created this group and now it is such a convenience. If you don't know anything you can open the chat and ask and will be immediately responded to"; "as I am leading those groups and I feel a responsibility, but as for all other groups I mostly receive information". Consistent with the findings of this study, recent empirical research on the process of curriculum renewal in Kazakhstan also noted the rise of professional networks established following professional development courses initiated not only under the guidance of educational authorities but also by teachers (Fim'yar et al., 2023). Highlighting collaboration within and beyond the school as a vital aspect of implementing the revised curriculum, another recent study in Kazakhstan indicated that teachers were keen on staying connected through emails and social media platforms (including WhatsApp) that enabled them to share their experiences and seek clarification (Yakavets et al., 2023). Thus, emphasising the importance of teachers' professional networks in their ongoing professional learning, this chapter reinforces the idea that teachers' agency plays a crucial role in fostering professional interactions within virtual professional communities. In this way, our study echoes the plea for facilitating teachers' agency, which could be associated not only with individual teachers' professional learning but also with the collective capacity for educational improvements (Durrant, 2020).

Highlighting the value of learning from other people, Eraut (2004) points out that informal learning implies the need for individual agency. Drawing connections between teacher agency and virtual professional communities, a recent study suggests that teacher agency contributes to shaping teacher leadership in virtual communities of practice by enabling teachers to assume responsibility for their learning, fostering experimentation, encouraging collaboration and the exchange of knowledge as well as nurturing a culture of ongoing learning (Shal et al., 2024). In this regard, with the understanding that agency could be theorised following various intellectual traditions and disciplines, it could also be seen through an ecological view where teacher agency is considered to arise from the interplay between individual 'capacity' and surrounding 'conditions' (Priestley et al., 2015). Therefore, aiming to facilitate teacher agency, policymakers and leaders in educational organisations should give greater consideration to the significance of the available conditions as the context may impede teachers who otherwise possess significant agency potential.

5 Conclusion

While the study presented in this chapter is constrained by its use of volunteer-convenience sampling, which could suggest self-selection bias (Olsen, 2011), the presented insights align with the broader international literature indicating widespread adoption of social media for virtual professional communities among teachers (Greenhow et al., 2020; Lantz-Andersson et al., 2018). Acknowledging the multifaceted nature of teachers' professional learning and the need for a holistic perspective on this process, this chapter advocates for the recognition that effective learning conditions for teachers involve a combination and interconnection of formal and informal learning opportunities, including the use of virtual professional communities. The discussion in this chapter joins the call for considering the importance of a social-ecological approach to professional learning rather than solely relying on the human capital approach, highlighting the crucial importance of the school structure in fostering, leveraging, and maintaining the enthusiasm and commitment of teachers (Gu, 2023).

The study discussed demonstrates that virtual professional communities were initiated and led by both formal leaders and teachers themselves. Therefore, to promote teachers' professional learning, it could be recommended that policymakers and educational leaders place greater emphasis on the importance of the contextual factors that can hinder teachers' agency. The reported participation in virtual professional communities mirrored the formal organizational structure and processes within schools, particularly Subject Methodological Units. Therefore, one of the key recommended competencies for these formal school leaders is the development of skills to facilitate virtual professional communities, specifically, to focus interactions on instructional matters and to promote a collaborative culture. In this regard, reflecting on the work on collaboration among educators, Hargreaves (2019) argues that it is essential that teachers not only collaborate but do so effectively, with school and system leaders supporting and empowering them in this endeavour.

The growing body of research, including the one discussed in this chapter, indicates that professional learning can be enhanced by incorporating diverse formats. However, findings from the OECD's Teaching and Learning International Survey (TALIS) demonstrate that while a significant number of teachers engage in courses and seminars, participation in other forms of learning, particularly those emphasising teacher-centred and collaborative approaches, remains low. Similarly, numerous schools have not adopted a culture that promotes collaborative learning or established the infrastructure needed to maintain it. In various settings, teachers continue to work in isolation from one another, with few chances for collaboration (Boeskens et al., 2020). Although there is undoubtedly a significant amount of work ahead, there are observable signs that research on teacher-professional networks may have influenced political discussions, leading to a renewed focus on the significance of teacher collaboration. Particularly, to move forward, the International Commission on the Futures of Education has emphasised the importance of reimagining the teaching profession as a collaborative one (UNESCO & International Task Force on Teachers for Education, 2024).

References

Alwafi, E. (2021). Tracing changes in teachers' professional learning network on Twitter: Comparison of teachers' social network structure and content of interaction before and during the COVID-19 pandemic. *Journal of Computer Assisted Learning, 37*(6), 1653–1665. https://doi.org/10.1111/jcal.12607

Ayubayeva, N. (2018). *Teacher collaboration for professional learning: Case studies of three schools in Kazakhstan* [Doctoral dissertation]. https://doi.org/10.17863/CAM.20729

Baker-Doyle, K. J., & Yoon, S. A. (2020). The social side of teacher education: Implications of social network research for the design of professional development. *International Journal of Educational Research, 101.* https://doi.org/10.1016/j.ijer.2020.101563

Boeskens, L., Nusche, D., & Yurita, M. (2020). Policies to support teachers' continuing professional learning: A conceptual framework and mapping of OECD data. *OECD Education Working Papers, 235.*

Braun, V., & Clarke, V. (2006). Using thematic analysis in psychology. *Qualitative Research in Psychology, 3*(2), 77–101. https://doi.org/10.1191/1478088706qp063oa

Caduff, A., Lockton, M., Daly, A. J., & Rehm, M. (2023). Beyond sharing knowledge: Knowledge brokers' strategies to build capacity in education systems. *Journal of Professional Capital and Community, 8*(2), 109–124. https://doi.org/10.1108/JPCC-10-2022-0058

Chankseliani, M., & Silova, I. (2018). Reconfiguring Education Purposes, Policies and Practices during Post-socialist Transformations: setting the stage. In M. Chankseliani & I. Silova (Eds.), *Comparing post-socialist transformations: Purposes, policies, and practices in education.* Symposium Books Ltd.

Chernobay, E., & Tashibaeva, D. (2020). Teacher professional development in Russia and Kazakhstan: Evidence from TALIS-2018. *Voprosy obrazovaniya/Educational Studies Moscow,* (4), 141–164.

Clandinin, D. J., Long, J., Schaefer, L., Downey, C. A., Steeves, P., Pinnegar, E., McKenzie Robblee, S., & Wnuk, S. (2015). Early career teacher attrition: intentions of teachers beginning. *Teaching Education, 26*(1), 1–16. https://doi.org/10.1080/10476210.2014.996746

Coburn, C. E., Choi, L., & Mata, W. S. (2010). 'I would go to her because her mind is math': Network formation in the context of district-based mathematics reform. In A. J. Daly (Ed.), *Social network theory and educational change* (pp. 33–50). Harvard Education Press.

Coburn, C. E., & Russell, J. L. (2008). District policy and teachers' social networks. *Educational Evaluation and Policy Analysis, 30*(3), 203–235. https://doi.org/10.3102/0162373708321829

Coppe, T. (2024). Teacher networks: From a catalyst for enactment of professional development to a source of professional development. *Teachers and Teaching, 30*(3), 380–393. https://doi.org/10.1080/13540602.2023.2263734

Daly, A. J., & Stoll, L. (2018). Looking back and moving forward: Where to next for networks of learning?. In C. Brown, & C. L. Poortman (Eds.), *Networks for learning: Effective collaboration for teacher, school and system improvement* (pp. 205–214). Routledge.

Davis, K. (2015). Teachers' perceptions of Twitter for professional development. *Disability and Rehabilitation, 37*(17), 1551–1558. https://doi.org/10.3109/09638288.2015.1052576

Day, C. (2017). *Teachers' worlds and work: Understanding complexity, building quality.* Routledge.

De Laat, M. (2012). *Enabling professional development networks: How connected are you?* Open Universiteit.

Demir, E. K. (2021). The role of social capital for teacher professional learning and student achievement: A systematic literature review. *Educational Research Review, 33.* https://doi.org/10.1016/j.edurev.2021.100391

Durrani, N., Qanay, G., Mir, G., Helmer, J., Polat, F., Karimova, N., & Temirbekova, A. (2023). Achieving SDG 4, equitable quality education after COVID-19: Global evidence and a case study of Kazakhstan. *Sustainability*, *15*(20), 1–13. https://doi.org/10.3390/su152014725

Durrant, J. (2020). *Teacher agency, professional development and school improvement*. Routledge.

Eraut, M. (2004). Informal learning in the workplace. *Studies in Continuing Education*, *26*(2), 247–273. https://doi.org/10.1080/158037042000225245

Fancera, S. F. (2020). School leadership for professional development: the role of social media and networks. *Professional Development in Education*, *46*(4), 664–676. https://doi.org/10.1080/19415257.2019.1629615

Fim'yar, O., Helmer, J., Tursunbayeva, X., & Aringazina, L. (2023). Regional case study 2: A regional study of stakeholders' perspectives on education reform in Kazakhstan. In C. McLaughlin, L. Winter, & N. Yakavets (Eds.), *Mapping educational change in Kazakhstan* (pp. 237–256). Cambridge University Press.

Fox, A. R. C., & Wilson, E. G. (2015). Networking and the development of professionals: Beginning teachers building social capital. *Teaching and Teacher Education*, *47*, 93–107. https://doi.org/10.1016/j.tate.2014.12.004

Ghamrawi, N. (2022). Teachers' virtual communities of practice: A strong response in times of crisis or just another Fad? *Education and Information Technologies*, *27*(5), 5889–5915. https://doi.org/10.1007/s10639-021-10857-w

Greenhow, C., Galvin, S. M., Brandon, D. L., & Askari, E. (2020). A decade of research on K-12 teaching and teacher learning with social media: Insights on the state of the field. *Teachers College Record*, *122*(6), 1–72. https://doi.org/10.1177/016146812012200602

Greenhow, C., Lewin, C., & Staudt Willet, K. B. (2023). Teachers without borders: professional learning spanning social media, place, and time. *Learning, Media and Technology*, *48*(4), 666–684. https://doi.org/10.1080/17439884.2023.2209326

Grunspan, D. Z., Holt, E. A., & Keenan, S. M. (2021). Instructional Communities of Practice during COVID-19: Social Networks and Their Implications for Resilience †. *Journal of Microbiology & Biology Education*, *22*(1), 10–1128. https://doi.org/10.1128/jmbe.v22i1.2505

Gu, Q. (2023). Anchoring teacher professional learning and development in context: how schools enable teachers to thrive. In *The Palgrave handbook of teacher education research* (pp. 745–761). Springer International Publishing.

Hargreaves, A. (2019). Teacher collaboration: 30 years of research on its nature, forms, limitations and effects. *Teachers and Teaching: Theory and Practice*, *25*(5), 603–621. https://doi.org/10.1080/13540602.2019.1639499

Hargreaves, A., & Fullan, M. (2012). *Professional capital: Transforming teaching in every school*. Routledge.

Hargreaves, A., & O'Connor, M. T. (2018). *Collaborative professionalism: When teaching together means learning for all*. Corwin Press.

Hiebert, J., & Morris, A. K. (2012). Teaching, rather than teachers, as a path toward improving classroom instruction. *Journal of Teacher Education, 63*(2), 92–102. https://doi.org/10.1177/0022487111428328

Hu, S., Torphy, K. T., Opperman, A., Jansen, K., & Lo, Y. J. (2018). What do teachers share within Socialized Knowledge Communities: a case of Pinterest. *Journal of Professional Capital and Community, 3*(2), 97–122. https://doi.org/10.1108/JPCC-11-2017-0025

Hur, J. W., & Brush, T. A. (2009). Teacher participation in online communities: Why do teachers want to participate in self-generated online communities of K—12 teachers? *Journal of Research on Technology in Education, 41*(3), 279–303. https://doi.org/10.1080/15391523.2009.10782532

Information Analytic Center (IAC). (2018). *National Report on the state and development of the education system of the Republic of Kazakhstan.*

Kanayeva, G. (2019). *Facilitating teacher leadership in Kazakhstan* [Doctoral dissertation]. https://doi.org/10.17863/CAM.41620

Kyndt, E., Gijbels, D., Grosemans, I., & Donche, V. (2016). Teachers' everyday professional development: Mapping informal learning activities, antecedents, and learning outcomes. *Review of Educational Research, 86*(4), 1111–1150. https://doi.org/10.3102/0034654315627864

Lantz-Andersson, A., Lundin, M., & Selwyn, N. (2018). Twenty years of online teacher communities: A systematic review of formally-organized and informally-developed professional learning groups. In *Teaching and Teacher Education* 75, 302–315. https://doi.org/10.1016/j.tate.2018.07.008

Le Cornu, R. (2013). Building early career teacher resilience: The role of relationships. *Australian Journal of Teacher Education, 38*(4), 1–16. https://doi.org/10.14221/ajte.2013v38n4.4

Le, V. H., Maor, D., & McConney, A. (2022). The potential of social networking sites for continuing professional learning: investigating the experiences of teachers with limited resources. *Studies in Continuing Education, 44*(3), 546–562. https://doi.org/10.1080/0158037X.2021.1932453

Leana, C. R., & Pil, F. K. (2017). Social capital: An untapped resource for educational improvement. In E. Quintero (Ed.), *Teaching in Context: The social side of education reform* (pp. 113–130). Harvard Education Press.

Lieberman, A., & Mace, D. (2010). Making practice public: Teacher learning in the 21st century. *Journal of Teacher Education, 61*(1–2), 77–88. https://doi.org/10.1177/0022487109347319

Macià, M., & García, I. (2016). Informal online communities and networks as a source of teacher professional development: A review. *Teaching and Teacher Education, 55*, 291–307. https://doi.org/10.1016/j.tate.2016.01.021

McLaughlin, C., McLellan, R., Fordham, M., Chandler-Grevatt, A., Daubney, A. (2014). The role of the teacher in educational reform in Kazakhstan: Teacher enquiry as a vehicle for change. In Bridges, D. (Ed.), *Education reform and internationalisation: The case of school reform in Kazakhstan* (239–260). Cambridge University Press.

Mansfield, C., & Gu, Q. (2019). "I'm finally getting that help that I needed": Early career teacher induction and professional learning. *Australian Educational Researcher, 46*(4), 639–659. https://doi.org/10.1007/s13384-019-00338-y

Mourshed, M., Chijioke, C., & Barber, M. (2010). *Education ow the world's most improved school systems keep getting better*. McKinsey and Company

Nelimarkka, M., Leinonen, T., Durall, E., & Dean, P. (2021). Facebook is not a silver bullet for teachers' professional development: Anatomy of an eight-year-old social-media community. *Computers and Education, 173*. https://doi.org/10.1016/j.compedu.2021.104269

O'Brien, J., & Jones, K. (2014). Professional learning or professional development? Or continuing professional learning and development? Changing terminology, policy and practice. In *Professional Development in Education, 40*(5), 683–687. https://doi.org/10.1080/19415257.2014.960688

OECD. (2016). *Supporting teacher professionalism: Insights from TALIS 2013*. OECD Publishing. https://doi.org/10.1787/9789264248601-en

OECD. (2019). *TALIS 2018 results (Volume I): Teachers and school leaders as lifelong learners*. OECD Publishing.

OECD. (2020). *TALIS 2018 results (Volume II): Teachers and school leaders as valued professionals*. OECD Publishing.

Olsen, W. (2011). *Data collection: Key debates and methods in social research*. Sage.

Opfer, V. D., & Pedder, D. (2011). Conceptualizing teacher professional learning. *Review of Educational Research, 81*(3), 376–407. https://doi.org/10.3102/0034654311413609

Priestley, M., Priestley, M. R., Biesta, G., & Robinson, S. (2015). *Teacher agency: An ecological approach*. Bloomsbury Publishing.

Richter, D., Kunter, M., Klusmann, U., Lüdtke, O., & Baumert, J. (2011). Professional development across the teaching career: Teachers' uptake of formal and informal learning opportunities. *Teaching and Teacher Education, 27*(1), 116–126. https://doi.org/10.1016/j.tate.2010.07.008

Ronfeldt, M. (2017). Better collaboration, better teaching. In E. Quintero (Ed.), *Teaching in context: The social side of education reform* (pp. 71–93). Harvard Education Press.

Sancar, R., Atal, D., & Deryakulu, D. (2021). A new framework for teachers' professional development. *Teaching and Teacher Education, 101*, 103305. https://doi.org/10.1016/j.tate.2021.103305

Sarmurzin, Y., Menlibekova, G., & Orynbekova, A. (2023). "I Feel Abandoned": Exploring school principals' professional development in Kazakhstan. *The Asia-Pacific Education Researcher, 32*(5), 629–639. https://doi.org/10.1007/s40299-022-00682-1

Shal, T., Ghamrawi, N., Abu-Tineh, A., Al-Shaboul, Y. M., & Sellami, A. (2024). Teacher leadership and virtual communities: Unpacking teacher agency and distributed leadership. *Education and Information Technologies*, 1–18. https://doi.org/10.1007/s10639-023-12446-5

Shamshidinova, K., Ispusinova, S., Zhontayeva, Z., & McLaughlin, C. (2023). Rationale for and Perceptions of the Educational Reform in Kazakhstan. In C. McLaughlin, L. Winter, & N. Yakavets (Eds.), *Mapping Educational Change in Kazakhstan* (pp. 13–24). Cambridge University Press.

Shirley, D. (2016). *The new imperatives of educational change*. Routledge.

Shirrell, M., Hopkins, M., & Spillane, J. P. (2019). Educational infrastructure, professional learning, and changes in teachers' instructional practices and beliefs. *Professional Development in Education, 45*(4), 599–613. https://doi.org/10.1080/19415257.2018.1452784

Spillane, J. P., Hopkins, M., Sweet, T. M., & Shirrell, M. (2017). The social Side of Capability: supporting Classroom Instruction and Enabling Its Improvement. In E. Quintero (Ed.), *Teaching in context: the social side of education reform* (pp. 95–111). Harvard Education Press.

Struyve, C., Daly, A., Vandecandelaere, M., Meredith, C., Hannes, K., & De Fraine, B. (2016). More than a mentor: The role of social connectedness in early career and experienced teachers' intention to leave. *Journal of Professional Capital and Community, 1*(3), 198–218. https://doi.org/10.1108/JPCC-01-2016-0002

Taldau. (2023). 'Education Statistics of Kazakhstan' National collection.

Tran, L. T., & Pasura, R. (2023). How do teachers learn to teach international students? Teachers' informal professional learning in international vocational education. *Teacher Development, 27*(4), 431–446. https://doi.org/10.1080/13664530.2023.2223548

Turner, F., Wilson, E., Ispussinova, S., Kassymbekov, Y., Sharimova, A., Balgynbayeva, B., & Brownhill, S. (2014). Centres of excellence: Systemwide transformation of teaching practice. In D. Bridges (Ed), *Education reform and internationalisation: The case of school reform in Kazakhstan* (pp. 83–105). Cambridge University Press.

UNESCO & International Task Force on Teachers for Education 2030. (2024). *Global report on teachers addressing teacher shortages and transforming the profession.* UNESCO.

Van Dijck, J., Poell, T., & De Waal, M. (2018). *The platform society: Public values in a connective world*. Oxford University Press.

Wenger, E. 1999. *Communities of practice: Learning, meaning, and identity.* Cambridge University Press.

Wenger, E., Trayner, B., & de Laat, M. (2011). Promoting and assessing value creation in communities and networks: A conceptual framework. *Ruud de Moor Centrum 18*(August).

Wesely, P. M. (2013). Investigating the community of practice of world language educators on twitter. *Journal of Teacher Education, 64*(4), 305–318. https://doi.org/10.1177/0022487113489032

Wilson, E. (2017) Alternative paths to upgrading existing teacher qualifications: the Kazakhstan- based Centre of Excellence Teacher Education Programme. In M. Hartley & A. Ruby, (Eds.), *Higher education reform and development: The case of Kazakhstan* (pp. 107–124). Cambridge, Cambridge University Press.

Wilson, E., & Sharimova, A. (2019). Conceptualizing the implementation of Lesson Study in Kazakhstan within a social theory framework. *International Journal for Lesson and Learning Studies, 8*(4), 320–333. https://doi.org/10.1108/IJLLS-08-2019-0060

Yakavets, N., Winter, L., Malone, K., Zhontayeva, Z., & Khamidulina, Z. (2023). Educational reform and teachers' agency in reconstructing pedagogical practices in Kazakhstan. *Journal of Educational Change, 24*(4), 727–757. https://doi.org/10.1007/s10833-022-09463-5

CHAPTER 8

Teachers and Action Research in Kazakhstan

A Collaborative Action Research Case at a Technical Vocational Education and Training Institution

Arman Assanbayev and Tsediso Michael Makoelle

Abstract

This chapter presents the findings of a study on the use and impact of collaborative action research (CAR) by teachers at one of the TVET colleges in Kazakhstan. The study was conducted in four stages: planning, observation, action, and reflection. Data was interpreted in two stages: group interpretative analysis with collaborative action research participants and by the collaborating expert post-collaborative action research process. The findings highlight the applicability of CAR in a Kazakhstani context and its significant impact on teacher change. The chapter concludes with recommendations for the use of action research by teachers in a Kazakhstani context.

Keywords

collaborative action research – teachers – teacher education – technical and vocational education

1   Introduction

The application of any form of action research in Kazakhstan is a new and unexplored territory. In analysing the understanding of action research by Kazakhsnati teachers, Baitkayeva (2019) states that although teachers understand what action research entails, it seems they have not fully explored its benefits. It is stated that perhaps due to a lack of experience in conducting action research, Kazakhstani teachers are less likely to initiate action research as the nature of education is such that teachers are expected to comply with ministerial conditions rather than be innovative. These views are echoed by

© ARMAN ASSANBAYEV AND TSEDISO MICHAEL MAKOELLE, 2025 | DOI:10.1163/9789004726345_009

Nagibova (2019). Therefore, the goal of this study was to determine the benefits of the use of collaborative action research by Kazakhstani Teachers in the development of inclusive teaching practices at a TVET college. The study also wanted to explore collaborative action research's impact on teachers' knowledge about their teaching and professional growth.

2 Literature Review

2.1 *The Notion of Action Research*

There are multiple definitions of Action Research. It is assumed to be a particular form of research located in the real world, and it is grounded in practice (Anderson et al., 2015). The authors argued that Action Research is based on action for specific reasons/ purposes in order to address problems existing in practice and research to find better practical ways to do or to tackle the problem by the practitioner (s). The founder of Action Research, Kurt Levin (1946), argued that Action Research is for the problem-solving approach in social and organisational settings as well as applied for making a change in a group of people, organisation and even in a society (Dickens & Watkins, 1999, p. 127).

Action Research is designed to generate knowledge about a process by changing it for the better, and any action must be aimed at the best possible interest of the people involved (Hart & Bond, 1995). The change is the keyword for the purpose of doing action. Action Research is usually conducted systematically by practitioners, and it usually involves teachers in order to change the existing practice in their classrooms and schools. Their goal is to improve the existing practice, find better ways of teaching students, and find new solutions to existing problems (Efron & Ravid, 2013, p. 4). A common feature of variations of the definition of Action Research is the purpose of generating knowledge through inquiry in order to enhance or generate practice for the benefit of people involved in research.

This study adopted Action Research as a design. Action Research as an approach encourages the use of objective perspective combined with active intervention (Burton et al., 2008, p. 121). It employs a series of interventions, and its nature is an iterative process which promotes the initiatives to get the desired outcome by the researcher and research. As an intervention, it consists of a series of connected lessons which can be re-shaped due to the data gathered from previous lessons, and the intervention could be applied iteratively in order to further address the literature and shape the conceptual framework. The execution of CAR starts with the formation of the professional learning community, which is a driving force behind all activities.

2.2 *Professional Learning Community*

The collaborative action research team performed the Professional Learning Community (PLC). PLC is widely acknowledged as the capacity-building instrument for the emerging challenges in teaching within educational organisations. The concept of PLC has been acknowledged as the critical strategy towards achieving the involvement of teachers in collaborative learning and teaching as well as capacity building of educational institutions (Stoll et al., 2006; Louis et al., 1996; Derri et al., 2015). The concept of PLC is growing, and it can reflect multiple peculiarities: for this reason, it is essential to clarify what is to be discussed within PLC in this study. Despite many interpretations of the definition of the PLC, there is a common understanding indicating the purpose, which is continuous improvement. The definition of this section draws heavily on Stoll et al. (2006), who argued that PLC is a collaboration of school teachers and administrators who continuously look for learning opportunities, simultaneously share their learning, and use their learning attainments with the common aim to improve learning to students (p. 223). This definition espouses that teachers can change the existing practices and they can take responsibility for self-improvement, leading to capacity building as well as the improvement of students' learning.

The main benefit of such capacity building is the professional development of teachers, which can be facilitated through the collective efforts of teachers discussed by Stoll et al. (2006). The professional development of teachers can also be developed within the PLC without attracting external specialists or special programs because the PLC is also a powerful capacity which could have experienced experts. Thus, the PLC can raise the competence and attitudes of every teacher by contributing to one another's teaching capacity in organisations (Stoll et al., 2006, p. 234). The main point is that teachers' capacity and professional building can be built not only through additional upgrading of skills in formal training separately from the practice but from inner sources together with everyday practice.

Learning as a process is not an individual task but an obligation of the whole teaching community, which should learn together to improve people's learning (Stoll et al., 2006, p. 222). Derri et al. (2015) argued that professional development programs impact students' achievements, and they highlighted that *even short-term programs* raise the quality of teaching and engage students in learning (p. 247). Moreover, the culture of a constant learning community is the strength of any organisation, which helps to promptly respond to challenges collaboratively and establish common values and views among the members of the PLC. From the perspective of these definitions, PLC fosters that all teachers in the team should commit to employing the power, knowledge and skills of the team as well as teachers become learners committed to lifelong learning, aspiring for problem-solving and promoting PLC within the organisation, more specifically TVETIs in this thesis.

Special programs for teachers are beneficial to capacity building, provided every teacher as a learner learns something new and delivers that experience to his or her peers. Hoyle and John (1995) defined six features as the foundation of PLC: an emphasis on teaching and learning, an emphasis on inquiry and reflection, a commitment to life learning and the development of a learning community (p. 162). This definition of PLC asserts that the joint efforts of teachers can widen their horizons. Several teachers can bring several experiences to the common ground for further implementation. Such context facilitates learning for teachers with their colleagues, peer coaching, and individual learning, and the potential of every teacher contributes to sharing practical solutions to challenges and *deprivatisation of practice* (Louis et al., 1995, p. 8). The latter concept means that more experienced teachers share their effective solutions with their less experienced colleagues as sharing experience in a non-formal environment, and such exchange contributes to capacity building, which can be considered taken for granted. Avalos (2011) stressed the importance of interaction contexts (such as informal workplace interactions) that facilitate learning and stimulate teachers to change or reinforce teaching and educational practices. Educational practices can be considered from different perspectives, such as in a familiar environment with teachers- and peers. In other words, they can teach one another in a friendly environment. Less experienced teachers, mainly at the beginning of their career, can share their new vision to finding solutions based on the more recent theoretical knowledge from academia since they graduated from them more recently than their older colleagues. More experienced teachers can reinforce the capacity of institutions by providing feedback to less experienced teachers while watching their teaching practices during the teaching process (Derri, 2015, p. 237). Another point, the emphasis on inquiry and reflection within PLC, discussed by Hoyle and John (1995), was found by Derri (2015) as one of the critical strategies for establishing PLC. The author stressed that mutual inquiry and reflection of teachers' foster scientific and pedagogical advances to respond to challenges in teaching (Derri, 2015, p. 235).

Kazakhstani TVET teachers can incorporate the joint capacity of teachers to promote inclusion and change their environment and teaching, thus making it more inclusive. Despite their experience, teachers create the infrastructure of support within one organisation (Stoll et al., 2006, p. 221). Avalos (2011) argued that teacher co-learning is crucial to understanding how teachers work together and share practices for learning purposes. Furthermore, the author developed the idea that such collaboration among teachers contributes to teacher networks and teams, communities of practice and communities of learning, and peer coaching. Teachers can teach one another for free, even employing their capacity without external professional development programs, although the latter is essential, too.

Another benefit of PLC is that it fosters a shared vision towards commitment to life learning and the development of a learning community, as mentioned by Hoyle and John (1995). The capacity of the school can also be built through in-house and low-cost professional development of teachers continuously. Stoll et al. (2006) argued that professional development cannot be built by facilitating only formal professional development opportunities for the staff (p. 232). Avalos (2011) also argued that the PLC should look for non-formal learning opportunities and strive to engage all the teachers in learning from one another; thus, the school administrators should foster in-service learning. The professional learning community contributes to sharing experiences among teachers, and PLC develops their potential within professional development. Members of the professional learning community: school administrators, teachers and staff can use the potential of the workplace. The members of PLC can organise their workplace learning and thus promote professional development formally or informally without attracting outside facilitators (Avalos, 2011, p. 12). In the scope of workplace learning, teachers can mutually develop the design of teaching as well as implement effective training for the teachers (Derri, 2015, p. 237). Teachers' training could focus critically on examining selected teachers' teaching practices in order to improve practice for the benefit of learners. Such an approach to responding to challenges in the design and implementation of changes can contribute to positive learning, organisational conditions and a culture of support instead of unhealthy competition among teachers within one organisation (Stoll et al., 2006, p. 221). Finally, the capacity of the school's PLC can have a substantial impact on learners' academic achievement and involvement in the learning process. As the result of building the school's capacity through PLC, which enhances teachers' teaching practices, the students can benefit as learners (Stroll et al., 2006). The new solutions developed by the community of learners can respond to the needs of learners that have not been appropriately addressed before. Reinvented lessons and approaches in teaching can make the schools and lessons more inclusive, contributing to every learner's academic achievement. In the Kazakhstani context, learners' academic achievement is the indicator of success in schools, including TVETIs.

PLC is the collaboration of all the community aimed to make continuous improvements in teaching practices and student outcomes and foster professional learning within a community, making it a community of learners. The whole section focused on the definition of the PLC, which draws heavily on Derri (2016), Stroll et al. (2006), and Avalos (2011), as well as its benefits for the school and the school community. The conclusion is that shared efforts of the community of learners, which is open to the contribution of every teacher or staff engaged in their inquiries, can develop and promote inclusive teaching practices in the classroom. In the Kazakhstani context, PLC is instead a new phenomenon, so the current focus of school administrators is on individual teachers and their success. The present study revealed some attributes that testify to the administrators' attitude toward individual capacity and the development of teachers. For example, there are nominations which support the individual success of teachers rather than the collaboration of teachers within and outside of schools. The study found that there are nominations as "the best teacher of the year" and "the best teacher of the school". Such a method of measuring individual teacher's achievement creates competition among teachers within schools; moreover, it can lead to teachers' unwillingness to share experience and knowledge with their colleagues as well as to unhealthy competition among them instead of uniting the community of educators which fosters the development of a standard set of values and goals at the selected college. As the concluding remark, this study argues that PLC could be a good response to the insufficient capacity of the staff for inclusive education as well, and PLC could facilitate the culture of sharing knowledge and skills among teachers, leading to better inclusive teaching practices at the selected college.

3　Methods

3.1　*Research Paradigm*
The study adopts an interpretive ontological and epistemological paradigm. The interpretative paradigm assumes that reality is a construct, multidimensional, and changing depending on different frames used by the researcher (Burton et al., 2008, p. 61). Reality is constructed through a deeper understanding of the phenomena, shared meanings, interpretations, and insights by the researchers through qualitative data.

3.2　*Research Approach*
A qualitative approach for this study has been chosen, as it allows for exploring the experiences in detail. Qualitative research begins with assumptions and the use of the interpretive framework that informs the study of the research problem. It is assumed that the researcher and the team of teachers have assumptions about inclusion and inclusive teaching practices in the Kazakhstani TVET system.

3.3　*Research Design*
This study will adopt action research as a design. Action research encourages using an objective perspective combined with active intervention (Burton et al., 2008, p. 121). It employs a series of interventions, and its nature is an iterative process which promotes the initiatives to get the desired outcome by the researcher and

research. As an intervention, it consists of a series of connected lessons which can be reshaped due to the data gathered from previous lessons, and the intervention could be applied iteratively to address the literature further and shape the conceptual framework. There are different types of action research; however, for this study, collaborative action research was found to be more relevant and appropriate.

Collaborative-Action-Research (CAR) as a research design has been employed by the researcher in this research. CAR is the process which consists of identifying the issue to be addressed, forming a plan to solve the problem, collecting the data which reflects the data on the effects of the action, reflecting on the results of the action and creating actions to be taken (Levin & Rock, 2003, p. 136). Collaborative action research requires the collaboration of teachers and be goal-oriented in order to produce changes as insiders of the teaching process (Campbell, 2013, p. 1).

3.4 *Data Collection and Procedure*

The research data has been collected in four phases of the Action Research cycle, i.e. Planning, Observation, Action and Reflection, as Burton et al. (2008) suggested using CAR consisting of four stages (p. 133). Figure 8.1 shows the stages of CAR.

FIGURE 8.1   Collaborative action research cycle

The first step of action research requires describing the context and situation and identifying the problem (Goodnough, 2011, p. 8). As the problem is identified, then, the collaborative group plans the action to be applied; the next step is connected with the action or intervention, and the last step is to reflect on practice, make conclusions and make plans for the following action if necessary (Goodnough, 2011, p. 8). Burton et al. (2008) argued that reflection of actions applied provoke reflective dialogue and encourage generating evidence from experiences (p.126). Reflections follow actions, and actions follow reflections, thus making the research process systematic (p. 126).

3.5 *Data Collection Instruments*

3.5.1 Choosing a Research Site

This study used a purposeful sampling strategy. In this case, the researcher purposefully selected a research site, TVETI. More specifically, one of the TVETIs of Astana has been chosen as a research site. The site is one of the colleges that delivers TVET education to adult students in an inclusive environment, and it has adults with disabilities in its classes.

3.5.2 Recruiting Participants for CAR

Purposeful sampling has been used in this study. Sampling is defined as a strategy that helps understand the research question's central phenomenon (Creswell, 2014). In qualitative research, the researcher purposefully identifies the participants and the sites that can provide the necessary information (Creswell & Clark, 2007, p.112). Purposeful sampling means that the researchers *intentionally select the participants who have experience with the central phenomenon* (Creswell & Clark, 2007, p. 112

In the number of purposeful strategies, the group of TVET teachers and adults with disabilities, as students, has been chosen in one of the Kazakhstani TVET colleges described above. The sampling requirement was that only one group, which included students with disabilities, was chosen. The group under study has been mainstream, including adults with disabilities as students as well as other students who do not have any special educational needs, and they were the majority of the group. This study considered students who are 18 years old or older to be adults.

The criteria for the group of five teachers within TVET College have also been purposeful. Five teachers teaching to the selected group of students have been chosen. The study set the most important criteria for them as having inclusive teaching experience.

The collaborative action research team performed the Professional Learning Community (PLC). PLC is widely acknowledged as a capacity-building instrument for the emerging challenges in teaching within educational organisations. The concept of PLC has been acknowledged as the critical strategy for achieving teacher involvement in collaborative learning and teaching and capacity-building of educational institutions (Stoll et al., 2006; Louis et al., 1996; Derri et al., 2015).

3.5.3 Data Analysis

The different sets of data, i.e., one-on-one interviews, focus-group interviews, minutes of discussion and group-interpretative meetings, diaries, and observation data, were analyzed through an inductive qualitative data analysis process. The analysis included reading and coding the data, developing the data categories, and deriving themes from the data to generate the findings.

Data was analysed in two stages. Firstly, by the action research team during the action research process and, secondly, by the researcher after the action research process has been completed. During the action research, the data was analysed jointly with the research group. After each action research stage, the data was analysed through the Group Interpretative Method. The group interpretative method means going through the data with the research team to reflect on the process and make conclusions. At the end of every meeting, the researcher read aloud the agenda, objectives, and plans and verified them by all the meeting participants. Data analysis was conducted to systematise all the collected data and give meaning to the data. In order to get insights into the data, the data was grouped according to their meaning. The meaning is derived from the patterns, similarities, connections and relationships. As Bengtsson (2016) suggests, the texts are usually reduced, and then the data is grouped according to meaning and categories to understand the data in inductive content analysis (p. 8). In other words, inductive content analysis is an approach which sticks to the words and themes aimed to give meaning as well interpret results. In this study, the different sets of data were identified with codes, then those codes were labeled with themes and the latter was converted into structured sets of data deriving from the study.

3.5.4 Ethical Considerations

All the required documents, including certificates of CITI Training courses, were submitted to the IREC of Nazarbayev University, after which permission to conduct research was granted. The gatekeepers upon receiving the letter, granted access to the selected TVET College. All the participants were recruited on voluntary basis. To ensure, confidentiality and anonymity, the name of the college and all participants were anonymized.

3.5.5 Trustworthiness

Moser and Korstjens, (2018) suggested for maintaining trustworthiness it is of paramount importance to consider the issues of credibility, transferability, dependability and confirmability. Credibility was addressed through triangulation of the data derived from the study. All the data derived from the interviews in the form of scripts of the interviews was sent to the interviewed participants for checking whether the interpretation was the same what they had meant.

Transferability of this study was achieved by following a systematic data collection process. On the other hand, dependability of this study was achieved by aligning the process of data collection and analysis with the requirements of CAR. Confirmability of the study was achieved by constant interaction with the participants of the study. The researcher made summary after each interview and got confirmation of the data with the participants to avoiding researcher's any biases.

4 Findings

4.1 *Experiences of Participants during CAR*

The study revealed that all the teachers who participated in the CAR had positive attitude towards CAR after the research. They asserted that CAR was interesting experience and it produced impact on their teaching practices. The data from the study asserted that the teachers started to design and adapt their own teaching practices towards the needs of all the students in their classrooms. In addition, the teachers started to pay more attention to the preparation to the lessons. In other words, the teachers acquired a habit of making some research of their own teaching practices. For example, one of the teachers supported this and said:

> I think for me, as the person who probably will work in education, it was interesting experience and I reconsidered my attitude on my teaching strategies and it is possible to teach to students with disabilities differently.

Change of teaching practices was stressed by another teacher and stated:

> Well the research was very good for me. In terms of observing the lessons. I liked that students started to unlock their potential they started to work better than before it.

Some teachers asserted that CAR provided them opportunity for re-considering their teaching practices. During the CAR, they had choices for choosing the teaching strategies and the content of each lesson. Such opportunity for choice was appreciated by the CAR teachers. For instance, one of the teachers said:

> actually, it was the first experience for me, to be honest. I liked that I had the choice how to teach, the topic of the lesson. There was a big opportunity to choose anything else. I think there are enormous choices, so I liked them very much. To be honest. We chose the teams, teaching strategies and tried them. I attended the lessons of other teachers I should have attended before but we did not. We tried team teaching with two teachers as well.

The teachers also appreciated that observing one another's lessons geared them for developing new inclusive teaching practices. For instance, one of the teachers said:

> I observed my colleagues' lessons as we say exchange of experience and we evaluated their teaching and my teaching. I thought, I need to try another inclusive teaching practice for the next lesson and show it to the colleagues.

This study seemed to indicate that inclusion had to be promoted by administration at the selected college. Management should not push teachers to promote inclusive education practices but it must support teachers. As the testimony of that, one of the teachers said:

> Once the deputy director required me and the student with disability to develop a social project and write the whole social project proposal to the city contest in two days. She explained, we must submit a proposal by the municipal and she just got the letter requiring participation. We had only two days, we could do that because we had experience in participating in CAR and had understanding of inclusion. Moreover, we were rewarded as the authors of the second best project on the city level. It was tough and additional workload for me. I felt pressure from deputy to director, administration and in terms of power and time constraint but we could. Now, I understand that participation in CAR build my capacity as the teacher and innovator in my field and administration of the college as well as municipal know that.

This study found out that the teachers who participated at the CAR had positive impression and experience about the research. They stressed the importance of interaction between them such as observing the lesson which lead to development of inclusive teaching practices. The teachers also had positive feedback on the research because previously passive students became active and they unlocked their potential during the research. Observation of students' achievement books revealed that previously underrepresented students got better grades and they participated more actively. CAR changed the teachers' attitude towards their own inclusive teaching practices.

4.2 Skills Acquired during the CAR

The study has revealed that all the teachers acquired the skills associated with teaching to students with diverse educational needs. Those skills required planning the lesson, teaching as well as soft skills such as establishing effective communication. They also acquired not only research and collaborative skills. For instance, one of the teachers stated:

> Yes, yes, I learnt to listen and hear other teachers because I went one way the other teacher went the other way. What teaching practices he applied could be applied in other lessons too I mean. We can assign differentiated tasks. We can distribute lesson material in advance as the English teacher did. She distributed the assignment to students with disabilities in advance to allow them do it. The most important in my perspective is to be able to hear, listen and see. To see not teacher' mistakes but what benefit or good can be given to students. We do not have to focus on teacher's mistake because people can make mistakes by nature. It is necessary to get the best of every lesson and not bad staff.

The teachers also learnt listening not only to teachers but to students as well. As one of the teachers supported her statement with her evidence and asserted:

> Yes, I learnt, you need to understand your group at the 1-st of September or after one month with them to conduct mini sobranie (gathering together from the Russian language) to ask the students what they want to see themselves. It is necessary to listen to students and not to coerce them do what you want.

Ability to understand the students' needs and tailoring the learning staff keeping the students in mind was central teachers at the selected college. For instance, one of the teachers said:

> I acquired a lot during the lessons. I tried to adapt various teaching practices make them different and use them. Yes, for example talking with the

students with disabilities then as I said there are a lot of ways of explaining the lesson yes, orally and the connection between the student and the teacher. We call it collaboration as well.

While some teachers considered the skills like collaboration and establishing communication, the other teacher considered working in inclusive education environment as the skill. For instance, the teacher said:

> prior to this research, I did not know that inclusive education exists and it is possible to work deeper with students with special educational needs. I leant the skill that students with special educational needs can learn and they can understand the teachers and others.

The findings of the study asserted that the CAR teachers acquired the skills which helped them establish communication both among themselves and students. Moreover, the teachers seemed to acquire the skill of teaching to students with diverse educational needs in one classroom. As the findings suggested, some of the teachers did not have teaching skills to students with disabilities before. After the research, such teachers learnt how to teach to students with special needs.

4.3   *How CAR Changed Teaching Practices: Every Teacher's Voice*

The study found out that all CAR teachers changed their teaching practices during the CAR and after the research. They asserted that the CAR provided them a chance to look at their own teaching practices as outsiders due to multiple observations of the lessons. They stressed that different stages of CAR gave them chances to enhance their teaching practices and showed them the room for further development. For instance, one of the teachers said:

> Such research could be conducted not only with the students with disabilities. You can conduct such research with any students regardless of his health and it will be a push for the student and the research will give start to such students.

Analysis of data revealed that other teacher participant of the CAR had positive feelings about CAR and as the testimony, the teacher said:

> Ok in CAR I attended more than five lessons observed how the teachers taught them, their teaching practices. I observed the students with special educational needs who unlocked their potential when they worked

with others, their showed the ability to work and their capacity grew. Besides of observations we discussed after the lessons in group interpretative meetings with teachers and proposed how to improve the lesson and some teaching practices and how to conduct the next lesson aimed to impact on engaging students with special educational needs and to make the lesson more interesting.

Analysis of teacher reflections also pointed that they wished promotion of CAR on the whole school, department and entire education system. For instance, the teacher expressed her belief and said:

> it is necessary that such research could be applied and the CAR is required in our country. We can apply, develop and to research it further.

Evidence from data also indicated that CAR produced positive impact on teachers in terms of teachers' transformation towards achieving the best in their teachings and changed their attitude towards teaching practices. CAR made them focused on preparation to the lesson or planning stage. For instance, one of the teachers said:

> I thought a lot, contemplated and sought for such attitudes towards inclusive teaching practice. The teacher must have the goal to seek for knowledge here. And should not be like for example, tomorrow I have the lesson I need to distribute the cards, or something to students during the lesson and that is it. No, you cannot do like this. The teacher must prepare for the lesson and make some research for practice and it is obligatory. The teacher must be fully prepared taking into consideration all the aspects around.

5 Discussion of Findings

5.1 *Experiences of CAR Participants during CAR*

Forssten Seiser (2019) argued that participation in CAR would result in promoting non-hierarchic partnership and trustworthy relations among the participants in the Action Research practice (p. 13). Thus, Action Research makes a positive impact on teachers as well as affects teachers' teaching practices because the teachers make stages of Action Research part of their daily practice in the future after the research. Leeman et al. (2018) argued that teachers learn to develop a more elaborate and shared view of teaching practices, and they learn to respond to different views on teaching strategies during Action Research (p. 13). Thus, the steps of CAR, such as planning the lessons or actions, reflection, and observation, enhance the teachers' teaching process to teachers after the study. This study has found that the teachers who participated in the CAR had learnt how to design lessons responsive to various learning needs of students and acquired research skills such as looking for various solutions to challenges in their daily teaching practice. The teachers also learnt to accept and give positive feedback on further improvement of the lessons.

5.2   Skills Acquired during the CAR

Sampson (2020) argued that Action Research is more ethical form of research which allows participants to receive from it and give to participants via it because it works with participants (p. 13). In other words, Action Research is the form of conducting research where participants, the teachers, conduct research because they build their own capacity, implement their efforts and skills, then continue their teacher research and learn from it due to engagement in it. This claim is in line with Banegas and Cad (2020) that the teacher research is carried *by teachers and for teachers in their own* unique *teaching contexts* (p. 1). As the concluding remark, Action Research enables the teachers to pose questions, and look for answers to them, which leads to producing context-bound knowledge as the response to the emerging issues and questions, and all these endeavours contribute to developing skills for teachers required in their contexts.

The literature discussed above supports the findings of this study. The CAR teachers acquired skills that were appropriate and useful in their own context. As in the literature, during Action Research, some teachers could learn inclusive teaching skills from the research. Thus, the CAR built teachers' teaching capacity and their communication skills, which were developed during the study.

5.3   How CAR Changed Teaching Practices: Every Teacher's Voice

Research conducted by the teachers fosters change in teacher society and teaching practices by allowing the knowledge flow and democracy of knowledge as well and Action Research promotes teachers' communities of practices. Banegas and Cad (2020) argued that Action Research facilitates and strengthens the *knowledge flow and knowledge democracy to transform the society which produces, critiques, and uses its own generated knowledge* (p. 15). Heissenberger and Matischek-Jauk (2020) asserted that Action Research can be considered as the learning environment which allows teachers to make concrete conclusions in regard to future planning and conducting the lessons (p. 574). In other words, action research allows teachers to transfer the skills they acquired during their studies in the future.

The study has demonstrated that there is a strong tendency to improve the teaching practices of teachers and enhance the teaching practices of all the teachers who participated in the CAR. The CAR provided a platform where the teachers were enabled to reflect on their own teaching practices, discuss the existing challenges and collaboratively develop new teaching approaches which would be beneficial to both students and teachers. Different stages of CAR enhance daily teaching practices, and those teaching practices widen access to a more meaningful education for students at the selected college after conducting research in other contexts.

6 Conclusion

It is evident from the study that CAR has an impact on how teachers perceive, plan and understand their teaching and learning practices. Various practices have been inculcated into their teaching processes, i.e. reflexivity and criticality toward one's practice. Collaboration between teachers was enhanced, culminating in the teachers learning from one another. CAR created a platform for teacher engagement about inclusion, and thus, the meaning and practice of inclusion were illuminated. The study has demonstrated that teacher development and professional learning could be more effective if they are teacher-led. As a result, it is strongly recommended that action research be part of pre-service teacher preparation and in-service training. It could also be incorporated into teacher attestation, developmental appraisal systems, and policies. While this study was conducted in one college, findings could be valuable for colleges with similar contexts. We are mindful that action research is a new phenomenon in Kazakhstan and the Central Asian region, so developing it as part of the school/college institutional culture might take longer. However, this study forms a foundational basis for discussions about teacher-led action research and its relevance and significance in the Kazakhstani school context.

References

Avalos, B. (2011). Teacher professional development in teaching and teacher education over ten years. *Teaching and Teacher Education, 27*(1), 10–20.

Baitokayeva, L. (2019). *Teachers' understanding of action research: A qualitative case study of a specialized school in Kazakhstan* (Master's thesis, Nazarbayev University Graduate School of Education).

Banegas, D. L., & Cad, A. C. (2020). Knowledge flow in Argentinian English language teaching: A look at citation practices and perceptions. *Educational Action Research,* 1–18.

Bengtsson, M. (2016). How to plan and perform a qualitative study using content analysis. *Nursing Plus Open, 2,* 8–14.

Burton, N., Drundrett, M., & Jones, M. (2008). *Doing your education research project.* Sage.

Campbell, K. H. (2013). A call to action: Why we need more practitioner research. *Democracy & Education, 21*(2). http://democracyeducationjournal.org/cgi/viewcontent.cgi?article=1133&context=home

Creswell, J., & Clark, V. (2007). *Designing and conducting mixed methods research.* Sage Publications, Inc.

Creswell, J. W. (2013). *Qualitative inquiry & research design: Choosing among the five approaches* (3rd ed.). Sage.

Creswell, J. W. (2014). *Educational research: Planning, conducting, and evaluating quantitative and qualitative research.* Pearson Education Limited.

Derri, V., Vasiliadou, O., & Kioumourtzoglou, E. (2015). The effects of a short-term professional development program on physical education teachers' behavior and students' engagement in learning. *European Journal of Teacher Education, 38*(2), 234–262.

Efron, S. E., & Ravit, R. (2013). *Action research in education.* The Guilford Press.

Elliott, J. (1994). Research on teachers' knowledge and action research. *Educational Action Research, 2*(1), 133–137.

Forssten Seiser, A. (2019). Exploring enhanced pedagogical leadership: An action research study involving Swedish principals. *Educational Action Research,* 1–16.

Goodnough, K. (2011). Taking action in science classrooms through collaborative action research. Springer Science & Business Media.

Hart, E., & Bond, M. (1995). *Action research for health and social care: A guide to practice.* Open University Press.

Heissenberger, K., & Matischek-Jauk, M. (2020). "It's worth it": Practitioner research as a tool of professional learning: Starting points, conclusions, and benefits from the perspective of teacher-students. *Educational Action Research, 28*(4), 561–578.

Hoyle, E., & John, P. (1995). *Professional knowledge and professional practice.* Cassell.

Leeman, Y., Van Koeven, E., & Schaafsma, F. (2018). Inter-professional collaboration in action research. *Educational Action Research, 26*(1), 9–24.

Levin, B. B., & Rock, T. C. (2003). The effects of collaborative action research on preservice and experienced teacher partners in professional development schools. *Journal of Teacher Education, 54*(2), 135–149.

Li, Y. L. (2008). Teachers in action research: Assumptions and potentials. *Educational Action Research, 16*(2), 251–260.

Louis, K. S., & Marks, H. (1998). Does professional community affect the classroom? Teachers' work and student experiences in restructuring schools. http://files.eric.ed.gov/fulltext/ED412634.pdf

Moser, A., & Korstjens, I. (2018). Series: Practical guidance to qualitative research. Part 3: Sampling, data collection, and analysis. *European Journal of General Practice, 24*(1), 9–18.

Nagibova, G. (2019). Professional development: The challenges of action research implementation in Kazakhstan. *International Academy Journal Web of Scholar, 2*(9 (39)), 17–24.

Sampson, R. J. (2020). Evolving understandings of practitioner action research from the inside. *Educational Action Research,* 1–15.

Stoll, L., Bolam, R., McMahon, A., Wallace, M., & Thomas, S. (2006). Professional learning communities: A review of the literature. *Journal of Educational Change, 7*(4), 221–258.

CHAPTER 9

Teacher Leadership in Kazakhstan

Tsediso Michael Makoelle

Abstract

The curriculum reforms in Kazakhstan have seen an increase in the involvement of teachers in many education and school-related processes. However, teachers are still subjected to too much administrativism and managerialism from the Ministry of Education, and as a result, they play less role in decision-making. According to Kanayeva (2019), confirmed by Qanay, Courtney & Nam (2021), to improve schools teachers need to lead learning and innovation within and outside their schools. This chapter analyses the role of teachers as leaders in a Kazakhstani schooling context, how teachers conceptualize and enact teacher leadership, and the challenges they experience in this regard. Some lessons are drawn from the review on enhancing teacher leadership in Kazakhstan.

Keywords

collaborative culture – teacher leadership – distributed leadership – school leadership – school management

1 Introduction

Teacher leadership has become critical in leadership studies in post-soviet education systems such as Kazakhstan. According to Tajik & Yesselbayev (2024), leadership filtered through the government and the schools. As a result, school leadership was part of the bureaucratic order. Kazakhstani, thirty-one years after the fall of the Soviet Union, the education leadership still bears the hallmarks of the past bureaucratic leadership system. The leadership structure only offers a little space for the teachers, who are at the bottom of the leadership hierarchy to some extent, to make independent decisions. The leadership model is heavily based on principles of positional leadership and the execution of power. However, Kazakhstan has embarked on critical curriculum and other secondary education reforms that need the role of teachers to be more active

© TSEDISO MICHAEL MAKOELLE, 2025 | DOI:10.1163/9789004726345_010

participants rather than passive. Therefore, this chapter poses the following research questions as a guiding compass for the discussions in this chapter:

- What is the state of teacher leadership in Kazakhstan?
- Which challenges (if any) and opportunities are presented by teacher leadership in Kazakhstani schools?
- How can teacher leadership in Kazakhstan (if necessary) be enhanced?

A systematic literature review was conducted to answer these questions. The chapter conceptualizes school and teacher leadership both internationally and locally. It then discusses the frameworks and models of teacher leadership and outlines the benefits and challenges of leadership. The chapter concludes by providing the lessons learned from the review, presenting the conceptual framework of teacher leadership, and making recommendations for enhancing teacher leadership in Kazakhstan.

2 Method of Review

This review investigated the state of teacher leadership in Kazakhstan, it challenges and opportunities as well as how it could be enhanced.

The review was mapped to achieving the following objectives:

- Through literature, explore the state of teacher leadership in Kazakhstan;
- Identify (if any) challenges and opportunities presented by teacher leadership in Kazakhstani schools;
- To make recommendations based on the review on how teacher leadership in Kazakhstan (if necessary) could be enhanced.

The criteria used to select the literature were guided by the availability of supportive empirical evidence. Speculative literature was deliberately excluded. While the literature was reviewed for a study focused on leadership and teacher leadership, some of the reviewed work was inclined towards teacher education in general as closely related disciplines such as teacher professional learning and teachers' professional development.

I consulted several databases, such as Eric, Scopus, and Google Scholar. Further sources of relevant information were internationally accredited journals, including Educational Management & Administration and Teaching and Teacher Education. I also consulted the Nazarbayev University library and perused books, articles, theses, and electronic sources for relevant, up-to-date literature on the topic.

3 The Notions of School Leadership

Before we can understand the notion of school leadership, it is essential to unpack the concept of leadership. Although there are different interpretations of leadership regarding this concept, I share my view with that of Bush (2014), who contends that leadership is the influence a person may have toward others to direct their thoughts and actions toward accomplishing a specific goal. In his work, Bush (2014) quotes Gunter (2004), who postulates that the labels used to describe the field of leadership have changed from school administration to educational management and then to educational leadership. I beg to differ with Gunter's assertion; educational administration, management, leadership, and governance are the main components of school leadership and have always co-existed, but the differences between the four must be clearly defined. The field of school leadership is composed of these critical areas as depicted in Figure 9.1.

Although these components could be considered separate entities, they must be considered interwoven, and there is a thin line between them. While leadership is part of the four components, it differs from the three. The difference is that leadership does not necessarily require a position (it is non-positional) as it can be exercised from influence. However, management, administration and governance are always exercised within a particular position of authority. Although leadership can be exercised within management, administration, and governance, there is no direct link as we could have school managers, administrators, and governors who do not influence as such do not have leadership. More often than not, school managers, administrators and governors rely on their authority position to direct school activities. While school leadership refers to the influence the leader has to direct others to accomplish organisational goals, school management represents the daily activities that direct activities of the organisation. School management is planning (determining school goals and objectives), organising (mobilising both human and physical

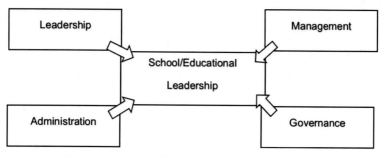

FIGURE 9.1 Components of school leadership

resources to achieve school goals and objectives), leading (distribution of roles and functions to subordinates) and controlling (monitoring and evaluation).

While school administration may be misconstrued as school management or leadership, it is a distinct part of the two. School administration is the arm of school leadership that supports the decision-making of school leaders and managers through recording, safekeeping, and sharing information. In most school contexts, these administrators are called school secretaries and clerks. School administrators do not make decisions but safely keep and inform stakeholders about the decisions of school leaders, managers, and governors. Therefore, their role is to process decisions rather than make them. School governance, on the other hand, denotes making decisions about school policies, rules and procedures that impact the general well-being of the school as an organisation and its immediate school community.

In this chapter, a particular focus is paid to the leadership as influence exercised by teachers who might or might not be in a position of authority. This notion is referred to as teacher leadership.

4   The Notion of Teacher Leadership

The notion of teacher leadership remains elusive. However, there are common elements in the way teacher leadership as a concept is understood. In their review, York-Barr and Duke (2004) associate teacher leadership with the process through which teachers become leaders because they have mastered the art of teaching and learning and contribute to the general effectiveness and improvement of the school. According to them, teacher leadership is more focused on school improvement as it determines how well teachers, as leaders of teaching and learning, may influence the quality of their teaching and thus impact student achievement. According to Lieberman, Saxl and Miles (2000), not only should teacher leaders be effective teachers, but they should also be able to lead and guide others. In their work, Nguyen, Harris and Ng (2019) postulate that the definition of teacher leadership is varied. Contrasting their definition with that of Wenner & Campbell (2017), which focuses on teacher leadership outside the classroom, theirs is premised on the following principles: being able to lead within and beyond the classroom; being part of and contributing to the community of students, teachers and leaders; being in the position to influence others to improve the education practice; able to take responsibility for achieving the outcomes of leadership. However, it is interesting that in the dimensions of teacher leadership emerging from their literature review about teacher leadership definitions of teacher leadership, we focused on the following areas: teacher leadership as influence rather than position, as the exercise of agency by teacher leaders to effect change and innovation; as influence beyond the classroom and being part of school collaborative culture; as leading teaching and learning excellence; as the influence of student outcomes and achievements and finally as impacting on school effectiveness and improvement.

5 The Nature and Practice of Teacher Leadership

Based on the literature review, this chapter's conceptual framework for teacher leadership is based on the following cardinal pillars: leadership, pedagogy, agency and change, community engagement, and school effectiveness and improvements.

5.1 *Leadership*

Most literature suggests that teacher leadership is an exercise of influence rather than a position of authority. It comes when one teacher's work in one or several school areas becomes so influential that it starts to set an example to other teachers and thus become a role model for an effective teacher who contributes to the improved outcomes of students and the general improvement of the school. Frost (2019) contends that such an influence on the teacher's role should be divorced from the hierarchical management structures of the school. Frost (2019) further mentions that the nature of teacher leadership requires a distributed leadership model as it allows teachers to take charge of their decision-making process, and this may be in the position to influence critical school processes. The networks teachers form with and through others create a collaborative culture, which may lead to teacher innovation and, thus, self-directed improvement (Frost, 2016).

5.2 *Agency and Change*

Teachers are at the heart of school development, and the teachers must implement any change at the school. Various scholars believe that change at the

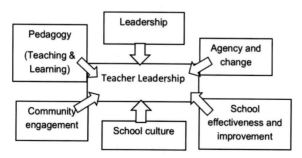

FIGURE 9.2   Conceptual framework for teacher leadership

school could be difficult to implement if teachers are not directly involved. McCay et al. (2001) postulate that teacher leadership enables a collaborative culture that can be used for reform, transformation and change. This view is echoed by Makoelle and Makhalemele (2020), who posit that teachers were agents of change who contributed immensely to the political transformation of the education system post-apartheid through their agency. Similarly, Cherian & Daniel (2008) believe teacher leaders have confidence in their abilities as change agents who positively influence school environments.

5.3 *School Effectiveness and Improvement*

According to Harris (2003), school improvement has been associated with the school leader, but according to Harris, such "heroic" leadership forms which are centred on one person have proved fruitless. As such, distributed leadership has emerged, which offers leadership opportunities at the teacher level, "teacher leadership". Muijs and Harris (2003) postulate that not only doe's teacher leadership impact school improvement but also on teacher motivation and retention. As a result, the change and improvement at the school become teacher-led thus leading to teacher empowerment (Muijs & Harris, 2006). According to Poekert (2016), teacher leadership could be an appropriate platform for professional development as teacher leaders can influence improvement and change that may directly or indirectly impact the skills, knowledge, attitudes and competencies of other teachers.

5.4 *School Culture*

While teacher leadership could offer hope for an effective school, Muijs & Harris (2006) indicate that the school culture has to set the right conditions for teacher leadership to thrive, several aspects such as trust and support, structures that are clear and transparency, the head teacher that enables a conducive environment for teacher leadership that promotes teacher innovation and teacher professional growth. Cansoy and Parlar (2017, p. 9) identify four school cultural dimensions which are critical for teacher leadership, these are:

The analysis of the four dimensions indicated that the support, task and success-oriented school culture enabled collaboration and ensured that teacher leadership thrives. This view is consistent with the views of Yusof, Osman, & Noor (2016), who contend that collaboration enables teacher professionalism and goal setting.

5.5 *Community Engagement*

Conan-Simpson (2021) postulates that teacher leadership not only benefits teachers and students but also has a direct bearing on parental involvement

TABLE 9.1   Cultural dimensions for teacher leadership (Adapted from Cansoy & Parlar, 2017)

support-oriented culture	emphasis on collaboration, personal relationships, and solving problems. The ability to mobilise, work with and through others
task-oriented culture	Ensure the attainment of organisational goals and objectives. It relies on the expertise of teachers, which equals leadership
success-oriented culture	Completion of tasks is followed with a reward. Because teacher want to be successful, they may engage in professional development that may enable them to be successful in their roles.
bureaucratic culture	Formal procedures and accountability measures. Because rules and procedures are emphasised, creativity and innovation could be negatively affected

in a school, as teacher leaders have a way of enabling conversations and activities that foster positive teacher-parent relationships. It is further stated that teacher leaders' influence could spill over to the wider community, including the education departments, which may impact policy development. Teacher leaders may influence school-community partnerships that directly or indirectly benefit teachers, parents, students and the general school community.

5.6   *Pedagogy*

The literature indicates that teacher leaders are pedagogical leaders who have mastered the art of teaching and learning, and pedagogies inform their social justice and equity practices and are likely to influence learning environments significantly. They may do so as individuals but also as communities of practice (Campbell et al., 2022) or professional learning communities (Moller, 2006). However, Male and Palaiologou (2015) caution that teacher leadership is not only concerned about teaching and learning but goes beyond as it encompasses aspects of social capital. Drawing from Freire's (1986) conception of "praxis", they believe pedagogical leadership entails reflection and action aimed at transforming social relations.

6   Teacher Leadership in Kazakhstan

Kazakhstan, as one of the post-soviet countries, has inherited the leadership model based on the top-down bureaucratic approach (Khoroshash, 2016), which centralises power and does not allow teachers autonomy. An important fact to note is that mainstream and ungraded schools and Nazarbayev

Intellectual School (NIS) present two streams of school leadership discourses. The mainstream and ungraded schools are riddled with leadership dilemmas characterized by bureaucratic practices. On the other hand, the NIS schools which have adopted international best practices are the ones that are likely to promote leadership by teachers.

Since the implementation of educational reforms in Kazakhstan, most studies have focused on the role of the teacher and the contributions teachers can make to modernising education in Kazakhstan. Some focus on teachers' professional learning and teacher leadership, which are about teachers and agents of change and reform. For instance, Ayubayeva (2018) postulates that teacher collaboration was critical for teachers' professional learning to address the legacy of the inflexible and bureaucratic soviet school leadership model, which constrained teacher autonomy and limited their decision-making. However, according to Yakavets, Frost and Khoroshash (2015), the leadership capacity in Kazakhstani schools has yet to be fully realized. According to Amirova (2016), teachers are afraid to exercise their leadership as this could be misconstrued as trying to undermine the positional leaders, so they may not be able to take the initiative and lead.

To enable teacher participation in curriculum and school reform, most authors believe teacher leadership could be a vehicle to achieve these ideals. For instance, Qanay and Frost (2022) conducted a study that explored how teacher leadership may contribute to educational reforms and the transformation of teacher learning in Kazakhstan, given the modernisation and internationalisation of education. The study postulates that teacher leadership would occur in the context of schools as learning organisations, which may enable teachers' professionalism and reflective practice. As a result, teacher leadership in Kazakhstan would serve as a vehicle for school improvement and, thus, school effectiveness (Kanayeva, 2019). However, according to Qanay and Frost (2023), building a culture that promotes teacher leadership will not happen overnight, and there are important conditions to achieve this. They believe that teacher leadership should be adopted as a model in schools but the following were important:

- There was a need for teachers to provide professional learning opportunities in schools;
- Non-positional leadership was necessary to change leadership culture and practices;
- Transformational leadership by school leaders might go a long way in enabling teacher leadership;
- Non-positional leadership may enable teachers' innovation, which is crucial for teacher leadership;

- Non-positional leadership could enable the application of constructivist pedagogy, which is student-centred;
- Collaborative school culture was necessary for enablement of teacher leadership and
- Schools need principals to adopt strategies to promote teacher leaders.

In some studies, evidence of the significance of some of the conditions has been collected. For instance, in their study by Qanay, Courtney and Nan (2021), it was found that teachers who were from schools with collaborative cultures capacity to enact teacher leadership was enhanced. On the other hand, Makoelle (2024) said that a distributed leadership approach was a prerequisite for distributed responsibilities and decentralized power to teachers if Kazakhstan redressed the centralized and bureaucratic decision-making model, thus enabling teacher learning and collaboration.

7 Lessons Learned

The state of teacher leadership is presented using the conceptual framework gleaned from the literature review in this chapter.

Non-positional leadership was crucial to teacher leadership. Findings from this review suggest that non-positional teacher leadership was important as teachers are better placed to implement educational reforms in Kazakhstan. The non-positional leadership allows teachers to move away from positional leadership, which in most cases still bears the hallmarks of the hierarchical and top-down leadership model of soviet education. The review also demonstrated that school principals and co-leaders must create a conducive school environment and climate that may promote teacher leadership. The transformational leadership model is a better place to enhance teacher leadership in a Kazakhstani school context. It is important to note from the review that distributed leadership is recommended as it could decentralise power and enable teachers to be part of the decision-making process.

The review also shows that teachers can be agents of change. In this review, evidence is mounting that teacher participation was important in the constraining, inflexible education structure. Thus, the application of their agency would enable them to navigate the effects of bureaucracy. Their exercise of agency would enable them to develop a sense of identity as leaders in their own right and thus influence the change and transformation that is needed to sustain a new democratic teacher leadership regime.

This review reveals that teacher leadership is associated with school improvement and effectiveness. It has also been confirmed that teacher leadership in Kazakhstan could contribute significantly to school improvement processes, given the curriculum and other educational reforms.

The review suggests that collaborative culture is a precondition for enabled teacher leadership. It became evident that collaborative culture was a necessity in Kazakhstani schools if teacher leadership was to become a reality.

The review suggests that the school and the community could benefit immensely from teacher leaders. In this review, there was scanty research about teacher leadership and communities; it is evident from the international literature that this was significant. More studies are needed in Kazakhstan to explore this topic. However, in the review, it became evident that teacher leadership goes beyond the classroom. It touches on aspects of school community building through collaborative networks and partnerships.

The current modenisation of curriculum and change of teaching and learning to student centred model would benefit from teacher leadership as highly effective and functional teacher leaders (as pedagogical teacher leaders) could act as role models for curriculum reform implementation and thus indirectly contribute to the professional development and mentoring of their peers thus changing and transforming teaching and learning practices.

8 Conclusion

This chapter has reviewed the state of teacher leadership in Kazakhstan. It provided a comprehensive account of studies that were conducted in this area. The international literature was used to develop a conceptual framework for understanding teacher leadership in Kazakhstan. The chapter, therefore, contributes knowledge about teacher leadership understandings and enactment in the Kazakhstani context. However, teacher leadership in an evolving area in Kazakhstan, the lessons learned from this review, and the recommendations might need to be more conclusive as Kazakhstani teacher education and educational processes are undergoing rapid changes. The whole of secondary education in Kazakhstan is undergoing reform, with teachers gradually being placed at the centre of the implementation of educational reforms. However, it must be understood that although teachers are beginning to be part of educational reforms, their ability to challenge bureaucratic structures and influence decisions is still very limited. However, the chapter contributes to the discussions and debates about teacher leadership in Kazakhstan.

References

Amirova, B. (2016). Teacher Leadership. In *ICIE 2016 Proceedings of the 4th international conference on innovation and entrepreneurship: ICIE2016* (p. 411). Academic Conferences and publishing limited.

Ayubayeva, N. (2018). *Teacher collaboration for professional learning: Case studies of three schools in Kazakhstan* [Doctoral dissertation].

Bush, T., & Glover, D. (2014). School leadership models: What do we know?. *School Leadership & Management, 34*(5), 553–571.

Campbell, T., Wenner, J. A., Brandon, L., & Waszkelewicz, M. (2022). A community of practice model as a theoretical perspective for teacher leadership. *International Journal of Leadership in Education, 25*(2), 173–196.

Cansoy, R., & Parlar, H. (2017). Examining the relationship between school culture and teacher leadership. *International Online Journal of Educational Sciences, 9*(2).

Cherian, F., & Daniel, Y. (2008). Principal Leadership in New Teacher Induction: Becoming Agents of Change. *International Journal of Education Policy and Leadership, 3*(2), 1–11.

Conan Simpson, J. (2021). Fostering teacher leadership in K-12 schools: A review of the literature. *Performance Improvement Quarterly, 34*(3), 229–246.

Freire, P. (1986). *Pedagogy of the oppressed.* Continuum.

Frost, D. (2016). From professional development to system change: Teacher leadership and innovation. In *Teacher leadership and professional development* (pp. 45–67). Routledge.

Frost, D. (2019). Teacher leadership and professionality. In *Oxford Research Encyclopedia of Education.*

Harris, A. (2003). Teacher leadership and school improvement. *Effective leadership for school improvement, 72–83.*

Kanayeva, G. (2019). *Facilitating teacher leadership in Kazakhstan* [Doctoral dissertation].

Khoroshash, A. (2016). *The exploration of teacher leadership at secondary schools in Kazakhstan* [Doctoral dissertation, Graduate School of Education].

Lieberman, A., Saxl, E. R., & Miles, M. B. (2000). Teacher leadership: Ideology and practice. *The Jossey-Bass Reader on Educational Leadership, 1*, 348–365.

Male, T., & Palaiologou, I. (2015). Pedagogical leadership in the 21st century: Evidence from the field. *Educational Management Administration & Leadership, 43*(2), 214–231.

Makoelle, T. M. (2024). Educational Leadership: Secondary Education Perspectives From Kazakhstan. In *Redefining educational leadership in central Asia* (pp. 37–48). Emerald Publishing Limited.

Makoelle, T. M., & Makhalemele, T. (2020). Teacher leadership in South African schools. *International Journal of Management in Education, 14*(3), 293–310.

McCay, L., Flora, J., Hamilton, A., & Riley, J. F. (2001). Reforming schools through teacher leadership: A program for classroom teachers as agents of change. *Educational Horizons, 79*(3), 135–142.

Moller, G. (2006). Teacher leadership emerges within professional learning communities. *Journal of School Leadership, 16*(5), 520–533.

Muijs, D., & Harris, A. (2003). Teacher leadership—Improvement through empowerment? An overview of the literature. *Educational Management & Administration, 31*(4), 437–448.

Muijs, D., & Harris, A. (2006). Teacher led school improvement: Teacher leadership in the UK. *Teaching and Teacher Education, 22*(8), 961–972.

Nguyen, D., Harris, A., & Ng, D. (2020). A review of the empirical research on teacher leadership (2003–2017) Evidence, patterns and implications. *Journal of Educational Administration, 58*(1), 60–80.

Poekert, P. E. (2016). Teacher leadership and professional development: Examining links between two concepts central to school improvement. *Teacher Leadership and Professional Development*, 9–28.

Qanay, G., Courtney, M., & Nam, A. (2021). Building teacher leadership capacity in schools in Kazakhstan: a mixed method study. *International Journal of Leadership in Education*, 1–27.

Qanay, G., & Frost, D. (2022). The teacher leadership in Kazakhstan initiative: Professional learning and leadership. *Professional Development in Education, 48*(3), 411–425.

Qanay, G., & Frost, D. (2023). Education reform in Kazakhstan and teacher leadership The success of education reforms depends ultimately on teachers (Darling-Hammond, 2000; OECD, 2014a; Fullan, 2016) and their capacity to partici-pate actively in reform. This requires a view of leadership as deliberate action to influence others in order to achieve common goals (Yukl, Gordon and. *Mapping Educational Change in Kazakhstan*, 173.

Tajik, M. A., & Yesselbayev, R. (2024). Educational Leadership in Post-Soviet Kazakhstan: Historical Evolution and Reconceptualization of Leadership. In *Redefining educational leadership in central Asia: Selected cases from Kazakhstan and Kyrgyzstan* (pp. 19–35). Emerald Publishing Limited.

Yakavets, N., Frost, D., & Khoroshash, A. (2017). School leadership and capacity building in Kazakhstan. *International Journal of Leadership in Education, 20*(3), 345–370.

York-Barr, J., & Duke, K. (2004). What do we know about teacher leadership? Findings from two decades of scholarship. *Review Of Educational Research, 74*(3), 255–316.

Yusof, H., Osman, M. N. A. H., & Noor, M. A. M. (2016). School culture and its relationship with teacher leadership. *International Journal of Academic Research in Business and Social Sciences, 6*(11), 272–286.

CHAPTER 10

Gender Equity and Equality in Teacher Education

Tsediso Michael Makoelle

Abstract

Gender equity has become an important topic in post-Soviet countries. This chapter, therefore, does a comprehensive systematic review of the literature to understand the nuances of gender equity in teachers' education in Kazakhstan. Through international and local literature, the notion of gender equity is conceptualized. The impact of gender inequity in teacher education is foregrounded. The chapter concludes by drawing lessons from the review about how Kazakhstan can move forward in ensuring that gender inequities in teacher education are addressed.

Keywords

feminism – gender – gender equity – gender equality – gender parity – teacher education

1 Introduction

Gender equity and equality in education have become an essential issue for most countries, including Kazakhstan. According to Vaughan (2016), the process of equalising gender can be traced back to the Universal Declaration of Human Rights, which was adopted in 1948. This led to the promulgation of other documents, such as the Convention of the Elimination of all Forms of Discrimination Against Women (CEDAR) in 1979, the Beijing Platform for Action in 1995, and the UN Security Council Resolution 1325 in 2000 on Women's Peace and Security. Recently, the Sustainable Development Goal (DSG) 5: "Achieve gender equality and empower all women and Girls" adopted in 2015 as part of Agenda 2030, has become a driving force towards gender equity and equality intersecting with DSG 4: Ensure inclusive and equitable quality education and promote lifelong learning opportunities for all, seek to ensure that gender inequality in educational opportunities was the thing of the past (Webb et al., 2017).

© TSEDISO MICHAEL MAKOELLE, 2025 | DOI:10.1163/9789004726345_011

About 143 countries have guaranteed equal rights for women and men in their constitutions. 132 legislated the marriage age at 18 and 119 for domestic violence. Then, in 125 countries, laws against sexual harassment were passed (Vaughan, 2016). However, gender inequalities persist in many countries.

The DSG 5 is set out to achieve gender equality. Although many countries have women's rights enshrined in the constitution, the reality often differs from what the rights are set to achieve. According to the UN Women (2015), as quoted in Vaughan (2016:4), in addition to the rights of women is the need for substantive equality for women, which could be achieved if three actions are taken: redressing women's socio-economic disadvantage; addressing stereotyping and violence as well as strengthening agency, voice and participation.

Kazakhstan, as a member of the international community, has also embarked on equalising opportunities between women and men; this occurs within the internationalisation of education. One area of education that has become the focus of reform is teacher education. The Ministry of Education has embarked on modernising teacher education and raising teacher education standards to make teacher education attractive to young people in Kazakhstan. Kazakhstan may not achieve its goals of ensuring the prosperity of its people without an effective teacher education system based on international practice. While Kazakhstan has achieved gender parity in some areas of the education system, the goal to achieve gender equity and equality in teacher education seems to have not yet been fully realized. In this chapter, the following question drove the arguments:

> What is the state of gender equity and equality in Kazakhstani education, particularly teacher education?

Therefore, in answering this research question, this review chapter aims to explore how gender equity and equality are conceptualised within Kazakhstan's teacher education, compare it to the international context, analyse the current state of affairs regarding gender equity and equality, and then make recommendations for the future.

2 Method of Review

This review investigated the notions of gender equity and equality within the teacher education of Kazakhstan.

The review was mapped to achieving the following objectives:
- To explore the concepts of gender equity and gender equality in teacher education;

GENDER EQUITY AND EQUALITY IN TEACHER EDUCATION

- To draw parallels of the notions about the international context;
- To recommend gender equity and equality in teacher education going forward.

The criteria used to select the literature were guided by the availability of supportive empirical evidence. Speculative literature was deliberately excluded. While the literature was reviewed for a study focused on equity and equality in teacher education, some of the reviewed work inclined towards equity and equality in education in general, as closely related disciplines such as political science, law, and sociology were considered.

I consulted several databases, such as Eric, Scopus, and Google Scholar. Further sources of relevant information were internationally accredited journals, including the International Journal of Inclusive Education. I also consulted the Nazarbayev University library and perused books, articles, theses, and electronic sources to find relevant, up-to-date literature on the topic.

3 The Notion of Gender Equity and Equality

Sanders (1995, p. 1) defines gender equity as "a set of behaviours and pieces of knowledge that permits teachers to recognize inequality in educational opportunities, to carry out specific interventions that constitute equal educational treatment and to ensure equal educational outcomes" This is echoed by Subrahmanian (2005) who characterizes the aim of gender equity as achieving both gender parity (equal participation) and gender equality (equal opportunities) regarding the Millennium Development Goals (UNESCO, 2000, p. 11). Gender equity may not be regarded as an isolated phenomenon in society; as Klein, Ortman & Friedman (2002) put it, gender equity is interwoven with other areas of social justice, such as human rights, to ensure fairness between males and females, i.e. achieving equitable outcomes for both by providing equal opportunities, decrease gender stereotyping in decision-making and removal of discriminatory practices. According to Magno and Silova (2007), the purpose of gender equity is to ensure "gender mainstreaming," which is an attempt to infuse gender-sensitive policies into the country's development policies that can ensure that gender does not become an impediment to progress at all levels and sectors of the economy and social life. While gender equity is about redress and closing the gap between women and men in terms of opportunities, gender equality is about ensuring equality. Esteves (2018), quoting UNESCO (2011), contends that gender equality occurs when men and women realize the same status, their human rights are ensured, and their participation in economic, political, social, and cultural spheres is enabled. Esteves further draws the definition of gender equality from the UN Sustainable Goal 5, which underscores gender equality as a fundamental right and provides women and girls with economic growth and livelihood opportunities. However, Pollard (2013) cautions that although gender could be equality and equity could be singled out as a challenge, it is often interwoven with aspects such as race and ethnicity; therefore, dealing with it might not be as straightforward.

4 Theoretical Frameworks for Understanding Gender Equity in Education

Various frameworks are applied to understand the impact of gender in education. Yokozeki (1998) identifies three critical frameworks used to illuminate the effect of gender in education. These are liberal feminism which assumes that women must obtain equal opportunities and equal rights in education and society; the socialist feminism (neo-Marxist) which departs from the underlying assumption that gender is a power relations issue i.e. power and society- gender as a mechanism to disempower women economically with sexist assumptions incorporated into schooling and school culture; radical feminism which means dealing with the monopolisation of culture and knowledge as well as challenging the current forms of schooling as it perpetuates gender imbalance. These frameworks are not immune to critique. Acker (1987) posits that liberal feminism's weakness is that there is reluctance to confront power and patriarchy. Socialist feminism is caught up in theory, and there is little movement toward action. On the other hand, radical feminism is criticised for its biological reductionism. On the contrary, Khairullayeva et al. (2022) contend that these frameworks are not relevant for analysing Kazakh gender issues. They postulate that understanding gender equality in Kazakhstan, Asian and post-colonial feminism, which probes deep into the Kazakh culture, could be valuable. They also believe that gender equality has always been maintained in the Kazakh traditions, albeit in a different way.

5 Practice and Policy Framework for Equity in Teacher Education

Policy and practice framework is crucial for understanding gender equity in teacher education. In this chapter, the Lamptey et al. (2015) UNESCO policy and practice framework is adopted as a conceptual framework. According to this model, the policy and practice framework is based on ten cardinal pillars, i.e. understanding of gender, availability of a responsive policy, institutional culture and environment, gender-sensitive support services, teacher education curriculum, pedagogy, management and leadership practices, mainstreaming and research, monitoring and evaluation, advocacy for gender equality.

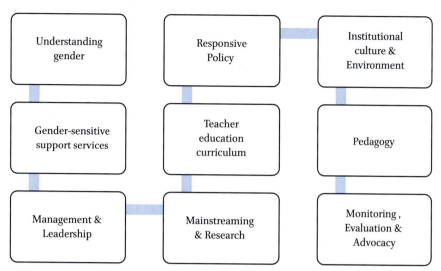

FIGURE 10.1   Gender policy and practice framework (Lamptey et al., 2015)

According to this framework, it is important that the concept of gender is clarified and its characteristics outlined to foster a coherent understanding. There is a belief that an articulated policy aimed at gender mainstreaming is pivotal. To address gender equality the institutional culture and environment must encapsulate such values and norms that promote gender equity. The role of gender-sensitive support services is vital as they are charged with the responsibility of providing guidance and support. The teacher education curriculum must inform both the teacher education and pre-service teachers about the prevalence of gender-related barriers and enablers. Clear guidelines about pedagogy and pedagogical content knowledge should promote gender-sensitive pedagogical practices, attitudes, and beliefs. The leadership and management practices such as in financing or strategic planning must be mindful of the gender mainstreaming goals. It is crucial that gender mainstreaming is adopted through practitioner-based engagements such as action research. The institutions should continuously reflect on the successes hence monitoring and evaluation are essential. Letting the stakeholders know about institutional gender equity goals through advocacy is significant.

6   Gender Equity and Teacher Education: Global Perspective

Gender equity is thought of as a phenomenon that affects people's roles as individuals in the classroom and the educational institution in general (Andrews et al., 2020). According to UNESCO (2021), Gender equality is critical in implementing the 2030 Agenda for Sustainable Development. It empowers women and girls (Goal 5) and ensures inclusive and equitable quality education (Goal 4). Gender equality is a strategic goal for UNESCO's Gender Equality Action Plan 2014–2021 and UNESCO Strategy for Gender Equality in and through Education 2019-2025.

According to Sanders (1997), it was only in the nineties that gender equality in teacher education became a priority in US education. Studies on gender and teacher education have become significant because teacher education in many contexts is viewed as a *"women's profession"*, and as Hollingsworth (1995) believes, this could, to a great extent, cover the reality of gender inequities in teacher education. Cochran-Smith (2020) believe that issues of diversity, equality and justice in teacher education can sometimes be masked by the standard "professional teacher" notion, which seems to neutralise inequality. Cochran-Smith (2020) postulate that the preparation of teachers should be equity-centred, which means teacher preparation becomes a vehicle for social justice. This view is echoed by Grant and Agosto (2008).

In many contexts, teacher recruitment is often embedded in gendered policy frameworks that do not advocate for change but perpetuate the current status (Skelton, 2007). As a result, there is a view that gender-related education has to be integrated into teacher education if social justice and inclusiveness are to be achieved in the teaching profession.

For instance, Weiner (2000) states that in Europe, despite female dominance in teacher education, it took a long time for issues of gender in teacher education to be taken note of. As a result, no radical position was taken; Weiner calls fear of feminism.

There are attempts to infuse gender equity in teacher education. However, it seems as though the current teacher education programs fall short of implementing gender equity. For instance, Sadker et al. (2007) postulate that the current teacher education programs do not prepare students to see the gender inequalities and disparities in teacher education. This thus influences the pre-service teacher conceptions and understandings of the impact of gender inequities. Monagham (2014) postulates that although pre-service teachers in the USA are aware of the influence of gender in the classroom, they think it is not necessarily an issue due to the dominant discourse of gendered curriculum. As Zittleman and Sadker (2002) postulate, although attempts are made to voice gender inequality in teacher education, textbooks often characterise the text as lacking strategies to deal with inequalities. Similarly, Flintoff (1993) believes that some school subjects continue to be gendered, i.e. physical education and dance are seen as either feminine or masculine. In an attempt to clarify how teacher education can promote equity and equality, Blackwell

GENDER EQUITY AND EQUALITY IN TEACHER EDUCATION 209

& Smiley (2010) use this citation from Delpit (1995, p. 134) to describe what teacher education needs to do to achieve equity and equality:

> Teach across the boundaries of race, class or gender, ... we must recognize and overcome the power differential, the stereotypes and other barriers which prevent us from seeing each other. Those efforts must drive our teacher education, our curriculum development, our instructional strategies and every aspect of the educational enterprise. Until we can see the world as others see it, all the educational reforms in the world will come to nought. (Delpit, 1995, p. 134)

The statement aims to emphasise the need for equal treatment for all, including different genders. In order to achieve what is encapsulated in the quote above, Erden (2009) postulates that institutions of teacher preparation need to develop a course specifically devoted to addressing issued of gender equity and equality.

7 Gender Equity and Equality in Kazakhstan

Gender equity has become a hotly debated topic in teacher education globally. Silova and Magno (2004) postulate that the fall of the Soviet Union provided women with the opportunity to re-imagine their status as citizens in the post-soviet world. They assert that although the post-soviet countries masquerade equality for women, reality tells a different story. Gender-related issues affect education and teacher education and permeate beyond aspects of the labour market and employment (Ryskaliyev et al., 2019). Be that as it may, Kazakhstan's labour market has high female participation, with the unemployment rate of women standing at 6.2% and is ranked 37th in the world regarding the treatment of women (Litjens & Taguma, 2017). However, there is less representation of women in government, with only 16% of ministers being female and 24% being parliamentary deputies.

In Kazakhstan, the proportionate number of women in secondary school is significantly higher than their male counterparts, i.e. 81.3%. According to OECD (TALIS) (2018, p. 2), "In Kazakhstan, only 53% of principals are women, compared to 76% of teachers. This can be benchmarked against the OECD averages of 47% of women among school leaders and 68% among teachers". This chapter analyses the role of gender in the Kazakhstani teacher education context and highlights the gender imbalances, their impact, and mechanisms put in place to address them.

According to Buribayev and Khamzina (2019), women comprise 70% of the health, education, and social services employees. They postulate that although legislatively, the system is transformed to ensure gender equity, the patriarchal family structure militates against these goals. However, in education, Almukhambetova (2024) avers that women are underrepresented in STEM education. Similarly, UNESCO (2021) states that women are more represented in pre-, primary, and secondary education but less in higher education than their male counterparts. In analysing school textbooks, Durrani et al. (2022) found that textbooks entrench gender power relations, constructing dominant masculinities and embedded femininities that produce gender hierarchies that perpetuate gender imbalance. While there is hope that gender equity and equality could be achieved in Kazakhstan, Khamzina et al. (2020), albeit in the field of law, postulate that gender equity and equality are neither evaluated nor monitored, making it difficult to achieve. Although there are efforts to ensure gender equity and equality in Kazakhstan, Shakirova (2015) laments the superficial way in which it was driven. Shakirova thinks gender equity and equality were used as political tokenism and mainly was not part of a critical transformational agenda, albeit slogans and numerous policy slogans. To achieve gender equity and equality, Yelibay (2021) suggests that a mentoring system whereby women are mentors and role models could go a long way in developing other women and thus ensure they are competent and equal to the tasks in their respective fields.

8 Lessons from the Review

Using Lamptey et al. (2015) UNESCO policy and practice framework, the lessons drawn from the review are responsive to the ten (10) cardinal pillars of gender equity, i.e. understanding of gender, availability of a responsive policy, institutional culture, and environment, gender-sensitive support services, teacher education curriculum, pedagogy, management and leadership practices, mainstreaming and research, monitoring and evaluation, advocacy for gender equality.

The analysis of the Kazakhstani context seems inclined to the liberal feminism approach as there is much emphasis on the provision of equal opportunities and equal rights to both sexes. However, there is an element of socialist feminism as the provisions of equity and equality seem to be tokenism rather than actionable. The feminization of teacher education is an indication that radical feminism is needed as the education sector has more women, but in positions of power, males still dominate. However, the Asian and post-colonial conceptions of gender equity seem to prevail. Although there is a belief that the Kazakh culture promotes gender equity, the description of the notion of gender equity contrasts with that of the Western liberal forms (Khairullayeva et al., 2022). Although on the surface the teacher education institutions' culture and environment might appear to be gender friendly it is apparent that gender equity issues are not explicitly talked about. There is a general lack of gender-sensitive services in most teacher education institutions and thus teacher education curriculum is gender neutral. While there are efforts to practice a gender-sensitive pedagogy in teacher education, indications from this review are that the curriculum and pedagogical material still present masculinities and femininities, perpetuating gender stereotypes (Durrani et al., 2022) and gender stereotypes influence teacher subject choices (Almukhambetova, 2024). The leadership and management seem to portray toughness oriented on projecting power rather than softness. Even when the leadership is female, the character, nature, and practice of leadership show masculine attributes. Although it seems as though gender equity is taken note of, the teacher education institutions do not seem to have an articulated gender mainstreaming program and it does not appear as though the gender equity processes are monitored nor evaluated (UNESCO, 2021; Khamzina, et al., 2020). While gender equity has been talked about in general terms, it seems that it has not been advocated formally in teacher education institutions (UNESCO, 2021).

9 Conclusion

From this review chapter, several conclusions are drawn. The gap between policy and practice regarding gender equity and equality in Kazakhstani teacher education is still vast. Although there seems to be a general view to empower female teachers, the practical and procedural processes of achieving this have not been instrumentalised. Gender equity and equality in teacher education occur within the broader social, cultural, economic, and political context and may not be treated in isolation. There seems to be a need for strengthening advocacy, curriculum relevance, pedagogical, leadership, reflective, and monitoring practices to ensure that gender equity and equality stay as the central part of the educational reform agenda. It must be borne in mind that Kazkahstan's educational fraternity is rapidly changing, and as such, some conclusions in this chapter could have already been achieved. However, this chapter serves as an important contribution toward the debates about gender equity and equality in the Kazakhstani teacher education sector.

References

Acker, S. (1987). Feminist theory and the study of gender and education. *International Review of Education, 33*, 419–435.

Almukhambetova, A. (2024). Exploring STEM Teacher Educators' Gender Awareness and Understanding of Gender-responsive Pedagogies in Kazakhstan. In *The political economy of education in central Asia: Evidence from the field* (pp. 97–115). Springer Nature Singapore.

Andrews, N. C. Z., Cook, R. E., Nielson, M. G., Xiao, S. X., & Martin, C. L. (2020). Gender in education. In T. L. Spinrad & J. Liew (Eds.), *Social and emotional learning section; D. Fisher (Ed.), Routledge encyclopedia of education* (online). Taylor & Francis.

Blackwell, S., & Smiley, A. D. (2010). Addressing equity in teacher education. *AILACTE Journal, 7*(1), 1–13.

Buribayev, Y. A., & Khamzina, Z. A. (2019). Gender equality in employment: The experience of Kazakhstan. *International Journal of Discrimination and the Law, 19*(2), 110–124.

Cochran-Smith, M. (2020). Teacher education for justice and equity: 40 years of advocacy. *Action in Teacher Education, 42*(1), 49–59.

Delpit, L. (1995). *Other people's children: Cultural conflict in the classroom*. The New Press.

Durrani, N., CohenMiller, A., Kataeva, Z., Bekzhanova, Z., Seitkhadyrova, A., & Badanova, A. (2022). 'The fearful khan and the delightful beauties': The construction of gender in secondary school textbooks in Kazakhstan. *International Journal of Educational Development, 88*, 102508.

Esteves, M. (2018). Gender Equality in Education: a challenge for policy makers. *International Journal of Social Sciences, 4*(2), 893–905.

Erden, F. T. (2009). A course on gender equity in education: Does it affect gender role attitudes of preservice teachers? *Teaching and Teacher Education, 25*(3), 409–414.

Flintoff, A. (1993). Gender, physical education, and initial teacher education. In J. Evans (Ed.), *Equality, education and physical education* (pp. 184–204). Falmer Press.

Grant, C. A., & Agosto, V. (2008). Teacher capacity and social justice in teacher education. In *Handbook of research on teacher education* (pp. 175–200). Routledge.

Hollingsworth, S. (1995). The "problem" of gender in teacher education. *Mid-Western Educational Researcher, 8*(2), 3–11.

Khairullayeva, V., Sarybayev, M., Kuzembayeva, A., Yermekbayev, A., & Baikushikova, G. (2022). Gender policy in Kazakhstan. *Journal of International Women's Studies, 24*(1), 25.

Khamzina, Z., Buribayev, Y., Yermukanov, Y., & Alshurazova, A. (2020). Is it possible to achieve gender equality in Kazakhstan: Focus on employment and social protection? *International Journal of Discrimination and the Law, 20*(1), 5–20.

Klein, S., Ortman, B., & Friedman, B. (2002). What is the field of gender equity in education? *Defining and Redefining Gender Equity in Education*, 3–29.

Lamptey, A., Gaidzanwa, R. B., Mulugeta, E., Samra, S., Shumba, O., Assie-Lumumba, N. D. T., Oliphant, J., Sunnari, V., Ssereo, F., & Kurki, T. (2015). *A guide for gender equality in teacher education policy and practices*. UNESCO. https://unesdoc.unesco.org/ark:/48223/pf0000231646

Litjens, I., & Taguma, M. (2017). *Kazakhstan*. OECD. https://www.oecd.org/education/school/Early-Childhood-Education-and-Care-Policy-Review-Kazakhstan.pdf

Magno, C., & Silova, I. (2007). Teaching in transition: Examining school-based gender inequities in Central/Southeastern Europe and the former Soviet Union. *International Journal of Educational Development, 27*(6), 647–660.

Monaghan, M. M. (2014). Gender equity and education: Examining preservice teachers' perceptions. *GEMS (Gender, Education, Music, and Society), 7*(8).

Peppin Vaughan, R. (2016). Gender equality and education in the Sustainable Development Goals. *UNESCO.*

Pollard, D. S. (2013). Understanding and supporting gender equity in schools. In *Multicultural education: Issues and perspectives* (pp. 145–160).

Ryskaliyev, D. U., Mirzaliyeva, A., Tursynbayeva, G., Muratova, E. M., Buribayev, Y. A., & Khamzina, Z. A. (2019). Gender inequality among employees in Kazakhstan. *The Lawyer Quarterly, 9*(4).

Sadker, D., Earley, K. Z. P., McCormick, T., Strawn, C., & Preston, J. (2014). The treatment of gender equity in teacher education. In *Handbook for achieving gender equity through education* (pp. 161–180). Routledge.

Sanders, J. (1997). Teacher education and gender equity. *ERIC Digest.*

Shakirova, S. (2015). Gender equality in Kazakhstan and the role of international actors in its institutionalization. In *Institutionalizing gender equality: Historical and global perspectives* (pp. 211–225).

Silova, I., & Magno, C. (2004). Gender equity unmasked: Democracy, gender, and education in Central/Southeastern Europe and the former Soviet Union. *Comparative Education Review, 48*(4), 417–442.

Skelton, C. (2007). Gender, policy, and initial teacher education. *Gender and Education, 19*(6), 677–690. https://doi.org/10.1080/09540250701650059

Subrahmanian, R. (2005). Gender equality in education: Definitions and measurements. *International Journal of Educational Development, 25*(4), 395–407.

UNESCO. (2021). *Policy brief: Gender equality in and through education in Central Asia*. UNESCO.

Webb, S., Holford, J., Hodge, S., Milana, M., & Waller, R. (2017). Lifelong learning for quality education: Exploring the neglected aspect of sustainable development goal 4. *International Journal of Lifelong Education, 36*(5), 509–511.

Weiner, G. (2000). A critical review of gender and teacher education in Europe. *Pedagogy, Culture and Society, 8*(2), 233–247.

Yelibay, M. (2021). Department chair as mentor: Perceptions of young female faculty members from Kazakhstan. *Journal of Professional Capital and Community, 6*(4), 318–335.

Yokozeki, Y. (1998). Gender in education and development. *Journal of International Cooperation in Education, 1*(1), 45–63.

Zittleman, K., & Sadker, D. (2002). Gender bias in teacher education texts: New (and old) lessons. *Journal of Teacher Education, 53*(2), 168–180.

CHAPTER 11

Running on Fumes in the Steppe

An In-Depth Exploration of Teacher Burnout in Kazakhstan

Dana Nygmetzhanova and Daniel Hernández-Torrano

Abstract

Teacher burnout can affect teachers' well-being, efficiency, and performance. This chapter reports on a quantitative study that investigated teacher burnout in five schools in Astana, Kazakhstan. An adapted version of the Copenhagen Burnout Inventory (CBI) self-report questionnaire was used to evaluate three dimensions of teacher burnout. Data was analysed in four stages using various analytic frameworks. The findings revealed that teacher burnout is widespread in Kazakhstan, with 73% of participating teachers experiencing moderate levels of burnout. Being female, single, childless, and less experienced was associated with higher burnout rates. However, variables like teaching hours, teaching level (primary vs. secondary), and educational background (TVET, bachelor's, master's) did not significantly impact teacher burnout. Moreover, high levels of burnout were found to negatively affect teachers' health, well-being, self-efficacy, and job satisfaction. This study offers valuable insights for policymakers and superintendents to develop practices and services that support teachers' well-being and prevent burnout.

Keywords

teacher burnout – teacher well-being – emotional exhaustion – depersonalization – self-efficacy – Kazakhstan

1   Introduction

There is empirical evidence that teachers are at high risk of burnout syndrome, which has become a concern for educational institutions and organizations (Iancu et al., 2018; García-Carmona et al., 2019). Burnout is considered a pervasive phenomenon that may increase teachers' absenteeism and attrition and may negatively influence the quality of students' learning (Akin, 2019; Herman

© DANA NYGMETZHANOVA AND DANIEL HERNÁNDEZ-TORRANO, 2025
DOI:10.1163/9789004726345_012

et al., 2018). Besides, there is empirical evidence that teacher burnout may negatively impact students' academic and non-academic outcomes (Brunsting et al., 2014; Herman et al., 2019; Madigan & Kim, 2021).

Although various interpretations of burnout are available in the literature, many authors refer to the original definition of the term by clinical psychologist Freudenberger (Akin, 2019). In that definition, burnout is understood as "failure, exhaustion, loss of energy, in other words, the state of exhaustion that occurs as a result of unsatisfied desires by internal resources of the individual" (p. 49).

Teachers' burnout is a complicated issue and its consequences are poorly understood (e.g., Akin, 2019; Rumschlag, 2017), especially in non-Western contexts (Herman et al., 2018). This study offers an in-depth exploration of teacher burnout in Kazakhstan, a country in Central Asia that has embarked on measures to improve the training, support, and prestige of the teaching profession in different fronts. For instance, a new model of teachers' attestation was introduced in 2018 to encourage professional development and excellence (MOES, 2019a). Similarly, a new law "On the status of a teacher" was passed to "determine the status of the teacher, establish their rights, social guarantees, and restrictions, duties and responsibilities" (MOES, 2019a), and "State Program of Education Development for 2020–2025" (MOES, 2019b) contributed to gradually raise teacher salary up to 25% each year until 2025.

However, the extent to which these and other actions have contributed to improving teachers' satisfaction, motivation, and engagement with their profession is uncertain (Yembergenova, 2019). The limited information available suggests that, in recent years, the number of people entering the teaching profession is on the decline (Rodionov, 2019). In addition, only 58% of teachers plan to continue their teaching careers due to their retirement age (IAC, 2019) and every fifth teacher plans to quit teaching in the following five years (Irsaliyev et al., 2019). Also, the national report on Teaching and Learning International Survey (TALIS) 2018 results illustrate that only 28% of urban secondary school teachers and 45% of rural schools' educators are satisfied with their salaries (OECD, 2019).

The purpose of this study was to explore the burnout levels of teachers in Kazakhstan and to investigate the causal relationship between burnout levels, influencing factors, and possible consequences of burnout. Three research questions guided the study:

– What is the level of mainstream teachers' burnout in Kazakhstani schools?
– What factors contribute to teacher burnout in Kazakhstan?
– What are the consequences of teacher burnout in the context of Kazakhstan?

2 Literature Review

2.1 *The Development of Teacher Burnout*

Burnout is a process that develops over time and is characterized by the gradual depletion of an individual's internal resources (Maslach, 2018; Toker & Biron, 2012). Specifically, Maslach (2018) emphasizes that this process happens in several interconnected stages: emotional exhaustion, depersonalization, and low self-efficacy. The emotional exhaustion stage is a response to the excessive amount of external demands (Herman et al., 2018) and it is characterized by the depletion of one's emotional resources (Maslach & Leiter, 2005). The depersonalization phase refers to a reaction to long-term exhaustion and is expressed by a detached attitude toward one's work responsibilities (Herman et al., 2018). In other words, due to prolonged fatigue, a worker usually becomes self-protective and creates an emotional buffer of "detached concern" (Maslach & Leiter, 2005). Over time, this person can reduce the quantity of work, and a negative or mechanical attitude toward people and jobs can be developed. Finally, the reduced self-efficacy stage represents the feeling of self-perceived ineffectiveness (Herman et al., 2018).

2.2 *Causes of Teacher Burnout*

Various factors contribute to teacher burnout within and outside school settings (Akin, 2019; Dorman, 2003). According to Mota et al. (2021a), teachers' burnout can be explained by factors at three levels: personal, organizational, and classroom.

The *personal dimension* encompasses the personal and professional identity of the teacher leading to burnout. Personal predictors include the management of teachers' life roles (e.g., mother, wife, daughter, or daughter-in-law), coping mechanisms, and capabilities. Additionally, sociodemographic factors like gender, marital status, and the number of children have been identified as possible predictors of burnout at the personal level (Akin, 2018; Herman et al., 2018; Mota et al., 2021a). Concerning the professional identity of the teacher, the lack of recognition, dissatisfaction with job or salary, and status in society may facilitate the development of burnout (Bataineh & Alsagheer, 2012; Montero-Marin et al., 2011; Mota et al., 2021b).

The *organizational dimension* encompasses issues at the school structure, system, and context levels. Heavy workload stands out as a primary contributor to teacher burnout in terms of school structure (Akin, 2018; Mota et al., 2021b; Noushad, 2008; Pressley, 2021). In addition to scheduled teaching hours, excessive work (Bataineh & Alsagheer, 2012), bureaucracy (Mota et al., 2021b), meaningless tasks (Maslach & Leiter, 2005), as well as programs, schedules, time pressure, inadequate policy, and legislation (Mota et al., 2021b) also impact teachers' workload and contribute to burnout. At the system level, low decision-making power and teacher autonomy have been identified as burnout-related factors (Akin, 2019; Mota et al., 2021b). At the context level, a lack of community is one of the major causes of burnout at work (Maslach & Leiter, 2008; Rankin, 2016; Skovholt & Trotter-Mathison, 2011). Similarly, poor school climate (Mota et al., 2021a) and strained relationships with colleagues and supervisors (Akin, 2019) lead to teachers burning out. Injustice (Mota et al., 2021b) in the school community and lack of control (Montero-Marin, 2011) can also cause teachers' exhaustion and depersonalization.

The *classroom dimension* involves classroom and students' characteristics. Students' misbehavior is one of the commonly causes of burnout among teachers (Bataineh & Alsagheer, 2012; Mota et al., 2021a). Indiscipline and disruptive student behavior reinforce teachers' mental exhaustion, demand more emotional resources, and may lead to a detached manner of teaching (Mota et al., 2021b). Also, students' low academic performance and lack of motivation may have a negative effect on teaching and cause teacher burnout (Mota et al., 2021a).

2.3   *Consequences of Teacher Burnout*

The outcomes of teacher burnout can be divided into two categories: personal and professional. At the *personal level*, accumulated empirical evidence indicates that burnout adversely affects individuals' health and well-being (Bataineh & Alsagheer, 2012; Brunsting, 2014; Milfont et al., 2012; Rumschlag, 2017). Physical manifestations such as bowel difficulties, weight fluctuations, and hypertension are commonly cited as negative health consequences of burnout (Bataineh & Alsagheer, 2012). Additionally, Milfont et al. (2008) associate burnout with mental health problems and increased anxiety levels. Another range of negative consequences on teachers' well-being includes educators' social behavior and emotional state. Moreover, teachers may act rigidly and be harsh, less tolerant toward their pupils, and hold negative and low expectations of students.

Professional outcomes of burnout consist of its influence on teachers professionally and their students. According to Rumschlag (2017), teacher burnout is a chronic issue that remains a major cause of teacher exodus in the twenty-first century. This underscores the observation that teacher attrition is usually preceded by burnout (O'Brien et al., 2008). Furthermore, some scholars emphasize the negative influence of this phenomenon on the quality of teachers' practices. Skaalvik and Skaalvik (2007) claim that exhausted and stressed teachers exhibit lower quality of teaching. Consequently, Herman et al. (2018) suggest that teachers with high burnout or emotionally drained deliver poorer instructions and have strained relationships.

2.4 Conceptual Framework

The conceptualization of teacher burnout in this study is presented in Figure 11.1. The main focus of this study, teacher burnout, is located in the center of the figure. In this study, teacher burnout will be considered as a combination of three types of burnout: general burnout, work-related burnout, client-related burnout (Kristensen et al., 2005).

On the left side, the main predictors of burnout are presented. Aligned with the literature reviewed, the causes of burnout are divided into three dimensions: personal, school, and classroom predictors. Firstly, the personal dimension refers to teachers' personal (age, gender) and professional identities (salary, job satisfaction level). Secondly, school-related contributors to burnout include factors associated with the school system (school policy, schedule) and school context (relationships with school administrators and colleagues, school climate). Finally, the classroom section consists of factors related to classroom climate (class size, behavior) and students (motivation, parental involvement).

The right side accounts for the possible ramifications of burnout. Personal and professional outcomes of burnout will be explored in the present research. Personal consequences include psychological distress and negative effects on teachers' well-being (e.g., emotional breakdown and depression) and physical symptomatology (e.g., headache). In addition, professional consequences such as the intention to leave and attrition, low quality of teaching, reduced self-efficacy, and strained relationships with school administrators, colleagues, students, and their parents will be investigated.

3 Methods

3.1 Design

A quantitative approach was employed in this study to determine levels of teacher burnout in Kazakhstan and to examine the relationships among these levels, the causes of burnout, and its possible consequences. This approach was appropriate as it "investigates a research problem through a description of trends or a need for an explanation of the relationship among variables" (Creswell, 2014, p. 13). Specifically, a non-experimental, cross-sectional survey design was applied to address the research questions. This flexible design

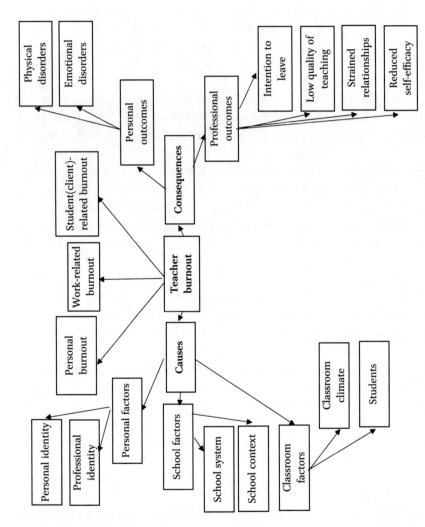

FIGURE 11.1 The conceptualization of teacher burnout, its causes, and consequences

allows for collecting data from a large group of people simultaneously (Muijs, 2011). Additionally, this design has the advantage of being able to assess the current attitudes or practices of participants (Creswell, 2014), and it allows for the examination of "the nature of existing conditions, or identifying standards against which existing conditions can be compared, or determining the relationships that exist between specific events" (Cohen et al., 2007).

3.2 *Participants*
A non-probabilistic convenience sample of 161 teachers working in five private schools in Astana participated in the study. Table 11.1 provides a detailed account of participants' background characteristics. Most respondents were female teachers (83%), aligning with the general trend of higher representation of females in education. Additionally, over half (58.8%) were under 35. Furthermore, 52% of the teachers were unmarried, and 41% reported not having children. Approximately 40% of the participants had five or fewer years of teaching experience. Also, more than half (57.4%) of respondents reported working more than 25 hours per week, exceeding the standard national workload of 16 hours. Similarly, nearly 40% of the participants reported working more than 8 hours per day. Also, slightly more than half of educators (51.9%) reported teaching a class size of 21–25 students.

3.3 *Data Collection Tools*
The Copenhagen Burnout Inventory (CBI; Kristensen et al., 2005) was employed in this study to assess teachers' burnout levels. The CBI, a self-report questionnaire with 19 items, evaluates three dimensions of burnout: personal, job-related, and client-related burnout. To measure personal burnout, six items were included, assessing physical and mental weariness. Job-related burnout, reflecting exhaustion caused by work, was measured with seven items. Client-related burnout, gauging exhaustion experienced by those working with students, was assessed with six items. Respondents rated their agreement with the 19 statements on a 5-point Likert scale.

Teachers were also asked complementary questions to account for predictors and outcomes of burnout. These questions included personal, professional, and school context predictors, as well as classroom-related indicators. Respondents also evaluated items on health and well-being consequences based on the General Health Questionnaire 12 (GHQ) and the Mental Health Continuum – Short Form (MHC-SF). In addition, to evaluate the current level of job satisfaction, items of the Teachers' Job Satisfaction Questionnaire (TJSQ) and the Teacher Self-Efficacy Questionnaire (TSE) were used. The complete survey questionnaire was distributed online via Qualtrics using an anonymous link.

TABLE 11.1 Demographic characteristics of participants

	n	%
Gender		
Male	19	14.73
Female	108	83.72
Age		
20–25	34	26.36
26–35	42	32.56
36–45	24	18.61
46–55	20	15.50
56+	8	6.20
Marital status		
Married	68	52.71
Not married	58	44.96
Number of children		
No Children	54	41.86
One	22	17.05
Two	28	21.71
Three	14	10.85
Four or more	9	6.98
Education background		
TVET	2	1.55
Bachelor degree	84	65.17
Master degree	41	31.78
Years of experience		
0–5	51	39.54
6–10	22	17.05
10–15	16	12.40
15–25	19	14.73
26+	21	16.28
Teaching hours (week)		
Up to 8 hours	6	4.65
9–16 hours	13	10.08
17–24 hours	36	27.91
25+ hours	74	57.36
Working hours (day)		
up to 4 hours	9	6.98
4–8 hours	71	55.04
more than 8 hours	48	37.21

(*cont.*)

RUNNING ON FUMES IN THE STEPPE

TABLE 11.1   Demographic characteristics of participants (*cont.*)

	n	%
Teaching level*		
Primary (1–4 grades)	37	28.68
Secondary (5–8 grades)	76	58.91
Higher (9–11 grades)	55	42.64
Number of students		
less than 15	37	28.68
15–20	5	3.88
21–25	67	51.94
26–30	18	13.95
30+	2	1.55

Note: * Participants can teach at multiple levels (i.e., total percentage can be above 100%)

Overall, the CFAs demonstrated satisfactory fit indices for the presupposed dimensional structures of the CBI, GHQ, MHC-SF, TJSQ, and TSE measures (see Table 11.2). However, a poor fit was evidenced with regards to the SRMR index for the CBI and TSE and the RMSE measure for the TJSQ, CBI, GHQ, and TSE. The poor fit of these models can be due to the simplicity of the models and the small number of degrees of freedom, as suggested by Kenny et al. (2015).

TABLE 11.2   Reliability and confirmatory factor analysis fit measures for the models tested

						RMSEA 90% CI	
Measure	Model tested	CFI	TLI	SRMR	RMSEA	Lower	Upper
TJSQ	1 factor (Job Satisfaction)	.99	.98	.07	.40	.00	.13
CBI	3 factors (Personal, Client, and Work)	.98	.98	.13	.19	.17	.20
GHQ	1 factor (Physical Health)	1.00	1.01	.05	.85	.00	.10
MHC-SF	1 factor (Well-being)	.99	.98	.05	.01	.09	.25
TSE	1 factor (Self-efficacy)	.99	.98	.10	.21	.16	.28

Note: TJSQ = Teacher Job Satisfaction Questionnaire, CBI = Copenhagen Burnout Inventory, GHQ = General Health Questionnaire, MHQ= Mental Health Questionnaire, TSE = Teacher Self-Efficacy

Therefore, the models tested were considered to demonstrate a relatively appropriate fit based on the CFI, TLI, and SRMR indices.

3.4 Data Analysis

Data analysis was conducted in four stages. First, confirmatory factor analyses were then conducted to determine if the presumptive dimensions of the measures used in the study were supported. Second, descriptive analyses identified three levels of burnout based on CBI survey responses. Pearson's correlation coefficients were calculated to examine relationships between key variables, and internal consistency was assessed using Cronbach's alpha to assess the reliability of the scores. Third, parametric and non-parametric tests were conducted to compare total burnout mean scores across groups. Fourth, linear regression modeling estimated the relationship between burnout and its consequences, including health and well-being. Fifth, path analysis was employed to test the fit of the correlation matrix against causal models, examining the relationships between multiple measurements and disentangling causal processes underlying specific outcomes. All analyses were performed in *jamovi* v.2.3 (The jamovi project, 2023).

3.5 Procedures

This study did not involve more than minimal risk and was approved by the Nazarbayev University Graduate School Education Institutional Research Ethical Committee. Meetings were conducted with school officials to obtain access to the research sites. The questionnaire was distributed online using an anonymous survey link by the first author through school WhatsApp groups. Participants provided informed consent emphasizing voluntary participation, and only the researcher and supervisor had access to the data.

3.6 Ethical Considerations

This study posed no more than minimal risk to participants. Anonymity was ensured as the questionnaire was conducted online, and no information that could reveal the identity of the participants was collected, including name, surname, and IP address. Also, to keep the identity of the participants private, each participant was assigned an alphanumeric code (e.g., P001). Confidentiality of the research data was warranted as the gathered data was not shared or discussed with anyone except the supervisor. Only the researcher and the research supervisor had access to the data, which was stored on the researcher's personal password-protected laptop. The paper variants of protocols and notes were stored in a locked cabinet in the researcher's office. Also, given that the research could require participants to remember negative experiences related to burnout, teachers can experience some discomfort. To minimize those risks, the researcher reminded participants about the voluntary nature of the study, their right to withdraw from the study at any survey stage, and that they could skip any question in the survey questionnaire if they were not comfortable answering. Moreover, the respondents answered the questions at a convenient time and place for them.

4 Findings

4.1 Descriptive, Correlation, and Reliability Analyses

Table 11.3 displays the descriptive statistics, intercorrelation matrix and internal consistency coefficients for the key variables under examination. Pearson's bivariate correlation coefficients were calculated and ranged from $r = -.65$ to .92. These indices contribute to a better understanding of the relationships between the major variables. Interestingly, the correlation coefficients demonstrate a weak relationship within burnout components (i.e., personal, work and client-oriented burnout [student burnout]) themselves. Notably, correlation coefficients of physical health and well-being are equal across all other variables. Moreover, there is a positive moderate ($r = .42$) association between both physical health and well-being with teacher's job satisfaction. As expected, there are strong negative correlations between physical health and well-being with personal burnout and work burnout. Cronbach's alpha coefficients across measures ranged from $\alpha = .65$ (CBI Student burnout) to $\alpha = .93$ (CBI Personal burnout), indicating that the internal consistency of the sample's results is satisfactory to good (Gaciu, 2020).

TABLE 11.3   Descriptive, reliability, and correlation coefficients for the key variables

	M	SD	α	1	2	3	4	5	6	7	8
1 Personal burnout	18.70	5.81	.93	–							
2 Work burnout	19.42	6.80	.90	.87***	–						
3 Student burnout	9.36	3.08	.65	.08	.18	–					
4 Total burnout	47.65	13.13	.92	.92***	.96***	.37***	–				
5 Job satisfaction	21.52	4.38	.66	−.34***	−.34***	.03	−.32**	–			
6 Physical health	15.98	2.98	.79	−.63***	−.66***	−.21	−.68***	.28**	–		
7 Well-being	20.24	5.64	.85	−.64***	−.64***	−.09	−.65***	.42***	.48***	–	
8 Self-efficacy	19.46	3.92	.88	−.25*	−.35	−.37***	−.39***	−.04	.21*	.29**	–

Note: * $p < .05$, ** $p < .01$, *** $p < .001$

TABLE 11.4   Distribution of teacher burnout across the diagnosis categories

	Low		Moderate		High	
	n	%	n	%	n	%
Personal	10	9.7	64	62.1	29	28.2
Work	25	24.5	62	60.8	15	14.7
Student	27	27.8	66	68.0	4	4.1
Total	16	16.5	71	73.2	10	10.3

4.2   Prevalence of Burnout among Teachers

The distribution of teacher burnout across the diagnosis categories is presented in Table 11.4. The results of this study indicate that approximately 73% of the participating teachers reported moderate levels of burnout, as determined by the diagnostic criteria of the teacher burnout measurement tool (i.e., CBI). A total of 16.5% of the sample was categorized as having low burnout, while 10.3% reported experiencing high levels of burnout. This indicates that approximately nine out of every ten teachers in the sample displayed symptoms of moderate or high burnout.

4.3   Causes of Teacher Burnout

A series of independent-samples t-test were performed to compare the total burnout scores across several subgroups, including gender (male/female), marital status (not married/married), age (below 35/35 years and above), presence of children (no children/have children), teaching experience (less than 10 years/more than 10 years), weekly teaching hours (less than 25/more than 25 teaching hours), and weekly working hours (8 hours or less/ more than 8 hours). The normality and homogeneity of variances assumptions were checked and met for all variables in the analyses (Ghasemi & Zahedias, 2019).

The results of the group comparison analyses are presented in Table 11.5. Overall, the results indicate that there were statistically significant differences in total burnout scores between the groups based on gender, age, marital status, children, and years of experience. Conversely, no statistically significant differences were found between groups based on a number of teaching hours per week and number of working hours per week.

Female teachers (M = 49.07, SD = 12.77) reported statistically significant higher burnout scores than their male counterparts (M = 39.21, SD = 12.47) in

TABLE 11.5   Group comparisons on teacher burnout scores across socio-demographic variables

	t	df	p	Cohen's d
Gender	−2.68	95.0	0.009**	−0.77
Age	2.29	95	0.020*	0.48
Marital status	−2.79	94	0.006**	−0.54
Children	3.62	95	0.006**	0.74
Years of experience	2.50	95	0.010*	0.51
Teaching hours per week	−0.37	95.00	0.710	−0.08
Working hours per week	0.48	95.00	0.630	0.10

$* p < .05, ** p < .01, *** p < .001$

this sample, $t(95)$ = -2.68, p = 0.009, d = - .77. Teachers younger than 35 years-old (M = 50.10, SD = 13.80) demonstrated statistically significant levels of burnout compared to teachers 35 years old and older (M = 44.00, SD = 11.27); t (95) = 2.29, p = 0.02, d = 0.48). Burnout mean scores of married teachers (M = 44.02, SD = 10.94) were statistically significant lower than their non-married co-workers (M = 51.27, SD = 14.25), t (94) = -2.79, p = 0.006, d = - 0.54, pointing towards a moderate relationship between marital status and burnout levels. Moreover, teachers who have no children (M = 52.86, SD = 13.90) indicated higher levels of burnout in comparison with educators who have children (M = 43.67, SD = 11.07), t (95) = 3.62, p = 0.006, d = 0.74), which means that the (no) presence of children has a large effect on teacher burnout. Substantial differences were also found between teachers with different years of teaching experience, suggesting that teachers with less than 10 years of experience (M = 50.43, SD = 14.24) are more likely to report higher levels of burnout than experienced teachers (M = 43.85, SD =10.45), t (95) = 2.50, p = 0.01, d = 0.51. The group comparison for teaching hours t (95) = -0.37, p = 0.71) demonstrated no significant effect of teaching hours on teachers' burnout level. Moreover, the quantity of working hours per week had a minimal effect on teachers' burnout t (95) = 0.48, p = 0.63.

A series of one-way ANOVA were performed to compare the total burnout scores across several subgroups, including class sizes (less than 20, 20–25, more than 25 pupils), teaching level (primary, secondary, higher, more than one level), and educational background (TVET, a bachelor and master's degrees). The normality and homogeneity of variances assumptions were checked and met for all variables in the analyses (p > 0.05).

TABLE 11.6   Group comparisons on teacher burnout scores across socio-demographic variables

	Sum of squares	df	Mean square	F	p	η^2
Class-size	1260.96	(2, 94)	630.48	3.88	0.02*	0.080
Teaching level	63.30	(3, 93)	21.10	0.12	0.95	0.004
Educational background	185.75	(2, 93)	92.87	0.53	0.59	0.010

*$p < .05$, **$p < .01$, ***$p < .001$

The results of the group comparison analyses are presented in Table 11.6. Overall, the results indicate that there were statistically significant differences in total burnout scores between the groups based on class size, but no statistically significant differences were found between groups based on teaching level and teachers education background.

There was a significant effect of class size on teacher burnout at the $p < .05$ level for the three groups, $F(2, 94) = 3.88$, $p = 0.02$, $\eta^2 = 0.08$. However, a low eta-squared effect coefficient of 0.08 denoted a weak effect of class-size on teacher burnout. Post-hoc analyses using the Scheffe test indicated that the mean burnout score reported by teachers in classes with less than 20 students ($M = 52.30$, $SD = 12.91$) was significantly higher than the scores of teachers in classes with 20–25 students ($M = 44.49$, $SD = 12.90$), $t = 2.76$, $p = .03$, $d = .61$. However, burnout scores of teachers teaching in classes with more than 25 students ($M = 48.91$, $SD = 11.43$) did not significantly differ from the other two groups in their burnout levels. Taking this into account, the results suggest that class-size has a weak but statistically significant effect on teacher burnout level. There was no statistically significant difference in burnout scores between participants teaching in primary, secondary, and more than one level, $F(3, 93) = 0.12$, $p = 0.95$. Similarly, the results of the study demonstrated that there were no statistically significant differences in burnout scores between teachers holding TVET, bachelors, and master's degrees, $F(2, 93) = 0.53$, $p = 0.59$.

4.4   Consequences of Teacher Burnout

A series of simple linear regression analyses explored the impact of teacher burnout on various teacher outcomes, including teacher self-efficacy, health, well-being, and job satisfaction. In the first regression model, burnout significantly predicted changes in self-efficacy ($F = 15.8$, $p < .001$, $R^2 = 0.15$, $\beta = -.039$). The second model revealed that burnout had a substantial adverse effect on health ($F = 74.5$, $p < .001$, $R^2 = 0.46$, $\beta = -.39$). Similarly, the third regression showed a negative influence on well-being ($F = 63.6, p < .001, R^2 = 0.42, \beta = -.68$). The last regression analysis indicated that teacher burnout predicted low job satisfaction ($F = 10.7, p = .002, R^2 = 0.10$).

4.5 Path Analysis: Relationship between Predictors and Outcomes of Teacher Burnout

A path analysis was applied to further examine the hypothesized relationships of burnout with its causes (age, experience, gender, marital status, presence of children) and consequences (health, wellbeing, self-efficacy, and job satisfaction). This analysis consisted of five steps: specification, identification, estimation, evaluation, and interpretation of the model. At specification and identification stages, gender, age, marital status, years of experience were considered as exogenous variables while burnout, general health, wellbeing, self-efficacy, job satisfaction levels were endogenous variables.

At estimation and evaluation phases, the model fit the data well, $\chi^2 = 178.4$, $df = 35, p < .001$. Furthermore, the model demonstrated good fit indices: RMSEA = 0.04, SRMR = 0.05, TLI = 0.96, CFI = 0.97. The interpretation of the parameter estimates of the model demonstrated interesting results (see Figure 11.2). Among predictors of teacher burnout, the results suggest that only gender has a statistically significant effect on teacher burnout ($p = 0.002$). More specifically,

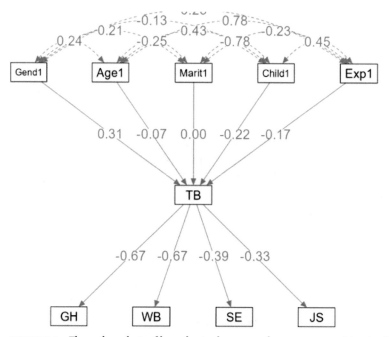

FIGURE 11.2   The path analysis of hypothesized causes and consequences of teacher burnout

the results suggest female teachers are more likely to report higher levels of overall burnout in this sample. All other potential causes of teacher burnout (i.e., age, marital status, having children, and years of working experience) did not demonstrate predictive power on teacher burnout ($p > .05$). Besides, according to the coefficients of hypothesized ramifications of burnout, all proposed consequences had meaningful relationships with burnout ($p < .001$). The most significant outcomes of burnout, according to our analyses, include health ($\beta = -.67$) and wellbeing ($\beta = -.67$) variables. Still, teacher burnout demonstrated to have a moderate effect on the other two variables of interest, job satisfaction ($\beta = -.33$) and self-efficacy ($\beta = -.39$).

5 Discussion

5.1 Levels of Mainstream Teachers' Burnout in Kazakhstani Schools

This study revealed that a substantial proportion of teachers experience burnout, with nearly three fourths (73%) of participants reporting moderate levels of burnout and 10.3% reporting high levels. These findings are consistent with previously reported rates of burnout among educators in other countries (García-Carmona et al., 2019; Rankin, 2016).

There might be several reasons for such a significant proportion of teachers experiencing burnout in the Kazakhstani context. Firstly, all five participating schools are newly-opened educational institutions (the oldest was established in December 2021). Hence, new schools usually face additional challenges such as setting the culture of the institution, staff retention, community engagement (Holmes, 2009). Rankin (2016) states that one of the most influential causes of burnout is a lack of community. In addition to that, a teacher has to adapt to a new environment and learners, which may cause an additional increase in teacher burnout level. Secondly, based on socio-demographic characteristics of participants, almost 40% of teachers are novice teachers with experience less than five years. According to Saloviita and Pakarinen (2021), young teachers are prone to have high exhaustion rates, resulting in burnout, in comparison to their more experienced colleagues. Finally, more than half of the sample (58%) reported that their teaching workload consisted of more than 25 hours which is nine hours more than ordinary workload. Moreover, two fifths (39%) of teachers indicated that they work more than 8 hours a day. These two factors compoundly denote the high workload which can be attributed to burnout.

This finding highlights the importance of creating mechanisms to prevent and cope with burnout. Schools should design programs to support teachers' well-being, prevent excessive workload and to unite the community in the given context. Additionally, the work of psychologists within these schools should be accelerated and consultations on coping strategies with burnout should be organized if needed.

One interesting outcome of this study is the identification of work-related burnout as the most prevalent form of burnout among teachers, in contrast to student-related and personal burnout. This finding contradicts the assumption made by Mota et al. (2021a) that personal factors, such as gender, age, and work experience, are the dominant predictors of depersonalization and exhaustion among teachers. However, it aligns with the perspective of Skovholt and Trotter-Mathison (2011) that burnout is typically induced by work-related factors rather than personal dimension predictors. Notably, the study found that student-related factors contributed the least to burnout levels. This conflicts with the assertion made by Bataineh and Alsagneer (2012) that classroom climate or student-related factors heavily reinforce teacher burnout levels in comparison to other predictors. The discrepancy between these findings could be attributed to variations in sample size, methodology, or other factors in these studies.

There might be a number of explanations for workplace burnout being more widespread among teachers. CBI work-related stressors include factors such as a lack of recognition, opportunity for professional development, income, working conditions, teacher's autonomy, support from administrators, role ambiguity, meaningless tasks. Apart from salaries, which are appointed by legislative documents, other predictors might be explained by a lack of communication between administrators and employees in the given educational settings (Rankin, 2016). Accordingly, the president Tokayev (Karina, 2023) emphasized the urgent necessity for skilled managers in the educational field and highlighted the importance of having professional superintendents who can manage schools expertly. This might prevent issues such as inadequate school policy, and ambiguous tasks. In addition, the shift from top-down to bottom-up approaches is needed in Kazakhstani schools. Giving more authority to educators and bottom-up approach to professional development and change may bring positive effects in the field (Bridges, 2014).

5.2 Factors Contributing to Teacher Burnout in Kazakhstan

The results of the study demonstrated that there were statistically significant differences in total burnout scores between the groups based on gender, age, marital status, children, and years of experience. Burnout demonstrated to be more pervasive among female teachers compared to their male counterparts. The impact of gender on burnout had provided inconsistent results in the literature. On the one hand, there is research evidence that female teachers are more likely to experience burnout rather than male educators (Mota et al., 2021a, Saloviita & Pakarinen, 2021). On the other hand, other scholars state that male educators tend to report higher levels of burnout (Unterbrink et al., 2007). A plausible explanation for the higher levels of burnout reported by female teachers in this study is that they may face more challenges in balancing work and "experiencing higher occupational stress" (p. 697) due to social roles such as being a mother, wife, daughter, daughter-in-law (Akin, 2019), which could lead to increased stress and burnout (Mota et al., 2021). This finding emphasizes the importance of addressing the unique needs of female teachers in schools and providing them with adequate support and resources to prevent burnout. Schools could offer programs that help female teachers to organize their time wisely and cope with stress, balance work-life. Additionally, there is need for programs to support women after maternity leave as this period is associated with higher depression, negative influence on mother's self-esteem and marriage (Feldman et al., 2004).

There were some differences between age, years of experience, marital status and presence of children groups. Thus, both age and years of experience groups had consistent results stating that young novice teachers report levels of burnout in the given sample. These results can be associated with lower levels of personal accomplishment among beginning teachers and a lack of supporting systems of novice teachers within educational institutions (O'Brien, 2007).

5.3   *The Effect of Teacher Burnout on Personal and Professional Outcomes*

The results of this study revealed a significant relationship between teacher burnout and various aspects of teachers personal and professional lives. More specifically, this study provides compelling evidence that high levels of burnout have significant adverse effects on the health and well-being of teachers. This aligns with previous empirical research indicating that burnout can negatively impact individuals' overall health and well-being (Milfont et al., 2012). Moreover, Bianchi et al. (2015) highlighted that burnout is characterized by feelings of being "emotionally drained" (p. 4), which can further exacerbate the detrimental effects on teachers' health and well-being.

This study also provides support for the idea that burnout has a significant negative relationship with teacher self-efficacy, in alignment with previous research in the field. For instance, Maslach et al. (1997) identified reduced self-efficacy as one of the key components of burnout, along with exhaustion and depersonalization. Similarly, Noushad (2008) posited that low self-efficacy is the ultimate phase of burnout, which follows a period of extreme exhaustion, absenteeism, and cynicism toward students and colleagues. Friedman (2003) contended that low self-efficacy has a longitudinal effect on personal accomplishment, emotional exhaustion, and can serve as a predictor of burnout. Recent findings by Madigan and Kim (2021) observed that burnout was associated with reduced self-efficacy, but not the other way around (p. 10), echoing the earlier studies.

There are several plausible explanations behind this finding. Firstly, Herman et al. (2018) have highlighted the detrimental effects of burnout and low self-efficacy levels over time, which could lead to reduced effectiveness in teaching and, ultimately, lower self-efficacy. Secondly, burnout teachers may experience decreased productivity at work and home, which can invite criticism from stakeholders such as administrators, parents, and family members (Rankin, 2016). Thirdly, a high level of burnout and persistent stress may result in workload imbalances (too much work, insufficient resources) and community mismatches (isolation, conflict, disrespect), leading to low levels of self-efficacy (Maslach & Leiter, 2005).

Finally, this study highlights the adverse effects of high levels of burnout on teachers' job satisfaction in the context of Kazakhstan. The findings of this study align with the existing literature, indicating that burnout can negatively impact one's job satisfaction. For instance, Bataineh and Alsagheer (2012) indicated that one of the consequences of burnout is diminished job satisfaction.

5.4   *Limitations and Future Research*
The findings of the study should be interpreted in light of several limitations that needed to be taken into account. Firstly, the survey design limited participants' responses, possibly restricting the depth of information (Muijs, 2011). Secondly, the self-report questionnaire might also be viewed as a drawback because it "only captures what people think rather than what they do" (Cresswell, 2014, p. 403). Thirdly, the validity of study findings is compromised, as teachers' burnout level (CBI) was determined using only one method without triangulation. Fourthly, the use of non-probabilistic convenience sampling limits the representativeness of the results, making them not necessarily generalizable to all teachers in Kazakhstan. Finally, the small sample size (161 participants) also restricts the broader applicability of the findings.

Based on the results of the study and the limitations mentioned above, some recommendations for future research can be outlined. For instance, future research could replicate the findings of the study using larger sample sizes. In addition, other studies could consider exploring burnout by investigating the voices of teachers in qualitative research. Also, further research may consider using Maslach Burnout Inventory for Teachers designed to examine teacher burnout. This may help to further explore burnout from different angles.

6 Conclusion

The present study highlights the importance of acknowledging teacher burnout, its causes and consequences. Overall, the study suggests that burnout is a pervasive phenomenon which may go far from school and classroom settings. This study was consistent with available empirical evidence suggesting that personal, organizational and student-related burnout factors may cause burnout and provided the understanding of how spread burnout in the local community and determined burnout predictors and outcomes. Interestingly, the findings have not confirmed widespread theories regarding burnout causes but corroborated adverse effects of burnout. Available empirical data suggested that there is strong correlation between workload and burnout (Herman et al., 2018; Noushad, 2008). However, in this study, no significant effect was identified among groups divided by number of working and teaching hours.

The study results highlighted the necessity to pay heed to teachers' wellbeing and other ramifications of burnout. Research with larger sample sizes and in-depth interviews with educators may further disclose burnout in schools and address the limitations of the current study. Hopefully, the empirical findings will urge school administrators and policymakers to promote positive working conditions, provide resources on wellbeing and support services for teachers, and take into account challenges faced by female and novice teachers to address burnout.

Acknowledgments

This chapter is adapted from Nygmetzhanova, D. (2022). Teacher burnout in Kazakhstan: Prevalence, causes and consequences. [Master's thesis, Nazarbayev University]. http://nur.nu.edu.kz/handle/123456789/7317

References

Akin, M. A. (2019). An investigation into teacher burnout in relation to some variables. *International Journal of Progressive Education, 15*(4), 47–65.

Bataineh, O., & Alsagheer, A. (2012). An investigation of social support and burnout among special education teachers in the United Arab Emirates. *International Journal of Special Education, 27*(2), 5–13.

Bianchi, R., Schonfeld, I. S., & Laurent, E. (2015). Burnout–depression overlap: A review. *Clinical Psychology Review, 36,* 28–41.

Bridges, D. (Ed.). (2014). *Education reform and internationalisation: The case of school reform in Kazakhstan.* Cambridge University Press.

Brunsting, N. C., Sreckovic, M. A., & Lane, K. L. (2014). Special education teacher burnout: A synthesis of research from 1979 to 2013. *Education and Treatment of Children, 37*(4), 681–711.

Cohen, L., Manion, L., & Morrison, K. (2007). *Research methods in education* (6th ed.). Routledge.

Creswell, J. (2014). *Research design: Qualitative, quantitative, and mixed methods approaches.* Sage.

Dorman, J. (2003). Testing a model for teacher burnout. *Australian Journal of Educational & Developmental Psychology, 3*(1), 35–47.

Feldman, R., Sussman, A. L., & Zigler, E. (2004). Parental leave and work adaptation at the transition to parenthood: Individual, marital, and social correlates. *Journal of Applied Developmental Psychology, 25*(4), 459–479.

Freudenberger, H. J. (1974). Staff burn-out. *Journal of Social Issues, 30*(1), 159–165.

Gaciu, N. (2020). *Understanding quantitative data in educational research.* Sage.

García-Carmona, M., Marín, M. D., & Aguayo, R. (2019). Burnout syndrome in secondary school teachers: A systematic review and meta-analysis. *Social Psychology of Education, 22,* 189–208.

Ghasemi, A., & Zahediasl, S. (2012). Normality tests for statistical analysis: A guide for non-statisticians. *International Journal of Endocrinology and Metabolism, 10*(2), 486.

Herman, K. C., Hickmon-Rosa, J. E., & Reinke, W. M. (2018). Empirically derived profiles of teacher stress, burnout, self-efficacy, and coping and associated student outcomes. *Journal of Positive Behavior Interventions, 20*(2), 90–100.

Holmes, M. T. (2009). *Creating a positive school culture in newly opened schools.* North Carolina State University.

IAC. (2019). *National report: Chapter 1. Teaching and Learning International Survey TALIS-2018: The initial results of Kazakhstan.*

Iancu, A. E., Rusu, A., Măroiu, C., Păcurar, R., & Maricuțoiu, L. P. (2018). The effectiveness of interventions aimed at reducing teacher burnout: A meta-analysis. *Educational Psychology Review, 30,* 373–396.

Irsaliyev, S. A., Kamzoldayev, M. B., Tashibayeva, D. N., & Kopeyeva, A. T. (2019). Teachers of Kazakhstan: Why young people choose this profession and what motivates them to stay. *Beles.*

Karina, D. (2023, March 27). Tokayev: It is necessary to attract professionals to the management of education. *Inbusiness.kz*. Retrieved from https://inbusiness.kz/ru/news/tokaev-neobhodimo-privlech-professionalov-v-menedzhment-sfery-obrazovaniya

Kenny, D. A., Kaniskan, B., & McCoach, D. B. (2015). The performance of RMSEA in models with small degrees of freedom. *Sociological Methods & Research, 44*(3), 486–507.

Kristensen, T. S., Borritz, M., Villadsen, E., & Christensen, K. B. (2005). The Copenhagen Burnout Inventory: A new tool for the assessment of burnout. *Work & Stress, 19*(3), 192–207.

Madigan, D. J., & Kim, L. E. (2021). Does teacher burnout affect students? A systematic review of its association with academic achievement and student-reported outcomes. *International Journal of Educational Research, 105*, 101714.

Maslach, C. (2018). Burnout: A multidimensional perspective. In *Professional burnout: Recent developments in theory and research* (pp. 19–32). CRC Press.

Maslach, C., Jackson, S. E., & Leiter, M. P. (1997). *Maslach Burnout Inventory*. Scarecrow Education.

Maslach, C., & Leiter, M. P. (2005). Reversing burnout. *Stanford Social Innovation Review*, 43–49.

Maslach, C., & Leiter, M. P. (2008). *The truth about burnout: How organizations cause personal stress and what to do about it*. John Wiley & Sons.

Milfont, T. L., Denny, S., Ameratunga, S., Robinson, E., & Merry, S. (2008). Burnout and wellbeing: Testing the Copenhagen Burnout Inventory in New Zealand teachers. *Social Indicators Research, 89*(1), 169–177.

Ministry of Education and Science of the Republic of Kazakhstan. (2019a). *Law on the status of a teacher*. Retrieved from https://adilet.zan.kz/eng/docs/Z1900000293

Ministry of Education and Science of the Republic of Kazakhstan. (2019b). *State program of educational development for 2020–2025*. Retrieved from https://adilet.zan.kz/rus/docs/P1900000988

Montero-Marín, J., Skapinakis, P., Araya, R., Gili, M., & García-Campayo, J. (2011). Towards a brief definition of burnout syndrome by subtypes: Development of the "Burnout Clinical Subtypes Questionnaire" (BCSQ-12). *Health and Quality of Life Outcomes, 9*(1), 1–12.

Mota, A. I., Lopes, J., & Oliveira, C. (2021a). Teachers' voices: A qualitative study on burnout in the Portuguese educational system. *Education Sciences, 11*(8), 392.

Mota, A. I., Lopes, J. A. L., & Oliveira, C. R. G. (2021b). Burnout in Portuguese teachers: A systematic review. *European Journal of Educational Research, 10*(2), 693–703.

Muijs, D. (2011). *Doing quantitative research in education with SPSS*. Sage.

Noushad, P. P. (2008). From teacher burnout to student burnout. *Online Submission*. Retrieved from https://files.eric.ed.gov/fulltext/ED502150.pdf

O'Brien, P., Goddard, R., & Keeffe, M. (2008, January). Burnout confirmed as a viable explanation for beginning teacher attrition. In *Proceedings of the Australian Association for Research in Education Annual Conference (AARE 2007)*.

Osipov, V. (2019). Real support for teachers. *Kazakhstanskaya Pravda*. Retrieved from https://kazpravda.kz/n/uchitelyam-realnaya-podderzhka/

Pressley, T. (2021). Factors contributing to teacher burnout during COVID-19. *Educational Researcher, 50*(5), 325–327.

Rankin, J. G. (2016). *First aid for teacher burnout: How you can find peace and success*. Routledge.

Rodiniov, V. (2022). Teachers should stop being treated as slaves. *Internet Newspaper ZonaKZ*. Retrieved from https://zonakz.net/2019/01/30/olga-beder-uchitelej-nado-perestat-schitat-za-rabov/

Rumschlag, K. E. (2017). Teacher burnout: A quantitative analysis of emotional exhaustion, personal accomplishment, and depersonalization. *International Management Review, 13*(1), 22–36.

Saloviita, T., & Pakarinen, E. (2021). Teacher burnout explained: Teacher-, student-, and organization-level variables. *Teaching and Teacher Education, 97*, 103221.

Skaalvik, E. M., & Skaalvik, S. (2007). Dimensions of teacher self-efficacy and relations with strain factors, perceived collective teacher efficacy, and teacher burnout. *Journal of Educational Psychology, 99*(3), 611.

Skovholt, T. M., & Trotter-Mathison, M. J. (2011). *The resilient practitioner: Burnout prevention and self-care strategies for counselors, therapists, teachers, and health professionals* (2nd ed.). Routledge, Taylor, and Francis Group, LLC.

Toker, S., & Biron, M. (2012). Job burnout and depression: Unraveling their temporal relationship and considering the role of physical activity. *Journal of Applied Psychology, 97*(3), 699.

The Jamovi Project. (2023). *Jamovi (Version 2.3) [Computer software]*. Retrieved from https://www.jamovi.org

Unterbrink, T., Hack, A., Pfeifer, R., Buhl-Griesshaber, V., Müller, U., Wesche, H., & Bauer, J. (2007). Burnout and effort–reward-imbalance in a sample of 949 German teachers. *International Archives of Occupational and Environmental Health, 80*, 433–441.

Yembergenova, A. (2015). Teachers addressing intensification at one of Nazarbayev Intellectual Schools in Kazakhstan (Unpublished master's thesis). Graduate School of Education, Nazarbayev University, Astana, Kazakhstan.

CHAPTER 12

Mentoring in ITE Practicum Programs in Kazakhstan

Lyazat Turmukhambetova

Abstract

Kazakhstani educational landscape has been in the process of dramatic transformation in the recent decade, with teachers being viewed as "central planks" of the school reform (McLaughlin et al., 2021). However, the preparation of highly qualified teacher candidates, which relies on the Initial Teacher Education (ITE) programmes, seems to lag behind in providing quality practical experiences for the student teachers, which is represented by the lack of provision of pre-service mentoring support. This multiple case study explored mentoring practices within Kazakhstani ITE practicum programmes, employing Ambrosetti et al.'s (2014) mentoring framework for maximising mentoring potential. As the research found, at the micro-level, various elements of the mentoring programme were fulfilled only partially or were absent (such as expectations/goal-setting, irregular communication within the mentoring triad, lack of explicit guidelines for evaluation, etc.). However, the misalignment at every mentoring stage stems from the lack of agency given to the school-based mentors in the partnering schools and the lack of agreement and involvement within the meso-level of the school-university partnerships. Therefore, this research may inform the existing school-university collaborative strategies for further development and better integration of the practical component of the ITE programmes and mentoring provided. Additionally, it can inform the educational policies and practices related to teaching mentoring at a macro level.

Keywords

teacher education – practicum – mentoring – pre-service teacher – mentor

1 Introduction

The Law on the Status of a Teacher (Institute of Legislation and Legal Information of the Republic of Kazakhstan, 2019) defines mentoring as a form of

© LYAZAT TURMUKHAMBETOVA, 2025 | DOI:10.1163/9789004726345_013 professional help for professional adaptation for a novice teacher in secondary school (Article 13, para. 4) through coaching practices such as observation, professional discussion, and collaborative administrative work (MoES, 2020). Mentors, in light of the introduction of the new attestation mechanism (Fitzpatrick et al., 2018), precipitated by the nationwide shift to Renewed Content of Education (RCE), are expected to possess the following minimum required categories as teacher-researcher or teacher-master, while being eligible for the compensatory remuneration for their mentoring work (Institute of Legislation and Legal Information of the Republic of Kazakhstan, 2019, Article 13, para. 1; MoES, 2020, para. 14).

While the in-service mentoring programme has been acknowledged in the policy documents (see *The Law on the Status of a Teacher*) and is increasingly addressed in the research studies (Ayubayeva, 2018; Karimova, 2020), pre-service teacher mentoring programmes were overlooked in public discourse and received scant attention until very recently (Turmukhambetova, 2022). Although the matter of the quality mentoring during the practical component of the ITE programme plays significant role in the quality professional preparation for the teacher candidates, it remains unclear how the pre-service mentoring programmes operate and whether there are any regulations regarding their structure.

All in all, the purpose of this research was to contribute to the mentoring research landscape by exploring the mentoring practices within the ITE practicum programmes (by engaging the mentoring triad, including practicum advisors) and by understanding the role of the school-university partnership for the praxis of mentoring. To shed light on the mentoring practices during the pedagogical practicum, this doctoral research study (see Turmukhambetova, 2022) was guided by the following general research question: "How is the pre-service teacher mentoring program during the pedagogical practicum between universities and secondary schools in Kazakhstan understood and practised?" Therefore, this chapter will unearth and discuss the first part of the question, which relates to mentoring practices.

2 Literature Review

2.1 *The Notion of Pre-Service Teacher Practicum*
In the literature, terminology for the student teachers' practical teaching experiences during the teacher education programmes vary from "student teaching; teaching practice; practice teaching; fieldwork; professional experience; internship; teaching round; and, clinical practice" (White & Forgasz, 2016, p. 231),

whilst the word "practicum" is considered to be the most commonly used name in the professional literature. To diversify between the practicum models, Le Cornu and Ewing (2008) divided them into three major types: a traditional professional experience (with the attributes of behaviourist approach to education – by transmitting the "knowledge"), a reflective/laboratory practicum founded on the principles of teachers as reflective practitioners, and learning communities/transformative practicum inspired by the notion of communities of practice (Lave & Wenger, 1991) and action research. Nevertheless, regardless of the type of the practicum or its name, this part of the teaching program remains one of the most pivotal stages within the teaching candidate's learning journey. It is during this stage that student teachers experience intensive teaching in the classroom while having an opportunity to gain more practical knowledge about the teaching profession and apply the teaching theories in practice (Cohen et al., 2013; Darling-Hammond & Baratz-Snowden, 2007; Flores, 2010; Kitchen & Petrarca, 2016; OECD, 2005; Smith & Lev-Ari, 2005).

Whereas ITE practitioners tend to delineate between the theoretical and practical elements of teaching, this status-quo dichotomy is being actively debated and criticized in the literature. Thereby, the so-called "academic knowledge" (theory) is perceived to be of higher importance as it is being taught at the universities or "ivory towers" (Kameniar et al., 2017; Loughran & Hamilton, 2016), whereas the practicums are often seen as a "*poor cousin*" of theory (Kameniar et al., 2017, p. 54). However, it is evident that the ITE programmes need to support school-based mentors and incorporate all the necessary theoretical foundations within the provided mentoring support in a joint way, emphasising the importance of collaboration in teacher education. As Rawlings Smith (2022) proposed, the ITE practicum programmes should be viewed as a zip, where teeth symbolize the merge of the theory and practice, and the student teacher is seen as a slider, who combines the both elements.

2.2 Practicum Programme in Kazakhstan

Since being included in the Bologna process, Kazakhstan aims to embody European standards and values within its higher education programmes (MoES, 2010), comparing the practicum programmes in Kazakhstan with the European countries was justified. The European practicum programme is defined as "an integral part of professional training that can include observation of teaching and sometimes teaching itself" (European Commission/EACEA/ Eurydice, 2021, p. 67), which resonates with the practicum programme format in Kazakhstan. Likewise, the European practicum programme is usually not remunerated for the student teachers and is conducted primarily in the natural working environment of schools (p. 67).

As highlighted in the Eurydice report, the duration of practicum programs varies across countries, with Romania setting a minimum of 5 European Credit Transfer and Accumulation System (ECTS) credits and Ireland establishing a maximum of 60 ECTS credits (European Commission/EACEA/Eurydice, 2021, p. 67). In Kazakhstan, institutions providing ITE previously adhered to a range of practicum hours outlined in the former state educational standards for undergraduate programs, spanning from a minimum of 6 to a maximum of 20 ECTS credits (MoES, 2011, Clause 7.9), until the adoption of revised state compulsory educational standards for higher education institutions in 2018 (MoES, 2018). These updated standards grant flexibility to university programs in determining and assigning the duration and ECTS credits for practicum, aligned with a module-based system where practicum hours are calculated based on core subject cycle (CS) and major subject cycle (MS) components within the mandatory 240 ECTS framework.

Drawing on the literature, it was found that Kazakhstan shares the most common practicum challenges with other countries in the same way. For instance, the inadequate collaboration between schools and universities remains a crucial issue in Kazakhstan's ITE program. Yakavets et al. (2017a) found that schools often reluctantly accept student teachers due to minimal financial support, echoing Darling-Hammond and Baratz-Snowden's (2007) observation that short placements burden schools with low student contributions. Kourieos (2019) noted this perception in Cyprus's primary school practicum programmes.

Furthemore, Kazakhstan lacks a standardised ITE practicum curriculum or guidelines, despite similar program content nationwide, as each higher institution develops its practicum program based on various legal requirements such as the State Regulations of Practicum Conduct (MoES, 2016c), the Law on Education (2007), and the Labour Code (2015). A comprehensive set of guidelines for the pedagogical practicum was introduced only in 2022. As the guidelines distinguish, there are essentially four types of practicums, starting from the introductory/observational (Year 1) practicum (60h), psychological-pedagogical (Year 2) practicum (60h), pedagogical (Year 3) (180h), and pedagogical full-time practicums (Year 4) (450h). However, a concise memorandum briefly touches upon the roles and expectations of the mentors' roles and the character of the assessment, with no outlined description and goals for each type of practicum (Enic-Kazakhstan, 2022). Following the outlined professional competencies within the professional teaching standards introduced by the National Chamber of Entrepreneurs of the Republic of Kazakhstan, it is expected that the teacher candidates will integrate research-based teaching practices in the school using the academic literature (Atameken, 2017, p. 62) implying the presence of the enquiry-based type of the practicum (see Dewey, 1904; Lave & Wenger, 1991).

Among other challenges revealed in the literature about Kazakhstani practicum programs were the lack of appropriate level of practical preparation in the schools and the deficit of subject mentors to provide enough subject teaching opportunities (Aimagambetov, 2020; Yakavets et al., 2017a, p. 25), which, therefore, may result in high attrition and low prestige and status of the teaching profession in public discourse (see Irsaliyev et al., 2018).

Another problem within the practicum related to miscommunication between mentors and practicum advisors (Beck & Kosnik, 2002; Clarke, 2000; Ralph et al., 2015). This issue stemmed from the lack of explicit understanding of the role and main functions of the practicum advisors - university-based teacher educators who supervise the practicum from the university side and evaluate its outcome. The role of the practicum advisor as a liaison between the ITE and the practicum school was not well-illuminated, both in Kazakhstani and international literature, often leaving the functions and roles of the teacher educators confusing and ambiguous within the mentoring triad, often leaving the practicum advisors reduced to administrators rather than educators (Bruneel & Vanassche, 2021; Williams & Soares, 2002).

2.3 *Mentoring Programmes in Kazakhstan*

As suggested in the literature, the success of any practicum experience hinges on a central figure: the mentor or teacher educator. Mentors guide the practicum process and serve as the primary facilitator of student teachers' learning within school settings, acting in roles such as associate teacher or mentor (see Beck & Kosnik, 2002; Clarke et al., 2014; Ellis et al., 2020; Ferrier-Kerr, 2009; Hudson, 2016; Mackie, 2020; White & Forgasz, 2016, etc.).

The existing definitions of mentoring in the mentoring research are similar, suggesting various nuances in the context (organisational/educational/formal/informal). However, they all maintain the parallel roles between the mentor and the mentee. All in all, mentoring in literature is defined as a multifaceted and dynamic process involving a more experienced professional providing support, oversight, and encouragement to facilitate the career and personal development of a less experienced mentee/protege to foster learning, development, and well-being (see Fairbanks et al., 2000; Dominguez & Kochan, 2020; Hobson et al., 2017, 2020; Kram & Isabella, 1985; Roberts, 2000).

While mentoring programmes have garnered increased attention following enacting the *Law on the Status of a Teacher* (Institute of Legislation and Legal Information of the Republic of Kazakhstan, 2019), the discourse primarily revolves around in-service teacher mentoring. However, more information is needed about mentoring programs designed for student teachers during the compulsory ITE practicum.

The in-service mentoring program for beginning teachers is known as *the School of a Young Teacher* (from 24.10.11), devised under the *Law on Education* (Government of the Republic of Kazakhstan, 2007). This program mandates the provision of a designated mentor within the school to aid in the professional induction of newly appointed teachers.

Complying with the program guidelines, beginning teachers must sign a one-year mentoring contract (OECD, 2015). In the end, mentors compose a novice teacher's portfolio, including all their professional activities, achievements, feedback, and self-reflection. Afterwards, this portfolio undergoes examination by the school committee and the principal to determine the final decision regarding the teacher's candidacy (Ayubayeva, 2018; OECD, 2014). While the OECD (2014) concluded that *the School of a Young Teacher* constitutes a part of an effective induction system, with nearly 97% of the interviewed principals reporting a supportive mentoring culture, recent research on this topic presents contrasting findings. Much of the criticism of the existing mentoring mechanisms focuses on their inefficiency (Ayubayeva, 2018), inadequate implementation, lack of formal preparation for mentors, and the formalistic approach (Ayubayeva, 2018; Karimova, 2020). This evidence underscores the significance of delving deeper into the current mentoring practices within both pre-service and in-service teacher training.

2.4   *The Conceptual Framework*

Many empirical studies in mentoring research employ Kathy Kram's (1983) stage-based theoretical framework, which focuses on the most critical phases of the mentoring experience within the mentoring dyad (a mentor and a mentee). However, while Kram's (1983) work hinges on the informal long-term mentoring relationships in the professional organisational/managerial context, the conceptual framework by Ambrosetti et al. (2014), inspired by Kram (1983), is perfectly tailored to the context of the ITE (as it also includes the presence of the third party - the practicum advisor, which was critical for this study). It also assumes a short-term nature of the relationship (as the formal mentoring programme in Kazakhstan lasts approximately two to ten weeks). Furthermore, the chosen framework encapsulates all the essential elements (main concepts) that were found in other ITE mentoring frameworks, for example, goal-setting, modelling, feedback, and reflection (see Clarke et al., 2014; Crutcher & Naseem, 2016; Nielsen et al., 2022).

Moreover, all the framework elements are presented in the stage-based model, helping the researcher identify the presence/lack of the critical elements at each stage (See Table 12.1). Therefore, using this framework benefitted this study by helping to explore the existing mentoring practices in Kazakhstan comprehensively.

TABLE 12.1 Phases of implementation framework for maximising the potential of mentoring (Ambrosetti et al., 2014)

Stage	Phase focus	Considerations
Preparation for mentoring	Training for mentors and mentees before the participants meet	Training that centres on: – The nature of mentoring – Processes of mentoring – Roles of the mentor and mentee – Conflict resolution – Defining expectations for the relationship
Pre-mentoring	Initial meeting before the professional placement begins	– Outlining goals for each participant – Defining roles for the mentor and mentee – Mapping out a timeline – Setting up communication channels – Setting up a meeting schedule – Induction (to the school) – Socialisation
Mentoring	Development of the relationship and progression towards the achievement of goals	– Opportunities for development of competencies and capabilities (skills, knowledge and processes) through teaching and coaching, active participation – Feedback approaches – Reflective opportunities – Interactions that endorse reciprocity (sharing, modelling, facilitation)
Post-mentoring	Continuation or completion of the relationship	Continuation: – Progress review (formal tasks and duties) – Redefining needs/goals and mentoring roles Completion – Assessment – Relationship evaluation

3 Methodology

3.1 *Research Philosophy and Design*

Given the focus of this study on the personal experiences and perceptions of mentoring, the constructivist/interpretivist approach was deemed crucial. Unlike the positivist paradigm, which is rooted in a single objective reality, this approach allows for the inclusion of multiple realities and contexts, thereby enriching the research (Creswell & Poth, 2018; Denzin & Lincoln, 2018). Drawing on the fact that the mentoring program during the practicum functions on behalf of the university and school partnership, it was decided to focus on the two universities' practicum programs and their partnerships with the secondary schools to produce an in-depth and detailed analysis of the existing mentoring stages during the practicum. Thus, the case study method was selected as it allowed exploring the program "in-depth and within its real-world context" (Yin, 2018, p. 15).

Therefore, this multiple-case study explored two ITE practicum programs in two Kazakhstani universities located in the two most populated cities: Astana and Almaty. Following the principles of the multiple-case research design (Yin, 2018), the two practicum programs represent the typical practicum programs within ITE as they both organize their practicums drawing on the national regulations of the practicum program prescribed by the State Regulations of the Practicum Conduct (MoES, 2016c) and *Law on Education* (from 27.07.2007) in terms of the practicum organisation and conduct.

3.2 *Data Collection and Analysis*

This study drew on a variety of sources, including 23 semi-structured one-on-one interviews, one paired interview, four focus groups, and document analysis. Apart from the university practicum documents and the accounts of the mentors and the student teachers at the schools, it was also important to include the voices of the university-based teacher educators (practicum advisors), whose voices were underrepresented in the literature (see Bruneel & Vanassche, 2021; Hart, 2018). Therefore, this study filled the population gap (Miles, 2017). All in all, 26 people participated in this research after giving informed consent. The internal and external confidentiality of the participants was also ensured (Sieber & Tolich, 2012), and participants were given pseudonyms (e.g., student teachers – STs, mentors – Ms, practicum advisors – PAs).

These diverse data sources were analysed using a combination of approaches. Yin's (2016) five-phased qualitative analysis approach served as a broad analytical framework, while Tracy's (2020) iterative phronetic approach provided a more focused analytical perspective. This combined approach facilitated a comprehensive and nuanced interpretation of the data, aligning with the research questions and across cases.

3.3 Ethical Considerations

This study was conducted in accordance with the KERA (2020) ethical code's values for educational research, which hinge on respect for the participants' rights, fairness of the participants' selection, promoting beneficence by minimising risks, and trustworthiness and accountability in terms of the study results' dissemination (pp. 22–23).

3.4 Trustworthiness of the Research

The trustworthiness/credibility of the study was accomplished by several means. The prolonged engagement, member checking with the participants, and triangulation of sources and methods (see Beitin, 2012; Silverman, 2013; Yin, 2018) helped address the credibility criteria essential to the constructivist paradigm (Lincoln & Guba, 2013). The dependability and confirmability (internal validity) of the data (Lincoln & Guba, 2013) were addressed through regular communication and discussions with the PhD supervisory committee, along with asking doctoral colleagues to peer-review the chapters and discuss possible rival explanations (Yin, 2018).

4 Findings and Discussion

Being guided by the stagewise mentoring framework by Ambrosetti et al. (2014) (see Table 12.1), seven themes were developed.

4.1 Practicum Advisors' Roles and Responsibilities

As the study unfolded, the role of the university-based teacher educator was critical in terms of the quality practicum provision and mentoring by extension. Therefore, it was deemed crucial to shed light on the practicum advisors' responsibilities in preparing student teachers for the practicum and the challenges surrounding student teachers' readiness for educational reforms. While requirements for practicum advisors vary between institutions, their roles typically include organising pre- and post-practicum conferences, managing documentation, liaising with schools, and ensuring student teachers' preparedness. This finding was in line with the literature on the practicum advisors' managerial duties in the international literature (see (Bruneel & Vanassche, 2021; Cohen et al., 2013).

Practicum advisors were also assigned to prepare student teachers for the practical aspects of teaching, including methodological guidance and orientation. However, several discrepancies were found in the effectiveness of this preparation, with some mentors expressing concerns over student teachers' readiness for the practicum, especially in Case 1. Many mentors and student teachers voiced their concerns regarding the inadequate institutional preparation for new teaching approaches in light of the RCE and a lack of clarity in practicum expectations. Inadequate alignment between university instruction and practical school requirements exacerbates this issue, hindering student teachers' ability to engage with ongoing educational changes effectively.

> I have [...] year-7 pupils, and I was asked by the principal to take some mentees for this class, because we had to teach the "obnovlyonka" [RCE] and we also organized teaching seminars on that terrible "obnovlyonka" [RCE] [laughs]. Of course, I took them [mentees]. And for them, it was a frightening experience. I would like you to especially note this. Unfortunately, according to this updated curricular programme our school was well-trained, and we are now running ahead even of those pedagogical universities which we are partners with. Now, when I have my mentees from different pedagogical institutions, and when their practicum advisors brought them here, they tell me: "We do not know what this programme is about; we do not give them that methodological material yet". (University 1 stage 2\M 4: 18)

While the practicum advisors' role at this stage is crucial in terms of preparing the student teachers for the practicum, many of them failed at this stage, which resulted in the student teachers' lack of the methodological and practical understanding of the educational reform, which supports the McLaughlin et al.'s (2021) proposition about the insufficient preparation and lack of professional readiness provided by the ITE institutions in Kazakhstan. While practicum advisors show themselves incapable of offering the necessary theoretical provision, school-based mentors can take advantage of this state of things and provide student teachers with the necessary RCE-related training, thereby shifting the perception of the school-based mentors as the stakeholders in the "diminished position of power" (Brown et al., 2016, p. 2016; Manderstedt et al., 2023) to a more robust and more influential position within the school-university partnership.

Despite differing perceptions of their roles' significance, practicum advisors play a crucial part in programme execution, though some interviewed advisors viewed their duties as formalities.

> my duty only revolved around collecting the papers necessary for the practicum report. Well, I think it is the same around Kazakhstan, because

> I know it from other universities' experiences. As with my experience, it is usually a formality, mainly related to the submission of the necessary documents. (University 2\Practicum advisor 1: 9–10)

This perception may be connected to the perceived low prestige of the practicum advisors' role at the ITE universities and the lack of clearly defined criteria for this role (see Beck & Kosnik, 2002). It stresses the importance of prioritising the practicum programs and having the practicum advisors' functions and responsibilities delineated when they are assigned to this position.

4.2   Sharing Expectations and Defining Goals of the Mentoring Process

In Theme 2, "Sharing Expectations and Defining Goals of the Mentoring Process," the initiation stage of mentoring involves discussions between mentors and mentees to establish conditions and working schedules, aligning with Ambrosetti et al.'s (2014) framework for maximising mentoring potential. Expectations play a crucial role in formal mentoring relationships, as they differ significantly from those in naturally formed informal mentoring relationships (Baugh & Fagenson-Eland, 2007; Ghosh, 2011).

Clear communication of expectations was reported crucial by all mentors yet often overlooked in practice. While mentors harboured implicit expectations, student teachers typically lacked articulated expectations beyond meeting practicum requirements, leading to a disconnect between perceived goals and actual outcomes. This finding differed from the literature that maintains that shared expectations are paramount for the mentoring relationship as it helps set trustful and open communication (Chao, 2007; Rajuan et al., 2010; Zachary, 2012).

This attitude towards shared expectations may stem from various factors such as time constraints, cultural norms, or assumptions about shared understanding. For example, open discussions about the expectations could seem a challenge for Kazakhstani teachers of older generations, given that some schoolteachers come from a Soviet background known for the autocratic principles of leadership (Ardichvili & Gasparishvili, 2001) and the high-power distance culture (Hofstede, 2001). That is why the role of practicum advisors is particularly valuable, as they can facilitate negotiations between students and mentors from an equal position of power on behalf of the students (Rikard & Veal, 1998; Slick, 1998; Stanulis, 1995).

Furthermore, it is even more crucial for all the participants of the mentoring relationship to know and agree on each other's understanding of mentoring and have clarity over the assigned roles to avoid any confusion or disappointment throughout the mentoring process (Kochan & Freeman, 2020; Zachary, 2012).

As participants shared, mentors generally expected mentees to be proactive, engaged, and receptive to guidance. Mentees, on the other hand, had their expectations shaped by institutional requirements or personal aspirations. "We all know that we go to the practicum just for the sake of passing it, to get the pass for the practicum." (University 1 stage 2\ST 2: 32).

> [...] initially I went to the practicum driven by the requirement of submitting the practicum documents to her [PA] afterwards. Initially, we [group] were not motivated in the right way, and mostly I think it is because of the practicum advisor. (University 1 stage 1\Student teacher 1: 34)

While the students' responsibility for preparing for the practicum remains, the practicum advisors needed to spend more time discussing the students' expectations and understanding of the mentoring practices before starting the practicum. This was further demonstrated in their attitudes towards their reflective practices, which were recorded in their practicum diaries.

The lack of agreement over the practicum goals and roles was also evident in the mentors' accounts, who criticized the generic nature of some practicum goals (represented in the attainment of practical teaching skills), highlighting the need for more explicit articulation and alignment with the roles of practicum advisors.

> M2: Unfortunately, sometimes the goals and objectives of the practicum of those partnering institutions are not clearly articulated, or they are very generic. I mean, when working with the [pedagogical] colleges, you clearly know that they see practicum as a future possibility of their students' [future] employment, whereas most of the ITE universities, including this partnering university, are quite nebulous. For example, I do not know how the practicum advisors of that university perceive the practicum, it is not written or stated anywhere in the documents. What I can see from that attitude is that this university administration perceives practicum more as a formality, rather than a serious work. And that is upsetting, such an attitude. (University 1 stage 1\Focus Group 3 Mentors University 1 Case 1: 14)

Overall, as the research demonstrated, the success of the mentoring process hinges on transparent communication among all the participants of the mentoring triad, and ITE universities and their partnering schools should approach the negotiations with clearly stated intentions and outlined goals that would benefit everyone.

As the research showed, mentors and student teachers did not distinguish between the practicum goals and mentoring goals. Thus, the mentoring process was entirely based on the guidelines provided by the ITE program, which puts the university-based advisors in a position of power and leaves mentors with no opportunity to voice their preferences and inclinations towards the teaching approaches used. Following Cohen's (2013) review of practicum experiences, this model of mentoring practices is considered to be "slanted towards the teacher education program" (p. 27). This evidence again highlights the domineering positionality of the Kazakhstani ITE programs, or "ivory towers" (Kameniar et al., 2017; Loughran & Hamilton, 2016) that keep dictating all the rules of the practicum, whereas evidently, it is public schools in Kazakhstan that are now advancing the educational reform and implement the RCE. Moreover, as the study by Manderstedt et al. (2023) demonstrated, disputes and signs of asymmetric power will persist in the mentoring triad as long as mentoring operates on one-sided terms.

4.3 Socialisation to School

The process of socialisation in the school environment plays a crucial role in preparing student teachers for their practicum experience. This theme delves into how student teachers are introduced to the school's culture, values, and internal workings, primarily facilitated by their mentors and practicum assignments.

Mentors in both cases adopted diverse approaches to socialising student teachers into the school community. While some student teachers in Case 2 experienced a warm reception from the school staff, others in Case 1 faced challenges, feeling neglected or abandoned by their mentors. One student teacher observed unethical behaviour within the teaching collective, demonstrated by her mentor, who permitted herself mocking other teaching candidates in front of the student teacher and pupils. Therefore, it is safe to assume that positive role modelling from the mentor's side enhances student teachers' integration into the teaching community. In contrast, instances of unprofessional conduct, such as mocking colleagues, can impede this integration and tarnish the teaching image within the specific school. Consequently, as organisational mentoring research demonstrates, poorly arranged socialisation opportunities may deter teacher candidates from further engagement with the school and the mentor and subsequent attrition from the profession (see Chao, 2007). This may partially explain the existing shortage of teachers in public secondary schools in Kazakhstan and their perceived lack of interest during their practicum program (MoES, 2019; OECD, 2014; Tastanbekova, 2018).

Along with the mentors, practicum advisors were also found to play a critical role in the student teachers' socialisation in the school community, as they oversaw briefing student teachers about the school culture and expectations. It were practicum advisors who could emphasize the importance of student teachers making meaningful contributions to the school community through extracurricular events, projects, or initiatives.

This finding was in line with the description of the socialisation activities revealed in the literature review on student teachers' practicum experiences by Cohen et al. (2013). Practicum advisors at University 2 even devised practicum assignments encouraging student teachers to engage with the school community and build professional networks.

> PA3: I also recommend our students to contribute to the schools with some additional projects, for example, this year I will probably insist on it [...]. For example, most schools don't have websites in English. [...] This year [year-4] they are going to be there for ten weeks, so ten weeks is enough time to prepare some materials with their students about the school, official school website or unofficial school website, or the Facebook account for this school institutional account. They can prepare it with their pupils, a kind of a project- based approach, and when they finish their practicum, they can give it as a gift, as a present to the school principal – why not? (University 2\Practicum Advisors Focus Group 2: 184–187)

This finding once again demonstrates the need and importance for the mentoring triad to act cooperatively, and the school-university partnerships to reconsider and re-evaluate their mentoring strategies during the practicum programme.

4.4 Developmental Opportunities

This theme focused on the mutual benefits of mentor-student-teacher collaboration in terms of improving professional competencies during observational and independent teaching stages.

The first observational stage emphasises the importance of observing mentors' teaching styles and classroom dynamics. Observations provided insights into schoolteachers' (not only mentors but other subject teachers', too) teaching methods and pupil behaviour. These findings were also in line with Bozack and Salvaggio (2016), who empirically concluded that observations should not be confined to the particular subject teaching practices only, as those teachers who had an opportunity to observe other subject teachers gained more new pedagogical knowledge.

While the observational stage was considered significant for the student teachers in terms of acquiring vicarious knowledge about teaching, it was also mentioned several times in both cases that the mentors' pedagogical approaches were somewhat outdated and reminded of the "Soviet-style", teacher-centred way of teaching. For that reason, some students in both cases mentioned having to retort to the transmissive teaching approaches over the constructivist teaching strategies following their mentors' lead.

> ST3: Traditionality in a sense like how we were taught at school, [...] old-fashioned teaching styles, you know, grammar-translational methods, when we are given one sentence and we should translate it. And these methods are still widely used in most of the schools. My mentor did not use it much, fortunately. [...] However, even with her, the lessons were mainly teacher-centred, although teaching methodology now is promoting student-centred learning. Lots of theory, no ICT equipment involved. [...]

> ST1: Even if the coursebook is defined to use the direct teaching method, the teaching approaches are still widely grammar-translation-based. [...] so even if they have new coursebooks they would adjust it to their own accustomed way of teaching.

> ST3: Almost all lessons I observed showed that students could not discuss or provide argumentation during the lesson [...]. I think students lack some critical thinking. [...] (University 1 stage 1\Focus Group 1 ST University 1 Case 1: 164–174)

A similar situation was observed in the German longitudinal research by Voss and Kunter (2020), who found that secondary school teacher candidates were more prone to adapt to the schools' teaching approaches and abandon their constructivist teaching approaches during their induction period due to the "reality aftershock" (p. 293). To tackle this lack of clarity over the selected methodology between the student teachers and their mentors, it is necessary for the mentors to offer their explanation of the lessons in the so-called "deconstruction" sessions after the observations, where student teachers and mentors may discuss the lesson step-by-step and shed light onto the chosen activities/ strategies and justification of their use (see Arthur et al., 2003; Mok & Staub, 2021; Nielsen et al., 2022). The practice of deconstructing the lesson would be especially beneficial for developing the culture of "reflective teaching" for the teacher candidates, as they may incorporate the habit of critically reflecting on their decisions during independent teaching, following the principles of "reflection-on-action" introduced by Schön (1987).

The second and final stage of independent teaching underscores the importance of mentors in developing pedagogical, subject-specific, and classroom management skills. Mentors prioritized building rapport with students and fostering differentiated learning. Student teachers acknowledged improvements in understanding pupil needs and managing classroom dynamics, facilitated by mentor guidance. This finding was also in line with Hudson's (2013) and Bird and Hudson's (2015) studies, which revealed that classroom management was one of the skills mentors and mentees prioritized the most in practicum settings.

4.5 Facilitating Reflective Practices through the Practicum Diaries

As the study revealed, the practicum diaries served as a means for student teachers to reflect on their experiences during the mentoring process, which aimed to facilitate attaining their practical knowledge. Surprisingly, the practicum program documents provided by both universities did not explicitly state the purpose of reflective writing or explain its importance—the reflective diaries also lacked structure or any guiding questions to encourage reflection. This evidence again underscored the lack of the ITE program engagement with the student teachers' actual teaching practice on site.

As a probable consequence, all the practicum participants viewed the diaries primarily as a formative assessment tool rather than a tool for in-depth reflection. Such a perception led to a lack of engagement in guiding or evaluating the written reflections.

> These practicum diaries – it is not a serious document for them [students], they don't treat them seriously. Once, I was asked to write a reference letter within that practicum diary, and I read what they had written there, and I was shocked. "...Seriously?" Their response was that everybody wrote like this, so it was not their fault. Of course, I was a bit disappointed, but they thought it was normal to write about their practicum like that. (University 1 stage 1\Mentor 2: 85)

The content of the practicum diaries provided for the document analysis tended to be descriptive rather than analytical, with little connection to academic literature. Some students' diary logs seemed similar to the content of other students' diaries, highlighting a lack of understanding of the importance of reflection among some student teachers. Participants also voiced their suggestions for improving the diaries to facilitate reflective teaching, which included exploring alternative formats and providing clearer instructions to students about the importance of reflective practice.

As literature demonstrates, it is pivotal for student teachers and mentors to agree on the definition of reflective teaching to yield meaningful practicum results and master their teaching skills (Gadsby, 2022; Gillies, 2017; Ward & McCotter, 2004). Following the introduced professional teaching standards (Atameken, 2017), it is essential for the ITE programs to be inquiry-based, and for that reason, practicum advisors need to work and emphasize the need for reflection at the school-based practicums too and, therefore, agree on the common definition and structure of those reflective thinking skills and require student teachers to base their reflections on the scholarly literature (Gadsby, 2022; Gillies, 2017; Hudson, 2013). The observed reflections in the provided practicum diaries can be defined as unproductive, following Davis's (2006) typology of productive and unproductive reflections, because they were not focused, highly descriptive and mostly entailed participants' personal judgement (e.g., "I liked..."), while productive reflections include analysis, assumption challenging and connecting the teaching practice with the academic literature.

Apart from the structure of the reflective diaries, format revision is necessary. While the reflective diary remains one of the most common formats for student teachers (Flores, 2020; Gadsby, 2022; Graves, 2010; Larrivee, 2000), several participants of the study mentioned the outdatedness of this instrument, suggesting other formats, including voice recording. Furthermore, it would be helpful to reconsider the existing format and allow student teachers to express their reflections in the ways they find more compelling. Hourani (2013) discussed the use of social network platforms or blogging, along with peer-reflective groups and forums, where student teachers can discuss and share their experiences with peers, thereby being ready to challenge or defend their practices by supporting them with the literature. E-portfolios were also identified as alternative reflection tools, given their capacity to incorporate diverse evidence of the learning journey, alongside their accessibility and user-friendly nature (Hourani, 2013; Oakley et al., 2014; Oner & Adadan, 2011).

4.6　Relational Opportunities

The organisation of the mentored practicum involves a complex communication system among mentors, student teachers, and practicum advisors, which undergirds the learning process along with support provided during this critical phase of teacher training.

As the study demonstrated, the interaction between mentors and student teachers was mainly characterised by a supportive and friendly approach, with mentors regularly engaging with mentees and playing the "parental figure" role, except for two cases of dysfunctional mentoring experiences that occurred with students from both cases. While interactions are often informal and personal, mentors maintain a balance between friendliness and professionalism, ensuring that trust remains central to their relationship. Trust, in turn, enhances student teachers' self-efficacy beliefs, contributing to their confidence in practical teaching.

> Sometimes, we have partnerships like friends, we can have a friendly relationship and discuss something not related to the school issues, but it is usually when the work is done and when it is appropriate. Of course, when the student teachers have any problems or something was upsetting the student, I can feel it, and we can discuss it together. (University 2\Mentor 3: 60)

This personal/professional duality between mentors and student teachers was also evident in the literature (see Mackie, 2017). Furthermore, the analysis of the mentors' vocalized perceptions of the student teachers as "children" would also indicate the implicit parental figure the mentors could undertake, as evident in Karimova's (2020) study on Kazakhstani in-service mentors. Overall, these findings indicate the psychosocial approach to mentoring (Kram, 1983), where mentors focus on accommodating the student teachers' psychosocial needs in the new environment through support and encouragement.

Following the classification of Wang and Odell (2002), teacher mentoring approaches can be divided into three significant perspectives, such as humanistic, situated apprentice, and critical constructivist. Therefore, given that mentors and mentees in both cases were oriented towards the attainment of practical knowledge during the practicum while at the same time expressing their willingness to be supported emotionally, it can be assumed that mentoring practices in both cases entailed the elements of the humanistic mentoring approach and situated apprenticeship, represented in a traditional hierarchical mentoring model.

As mentors from both cases pointed out, while maintaining a friendly relationship with students, it was critical for them not to cross professional boundaries. This attitude towards the hierarchy and asymmetric relationships between the mentors and mentees can be explained by the socio-cultural factor of high-power distance society which favours acquiescence towards the authority (Hofstede, 2001), as was also in line with Yakavets's (2017) study on the schooling culture in Kazakhstan, and which was also aggravated by the historical factor of Soviet-influenced autocratic understanding of leadership (Ardichvili & Gasparishvili, 2001; Fimyar & Kurakbayev, 2016).

Practicum advisors also play a crucial role in monitoring student teacher performance at the partnering schools, although their level of interaction with the students varied. In some cases, student teachers hesitated to seek direct assistance from practicum advisors, fearing it may negatively affect their competence. In case of uncertainty at the practicum site, student teachers would seek help from their peers in the social media group chat. This reluctance highlights a potential gap in support systems, particularly when mentor-student teacher relationships may become dysfunctional, and students do not have any mechanisms to protect themselves. Some practicum advisors openly admitted they wanted the partnering schools to take responsibility for their students, and thus, there was no point for the latter to complain.

> I always tell them [student teachers]: "Be grateful you do not dig potatoes at the mentor's garden – you do a teacher's work instead!" And they immediately stop nagging and get to work instead. I mean, of course, if they were asked to pay their communal services or pick their children from kindergarten – it is a different matter, but when the mentor asks to do some work around the classroom – it is student's duty to do it. [...].
> (University 1 stage 1\Senior Faculty Member: 57–59)

This evidence of the lack of contact between the student teachers and their practicum advisors can be interpreted as asymmetrical as opposed to collaborative, and their assistance was heavily managerial, which is also in line with the literature (Bruneel & Vanassche, 2021). For that reason, it is essential for the ITE programs and practicum guidelines to explicitly outline the responsibilities of the practicum advisors to increase their accountability and give them more responsibility within the mentoring triad.

It was especially alarming to learn that the communication system between the practicum advisors and mentors was almost non-existent or very limited, with practicum advisors preferring to communicate with school administration rather than directly with mentors. Given the rare frequency of communication, this approach may leave mentors feeling undervalued or neglected, particularly when facing challenges within the mentor-student-teacher relationship. Therefore, mentors may find themselves predicated between the ITE university requirements and the duty of providing quality lessons to their students through the help of the student teachers, which limits their sense of agency and their value within the whole practicum program, thereby hampering their intrinsic motivation to be helpful.

> M2: Maybe we should demand the response from those teacher educators who taught them that way of teaching? Maybe [we should] ask for the student teachers' academic transcript, to know how well they are doing

at the university? This is what I am talking about, about the partnership with the university, it should be a two-way street, we should not work alone with this student "material", we should know more about them, what they know, what they can do. Maybe it would be more helpful if our practicum grade would have more value and would stay within the student teachers' "zachyotka" [academic transcript]. Because in the end, it is still the practicum advisors who put their final grade for the practicum, not us. They [student teachers] do not perceive us very seriously [...]. (University 1 stage 1\Focus Group 3 Mentors University 1 Case 1: 89–90)

At the same time, mentors found the lack of interaction with the practicum advisors acceptable by stating that they found it easier to address the potential problems with their mentees directly or with the help of the vice-principals. As Veal and Rikard's study (1998) defined, this type of interaction mostly resembled a so-called "bureaucratic type of relationship", which is akin to a "contrived collegiality" type of teacher collaboration (Hargreaves & Fullan, 2012) which is mostly represented in papers rather than in reality.

Following Burroughs et al. (2020), this lack of communication within the school-university partnership may signify Level 1 and Level 2 of the partnership, defined as "Taking from schools" and "Borrowing from schools" and manifested in the lowest frequency of interaction between the university faculty and the mentors. These levels contradict the higher levels of the partnership within the framework: Level 5: Co-constructed partnership and Level 6: Learning community. Therefore, the findings indicate a lack of systematic interaction within the partnership, which may have implications for the whole mentoring process during the practicum and the practicum programme alignment with the ITE programmes' goals (Burroughs et al., 2020). To conclude, clear communication, trust-building, and mutual respect are essential for creating supportive environments conducive to student teacher development.

This finding also corroborates the hypothesis proposed by Andreasen et al. (2019), who posited that: "there are reasons to believe that the unfortunate cooperative climate between [...] institutions might prevent the development of a shared professional identity as teacher educators" (p. 288). For this reason, as the findings demonstrated, inadequate cooperation between the mentors and university practicum advisors may have detrimental effects on the quality of the practicum programme, as it may shape student teachers' attitudes towards the practicum and its goals, thereby informing their teaching and reflecting practices at the practicum site along with the mentoring culture at the partnering school too.

4.7 Assessment of the Mentoring Programme

This theme examined the evaluation of the mentoring program as the practicum draws to a close, which crowns the outcomes of the mentoring experience. As it was revealed, the practicum advisors play a significant role in the final stage of the mentoring program, as they undertake the assessment on par with the mentors. The commonalities between both cases included a similar approach to the practicum evaluation, represented in the students' portfolios, which entailed various documents such as practicum diaries, observations, lesson plans, and reference letters. The latter document was the most influential in the final deliberation of the grade, as was admitted by the Practicum advisor 3 in Case 1: "The mentor sees the student every day, both in mundane circumstances and during the lessons, so I guess the mentor's judgement in this matter is the priority."

This use of teacher portfolios for assessment is considered a widely common practice in ITE programs because they may entail various sources of evidence of the teaching work, such as: "planning, instruction, assessment, curriculum design, and communications with peers and parents" (Darling-Hammond & Snyder, 2000, p. 537).

At the same time, many participants (practicum advisors and student teachers) in both cases expressed their doubts regarding the effectiveness of the assessment tools. For example, Practicum advisor 1 in Case 2 admitted to seeing the practicum diaries as more of a formal requirement than a meaningful reflection tool. This perspective stemmed from the strict guidelines set by the university for internal and external evaluations of practicum programs, leading student teachers to write in diaries with the purpose of just filling the diary pages to meet these standards. This anxiety-driven approach to practicum evaluation may be explained by the "punitive function of assessment" (Fimyar & Kurakbayev, 2016, p. 96), which may happen due to the residues of the Soviet culture legacy among the university faculty. For that reason, it was critical to note the difference in the assessment system provided by the practicum advisors in Case 2, who devised a meticulous internal practicum assignment that would represent the student teachers' intrinsic teaching journey, helping to capture their thoughts throughout the practicum.

As a part of the university assessment, post-practicum conferences were noted as crucial for student teachers to share their experiences.

Along with the practicum assessment by the university-based teacher educator, there are assessment procedures by the school-based mentors. It was found that while mentors lacked explicit assessment criteria, their evaluations tended to centre on the professional growth and personal qualities of student teachers. Following van Ginkel et al.'s (2018) study, these two assessment criteria could be interpreted as dimensions of social judgement, represented in "social desirability" (personal qualities in relation to sociability and morality) and "social utility" (in relation to the student teachers' professional competencies and effort). Nevertheless, in both cases, instances of fairness concerns arose, as some mentors delegated the writing of reference letters to students, potentially hampering the reliability of assessments.

As the literature posits, it is unnatural for the mentor's role to evaluate their mentee, as it presents an additional "emotional labour" (Bullough Jr & Draper, 2004) and may compromize the fundamental trust between the participants (Marzano & Simms, 2016). In this regard, as the ONSIDE research project by Hobson (2017, 2020) demonstrated, mentoring assessment becomes less biased if the mentors are not directly associated with the specific school. Nevertheless, appointing external mentors might present logistical challenges in communication, particularly when time is already constrained, as highlighted by Aderibigbe et al. (2022).

Informal assessment methods, such as feedback sessions and observational journals, were highlighted as essential for fostering reflective teaching practices. However, satisfaction levels among student teachers varied, indicating the importance of an inquiry-based mentoring model for skill development and understanding student needs.

Overall, the findings indicate a lack of consensus regarding evaluative procedures between schools and universities in both cases, highlighting a discrepancy in student teachers' performance expectations during the practicum programs within both ITE programs and their partnering schools. Notably, a large-scale quantitative study by Soto-Lillo and Quiroga-Lobos (2021) provides compelling evidence that collaborative approaches to practicum evaluation between school-based and university-based teacher educators could enhance the reliability of assessment. This transparency can be achieved through a cooperative approach and open discussion of performance expectations. Therefore, these findings underscore the significance of shared practicum objectives between schools and universities and again stress the importance of collaboration between ITE programs and schools.

5 Conclusion

As findings revealed, following the stagewise model by Ambrosetti et al. (2014), the existing coordination within the school-university partnership affected all stages of mentoring. At the preparation for the mentoring stage, practicum advisors seemed to have unclear supervisory roles within the practicum, illustrating the lack of the Kazakhstani ITE programme to adequately prepare students for the school experience by informing them about the current educational reform and RCE along with helping student teachers focus on the learning goals and expectations during the practicum. In both cases, practicum advisors perceived their roles primarily in administrative or managerial capacities rather than as facilitators or agents of mentoring within the practicum program. They mainly communicated with school leadership representatives, such as principals or vice-principals. This evidence also underscored the mentors' low prestige within the school hierarchy, depriving them of decision-making authority and agency within the perceived mentoring triad and the practicum program. Therefore, recognising mentors' contributions can be considered a vital step towards enhancing the practicum experience for all stakeholders involved. The pre-mentoring stage revealed the inability of mentors to set the expectations and goals for the collaborative work that were entirely substituted by the practicum programme guidelines, implying the lack of informed understanding about mentoring and the lack of established mentoring practices within the schools in Kazakhstan. During the mentoring stage, it became evident that the lack of structured and guided observation methods hindered mentors' ability to provide effective cognitive modelling and foster productive reflective teaching practices, which implied the absence of an inquiry-based practicum model but rather an apprentice-based practicum model based on the reproduction of the existing teaching approaches. The final post-mentoring stage demonstrated the shortcomings of the existing assessment mechanisms, which were found uncoordinated and non-transparent.

While one might assume that the current mentoring approaches stem from underdeveloped mentoring practices, the issue is multifaceted. It primarily stems from a lack of communication between ITE practicum programmes and their affiliated schools. Although efforts within Kazakhstani ITE programmes to enhance the integration of theory and practice are underway, establishing well-arranged and sound partnerships remains an evolving issue.

This evidence contributes valuable insights to mentoring research by offering empirical support and extending upon the hypothesis proposed by Andreasen et al. (2019). Their hypothesis suggested a potential correlation between school-university partnerships and perceptions of mentoring. The present study reinforces these assumptions by demonstrating that such partnerships can impact the prevailing mentoring approaches within practicum programmes and the mentoring culture in general.

References

Aderibigbe, S. A., Holland, E., Marusic, I., & Shanks, R. (2022). A comparative study of barriers to mentoring student and new teachers. *Mentoring & Tutoring: Partnership in Learning, 30*(3), 1–22. https://doi.org/10.1080/13611267.2022.2070995

Aimagambetov, A. (2020, September 8). О подготовке будущих педагогов [On preparation of future teachers]. *Facebook*. https://www.facebook.com/askhat.aimagambetov/posts/10217037768752653

Ambrosetti, A., Knight, B. A., & Dekkers, J. (2014). Maximizing the potential of mentoring: A framework for pre-service teacher education. *Mentoring & Tutoring: Partnership in Learning, 22*(3), 224–239. https://doi.org/10.1080/13611267.2014.926662

Andreasen, J. K., Bjørndal, C. R., & Kovač, V. B. (2019). Being a teacher and teacher educator: The antecedents of teacher educator identity among mentor teachers. *Teaching and Teacher Education, 85*, 281–291. https://doi.org/10.1016/j.tate.2019.05.011

Ardichvili, A., & Gasparishvili, A. (2001). Socio-cultural values, internal work culture, and leadership styles in four post-communist countries: Russia, Georgia, Kazakhstan, and the Kyrgyz Republic. *International Journal of Cross-Cultural Management, 1*(2), 227–242. https://doi.org/10.1177%2F147059580112006

Arthur, J., Davison, J., & Moss, J. (2003). *Subject mentoring in the secondary school* (2nd ed.). Routledge.

Atameken. (2017). *Professional standards of the teaching profession*. Order №133. Addendum to the Order of the National Chamber of Entrepreneurs of the Republic of Kazakhstan from June 8, 2017. https://atameken.kz/uploads/content/files/ПС%20Педагог.pdf

Ayubayeva, N. (2018). *Teacher collaboration for professional learning: Case studies of three schools in Kazakhstan* [Unpublished doctoral dissertation]. University of Cambridge. https://doi.org/10.17863/CAM.20729

Baugh, S. G., & Fagenson-Eland, E. A. (2007). Formal mentoring programs: A "poor cousin" to informal relationships? In B. R. Ragins & K. E. Kram (Eds.), *The handbook of mentoring at work: Theory, research, and practice* (pp. 249–273). Sage Publications.

Beck, C., & Kosnik, C. (2002). Components of a good practicum placement: Student teacher perceptions. *Teacher Education Quarterly, 29*(2), 81–98. https://www.jstor.org/stable/23478294

Beitin, B. K. (2012). Interview and sampling: How many and whom. In J. F. Gubrium, J. A. Holstein, A. B. Marvasti, & K. D. McKinney (Eds.), *The Sage handbook of interview research: The complexity of the craft* (pp. 243–254). Sage Publications.

Bird, L., & Hudson, P. (2015). Investigating a model of mentoring for effective teaching. *Journal of Teaching Effectiveness and Student Achievement, 2*(2), 11–21. https://eprints.qut.edu.au/83687/23/__staffhome.qut.edu.au_staffgroupl%24_leaderj_Desktop_Mentoring%2BPractices%2Bfor%2BJTESA.pdf

Bloomfield, D., White, S., & Goulding, J. (2013). *Authentic assessment in practice settings: A participatory design approach.* Melbourne, Australia: Australian Teaching and Learning Council. https://ltr.edu.au/resources/PP10_1784_Reimann_Report_2013.pdf

Bozack, A. R., & Salvaggio, A. N. (2016). Impactful mentoring within a statewide, comprehensive. In L. Searby & S. K. Brondyk (Eds.), *Best practices in mentoring for teacher and leader development* (pp. 31–55). Information Age Publishing.

Brown, T., Rowson, H., & Smith, K. (2016). The beginnings of school-led teacher training: New challenges for university teacher education. *Manchester: MMU.* https://espace.mmu.ac.uk/602385/2/School%20Direct%20Research%20Report.pdf

Bruneel, S., & Vanassche, E. (2021). Conceptualising triadic mentoring as discursive practice: Positioning theory and frame analysis. *European Journal of Teacher Education, 1–17.* https://doi.org/10.1080/02619768.2021.1985456

Bullough Jr, R. V., & Draper, R. J. (2004). Making sense of a failed triad: Mentors, university supervisors, and positioning theory. *Journal of Teacher Education, 55*(5), 407–420. https://doi.org/10.1177/0022487104269804

Chao, G. T. (2007). Mentoring and organizational socialization: Networks for work adjustment. In B. R. Ragins & K. E. Kram (Eds.), *The handbook of mentoring at work: Theory, research, and practice* (pp. 179–196). Sage Publications.

Clarke, A. (2000). An advisory practicum for practicum advisors: A follow-up study. *Teaching Education, 11*(2), 131–146. https://doi.org/10.1080/713698970

Clarke, A., Triggs, V., & Nielsen, W. (2014). Cooperating teacher participation in teacher education: A review of the literature. *Review of Educational Research, 84*(2), 163–202. https://doi.org/10.3102/0034654313499618

Cohen, E., Hoz, R., & Kaplan, H. (2013). The practicum in preservice teacher education: A review of empirical studies. *Teaching Education, 24*(4), 345–380. https://doi.org/10.1080/10476210.2012.711815

Creswell, J. W., & Poth, C. N. (2018). *Qualitative inquiry and research design: Choosing among five approaches* (4th ed.). Sage Publications.

Crutcher, P. A., & Naseem, S. (2016). Cheerleading and cynicism of effective mentoring in current empirical research. *Educational Review, 68*(1), 40–55. https://doi.org/10.1080/00131911.2015.1058749

Darling-Hammond, L., & Baratz-Snowden, J. (2007). A good teacher in every classroom: Preparing the highly qualified teachers our children deserve. *Educational Horizons, 85*(2), 111–132. https://www.jstor.org/stable/42926597

Darling-Hammond, L., & Snyder, J. (2000). Authentic assessment of teaching in context. *Teaching and Teacher Education, 16*(5–6), 523–545. https://doi.org/10.1016/S0742-051X(00)00015-9

Davis, E. A. (2006). Characterizing productive reflection among preservice elementary teachers: Seeing what matters. *Teaching and Teacher Education, 22*(3), 281–301. https://doi.org/10.1016/j.tate.2005.11.005

Denzin, N. K., & Lincoln, Y. S. (2018). The discipline and practice of qualitative research. In N. K. Denzin & Y. S. Lincoln (Eds.), *The Sage handbook of qualitative research* (5th ed., pp. 29–71). Sage Publications.

Dewey, J. (1904). The relation of theory to practice in education. *Teachers College Record, 5*(6), 9–30. https://doi.org/10.1177/016146810400500601

Dominguez, N., & Kochan, F. (2020). Defining mentoring: An elusive search for meaning and a path for the future. In B. J. Irby, J. N. Boswell, L. J. Searby, F. Kochan, R. Garza, & N. Abdelrahman (Eds.), *The Wiley international handbook of mentoring: Paradigms, practices, programs, and possibilities* (pp. 3–18). John Wiley & Sons. https://doi.org/10.1002/9781119142973.ch1

Enic-Kazakhstan. (2022). Методические рекомендации по организации и проведению педагогической практики в организациях образования [Guidelines for organizing and conducting pedagogical practicum in educational institutions]. *Ministry of Education and Science of the Republic of Kazakhstan.* https://enic-kazakhstan.edu.kz/files/1651237257/metodicheskie-rekomendacii-po-provedeniyu-pedagogicheskoy-praktiki.pdf

European Commission/EACEA/Eurydice. (2021). *Teachers in Europe: Careers, development, and well-being. Eurydice report.* Luxembourg: Publications Office of the European Union. https://policies/eurydice/sites/default/files/teachers_in_europe_2020_chapter_2_0.pdf

Fairbanks, C. M., Freedman, D., & Kahn, C. (2000). The role of effective mentors in learning to teach. *Journal of Teacher Education, 51*(2), 102–112. https://doi.org/10.1177/0022487100051000204

Ferrier-Kerr, J. L. (2009). Establishing professional relationships in practicum settings. *Teaching and Teacher Education, 25*(6), 790–797. https://doi.org/10.1016/j.tate.2009.01.001

Fimyar, O., & Kurakbayev, K. (2016). "Soviet" in teachers' memories and professional beliefs in Kazakhstan: Points for reflection for reformers, international consultants and practitioners. *International Journal of Qualitative Studies in Education, 29*(1), 86–103. https://doi.org/10.1080/09518398.2015.1017850

Fitzpatrick, M., Figueroa, D. T., Golden, G., & Crosby, S. (2018). *Education policy outlook: Kazakhstan.* OECD Publishing. https://www.oecd.org/education/Education-Policy-Outlook-Country-Profile-Kazakhstan-2018.pdf

Flores, M. A. (2020). Feeling like a student but thinking like a teacher: A study of the development of professional identity in initial teacher education. *Journal of Education for Teaching, 46*(2), 145–158. https://doi.org/10.1080/02607476.2020.1724659

Gadsby, H. (2022). Fostering reflective practice in Post Graduate Certificate in Education students through the use of reflective journals: Developing a typology for reflection. *Reflective Practice, 23*(1), 1–12. https://doi.org/10.1080/14623943.2022.2028612

Ghosh, R., Dierkes, S., & Falletta, S. (2011). Incivility spiral in mentoring relationships: Reconceptualizing negative mentoring as deviant workplace behavior. *Advances in Developing Human Resources, 13*(1), 22–39. https://doi.org/10.1177/1523422311410639

Gillies, D. (2017). Developing the thoughtful practitioner. In M. A. Peters, B. Cowie, & I. A. Menter (Eds.), *A companion to research in teacher education* (pp. 23–35). Springer. https://doi.org/10.1007/978-981-10-4075-7_2

Van Ginkel, G., van Drie, J., & Verloop, N. (2018). Mentor teachers' views of their mentees. *Mentoring & Tutoring: Partnership in Learning, 26*(2), 122–147. https://doi.org/10.1080/13611267.2018.1472542

Government of the Republic of Kazakhstan. (2007). *Law on Education.* Amended effective in 04.07.2018. https://adilet.zan.kz/eng/docs/Z070000319_

Graham, B. (2006). Conditions for successful field experiences: Perceptions of cooperating teachers. *Teaching and Teacher Education, 22*(8), 1118–1129. https://doi.org/10.1016/j.tate.2006.07.007

Graves, S. (2010). Mentoring pre-service teachers: A case study. *Australasian Journal of Early Childhood, 35*(4), 14–20. https://doi.org/10.1177/183693911003500403

Hargreaves, A., & Fullan, M. (2012). *Professional capital: Transforming teaching in every school.* Teacher College Press.

Hart, A. E. (2018). Exploring the interpersonal dynamics of the supervisory triad of pre-service teacher education: A qualitative meta-synthesis. [Unpublished doctoral dissertation]. Kennesaw State University. https://digitalcommons.kennesaw.edu/cgi/viewcontent.cgi?article=1024&context=teachleaddoc_etd

Hobson, A. J. (2017). The terrors of judgementoring and the case for ONSIDE mentoring for early career teachers. In D. A. Clutterbuck, F. K. Kochan, L. Lunsford, N. Dominguez, & J. Haddock-Millar (Eds.), *The Sage handbook of mentoring* (pp. 335–357). Sage Publications Ltd.

Hobson, A. J. (2020). ONSIDE mentoring: A framework for supporting professional learning, development and well-being. In B. J. Irby, J. N. Boswell, L. J. Searby, F. Kochan, R. Garza, & N. Abdelrahman (Eds.), *The Wiley international handbook of mentoring: Paradigms, practices, programs, and possibilities* (pp. 521–545). John Wiley & Sons, Inc. https://doi.org/10.1002/9781119142973.ch32

Hofstede, G. (2001). *Culture's consequences: Comparing values, behaviors, institutions and organizations across nations* (2nd ed.). Sage Publications.

Hourani, R. B. (2013). Pre-service teachers' reflection: Perception, preparedness, and challenges. *Reflective Practice, 14*(1), 12–30. https://doi.org/10.1080/14623943.2012.732947

Hudson, P. (2013a). Desirable attributes and practices for mentees: Mentor teachers' expectations. *European Journal of Educational Research, 2*(3), 107–119. https://eprints.qut.edu.au/64234/

Hudson, P. (2013b). Mentoring as professional development: "Growth for both" mentor and mentee. *Professional Development in Education, 39*(5), 771–783. https://doi.org/10.1080/19415257.2012.749415

Hudson, P. (2016). Forming the mentor-mentee relationship. *Mentoring & Tutoring: Partnership in Learning, 24*(1), 30–43. https://doi.org/10.1080/13611267.2016.1163637

Institute of Legislation and Legal Information of the Republic of Kazakhstan. (2019, December 27). *On the Status of a Teacher.* No. 293-VI ЗРК. https://adilet.zan.kz/eng/docs/Z1900000293

Irsaliyev, S. A., Kamzoldayev, M. B., Tashibayeva, D. N., & Kopeeva, A. T. (2019). Учителя Казахстана: Почему молодые люди выбирают эту профессию и что их мотивирует оставаться в ней? [Teachers of Kazakhstan: Why do young people choose this profession and what motivates them to stay in it?]. Center of Analysis and Strategy "Beles." https://beles-cas.kz/images/teacher.pdf

Kameniar, B., Davies, L. M., Kinsman, J., Reid, C., Tyler, D., & Acquaro, D. (2017). Clinical praxis exams: Linking academic study with professional practice knowledge. In M. A. Peters, B. Cowie, & I. A. Menter (Eds.), *A companion to research in teacher education* (pp. 53–67). Springer.

Karimova, N. (2020). *Mentoring programs for novice teachers in Kazakhstani mainstream schools: Experiences and attitudes of main stakeholders* [Unpublished master's thesis]. Nazarbayev University. https://nur.nu.edu.kz/handle/123456789/4884

Kazakhstani Educational Research Association (KERA). (2020). *The code of ethics for researchers in education.*

Kitchen, J., & Petrarca, D. (2016). Approaches to teacher education. In J. Loughran & M. L. Hamilton (Eds.), *International handbook of teacher education* (Vol. 1, pp. 137–186). Springer. https://doi.org/10.1007/978-981-10-0366-0

Kochan, F., & Freeman, S. (2020). Mentoring across race, gender, and generation in higher education: A cross-cultural analysis. In B. J. Irby, J. N. Boswell, L. J. Searby, F. Kochan, R. Garza, & N. Abdelrahman (Eds.), *The Wiley international handbook of mentoring: Paradigms, practices, programs, and possibilities* (pp. 471–486). John Wiley & Sons. https://doi.org/10.1002/9781119142973.ch29

Kourieos, S. (2019). Problematising school-based mentoring for pre-service primary English language teachers. *Mentoring & Tutoring: Partnership in Learning, 27*(3), 272–294. https://doi.org/10.1080/13611267.2019.1630992

Kram, K. E. (1983). Phases of the mentor relationship. *Academy of Management Journal, 26*(4), 608–625. https://doi.org/10.5465/255910

Kram, K. E., & Isabella, L. A. (1985). Mentoring alternatives: The role of peer relationships in career development. *Academy of Management Journal, 28*(1), 110–132. https://doi.org/10.5465/256064

Larrivee, B. (2000). Transforming teaching practice: Becoming the critically reflective teacher. *Reflective Practice, 1*(3), 293–307. https://doi.org/10.1080/713693162

Lave, J., & Wenger, E. (1991). *Situated learning: Legitimate peripheral participation.* Cambridge University Press.

Le Cornu, R., & Ewing, R. (2008). Reconceptualising professional experiences in pre-service teacher education: Reconstructing the past to embrace the future. *Teaching and Teacher Education, 24*(7), 1799–1812. https://doi.org/10.1016/j.tate.2008.02.008

Lincoln, Y. S., & Guba, E. G. (2013). *The constructivist credo.* Left Coast Press.

Loughran, J., & Hamilton, M. L. (2016). Developing an understanding of teacher education. In J. Loughran & M. L. Hamilton (Eds.), *International handbook of teacher education* (Vol. 1, pp. 3–22). Springer. https://doi.org/10.1007/978-981-10-0366-0

Mackie, L. (2020). Understandings of mentoring in school placement settings within the context of initial teacher education in Scotland: Dimensions of collaboration and power. *Journal of Education for Teaching, 46*(3), 263–280. https://doi.org/10.1080/02607476.2020.1752555

Manderstedt, L., Viklund, S., Palo, A., & Lillsebbas, H. (2023). Meeting eye to eye: The power relations in triadic mentoring of the degree project in teacher education. *Mentoring & Tutoring: Partnership in Learning, 31*(4), 512–531. https://doi.org/10.1080/13611267.2023.2224256

Marzano, R. J., & Simms, J. A. (2016). Tips from Dr. Marzano. *Marzano Research.* https://www.marzanoresearch.com/resources/tips/cci_tips_archive

McLaughlin, C., Winter, L., Fimyar, O., & Yakavets, N. (2021). Reforming a whole school system: The case of Kazakhstan. In C. McLaughlin & A. Ruby (Eds.), *Implementing educational reform: Cases and challenges* (pp. 67–90). Cambridge University Press. https://doi.org/10.1017/9781108864800

Menter, I., & Flores, M. A. (2020). Connecting research and professionalism in teacher education. *European Journal of Teacher Education, 44*(1), 115–127. https://doi.org/10.1080/02619768.2020.1856811

Ministry of Education and Science (MoES). (2020). *On the organizational code of mentoring and the requirements to the teachers eligible for mentoring* (Order №160). Registered with the Ministry of Justice of the Republic of Kazakhstan on April 25, 2020, №20486. https://adilet.zan.kz/rus/docs/V2000020486

Ministry of Education and Science of the Republic of Kazakhstan (MoES). (2010). *State Program of Education Development in the Republic of Kazakhstan for 2011–2020.* Decree of the President of the Republic of Kazakhstan No. 1118, December 7, 2010. Astana: MoES.

Ministry of Education and Science of the Republic of Kazakhstan (MoES). (2011). *State compulsory educational standard of the Republic of Kazakhstan: Higher education.* https://online.zakon.kz/Document/?doc_id=31027312&pos=1;-16#pos=1;-16

Ministry of Education and Science of the Republic of Kazakhstan (MoES). (2016). *State Regulations of The Practicum Conduct. State Compulsory Educational Standard of the Republic of Kazakhstan.* Registered with the Ministry of Education and Science of the Republic of Kazakhstan on March 4, 2016, №13395. https://adilet.zan.kz/rus/archive/docs/V1600013395/29.01.2016

Ministry of Education and Science of the Republic of Kazakhstan (MoES). (2018). *The order on the approval of state compulsory educational standards for all levels of education №604*. Registered with the Ministry of Justice of the Republic of Kazakhstan on November 1, 2018, №17669. https://adilet.zan.kz/eng/docs/V1800017669

Mok, S. Y., & Staub, F. C. (2021). Does coaching, mentoring, and supervision matter for pre-service teachers' planning skills and clarity of instruction? A meta-analysis of (quasi-) experimental studies. *Teaching and Teacher Education, 107*, 103484. https://doi.org/10.1016/j.tate.2021.103484

Nielsen, W., Tindall-Ford, S., & Sheridan, L. (2022). Mentoring conversations in preservice teacher supervision: Knowledge for mentoring in categories of participation. *Mentoring & Tutoring: Partnership in Learning, 30*(1), 38–64. https://doi.org/10.1080/13611267.2022.2030185

Oakley, G., Pegrum, M., & Johnston, S. (2014). Introducing e-portfolios to pre-service teachers as tools for reflection and growth: Lessons learnt. *Asia-Pacific Journal of Teacher Education, 42*(1), 36–50. https://doi.org/10.1080/1359866X.2013.854860

Oner, D., & Adadan, E. (2011). Use of web-based portfolios as tools for reflection in preservice teacher education. *Journal of Teacher Education, 62*(5), 477–492. https://doi.org/10.1177/0022487111416123

Organisation for Economic Co-operation and Development (OECD). (2005). *Teachers matter: Attracting, developing and retaining effective teachers, education and training policy*. OECD Publishing. https://www.oecd.org/education/school/34990905.pdf

Organisation for Economic Co-operation and Development (OECD). (2014). *Reviews of national policies for education: Secondary education in Kazakhstan*. OECD Publishing. http://dx.doi.org/10.1787/9789264205208-en

Parliament of the Republic of Kazakhstan. (2015). *Labour Code of the Republic of Kazakhstan*. №414-V, 23 November 2015. Nur-Sultan, Kazakhstan. https://adilet.zan.kz/eng/docs/K1500000414

Rajuan, M., Beijaard, D., & Verloop, N. (2007). The role of the cooperating teacher: Bridging the gap between the expectations of cooperating teachers and student teachers. *Mentoring & Tutoring: Partnership in Learning, 15*(3), 223–242. https://doi.org/10.1080/13611260701201703

Ralph, E., Preston, J. P., & Walker, K. (2015). Mentorship in the teaching practicum: Partners' perspectives. *International Journal of Learning, Teaching and Educational Research, 13*(3), 1–16. http://mail.ijlter.org/index.php/ijlter/article/download/441/210

Rawlings Smith, E. (2022). Breaking the theory-practice relationship: Why decoupling universities from ITE would be illogical. *CollectivED Working Papers, 13*, 26–30. https://www.leedsbeckett.ac.uk/-/media/files/schools/school-of-education/collected-issue-13-final.pdf

Roberts, A. (2000). Mentoring revisited: A phenomenological reading of the literature. *Mentoring & Tutoring: Partnership in Learning, 8*(2), 145–170. https://doi.org/10.1080/713685524

Schön, D. A. (1987). *Educating the reflective practitioner.* Jossey-Bass.

Sieber, J. E., & Tolich, M. B. (2012). *Planning ethically responsible research* (Vol. 31). Sage Publications.

Silverman, D. (2013). *Doing qualitative research: A practical handbook* (4th ed.). Sage Publications.

Slick, S. K. (1998). The university supervisor: A disenfranchised outsider. *Teaching and Teacher Education, 14*(8), 821–834. https://doi.org/10.1016/S0742-051X(98)00028-6

Smith, K., & Lev-Ari, L. (2005). The place of the practicum in pre-service teacher education: The voice of the students. *Asia-Pacific Journal of Teacher Education, 33*(3), 289–302. https://doi.org/10.1080/13598660500286333

Soto-Lillo, P., & Quiroga-Lobos, M. (2021). University tutors and school mentors: Evaluators in the practical training of future teachers. *Teaching and Teacher Education, 107*, 103489. https://doi.org/10.1016/j.tate.2021.103489

Stanulis, R. N. (1995). Classroom teachers as mentors: Possibilities for participation in a professional development school context. *Teaching & Teacher Education, 11*(4), 331–344. https://doi.org/10.1016/0742-051X(94)00035-5

Tastanbekova, K. (2018). Teacher education reforms in Kazakhstan: Trends and issues. *Bulletin of Institute of Education, University of Tsukuba, 48*(2), 87–97. https://tsukuba.repo.nii.ac.jp/records/46586

Tracy, S. J. (2020). *Qualitative research methods: Collecting evidence, crafting analysis, communicating impact* (2nd ed.). John Wiley & Sons. https://www.wiley.com/en-es/Qualitative+Research+Methods%3A+Collecting+Evidence%2C+Crafting+Analysis%2C+Communicating+Impact%2C+2nd+Edition-p-9781119390800

Turmukhambetova, L. (2022). *Exploring formal mentoring programmes within the practicum programmes in Kazakhstan* [Unpublished doctoral dissertation]. Nazarbayev University. http://nur.nu.edu.kz/handle/123456789/7443

Veal, M. L., & Rikard, L. (1998). Cooperating teachers' perspectives on the student teaching triad. *Journal of Teacher Education, 49*(2), 108–119. https://doi.org/10.1177/0022487198049002004

Voss, T., & Kunter, M. (2020). "Reality shock" of beginning teachers? Changes in teacher candidates' emotional exhaustion and constructivist-oriented beliefs. *Journal of Teacher Education, 71*(3), 292–306. https://doi.org/10.1177/0022487119839700

Wang, J., & Odell, S. J. (2002). Mentored learning to teach according to standards-based reform: A critical review. *Review of Educational Research, 72*(3), 481–546. https://doi.org/10.3102/00346543072003481

Ward, J. R., & McCotter, S. S. (2004). Reflection as a visible outcome for preservice teachers. *Teaching and Teacher Education, 20*(3), 243–257. https://doi.org/10.1016/j.tate.2004.02.004

White, S., & Forgasz, R. (2016). The practicum: The place of experience? In J. Loughran & M. L. Hamilton (Eds.), *International handbook of teacher education* (Vol. 1, pp. 231–266). Springer. https://doi.org/10.1007/978-981-10-0366-0

Williams, A., & Soares, A. (2002). Sharing roles and responsibilities in initial teacher training: Perceptions of some key players. *Cambridge Journal of Education, 32*(1), 91–107.

Yakavets, N. (2017). Negotiating the principles and practice of school leadership: The Kazakhstan experience. *Educational Management Administration & Leadership, 45*(3), 445–465. https://doi.org/10.1177/1741143216628537

Yakavets, N., Bridges, D., & Shamatov, D. (2017). On constructs and the construction of teachers' professional knowledge in a post-Soviet context. *Journal of Education for Teaching: International Research and Pedagogy.* https://doi.org/10.1080/02607476.2017.1355086

Yin, R. K. (2016). *Qualitative research: From start to finish* (2nd ed.). The Guilford Press.

Yin, R. K. (2018). *Case study research and applications: Design and methods* (6th ed.). Sage Publications.

Zachary, L. (2012). *The mentor's guide* (2nd ed.). Jossey-Bass.

Zeichner, K. (1990). Changing directions in the practicum: Looking ahead to the 1990s. *Journal of Education for Teaching, 16*(2), 105–132. https://doi.org/10.1080/0260747900160201

CHAPTER 13

Navigating Transformations

Early Childhood Education and Care in Kazakhstan

Aiida Kulsary, Laura Ibrayeva and Daniel Hernández-Torrano

Abstract

Early childhood education and care (ECEC) has become one of the priorities of teacher education reforms in Kazakhstan. With this chapter we present a systematic review of the developments in its policies and practices. The review provides an account of its historical evolution since the Soviet education till to date. We then draw on some lesson from the review in order to make recommendations for the model of ECEC in Kazakhstan.

Keywords

early childhood education and care – pre-school education – initial teacher education – ECEC curriculum – professional development

1 Introduction

Early Childhood Education and Care (ECEC) has become a priority area for educational policy and practice worldwide, recognized for its significant impact on children's later developmental outcomes (Vandenbroeck, 2020). Supranational agencies such as UNESCO, UNICEF, and the OECD have played a crucial role in advocating for ECEC globally. For instance, the OECD's "Starting Strong" initiative has been instrumental in shaping policy development in Nordic countries (Karila, 2012). Similarly, Target 4.24 of the United Nations Sustainable Development Goals encourages member counties to ensure access to quality ECEC for all children (UN, 2015). As countries aim to meet agency recommendations, national reforms focus on expanding access through initiatives like public-private partnerships (Ruutiainen et al., 2020) and enhancing ECEC quality by improving curriculum standards and investing in professional development (Karila, 2012).

© AIIDA KULSARY, LAURA IBRAYEVA AND DANIEL HERNÁNDEZ-TORRANO, 2025
DOI:10.1163/9789004726345_014

A recent bibliometric study conducted by Ibrayeva et al. (under review), spanning nearly five decades, reveals a notable surge in ECEC research, particularly in the last two decades. This indicates ongoing growth and development in the field. The findings suggest that ECEC research has primarily focused on social scientific research. The extensive body of research on ECEC has consistently demonstrated that access to quality ECEC can promote cognitive (Davies et al., 2021; Ansari & Pianta, 2018), socio-emotional (Yang et al., 2019), and physical development while also playing a crucial role in reducing social inequalities (Van Belle, 2016). However, most of the research has been produced from the USA, other predominantly English-speaking countries, and Europe (Ibrayeva et al., under review). There is limited output from researchers in other regions, including the CIS region.

The landscape of ECEC in Kazakhstan has undergone significant transformations marked by historical developments and recent reforms. This chapter presents a comprehensive examination of these changes, offering a nuanced understanding of the current state of ECEC in the country. The chapter begins with an exploration of the historical context of preschool education during the Soviet era. It then navigates through the challenges encountered in the early years of independence, highlighting the efforts to expand access to the ECEC. Next, recent reforms aimed at enhancing the quality assurance of the ECEC are presented. Furthermore, the chapter sheds light on the pedagogical foundations shaping early childhood experiences and scrutinizes recent developments and government initiatives aimed at elevating the qualifications and capabilities of ECEC educators. Looking forward, the chapter touches upon the future developments in inclusive ECEC in Kazakhstan.

2 Method of Review

In order to provide a comprehensive account of changes in ECEC, so to offer a deeper understanding of the current state of ECEC in Kazakhstan, we conducted a systematic review of literature. We also conducted a policy review. The objectives of the review were to do the following:
- To provide a comprehensive overview of preschool education in the Soviet era;
- Identify challenges experienced in preschool education;
- To analyse the impact of reforms on ECEC quality assurance;
- Explore current trends in practices, ECEC teacher preparation, and professional development.
- Draw some lessons to make recommendations for ECEC in the future.

In selecting the relevant literature, we focused on scholarly papers and policy documents. Our criteria for scholarly papers were that they should have supportive empirical evidence. Papers which presented only the authors' opinions were deliberately excluded. Our search was aimed at papers that focused on the history of preschool education in the Soviet times, the conceptualisation of ECEC, its challenges, the reforms and current trends, ECEC teacher preparation, and professional development. The selection of policies reviewed was that they should be connected directly or indirectly to ECEC. For scholarly papers, we consulted various databases such as ERIC, Scopus, and Google Scholar. We also consulted the websites of the Kazakhstan Ministry of Education and Egov for policy documents. We consulted the Nazarbayev University library, and we perused books, articles, theses, and electronic sources to find relevant, up-to-date literature on the topic.

3 Historical Context of Preschool Education In Kazakhstan

3.1 The Development of Preschool Education in Soviet Kazakhstan

Preschool in Kazakhstan has historically been shaped by and built upon the practices and theories established during the Soviet period. This influence can be attributed to the fact that prior to the implementation of the Soviet educational system, childcare and upbringing were primarily provided by family members (Yakavets, 2017). However, following the events of the October Revolution in 1917, significant reforms in education took place in the Union Republics, including Kazakhstan. The new Soviet government acknowledged the significance of early childhood education in emancipating women and promoting child development in accordance with socialist values. This resulted in the integration of preschool education into the unified public education system and the establishment of widespread state preschool institutions accessible to all children (Zaporozhets & Kurbatova, 1974).

As a result, Kazakhstan established its first facility dedicated to ECEC in 1917 in the city of Verny, known today as Almaty. This pioneering institution accommodated 300 children and marked the beginning of an ECEC system in the region (UNESCO, 2004). By 1921, the country already had 115 kindergartens, and by 1940, 517 preschool organizations were operational across all regions, serving over 21,000 preschool-age children. Despite the challenges posed by the Great Patriotic War, the growth of preschool organizations continued uninterrupted. From 1940 to 1945, their numbers increased by 188 (IAC, 2022).

In the 1960s, the development of networks of preschool organizations in Kazakhstan took on a new magnitude, driven by the active development of various spheres of industry. At the beginning of the 1960s, there were 1,803 nurseries and kindergartens functioning in the country, and by the middle of the 1980s, these figures had tripled. By 1991, the republic boasted a remarkable count of 8,881 preschool institutions (IAC, 2022).

3.2 Navigating Challenges: Pre-School Education in the Early Years of Independence

Despite the high priority placed on preschool education in Soviet Kazakhstan, the sector encountered significant challenges following its independence in 1991. The economic crisis of the early and mid-1990s forced the government to introduce market-oriented reforms aimed at reducing government expenditure and increasing private investment in education. The 1999 education budget represented 3.9% of the GDP, compared with 4.5% in 1996 (UNESCO, 2004). In terms of the budget distribution within sub-sectors, preschool education was the most negatively affected. In 1999, preschool education received only 3.5% of the education budget, despite preschool-aged children representing 9% of the population (UNESCO, 2000).

During the Soviet period, about 60% of kindergartens were owned by state enterprises. After the privatization of these enterprises, most became unprofitable and could no longer financially support their associated kindergartens. As a result, 82% of preschool organizations were declared vacant and subsequently closed. By the year 2000, only 1,089 state preschool organizations remained operational, marking the lowest figure throughout Kazakhstan's period of independence, with rural areas being the most profoundly affected. In 1991, rural kindergartens held a numerical advantage over urban ones, but by 2000, they had lost over 95% of their network and student population (IAC, 2022).

It is also worth noting that despite the government's efforts to involve the private sector in the preschool provision, the number of non-governmental kindergartens decreased from 1071 in 1994 to 178 in 1999 (IAC, 2022). The operation of the private kindergartens was unprofitable because of the high utility costs, financial constraints among the population, and strict tax regulations. As a result, both the state and private preschool networks were unable to fully cover the educational and developmental needs of preschool-aged children, and during the period between 1991–2000, only 12.3% of the children aged 1-6 received preschool education (IAC, 2022).

Due to this issue, between 1995 and 1999, a significant number of children entered primary school without adequate ECEC training (IAC, 2022). Recognizing this educational gap, the government took proactive measures by introducing preschool preparation for 5 to 6-year-olds in 1999. Since then, pre-primary education has been both free and mandatory and can be conducted in

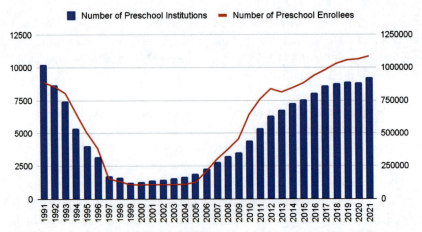

FIGURE 13.1   Evolution of preschool enrollees and preschool institutions in Kazakhstan (1911–2021)

preschool institutions, through pre-primary classes in general education schools, or within families (IAC, 2022). This initiative made Kazakhstan the first country in Central Asia to legislatively establish compulsory one-year free preschool preparation.

To effectively implement this policy, two services were introduced: pre-primary classes and pre-primary groups. Pre-primary classes are half-day programs designed for older preschool-aged children who had not previously received preschool education. These classes are typically established within secondary schools. On the other hand, pre-primary groups provide comprehensive, all-day pre-primary training and are set up within kindergartens (IAC, 2022).

As a result, in 1999, the country opened over 6,500 one-year preschool classes and successfully enrolled more than 130,000 children aged 5–6 years. Additionally, approximately 3,000 preschool groups were operating across the country, catering to more than 70,000 children. Following this initiative, in the academic year 2000–2001, more than 50% of first graders entered school prepared, a significant improvement from the 20% in 1999. This policy is considered a major accomplishment of the national education reform, Kazakhstan being the first Commonwealth of Independent States (CIS) country to implement compulsory pre-primary education legislation (IAC, 2022) (see Figure 13.1).

3.3   *Post-2000 Educational Reforms: Bridging Gaps and Enhancing Access*

Since 2000, Kazakhstan has witnessed substantial economic growth, which has cultivated favorable conditions for the transformation of the education sector. Recognizing education as a top national priority, the government has embarked on numerous reform initiatives to improve access to early childhood education and care (ECEC) services.

The State Program of Education (SPED) for 2000–2005 outlined the main development trajectories in education. Objectives included expanding accessibility, elevating educational quality, optimizing system management, improving the social status of educators, and fostering the integration of Kazakhstan's education system into the global educational landscape. In terms of ECEC provision, the primary emphasis was directed towards ensuring the school readiness of children and their transition into the formal education system (MES RK, 2000).

A further SPED for 2005–2010 was successful in improving the ECEC participation rates through increasing the number of preschool institutions. Between 2005 and 2010, the children's enrollment rate doubled, while the number of institutions increased from 1,283 units in 2005 to 6,446 units in 2010. The growth rate of ECEC networks during this period was significantly higher in rural areas than in urban. Rural institutions increased tenfold from 375 units in 2005 to 4,555 units in 2010 (IAC, 2022). The mini-centers were pivotal in this expansion, accounting for 64.9% of all ECEC institutions by 2010 (IAC, 2022). Shorter operating hours, fewer age groups, and flexible educational programs made them cost-effective and easy to set up in various settings, from private residences and community buildings to schools (UNESCO, 2010).

Kazakhstan has observed a notable increase in its birth rate since 2000. By 2010, the total fertility rate in the country reached 2.6 children per woman, significantly surpassing the OECD average of 1.75 (OECD, 2018). This uptrend has escalated the demand for preschool education institutions. In 2010, the government recorded approximately 296,700 applications for ECEC placement (IAC, 2022). In response to this challenge, the Balapan Preschool Education Program for 2010–2020 was approved. The program sought drastic measures to reduce the shortage of preschool institutions in the country and aimed to ensure 77.7% coverage of children with ECEC by 2015 and achieve 100% coverage by 2020, including pre-primary preparation for children aged 5–6 (MES RK, 2010).

To accomplish these objectives, the Balapan Program placed a strong emphasis on private-sector engagement. A range of public-private partnership initiatives, such as granting soft loans through the Damu credit program, were introduced to offer attractive terms that incentivize the private sector to establish preschool institutions (Galushko, 2019). Additionally, entrepreneurs who open daycare facilities can take advantage of government-provided tax privileges (Voronina, 2016).

Furthermore, in 2010, the licensing process for establishing private preschools was simplified. Instead of a formal licensing process, private preschools begin operations by notifying regional Departments of Education Control of their establishment. The requirements for opening are minimal and include possessing business registration, following construction standards for preschool facilities, obtaining approvals from emergency and sanitary control authorities, installing fire alarm systems, and providing essential equipment and educational materials (Kobenova, 2022).

Efforts to expand ECEC coverage through engaging the private sector have proven effective. By 2021, the network of private preschools had expanded significantly to reach 4,973 units, marking an eleven-fold increase from 2011. Private ECEC facilities constituted 45.7% of the total preschool institutions in 2021. The enrollment in private ECEC facilities accounted for 45.9%, encompassing a total of 424,302 children. In urban areas, 2,814 private ECEC establishments serve 234,228 children, while rural areas have 2,159 private ECEC facilities with 190,074 enrolled children (IAC, 2022) (see Figure 13.1).

3.4   *Setting Quality in Kazakhstani Ecec*

While Kazakhstan has achieved notable success in the expansion of ECEC services, both public and private, this rapid growth has raised concerns about the quality of the services provided. In particular, after a joint order from the Ministry of Internal Affairs and the Ministry of Education in 2019 to equip preschool institutions with video surveillance systems, there has been an increase in reported cases of child mistreatment, including physical abuse and violations of sanitary and educational standards (MES RK, 2022). International organizations have also noted low standards for preschool education in Kazakhstan compared to OECD countries (OECD, 2017).

The government's leniency towards private preschools has resulted in a notable decline in the quality of services provided by these institutions. While the government requires attestation for all educational organizations, reports indicate that this requirement is primarily enforced in state preschools, with only a minority of private preschools participating in the state attestation process. Despite private preschool teachers constituting over one-third of all educators in the field, most lack the necessary qualifications. Furthermore, over 60% of private preschools operate in non-standard buildings that do not provide safe, quality spaces for children due to the government's relaxed sanitary and hygiene standards for opening preschools (Buldybayeva, 2022).

In response to public concerns and growing media reports, the government has acknowledged the need to address the quality issues in preschool education. This commitment is reflected in the latest national education plan, the Concept of Development of Pre-School, Secondary, Technical, and Vocational Education for 2023–2029 (MoE RK, 2023). As part of this plan, Ensuring the Quality of Education at the Systemic Level has been identified as one of the seven key directions. The Concept aims to establish a comprehensive National Quality Assurance System with four levels: internal quality assurance, external quality assurance, quality assurance for accreditation bodies, and governmental quality assurance.

3.5 *Internal Quality Assurance: Monitoring Children's Development*

At the internal level, the quality of the ECEC services is ensured through a System for Monitoring the Development of Preschool Children's Skills and Abilities, which has been implemented since 2017. The primary method of monitoring is observation, conducted by teachers in children's natural environments. Three assessments are conducted throughout the academic year: one at the beginning of September, an intermediate assessment in January, and a final assessment in May. In these assessments, educators use a set of age-based indicators in line with the State Education Program to monitor a child's progress in educational areas such as Health, Communication, Cognition, Creativity, and Society. For each educational area, teachers record the outcomes of the assessments in separate Observation Sheets. These records are then compiled to create a comprehensive Summary Report for the entire group or class. Methodologists or vice principals review this report to make any necessary adjustments to the Education Program. Additionally, the assessment results are used to create an Individual Child Development Card, which serves as a guide for developing specific learning objectives for each child (IAC, 2022).

3.6 *External Quality Assurance*

Kazakhstan is actively working towards establishing a comprehensive system of external quality assurance. As part of this effort, there is an ongoing initiative to develop and implement an independent national quality assessment system for ECEC by the year 2026 (MoE RK, 2023). Presently, the external quality assurance framework includes regular state attestations, with plans to reintroduce licensing for the establishment of private preschools.

3.6.1 State Attestation

State attestation of ECEC institutions is one of the key vehicles used to ensure external ECEC quality in the country. The primary objectives of the attestation process are to ensure preschools' adherence to the State Education Standards, Education Plans and Programs, alignment with Organizational Requirements for Educational Institutions, and guarantee a secure environment for students and parents' satisfaction (MoE RK, 2023).

Despite its significance, the state attestation process faced challenges in the past. From 2012 to 2017, state attestation occurred regularly in educational organizations. However, it faced an interruption in 2016 due to identified corruption risks. Media reports from 2015 to 2018 highlighted at least seven criminal cases involving education department personnel (Kopeeva, 2018). Unclear qualification requirements and ethical guidelines for committee members were identified as contributing factors to the potential misuse of authority (Kopeeva, 2021).

Additionally, the high-stakes nature of the process, with binary results (attested or unattested), resulted in institutions facing excessive pressure and perceiving attestation as a means to avoid punishment rather than promoting genuine improvement. Further criticisms included the lack of consideration for the social context of educational organizations, the failure to measure the long-term development of education institutions, and the absence of mechanisms for pedagogical support. A significant communication gap existed between attestation results and key stakeholders such as teachers and parents, hindering the intended impact and limiting parental engagement in their child's educational journey (Kopeeva, 2021).

In 2021, state attestation was reinstated with modifications addressing some criticisms from previous years. For instance, during attestation, visiting educational organizations is prohibited, and the attestation commission, comprised of experts from a unified register, remains undisclosed until the conclusion to maintain anonymity. The assessment of learning outcomes has shifted to monitoring student skills and abilities, confirmed through parental surveys. Post-attestation, methodological recommendations are issued without initiating administrative offense proceedings but with mandatory clarification on the rectification process. For organizations that fully comply with standards, additional evaluative results are issued (excellent, good, or moderate). Results are publicly disclosed on the supervisory authority's official website and the educational organization's platform (Malgaeva, 2022).

According to Zeynep Makhsutova, Director of the Department for Quality Assurance in Education in East Kazakhstan, 80% of educational organizations in the region failed state attestation in 2022. The failure is attributed to the non-implementation of preschool education content, lack of initial monitoring of student's development, and failure to comply with requirements for study load, age grouping, and class composition in preschools (Plotnikova, 2022).

3.6.2 ECEC Licensing

While state attestation focuses on evaluating educational activities and students' mastery of programs, ECEC licenses are granted based on regulatory inspections to ensure basic conditions for children in preschools (Kobenova, 2022). As previously mentioned, preschool institutions currently operate on a notification basis, as the practice of licensing was abolished over 10 years ago. However, efforts have been made since 2020 to reintroduce licensing procedures for preschools. This initiative encountered opposition from key stakeholders, including the Chamber of Entrepreneurs and the Preschool Association (Makarov, 2022). A 2022 survey among private preschool leaders showed general support for licensing but highlighted two primary concerns: the risk of corruption in the licensing process and fears of reduced job opportunities and slower growth for new preschool organizations (Buldybayeva, 2022).

Nevertheless, during the 2022 Republican Conference on Education, Gulzat Kobenova, Chair of the Committee for Quality Assurance in Education and Science, announced the phased introduction of ECEC licensing starting in 2024. The initial phase targets newly established preschools, followed by those awaiting state attestation. Kobenova assured that the licensing process, excluding preschools, is well-established, transparent, and automated. Addressing concerns, she highlighted that examining licensed education levels has shown no adverse impact on new organizations; in fact, the number of newly opened schools has tripled in the last three years. Licensing requirements are now more lenient than those before 2011, with changes including tailored teacher requirements, medical services options, flexible catering facilities, and premises considerations, allowing for both owned and leased locations (Kobenova, 2022).

4 Preschool Education Content and ECEC Curriculum

In 2021, the Kazakhstani government conducted a comprehensive evaluation of Early Childhood Education and Care (ECEC) using the Early Childhood Environment Rating Scale – Third Edition (ECERS-3, Harms et al., 2015). The results revealed an overall score of 2.3 out of 7, indicating below-average quality. Specifically, within the Space and Furnishings subclass, certain indicators, such as play and provisions for children with special needs, scored below 3 points, entering the range of relatively low quality. For various activity types such as building blocks, mathematics, play, nature/science, music/movement, art, fine motor skills, and more, the assessment showed minimal scores within the Activities subcategory (Institute of Early Childhood Development, 2021).

Addressing these findings, the Model of ECEC Development (MES RK, 2021) was developed and implemented, providing a framework for quality improvement of the ECEC content in the country. Since the adoption of the new Model in 2021, nine regulatory documents governing the activities of preschool organizations have been amended. These changes encompass State Education Plans and Programs, which play a pivotal role in regulating the content of

ECEC services (Central Communications Service under the President of the Republic of Kazakhstan, 2023).

The primary objective of preschool education in today's Kazakhstan is to facilitate the comprehensive development and realization of each child's potential, grounded in both universal and national values (MoE RK, 2022). It recognizes the individuality of every child and takes into consideration their unique interests, characteristics, and needs. To accommodate the diverse developmental stages, the educational program is segmented into five age groups, catering to children from 1 to 5 years old: early age group – 1-year-old children; junior group – 2-year-old children; middle group – 3-year-old children; senior group – 4-year-old children; pre-school group – 5-year-old children (MoE RK, 2022). Within each age group, the program focuses on five key areas: physical development, communication skills, cognitive development, creativity and research, and emotional intelligence. Specific aims, objectives, and learning outcomes dictate the frequency and duration of instruction for each subject, tailoring the curriculum to the developmental needs of each age group. By encompassing a wide range of educational domains, a graduate of a preschool program is expected to be physically developed, inquisitive, initiative-driven, persistent, adaptable, communicative, self-confident, possess teamwork skills, be emotionally responsive, and have an initial understanding of self, family, society, the state, the world, and nature (MoE RK, 2022).

Despite these positive initiatives, Soviet educational philosophy continues influencing the ECEC curriculum, emphasizing regimented practices, planned activities, and cognitive development. The OECD's Policy of ECEC (2017) underscores the prescriptive nature of Kazakhstan's curriculum, limiting teachers' flexibility for creative methods or individualized attention. Notably, the studies by Needham et al. (2018) and Chukurova (2021) highlight the persistent challenge: educators feel pressured to adhere to the curriculum, hindering a shift towards more child-centered approaches and play-based methods.

5   ECEC Childcare Workforce

The evolution of Kazakhstan's ECEC workforce is closely tied to historical developments in ECEC provision. The 1990s marked a critical period characterized by a substantial reduction of the ECEC network, and subsequently the number of early childhood educators within the sector. A series of policy initiatives in the 2000s resulted in a significant increase in the number of preschool teachers, with a rate of 1.2 times in 2005, 2.6 times in 2010, and 5 times in 2015 (IAC, 2022). While there is a notable growth in the ECEC workforce in the country, it is becoming equally important to assess the skills, training, and overall performance of these educators as well as potential challenges within the ECEC workforce.

5.1 Initial Teacher Training in ECEC

In Kazakhstan, a preschool teacher must undergo formal training and achieve state certification. Regardless of their educational background, preschool teachers are referred to as "pedagogues" [педагог] or "educators" [воспитатель] (IAC, 2022). Unlike certain member countries of the OECD, where a minimum of a bachelor's degree, and in some cases a master's degree, is required for preschool teachers (IAC, 2022), the requirements for teachers in Kazakhstan are less stringent. Individuals may pursue this career path through technical-vocational colleges following lower secondary education (9th grade), and their diplomas would specifically reflect a specialization in vocational education. Those who graduate from these colleges have the option to continue their studies at a university in pursuit of a higher degree, which takes an additional three years.

Another option for higher education in the field of early childhood education is to attend a university after completing upper secondary education (11th grade). All pedagogical and comprehensive universities in Kazakhstan offer a 4-year program in "Preschool Education and Training," and currently, 31 Kazakhstani universities offer this program (Universities with Qualification, n.d.). The major "Preschool Education and Training" focuses on equipping educators with the necessary skills and knowledge to shape the development of young children (IAC, 2022).

Today, the profession of a teacher is highly valued and supported by the state, with increased grants, a high stipend, and the opportunity to obtain a pedagogical master's degree within a year. Moreover, university admission requirements for pedagogical majors have become stricter, with a minimum threshold score of 75 points (out of 140) in the Unified National Test (UNT) and a special pedagogic exam to determine professional suitability (IAC, 2022). This is in contrast to most other majors, where the minimum threshold scores for admission are 50 to 60 (NTC, June 2023)

5.2 Teacher Attestation

Upon graduating from a specialized institution, teachers must undergo professional certification to determine their level of training. To become a certified teacher, individuals must pass a national qualification test (IAC, 2022), also called teacher attestation. When teachers take the attestation test, they earn points based on their performance, which determines their category: Teacher,

Teacher-moderator, Teacher-expert, Teacher-researcher, or Teacher-master (National Centre for Testing, n.d.). The attestation is based on tests developed by an authorized body in education and training, with 30 tasks divided into two blocks. The first block assesses the teacher's knowledge of the State Education Standard and Standard Education Plans and Programs of Preschool Education and Training, while the second block focuses on methodology and developmental psychology. The evaluation takes 80 minutes, and the tasks are based on relevant regulatory documents, including standards and methodological recommendations (National Centre for Testing, n.d.).

Teacher attestation is not only important for determining the level of training of educators, but it also plays a crucial role in improving the overall quality of teaching in preschools. The decline in the qualified teaching staff, with a 20% decrease in the proportion of qualified teachers over 15 years (IAC, 2022), has also raised concerns about the shortage of high-category educators, emphasizing the need for regular assessments of preschool teachers in Kazakhstan. Thus, preschool teachers undergo state attestation every five years (Litjens & Taguma, 2017), and it serves as a vital tool for evaluating the quality and effectiveness of their teaching (IAC, 2022). The level of education and professionalism of teachers is one of the key factors in determining the quality of a preschool organization's practices (MoE RK, 2023).

5.3   *Professional Development*
To continuously improve the quality of preschool teachers, the country has a strong focus on professional development. Different institutes and organizations, including the JSC National Center of Professional Development "Orleu", the educational departments of rayons, cities, and oblasts (state administrative divisions), the Center of Pedagogical Mastery of JSC "Nazarbayev Intellectual Schools," and private institutes offer formal professional development courses, seminars and workshops (IAC, 2022; Menzhanova, 1992). For example, since 1996, the Republican Institute for Professional Development of Management and Research-Pedagogical Personnel of the Education System had been responsible for organizing and coordinating professional development until it was reorganized into "Orleu" in 2012 (IAC, 2022). Orleu's professorial pedagogical staff embarked on an internship in Singapore with the aim of studying the country's highly advanced preschool education system (Eskendirova, 2015). Through Orleu and the Center of Pedagogical Mastery, teachers are able to receive a comprehensive range of training courses for teachers covering the updated content of early childhood education and training, teaching methods for early childhood development, and inclusive education. In 2021, 7,495 teachers successfully

completed the training program organized by the Center of Pedagogical Mastery, of which 2,000 were preschool education teachers (IAC, 2022). In 2014, more than 12,000 early childhood education teachers took part in professional training in Kazakhstan (Litjens & Taguma, 2017). Moreover, Kazakhstan plans to establish competency centers and mobile groups in preschool organizations to promote the exchange of best practices and provide methodological support, which will take a comprehensive approach and address the issue of continuous professional development for teachers (MoE RK, 2023).

5.4   *Challenges and Current Trends Related to ECEC Educators*

The significant increase in preschools resulted in considerable growth of teachers, yet challenges remain. This is particularly evident in the shortage of educators in general and highly qualified educators due to the low requirements for preschool teacher qualifications (Litjens & Taguma, 2017; Tlemisov, 2016). Other challenges include low enrollment in preschool programs offered by pedagogical institutes, poor quality teacher training, and difficulties in the recruitment and retention of staff (Litjens et al., 2017; NUGSE, 2014). Factors including a rising number of young children, an aging workforce, inadequate influx of new professionals, and high turnover rates also caused the shortage of teachers (Litjens & Taguma, 2017). This was worsened by unfavorable working conditions, including low status, salaries, inadequate preparation for the job, heavy workloads and external pressures, and the lack of adequate opportunities for professional development (Litjens et al., 2017; Tlemisov, 2016).

Kazakhstan prioritizes efforts to address challenges in the ECEC workforce. This commitment is evident in multiple government documents, including the State Programs of Education Development for the periods of 2011–2020 and 2020–2025, and the Concept of Development of Pre-School, Secondary, Technical, and Vocational Education for 2023–2029, and reviews by the OECD (Litjens et al., 2017; MoE RK, 2023). OECD reviews recommended retraining current ECEC professionals who are not teachers, recognizing the importance of educators' roles, improving their status, offering comparable pay to teachers, providing professional development opportunities, and providing a positive work environment (Litjens & Taguma, 2017). Based on the recommendations, Kazakhstan launched initiatives such as the "Best Teacher" contest, opened the sector to non-specialists, salaries have increased, and free professional development opportunities are offered (Litjens & Taguma, 2017; MoE RK, 2023). Current qualified childcare professionals will receive additional training to enhance their skills further, and a teaching assistant position will be added to the staff (MoE RK, 2023).

6 Future Developments: Inclusive ECEC

In Kazakhstan, the development of the ECEC system has been marked by a progressive transformation towards inclusivity. Historically influenced by its Soviet past, the nation's education system predominantly emphasized standardized education with isolated institutions for children with special needs (Lubovski, 1981). However, post-independence, and especially over the last decade, there has been a shift toward committing to the principles of inclusive education, a change driven by both international and domestic advocacy.

The government demonstrated its dedication to inclusive education by ratifying the United Nations Convention on the Rights of Persons with Disabilities (UNCRPD) in 2015 (United Nations, 2019). Subsequently, Kazakhstan introduced amendments to its Law on Education (MES RK, 2007). The law outlines the right of persons with disabilities to education on an equal basis with others, without discrimination, at all levels and throughout life. It also empowers parents of children with disabilities to choose the educational establishment and form of education their child receives. Furthermore, the law emphasizes specialized curricula for children with disabilities, developed based on general preschool frameworks and tailored to their psychophysical and cognitive needs, in line with expert recommendations.

The Ministry of Education further reinforced this commitment by approving a policy outline for the development of inclusive education and a series of measures for its enhancement from 2015 to 2020. These measures and indicators are encapsulated in the 2011–2020 State Education Development Programme (MES, 2010). The program prioritized professional development, increasing state-sponsored training for specialists in inclusive education. Infrastructure improvements, such as ramps, driveways, and elevators, were emphasized to support inclusivity. The program also aimed to expand inclusive education in preschools, targeting an increase from 5% to 15%.

These policy reforms have led to notable improvements. In 2021, 69% of preschools ensured barrier-free access. This barrier-free environment is equipped to cater to children with special educational needs, ensuring they receive quality education. By 2021, there were 48 specialized preschool institutions, 73 units offering psychological, medical, and pedagogical consultations, and 186 psychological and pedagogical correction offices (IAC, 2022).

However, in 2018, there were 45,618 children aged 0 to 6 with special educational needs, which constituted 1.9% of the total population in this age group. Of these children, about 43.8% were accommodated in either specialized kindergartens, special groups within mainstream preschools, or inclusive groups within mainstream preschools. This means that the remaining 56.2% were not provided preschool services (IAC, 2022). The 2019 UNICEF report on education for children with disabilities in Kazakhstan underscores similar challenges despite the nation's progress towards inclusivity. The report highlights that the pace of achieving genuine inclusive education remains slow (UNICEF, 2019). A fundamental transformation in policies, approach to education, and addressing prevailing negative attitudes towards people with disabilities is essential for genuine progress. The report also suggests that educational decisions should not be based on a highly medicalized evaluation but should focus on providing reasonable accommodations to facilitate effective education for all children. This shows while there have been tangible improvements in infrastructure and provision for children with special educational needs, a significant portion still lacks access to high-quality preschool services.

7 Lesson Learned from the Review

7.1 *Soviet Legacy*

It is evident from the review that the evolution of ECEC in Kazakhstan has been shaped by historical, economic, and political factors. The Soviet era laid the foundation for the integration of preschool education into a unified public system, with remarkable growth in the number of institutions, however, Kazakhstan ECEC still bears the hallmarks of the Soviet pre-school education (Habibov, 2015).

7.2 *Policy on ECEC*

Despite the post-independence period posing significant challenges, notably economic downturns and privatization, which impacted the accessibility and quality of ECEC, government initiatives, such as the introduction of mandatory pre-primary education and strategic state programs, addressed these challenges. In that terms, Kazakhstan is not only country that when through significant ECEC policy reforms. This reflects a broader trend of significant ECEC policy reforms that have been happening internationally over the past 15 years. For example, Zhou (2011) outlines comprehensive changes in China aimed at enhancing ECEC quality and mitigating regional disparities. Similarly, Nordic countries have developed ECEC policies focusing on workforce quality and national curriculum guidelines, guided by OECD reports (Karila, 2012). While national policies have set minimum standards for ECEC service provision, the resent OECD's Starting Strong VI report (2021) stresses the importance of policies surpassing these standards to further enhance quality. It could be deduced that a clear policy framework and government initiatives are pivotal for the sustenance of ECEC.

7.3 *Private-Public Partnerships*

The Balapan Preschool Education Program (2010–2020), in particular, sought to alleviate the shortage of preschools by engaging the private sector through public-private partnerships, which resulted in a substantial increase in the number of private preschools. This trend mirrors international patterns; even in countries like Finland where ECEC services are predominantly publicly provided, private sector has been expanding due to public subsidies (Ruutiainen et al., 2020). However, a recent meta-analysis encompassing 15 studies across various countries found nuanced differences between public and private childcare providers when it comes to the ECEC quality (Brogaard & Petersen, 2022). While most studies indicated that public ECEC programs perform better in terms of structural features such as group sizes and staff qualifications, some studies showed no significant quality differences between public and private providers, with a few suggesting that private providers might offer higher quality (Brogaard & Petersen, 2022). The authors underscore several constraints in their research, including limited scholarly studies, variations across regions and eras, and a lack of evidence regarding how ownership impacts lasting educational outcomes. They call for more comprehensive studies examining outcomes of public and private ECEC providers on children's long-term educational, social, and cognitive growth.

7.4 *ECEC Quality Monitoring*

Quality assurance emerged as a critical concern amid the rapid expansion of ECEC services. Reports of mistreatment and low standards prompted governmental responses, including the reintroduction of licensing, reinstatement of state attestation, adoption of a new Model for Preschool Education, and significant revisions of the curriculum and content of preschool education. Although there has not been a detailed scientific study focusing on how monitoring can directly lead to concrete and measurable improvements in the quality of ECEC, there is some consensus that setting minimum standards can contribute to better development outcomes for children, promote transparency among private providers, and empower parents to make the best choices for their children's early education and care (OECD, 2012). International research that has investigated educators' perceptions of ECEC quality monitoring has shown simultaneous positive and negative viewpoints: while almost all educators believe there is a need for a monitoring mechanism to oversee the quality of ECEC services nationwide, concerns regarding its ability to accurately reflect service quality have been raised (Phillips & Fenech, 2023).

7.5 *ECEC Curriculum*

The focus on individualized development, diverse age groups, and key educational areas aligns with international standards (OECD, 2017), but the historical influence of Soviet educational philosophy remains evident, presenting challenges related to the prescriptive nature of the curriculum. This tension reflects a broader dichotomy seen internationally, wherein there's a simultaneous push for child-centered learning environments adaptable to diverse needs alongside the maintaining of standardized educational objectives (Trevor et al., 2020; Wood & Hedges, 2016). Recent analysis of ECEC policies in Australia, China, New Zealand, and Singapore has revealed this shift away from traditional knowledge-focused, subject-based learning towards integrated and authentic learning approaches. Notably, while China and Singapore maintain defined subject areas or disciplines with specific content and objectives their policies, Australia and New Zealand prioritize flexibility in curriculum design by refraining from prescribing specific subject content (Weipeng Yang et al., 2022).

7.6   *Teacher Preparation and Professional Development*
The qualifications of ECE teachers are crucial, as highly qualified teachers significantly impact children's learning, program quality, and developmental outcomes (Manning et al., 2019; Saracho, 2013). Higher education levels and specialized training among ECEC educators are strongly associated with enhanced quality in ECEC environments (Darling-Hammond et al., 2005; Manning et al., 2017). Therefore, many countries have high qualification requirements for ECEC educators. Some countries mandate a university degree, while others accept vocational qualifications or shorter certification programs. In Kazakhstan, the requirements for preschool teachers are less strict than in other OECD countries as bachelor's degree is not required. For example, in 2019, the minimum qualification level for pre-school teachers in OECD countries was generally a bachelor's degree or its equivalent (OECD, 2020a). However, some countries like Iceland, France, and Portugal require pre-school teachers to hold a master's degree (OECD, 2020a; 2020b). Although master's degree is not mandatory in Poland, most ECEC teachers begin their careers with this level (OECD, 2020b). While initial teacher education provides the foundational knowledge for ECEC teachers, continuous professional development is essential for improving the quality of the teaching workforce (Burchinal et al., 2008; OECD, 2020b; Sheridan et al., 2008). As previously noted in the context of Kazakhstan, the country places a strong emphasis on professional development, with the number of ECEC teachers participating in these programs increasing annually. This trend highlights the global recognition of the importance of both initial qualifications and ongoing professional development in ensuring high-quality ECEC.

7.7   *Inclusive ECEC*
Moreover, there has been a significant shift towards inclusive education, marked by policy changes and infrastructure improvements. Despite notable

progress, challenges persist, with a significant portion of children with special educational needs still lacking access to high-quality preschool services. Comparing international experiences sheds light on potential strategies for improvement. For instance, Ismiatun and Atika (2020) highlight the importance of government support in promoting inclusive education, emphasizing the need for teacher training to enhance competencies in catering to children with special educational needs. Similarly, Wertlieb (2019) discusses the Nurturing Care Framework (NCF) for Early Childhood Development (ECD), advocating for a rights-based approach and greater involvement of neuro-disability professionals. By incorporating insights from international studies, Kazakhstan can further develop its inclusive education policies and practices to ensure equitable access and quality for all children.

7.8   *Challenges of ECEC*

The review show that although Kazakhstan has shown a tremendous improvement in the implementation of the ECEC program, some challenges such as shortage of qualified ECEC teachers, quality of teacher preparation, recruitment and training, attrition and poor conditions of serve continue to pose a challenge. Comparatively, Kazakhstan shares similar challenges reflecting broader international trends. For instance, Leseman and Slot (2014) highlight issues within European ECEC systems, such as insufficient coverage, quality enhancement needs, and addressing cultural sensitivities for marginalized groups. Similarly, Qi and Melhuish (2017) discuss China's efforts to expand kindergarten access nationwide while struggling with disparities in development and concerns about maintaining program quality during rapid expansion. These challenges highlight the importance of learning from international experiences to address common obstacles and improve the effectiveness of Kazakhstan's ECEC initiatives.

8   Conclusion

In conclusion, Kazakhstan's ECEC journey shows a proactive response to challenges, with recent initiatives reflecting a commitment to high-quality, accessible early childhood education. The recent initiatives and reforms signal a recognition of the importance of ECEC in shaping the future of the nation, aligning with broader developmental goals outlined in national strategic documents. While this paper was an attempt to provide a comprehensive state of ECEC in Kazakhstan, we are aware that Kazakhstan ECED is undergoing rapid changes and that some conclusions in this chapter might not be applicable overtime. However, this chapter, contributes towards the discussions and debates about ECEC in Kazakhstan.

Acknowledgments

This paper is funded by the Central Asian Research Centre for Educational Innovation and Transformation (CARCEIT), Nazarbayev University (Grant No. GSE2023006, awarded to Daniel Hernández-Torrano).

References

Ansari, A., & Pianta, R. C. (2018). Variation in the long-term benefits of child care: The role of classroom quality in elementary school. *Developmental Psychology, 54*(10), 1854–1867. https://doi.org/10.1037/dev0000513

Asian Development Bank (ADB). (2004). *Education reforms in countries in transition: Policies and processes.* Six country case studies commissioned by the Asian Development Bank in Azerbaijan, Kazakhstan, Kyrgyz Republic, Mongolia, Tajikistan, and Uzbekistan.

Bennett, J. (2008). Benchmarks for early childhood services in OECD countries. *Innocenti Working Papers, 2008*(02). https://doi.org/10.18356/53c9dc0e-en

Brogaard, L., & Helby Petersen, O. (2022). Privatization of public services: A systematic review of quality differences between public and private daycare providers. *International Journal of Public Administration, 45*(10), 794–806. https://doi.org/10.1080/01900692.2021.1909619

Buldybayeva, M. (2022). Analiz politiki perekhoda na obyazatel'noe litsenzirovanie v doshkol'nom vospitanii i obuchenii: nadezhnyy li eto instrument dlya obespecheniya kachestva v chastnykh doshkol'nykh organizatsiyakh? [Analysis of the policy of transition to compulsory licensing in preschool education and training: Is it a reliable tool for ensuring quality in private preschool organizations?]. Soros Foundation-Kazakhstan. https://www.soros.kz/wp-content/uploads/2022/11/%D0%9C%D0%B5%D1%80%D1%83%D0%B5%D1%80%D1%82_%D0%91%D0%A3%D0%9B%D0%94%D0%AB%D0%91%D0%90%D0%95%D0%92%D0%90_.pdf

Burchinal, M., Hyson, M., & Zaslow, M. (2008). Competencies and credentials for early childhood educators: What do we know and what do we need to know? *NHSA Dialog Briefs, 11*(1), 1–8.

Central Communications Service under the President of the Republic of Kazakhstan. (2023, February 21). Model' razvitiya doshkol'nogo vospitaniya i obucheniya realizuetsya poetapno [Development model of preschool education and training is implemented step by step]. https://bilimdinews.kz/?p=229298

Chapter I. The preschool education system in the USSR. (1983). *Soviet Education, 25*(8), 10–34. https://doi.org/10.2753/RES1060-9393250810

Chukurova, S. (2021). Support for play in state kindergartens in Nur-Sultan: Early childhood educators' perspectives.

Darling-Hammond, L., Holtzman, D. J., Gatlin, S. J., & Heilig, J. V. (2005). Does teacher preparation matter? Evidence about teacher certification, Teach for America, and teacher effectiveness. *Education Policy Analysis Archives, 13*(1), 1–48. https://doi.org/10.14507/epaa.v13n42.2005

Davies, C., Hendry, A., Gibson, S. P., Gliga, T., McGillion, M., & Gonzalez-Gomez, N. (2021). Early childhood education and care (ECEC) during COVID-19 boosts growth in language and executive function. https://doi.org/10.31234/osf.io/74gkz

Early, D. M., & Winton, P. J. (2001). Preparing the workforce: Early childhood teacher preparation at 2- and 4-year institutions of higher education. *Early Childhood Research Quarterly, 16*(3), 285–306. https://doi.org/10.1016/S0885-2006(01)00106-5

Eskendirova, A. (2015). Early childhood education in Kazakhstan and Singapore. *New Impulse. Trainer-Education, Republican Informational Methodical Journal, 4*, 58–61.

Galushko, M. (2019, February 27). Chastnyy detskiy sad za gosudarstvennye den'gi [Private daycare funded by the state]. *Kapital.kz.* https://kapital.kz/business/76096/chastnyy-detskiy-sad-za-gosudarstvennyye-den-gi.html

Gradskova, Y. (2010). Educating parents: Public preschools and parenting in Soviet pedagogical publications, 1945–1989. *Journal of Family History, 35*(3), 271–285. https://doi.org/10.1177/0363199010368775

Habibov, N. (2015). On individual, household, and community factors explaining enrollment to early childhood education and care in post-Soviet transitional countries. *Child Indicators Research, 8*(4), 825–843. https://doi.org/10.1007/s12187-014-9277-z

Harms, T., Clifford, R. M., & Cryer, D. (2015). *Early Childhood Environment Rating Scale* (3rd ed.). Teachers College Press.

Harwin, J. E. (2005). Policy review report: Early childhood care and education in Kazakhstan. Early Childhood and Family Policy Series No. 12. UNESCO Institute for Education.

IAC (Informational Analytical Centre, MES RK). (2022). *National report on the condition and development of the education system of the Republic of Kazakhstan (for 30 years of Independence and 2021).*

Ibrayeva, L., Alpys, A., Kulsary, A., Kiikova, G., & Hernández-Torrano, D. (under review). Visualizing the early childhood education and care research: A bibliometric review. *Children and Youth Services Review.*

Institute of Early Childhood Development, MoE RK. (2021, December 22). Information on the conduct of the regional online seminar "Organization and Implementation of Assessment of the Quality of Preschool Education" within the framework of the implementation of the scientific and technical program "Scientific Foundations for Modernization of the Education and Science System." Retrieved from http://irrd.kz/news/read/Organizaciya_i_osucshestvlenie_ocenki_kachestva.html?lang=ru

Ismiatun, A. N., & Atika, A. R. (2020, August). Facing the challenges of inclusive education in early childhood education. In *International Conference on Early Childhood Education and Parenting 2019 (ECEP 2019)* (pp. 53–57). Atlantis Press.

Kaldybaeva, T. Z. (2001). Social problems of preschool education in Kazakhstan. *Russian Education & Society, 43*(3), 45–56. https://doi.org/10.2753/res1060-9393430345

Karila, K. (2012). A Nordic perspective on early childhood education and care policy. *European Journal of Education, 47*(4), 584–595. https://doi.org/10.1111/ejed.12007

Kobenova, G. I. (2022, August 10). Licensing of educational institutions. In *2022 Republican Conference on Implementing a New Model for Preschool Education and Development: Enriching Content and Quality Enhancement*. Astana, Kazakhstan. Retrieved from http://irrd.kz/news/read/Materialy_avgustovskoj_konferencii_2022.html?search=oLrQvtC9oYTQtQ

Kopeeva, A. (2018, February 7). Myths and truths about school state accreditation in Kazakhstan. *Factcheck.kz*. Retrieved from https://factcheck.kz/mify/mify-i-pravda-o-gosattestacii-shkol-v-kazaxstane

Kopeeva, A. (2021). Adequacy of the instrument of state attestation and its influence on school effectiveness. *Soros Foundation-Kazakhstan*. Retrieved from https://www.soros.kz/ru/adequacy-of-the-instrument-of-state-certification/

Lubovski, V. I. (1981). Basic principles of special education in the USSR. *Prospects: Quarterly Review of Education, 11*(4), 444–447.

Makarov, A. (2022, July 23). What will licensing of kindergartens in Kazakhstan bring in 2024? *Bizmedia.*

Malgaeva, A. S. (2022, January 18). Updated format of the state attestation procedure. *Department for Quality Assurance in the Field of Education of the Kostanay Region of the Republic of Kazakhstan*. Retrieved from https://kostanaycontrol.gov.kz/vvodite-tekst/

Manning, M., Wong, G. T., Fleming, C. M., & Garvis, S. (2019). Is teacher qualification associated with the quality of the early childhood education and care environment? A meta-analytic review. *Review of Educational Research, 89*(3), 370–415. https://doi.org/10.3102/0034654319837540

Menzhanova, A. (1992). *Mektepke deyingi pedagogiia [Pre-school pedagogy]*. Almaty: Rauan.

MES RK. (2000, September 20). *State program "Education."* Retrieved from https://adilet.zan.kz/rus/docs/U000000448_

MES RK. (2010). *Program for providing children with preschool education and training "Balapan" for 2010–2020.* Retrieved from https://adilet.zan.kz/rus/docs/P100000488_

MES RK. (2021). *State program for education development 2020–2025.* Retrieved from https://adilet.zan.kz/rus/docs/P1900000988

MES RK. (2021, March 15). *Model of development for preschool education and training.* Retrieved from https://adilet.zan.kz/rus/docs/P2100000137

MoE. (2023, March 28). *Concept of development of preschool, secondary, technical and vocational education of the Republic of Kazakhstan for 2023–2029.* Retrieved from https://adilet.zan.kz/rus/docs/P2300000249

MoE RK. (2022, July 25). Dozens of complaints about the work of private preschools are submitted to the Ministry of Education. [Press release]. Retrieved from https://www.gov.kz/memleket/entities/edu/press/news/details/404422?lang=ru

MoE RK. (2022, October 14). *Standard educational program for preschool education and training.* Retrieved from https://adilet.zan.kz/rus/docs/V1600014235

MoS RK. (2023, October 27). Quality education available to everyone. *Draft national report for the first congress of teachers.* Retrieved from https://www.gov.kz/memleket/entities/edu/press/article/details/135521?lang=ru

National Centre for Testing. (n.d.). Assessing the expertise of teachers in the field of preschool education institutions. Retrieved from https://testcenter.kz/ru/pedagogam/nkt/otsenka-znaniy-pedagogov-organizatsiy-doshkolnogo-obrazovaniya/

Nazarbayev University Graduate School of Education. (2014). *Development of strategic directions for education reforms in Kazakhstan for 2015–2020: Diagnostic report.* Astana: Indigo Print. Retrieved from https://nur.nu.edu.kz/bitstream/handle/123456789/335/DIAGNOSTIC%20REPORT.pdf?sequence=1&isAllowed=y

Needham, M., Kuleimenov, D., & Soltanbekova, A. (2018). Sticking and tipping points: A case study of preschool education policy and practice in Astana, Kazakhstan. *European Early Childhood Education Research Journal, 26*(3), 432–445. https://doi.org/10.1080/1350293X.2018.1463909

OECD. (2017). *Early childhood education and care policy review: Kazakhstan.* OECD Publishing. https://doi.org/10.1787/9789264283996-en

OECD. (2020a). *Building a high-quality early childhood education and care workforce: Further results from the Starting Strong Survey 2018.* TALIS, OECD Publishing. https://doi.org/10.1787/b90bba3d-en

OECD. (2020b). *Education at a glance 2020: OECD indicators.* OECD Publishing. https://doi.org/10.1787/69096873-en

OECD. (2012). *Starting Strong II: A quality toolbox for early childhood education and care.* OECD Publishing.

OECD. (2021). *Starting Strong VI: Supporting meaningful interactions in early childhood education and care.* OECD Publishing. https://doi.org/10.1787/f47a06ae-en

Phillips, A., & Fenech, M. (2023). Educators' perceptions of Australia's early childhood education and care quality assurance rating system. *European Early Childhood*

Education Research Journal, 31(6), 988–1000. https://doi.org/10.1080/
1350293X.2023.2211758

Plotnikova, I. (2022, May 13). V vko gosudarstvennaya attestatsiya organizatsiy obrazovaniya shokirovala rezultatami [In East Kazakhstan, the state accreditation of
educational organizations shocked with its results]. *yk-news.kz*. https://shorturl.at/
enx17

Pomfret, R. (2005). Kazakhstan's economy since independence: Does the oil boom
offer a second chance for sustainable development? *Europe-Asia Studies, 57*(6),
859–876. http://www.jstor.org/stable/30043927

Qi, X., & Melhuish, E. C. (2017). Early childhood education and care in China: History,
current trends, and challenges. *Early Years, 37*(3), 268–284.

Ruutiainen, V., Alasuutari, M., & Karila, K. (2020). Rationalising public support for
private early childhood education and care: The case of Finland. *British Journal of
Sociology of Education, 41*(1), 32–47. https://doi.org/10.1080/01425692.2019.1665497

Sheridan, S. M., Edwards, C. P., Marvin, C. A., & Knoche, L. L. (2009). Professional development in early childhood programs: Process issues and research needs. *Early Education
and Development, 20*(3), 377–401. https://doi.org/10.1080/10409280802582795

Tlemisov, S. (2016). On the issue of introducing a question-answer interface into a
knowledge testing system. *Bilim Research-Pedagogical Journal, №1*(76).

Trevor, G., Ince, A., & Ang, L. (2020). Towards a child-centred curriculum. In
Transforming early childhood in England: Towards a democratic education (pp.
100–118).

unesco. (2000). *Educational financing and budgeting in Kazakhstan.*
https://unesdoc.unesco.org/ark:/48223/pf0000123537

unesco. (2004). *The background report of Kazakhstan: The status of preschool
education in the Republic of Kazakhstan.* https://unesdoc.unesco.org/ark:/48223/
pf0000139025

United Nations. (2015). *Transforming our world: The 2030 agenda for sustainable development.* http://bit.ly/TransformAgendaSDG-pdf

United Nations. (2019, February 21). *Convention on the Rights of Persons with Disabilities.
Committee on the Rights of Persons with Disabilities.* https://docstore.ohchr.org/
SelfServices/FilesHandler.ashx?enc=6QkG1d%2FPPRiCAqhKb7yhsj2984V8b3r4
UhA5qrPxZmiMSohe%2Bz9YWLKwpxHsjWXMK%2F%2FzqQO1RLhr6UoU%
2Fs99DyEnRZgUDpRlKu%2B78uMsjhzTAGwYQn%2BqQvvr7kGuseb3

Universities with qualification (n.d.). *Vipusknik.kz.* Retrieved October 17, 2023, from
https://vipusknik.kz/university-specialties/doshkolnoe-obuchenie-i-vospitanie

Van Belle, J. (2016). *Early childhood education and care (ECEC) and its long-term effects
on educational and labour market outcomes.* rand Cooperation. https://doi.org/
10.7249/rr1667

Voronina, K. (2016, November 4). mon predlagaet nalogovye l'goty otkryvayushchim
detskie sady predprinimatelyam [Ministry of Education proposes tax benefits for

entrepreneurs opening daycare centers]. *Kazpravda.kz.* https://kazpravda.kz/n/mon-predlagaet-nalogovye-lgoty-otkryvayushchim-detskie-sady-predprinimatelyam/

Wood, E., & Hedges, H. (2016). Curriculum in early childhood education: Critical questions about content, coherence, and control. *The Curriculum Journal, 27*(3), 387–405. https://doi.org/10.1080/09585176.2015.1129981

Yakavets, N. (2017). Negotiating the principles and practice of school leadership: The Kazakhstan experience. *Educational Management Administration & Leadership, 45*(3), 445–465. https://doi.org/10.1177/1741143216628537

Yang, W., Datu, J. A., Lin, X., Lau, M. M., & Li, H. (2019). Can early childhood curriculum enhance social-emotional competence in low-income children? A meta-analysis of the educational effects. *Early Education and Development, 30*(1), 36–59. https://doi.org/10.1080/10409289.2018.1539557

Yang, W., Xu, P., Liu, H., & Li, H. (2022). Neoliberalism and sociocultural specificities: A discourse analysis of early childhood curriculum policies in Australia, China, New Zealand, and Singapore. *Early Child Development and Care, 192*(2), 203–219. https://doi.org/10.1080/03004430.2020.1754210

Zaporozhets, A. P., Markova, T. A., & Radina, E. I. (1968). Fifty years of Soviet preschool pedagogy. *Soviet Education, 10*(4), 3–14. https://doi.org/10.2753/RES1060-939310043

Zaporozhets, A. V., & Kurbatova, R. A. (1974). The half-century road of preschool education in the USSR. *Soviet Review, 15*(3), 43–59. https://doi.org/10.2753/RSS1061-1428150343

Zhou, X. (2011). Early childhood education policy development in China. *International Journal of Child Care and Education Policy, 5*(1), 29–39. https://doi.org/10.1007/2288-6729-5-1-29

Zhoumagozhina, R. (1973). From the history of early childhood development in country. *Journal of Primary School, 12*, 22–26.

CHAPTER 14

Exploring Opportunities and Challenges of Rural Teachers in Kazakhstan

Gulnara Namyssova and Mir Afzal Tajik

Abstract

Rural schools are an important part of Kazakhstan's educational system, providing education to the majority of children in the country. The role of teachers is pivotal in ensuring quality education in rural schools. Therefore, this study aimed to explore the opportunities and challenges encountered by rural school teachers in Kazakhstan. The study employed a mixed-method research design involving both quantitative and qualitative methods. However, the data presented in this chapter were collected only through the qualitative method. Specifically, semi-structured interviews and focus group discussions were held with rural teachers, school leaders, and students from different regions in the east, west, and south of the country. Professional development, financial incentives, and the opportunity to make a difference were perceived as the main drivers for teachers to work in rural schools, whereas excessive workload, poor infrastructure, and limited resources were considered the main challenges encountered by rural teachers.

Keywords

rural school – rural education – teacher development – challenges – Kazakhstan

1 Introduction

Kazakhstan is a relatively young country with a steadily growing population of about 20 million (Bureau of National Statistics, 2024). According to the Constitution and the Law on Education (2007), school education in Kazakhstan is secular, compulsory, and provided free of charge. The country's school system is complex and comprises various types of schools, such as public day schools, private schools, evening schools, special education establishments, international schools, republican schools, and Nazarbayev Intellectual Schools.

© GULNARA NAMYSSOVA AND MIR AFZAL TAJIK, 2025 | DOI:10.1163/9789004726345_015

According to the Constitution and the Law on Education, the state policy aims to ensure access/equality and quality/efficiency of free mandatory general secondary education. General secondary education consists of primary (1–4 grades), secondary basic (5–9(10) grades), and general secondary education (10(11)–11(12) grades).

Kazakhstan has achieved accessible universal primary education according to the Millennium Development Goals (MDGs). However, the goal of providing equal access to quality education remains critical for Kazakhstan. The problems related to school attendance and maintenance of school enrolment, and the presence of groups of at-risk children indicate that not all children have access to education (UN, 2007). According to the UN, factors such as poverty and unemployment, particularly in rural areas, and the presence of vulnerable population groups hinder the effective implementation of education policies. Challenges related to the low population density in vast territories and the reduction of the school network in rural regions also negatively affect the accessibility of education.

In the context of the Sustainable Development Goals (SDGs) adopted by the United Nations in 2015, rural schools can play a crucial role in achieving multiple SDGs by addressing the educational, social, economic, and environmental challenges faced by rural communities. Rural schools can contribute to improving access and quality of education, reducing gaps and inequalities between rural and urban areas, contributing to economic development, and fostering overall sustainable development in rural communities. For example, rural schools are essential in achieving SDG 4, which aims to ensure inclusive and equitable quality education and promote lifelong learning opportunities for all. Rural schools can contribute to improving literacy rates, enhance educational attainment, and foster the acquisition of knowledge, skills, and competencies necessary for sustainable development by providing access to education in rural areas, particularly for marginalized and disadvantaged populations. Similarly, rural schools can play a vital role in (i) addressing poverty and hunger (SDGs 1 & 2) by promoting sustainable livelihoods among rural communities through education and training that can empower individuals and enhance their productivity, (ii) improving health and well-being (SDG 3) of rural communities by incorporating health and hygiene education into the school curriculum and promoting healthy habits and behaviors among students, teachers, and parents, (iii) reducing gender and other inequalities (SDG 5 & 10) by ensuring equitable access to education, employment, and resources and addressing disparities and discrimination between boys and girls, rural and urban areas, and among different ethnic, religious, linguistic, and socio-economic groups. As rural communities around the globe suffer from the adverse effects of climate change, rural schools can contribute to protecting the environment by raising awareness about climate change and related issues and integrating environmental education, conservation practices, and strategies for protecting the ecosystem and mitigating the impact of climate change into the curriculum.

Although there have been some achievements concerning the Millennium Development Goals and the government of Kazakhstan is committed to achieving the SDGs as encapsulated in the Agenda 2030, rural schools and the teachers working there continue to face numerous challenges. Such challenges in rural schools have been extensively studied on a global scale, but empirical research within the Kazakhstani context is still lacking. Specifically, there is a scarcity of scholarly inquiries that delve into the challenges faced by rural teachers from the perspectives of both school leaders and teachers themselves. This study aimed to bridge this gap in the existing literature by conducting an in-depth examination of the challenges experienced by rural teachers in Kazakhstan. Therefore, this study provides valuable insights into the unique challenges encountered in rural education settings in Kazakhstan. It adds to the global understanding of rural education challenges and provides a foundation for future research and policy development aimed at improving rural education.

2 Literature Review

2.1 The Concepts of "Rurality" and "Rural Schools"

Defining rurality is a complex issue due to the absence of "a universally accepted definition of rural" (Miller, 2010, p. 1). Historically, rural areas have been conceptualized based on criteria such as population size or density, geographical isolation or proximity to urban centers, and land use patterns. However, Welsh (2024) argues that such conventional conceptualizations fail to capture the multifaceted nature of rurality, as rural areas encompass different socio-economic, cultural, and geographic dimensions. Furthermore, rural communities are characterized by their dynamism, and they often undergo demographic shifts, economic transformations, and cultural evolutions (Biddle et al., 2016). This dynamic nature necessitates a more flexible conceptualization of rurality that acknowledges the evolving contexts of rural areas (Echazzara & Radinger, 2019; Welsh, 2024).

Consequently, conceptualizing rural schools poses a similar challenge. As emphasized in the literature (Burrola et al., 2023; Welsh, 2024), the process of defining rural schools requires consideration of a diverse array of socio-economic, cultural, and demographic factors that shape the educational landscape. As Tajik et al. (2021) argue, a rural school in an isolated remote village is not only an important public institution that provides education to students, but it also serves as a 'rallying point for services to poor families and children and represents the economic lifeblood of the community' (Malhoit, 2005, p. 4). Therefore, the provision of quality education to children, particularly those in rural or disadvantaged areas, ought to be an important agenda for all stakeholders in education.

2.2 *Challenges and Opportunities of Rural Education*

An essential characteristic of Kazakhstan's school system is the abundance of rural schools, schools located in rural areas. With over 70% of schools situated and 45% of all students enrolled in rural areas, the role of rural schools in shaping Kazakhstan's future is significant. However, despite their pivotal role, these schools face various challenges. Issues such as declining academic performance, insufficient infrastructure, a shortage of qualified teachers, and limited access to quality education persist within rural educational settings (Tajik et al., 2021; Bridges & Sagyntayeva, 2014). These challenges stem from various factors, including declining enrollments, escalating dropout rates (Yakavets & Dzhandrina, 2014), poor performance in national assessments (Winter et al., 2014), low salaries of teachers (Frost et al., 2014), language barriers (Mehisto et al., 2014) and limited internet and insufficient computers (Tajik et al., 2021; Nurbayev, 2021). Furthermore, rural-urban disparity is still a critical issue in Kazakhstan. Children from city schools have more opportunities to receive better quality education than children from rural areas and, consequently, are more likely to have better performance (Smanova, 2021). As indicated by Tajik et al. (2021), this disparity is evident in both national and international achievement tests, with PISA-2018 results indicating a significant discrepancy of more than 30 points between rural and urban students, equivalent to approximately one year of education. Additionally, rural students scored an average of 8.98 points lower than their urban peers in the Unified National Test (UNT) for university entrance in 2017. This situation not only has serious implications for the work and life of teachers working in rural schools, but it also reflects the professional capacity and challenges of the teachers.

The rural-urban disparity is not only prevalent in Kazakhstan but also in other countries. A discrepancy of at least 20 percentage points between urban and rural schools can be observed in countries such as Australia, Austria, Belgium, Germany, New Zealand, Qatar, the United Arab Emirates, the United Kingdom, and the United States (Echazarra & Radinger, 2019). The studies find that the gap between rural and urban schools becomes even more pronounced during students' transitions to higher levels of education and in the educational expectations that precede their decisions to remain in the education system

(Echazarra & Radinger, 2019). This gap is linked to the low socio-economic status of rural people and other factors such as geographical isolation, a lack of career role models, and highly skilled jobs in rural areas.

The shortage of qualified teachers in rural Kazakhstani schools presents another challenge, significantly compromising the quality of education in rural schools (Tajik et al., 2021; Smanova, 2021). Despite governmental efforts to improve working conditions and implement initiatives aimed at attracting teachers to rural areas (e.g., the "Diploma to the Village" program), teacher quality remains far from ideal (Tajik, Shamatov & Fillipova, 2022). As highlighted by Smanova (2021), poor human resources are one of the "distinctive features" of rural schools in Kazakhstan. A comparative analysis conducted by Smanova (2021) revealed that, in comparison to their urban colleagues, rural teachers are less likely to pursue graduate studies. Furthermore, the study highlighted a notable difference in the proportion of teachers who have undergone professional development programs between rural and urban schools, with rural schools lagging by at least four percentage points. This gap can be attributed to limited opportunities for professional development, geographical remoteness, and a scarcity of training resources. Moreover, rural schools face the threat of losing proficient teachers to urban schools for gifted students, which attract teachers by providing additional resources (Tastanbekova, 2020).

In light of these challenges and considering the strong link between the quality of teachers and student performance (Darling-Hammond, 2000), there is a need to comprehensively study and understand the challenges encountered by rural teachers in Kazakhstan. This way, targeted interventions that address the specific needs of rural educators can be developed. This, in turn, will help enhance the academic performance of students, especially socio-economically vulnerable ones (Semke & Sheridan, 2012), in these areas and contribute to the advancement of the nation as a whole.

3   Methodology

3.1   *Research Design*
A mixed-method research design involving both quantitative and qualitative methods was employed in this study. However, this chapter is based only on the qualitative method. The qualitative methods of data collection offered greater flexibility for in-depth investigation of the phenomenon as well as for fostering rapport between researchers and participants (Bell, 2005). The semi-structured interviews allowed the researchers not only to paraphrase or change the wording and order of the questions but also to ask follow-up

questions to probe further depending on the answers provided by the respondents (Bell, 2005; Cohen et al., 2007).

3.2 *Research Sites and Participants*

This study was conducted with rural teachers, principals, vice-principals, and regional education managers in 16 rural schools from five different regions of the country. The regions included Almaty, Kyzylorda, Shymkent, Aktau, and Oskemen. Following the rules and policies concerning access to schools, the research team obtained permission from the Ministry of Education and Science (MoES) of the Republic of Kazakhstan to conduct this study in rural schools. The research team then approached the regional education authorities to get a list of rural schools from each region and approval to contact the schools. After the regional authorities provided a list of 3–4 schools from each region, the research team called individual schools and obtained permission from the gatekeepers (principals/directors) to visit and recruit participants at these schools.

The participants included teachers, school principals, vice-principals, and regional education managers/officials who voluntarily participated in the study. During their visit to each school, the research team met separately with the school leaders and teachers and presented details about the study including the purpose of the study, research questions, research design, data collection methods, ethical considerations, and informed consent forms. During these meetings, the research team invited school leaders and teachers to voluntarily participate in the study. Thus, a total of 116 participants took part in this study. Table 14.1 provides details about the participants and the number of individual and focus group interviews.

3.3 *Data Collection*

As shown in the Table 14.1, as many as 35 individual and 16 focus group interviews were conducted with teachers, principals, vice-principals, and regional education officials from 16 rural schools that participated in the study. These interviews and discussions, conducted in Kazakh or Russian according to participants' preferences, were transcribed and translated into English. The duration of each interview and focus group discussion lasted, on average, 40 minutes and one and a half hours, respectively. The interview questions focused on the opportunities and challenges the teachers experience in Kazakhstani rural schools.

3.4 *Data Analysis*

The data analysis process entailed both ongoing analysis starting from the first interview and summative analysis done after all interviews and focus-group discussions were conducted (Merriam and Tisdell, 2016). This process helped

EXPLORING OPPORTUNITIES AND CHALLENGES OF RURAL TEACHERS

TABLE 14.1   Summary of participants

Region	Number of individual interviews	Participants (individual interviews)	Number of FG interviews	Participants (FGD)
Kyzylorda	5	Principals (2) Dep Head (1), regional officials (2) Total: 5 participants	3	FGD teachers (9), Total: 9 participants
Turkestan	6	Regional officials (2), principals (2), Dep Head (1), Vice-principals (2 two persons in one interview) Total: 7 participants	2	FGD teachers (12), Total: 12 participants
Mangystau	9	Principals (3) Regional officials (3) Dep Heads (3) Total: 9 participants	3	FGD teachers (14), Total: 14 participants
Oskemen	11	Principals (3), Vice-principals (2) Regional officials (3), Dep Head (3) Total: 11 participants	5	FGD teachers (25), Total: 25 participants
Almaty	4	Principals (1), Principal (1) Principal and Vice-principal (2 persons in one interview) Principal and 2 vice-principals (3 persons in one interview) Total: 7 participants	3	FGD teachers (17), Total: 17 participants
Overall	35	39 participants (individual interviews)	16	77 participants (FGD)

keep the data focused and non-repetitive. Furthermore, the collected data was transcribed by research assistants from native Kazakh and Russian language backgrounds. The transcripts were then coded with text segments highlighted and coloured. The codes were then analyzed and organized into groups based on emerging patterns and relevance to the research purpose. Each group of codes was further analyzed to identify the themes and sub-themes, which are presented and interpreted as the findings in this chapter.

3.5   *Trustworthiness*

To streamline the data analysis process better, the researchers used NVIVO software, which allowed them to constantly review the data analysis and conduct co-coding and questioning to justify the findings (Merriam & Tisdell, 2016). This process helped the researchers ensure the rigor and trustworthiness of the findings. The authors also presented a clear audit trail to make sure that the outside reader can scrutinize the logic of the study and understand how the results were reached. A thick description of the context was provided such that other researchers could make a judgment about the replicability of the study with their context.

3.6   *Ethical Considerations*

It is important to mention that the study was approved by the Nazarbayev University Institutional Research Ethics Committee (IREC) before data collection started. The participants were provided with printed versions of the consent form. The form included a brief description of the study; time involvement; risks and benefits; an explanation of issues of confidentiality and privacy; participant's rights; and points of contact. The consent forms were signed by the participants.

The collected data were saved in password-protected files and a USB flash drive which is also password-protected. Pseudonyms were used to protect the identities of the participants and the schools where the participants work.

4   Findings

The study's findings are presented in two main themes: opportunities and challenges from rural teachers' and school leaders' perspectives. Each theme has several interrelated sub-themes.

4.1   *Opportunities*

Amid growing divides and inequalities between urban and rural schools across the country, the government of Kazakhstan has taken several initiatives to reduce the gaps and improve the overall conditions in rural schools. For example, the State Programme of Education Development for 2020–2025 outlined some comprehensive plans to improve education in rural schools. Specifically, setting goals for increasing the number of qualified teachers, revising teachers' pay scales, establishing mentorship programs, and supporting talented children from rural schools (Ministry of Education and Science, 2019). The participants in this study considered the following as important drivers behind teachers' motivation to continue to work in rural schools.

Professional development. Most participants discussed and appreciated the professional development (PD) opportunities available to rural teachers. The PD programs that teachers attend comprise courses such as updated curricula, trilingual education policy, ICT skills, etc. Overall, the participants, especially teachers, expressed satisfaction with the quality and relevance of these courses. They believed that such courses boost teachers' knowledge and skills, which in turn improves students' learning outcomes.

The participants also revealed that rural teachers are provided with opportunities to participate in seminars and training programs organized by Nazarbayev Intellectual Schools (NIS) and Nazarbayev University (NU). Moreover, representatives of these organizations usually visit rural schools and organize different training courses for the teachers. Some of the participants expressed that most courses they attended were too abstract and theoretical, and therefore, the participants could not apply what they had learned from the courses to their practice. The participants suggested that more practice-oriented courses would be beneficial for rural teachers.

Participants also noted that, in some schools, events are organized for teachers where they can share their knowledge and learn from their colleagues. One of the teachers said:

> I like this school because you can learn from other teachers. I learned a lot from [my fellow] teachers. And [the] administration greatly supports such events where we learn from each other.

The school principals, vice-principals and subject coordinators also mentioned that they support teachers' ongoing professional development so that teachers continue to upgrade the knowledge and skills they require to perform their duties effectively. One of the principals stated that she assigns experienced teachers to mentor novice teachers so that teachers work and learn from each other, as she said:

> The team [of teachers] is very good. We listen to each other, cooperate with [each] other, and then we all work together. In any case, we consult each other to solve the problems of our school collectively.

Financial incentives. During the survey and interviews, the participants in the study highlighted several positive aspects of working at rural schools. One of them is financial incentives provided to the rural teachers which keeps them motivated. For example, if teachers join a rural school, they can receive a one-time payment known as "fair credits" (подъёмные in Russian) which can be spent on purchasing a house. The government also runs a program called "With a Diploma to the Village," according to which young teachers who get employed at rural schools receive apartments. Moreover, teachers with higher qualifications receive an extra salary of 30 to 50% of their base salary. Also, those teachers who prepare students to participate in the Olympiads are eligible for additional financial support from the government. However, the focus group interviews revealed that not all rural schools have a consistent policy of providing financial incentives and bonuses to teachers. As an example, a teacher from the East of the country stated that in other schools of the region, teachers receive an additional payment if their students succeed in a competition, but such practice is not in place in their school. *"I know that some of the schools pay additional money to teachers with successful students, but it is not the case with our school",* said one of the participants.

Commitment to make a difference. Despite the various challenges (discussed in the following section), the interview data revealed that rural teachers are very committed to their work and students. Specifically, students mentioned in their focus group interviews that teachers, in addition to teaching, guide and help them with their application to Kazakhstani universities. Participants from all regions mentioned that rural teachers always conduct extra lessons for all students and try to discover each student's talent and potential. A principal in one of the Kazakhstani regions confirmed that teachers encourage their students to participate in contests and even cover the costs of their students' participation from their own salary.

The focus group interviews also revealed that teachers are committed to their profession and prioritize the well-being of their students. The participants recollected different cases they had to tackle as teachers of rural schools. For example, rural teachers often have to find sponsors or collect money from their salary to help disadvantaged students buy footwear, winter coats, and other necessary items. "There are cases when teachers buy from their salary firewood and coal," one of the teachers said.

Several teachers mentioned during the focus group interviews that they decided to stay and work in rural schools because they believed they were needed by the local community and students. Two teachers said they declined lucrative jobs offered by well-known schools in Astana and Almaty because they believed their services were needed at disadvantaged rural schools. Moreover, several other teachers stated that they want to continue to work in rural schools so that they can make a positive impact on students and local communities.

4.2 Challenges
The data also revealed several challenges teachers face in rural schools in Kazakhstan. These include but not limited to the following:

4.3 Workload
Extra hours of teaching. One of the main challenges identified by all respondents is related to the excessive workload placed on rural teachers, which goes beyond their primary teaching responsibilities. This additional workload includes but is not limited to teaching extra hours, supervising a classroom, organizing parent-teacher meetings, publishing articles, and preparing reports, etc. Many teachers in the southern and eastern regions admitted that they sometimes have to teach in two or even three shifts due to the overcrowded rural schools. Unfortunately, these teachers do not receive any additional compensation for their extra work. However, a principal in a southern region mentioned that their teachers are granted one day off per week, referred to as a "methodological day," to address this issue.

Excessive paperwork. Interview data about the challenges faced by rural teachers also spurred a discussion of the paperwork they have to fulfill on a daily basis. Teachers usually need to complete paperwork after their regular teaching duties. Some teachers struggle to complete all required forms during their workday, causing them to stay late in the evening to catch up on paperwork. Consequently, making them spend less time preparing their lessons. Additionally, teachers must use an electronic system called "Kundelik" to record student attendance and grades, which further reduces the time available for effective lesson preparation. It is further exacerbated by the fact that not all teachers have access to computers and a stable internet connection, therefore, sometimes teachers have to fill the register at home even at night.

New curriculum program requirements. The majority of participants in the study reported certain challenges associated with the implementation of the updated curriculum. According to the respondents, the new curriculum involves more homework, complicated content, and assignments that are time-consuming to prepare and assess. Moreover, teachers have to prepare materials for summative assignments, and sometimes, they have to buy school materials for their own money. The teachers reported that they take on these challenges because of the positive outcomes of the updated curriculum for their students. The teachers believed that due to the updated curriculum, students have started searching for information independently without teachers' support or involvement. The curriculum has also encouraged more student-centred learning instead of classical teacher-centred learning. For example, the students at one of the rural schools in east Kazakhstan stated that the lessons became more captivating and interesting as teachers used such methods as working in groups during the lessons and using ICT to deliver their lessons. Also, students collectively reported that after the new curriculum's incorporation, the materials and topics became clearer to them. Teachers were not only providing explanations but also conducting experiments to explain different concepts. One of the participants said the following about it:

> Now, after we switched to a new content (обновленка in Russian), everything is very clear, and teachers explain everything well and always thoroughly explain if you do not understand something.

Notwithstanding the updated curriculum's positive outcomes, teachers' workload has increased as they navigate its demands. Like any other change that brings a certain level of uncertainty and anxiety to teachers (primary implementers), the updated curriculum is also not free of such challenges, as the participants stated.

Classroom supervision. Another challenge rural teachers face is related to classroom supervision. According to the teachers, besides preparing their lessons, assessing homework, and doing heavy paperwork, they have the additional responsibility of supervising a certain class assigned to each teacher. Class supervision usually entails diverse sets of tasks, such as organizing parent meetings, visiting students' homes, conducting inspections, monitoring student attendance, and preparing for events like New Year's celebrations and others. Moreover, teachers are usually paid a minute amount of money for class supervision. Furthermore, rural teachers do not have anyone to assist them with these additional responsibilities, unlike NIS where teachers have teaching assistants who help them with class supervision and other tasks. One of the teachers described the issue as follows:

> Unfortunately, rural teachers do not have assistants who may help them with that duty. ... unlike in Nazarbayev Intellectual Schools, we do not have additional personnel for it [additional work such as class supervision]. As compulsory, every teacher has a class, and even if the salary is low, they [teachers] still have to work with children.

EXPLORING OPPORTUNITIES AND CHALLENGES OF RURAL TEACHERS 307

4.4 *Limited Resources*

The work of teachers in rural schools is also restrained by limited resources. There was a consensus among the teachers that one of the main challenges of the rural schools was the shortage of classrooms due to the increasing number of students. For example, one of the teachers mentioned that the number of students at their school reached 1600, even though the school was initially built for 600 students. This led to the shortage of classrooms and the closure of the teachers' room:

> Now we work in two shifts. In the afternoon, we don't have available classrooms as there are preparation classes, extra classes, and preparation for the UNT. In this regard, the shortage of classrooms affects our work. We also don't have teachers' room. Basically, we do not have a place to have a break, rest during the breaks, or change clothes.

Similarly, the shortage of computers and other equipment hinders teachers' delivery of lessons. Teachers complained that not all the classrooms were equipped with smartboards and projectors. And often there was not a sufficient number of computers which could be used by all students. Teachers opined the following about the shortage of technology:

> the lack of equipment is a big difficulty. For example, if I teach computer science and my class is divided into subgroups, it's good when I get a child sitting at each computer. But if a class is not divided into subgroups and there are 19 pupils for 10 computers. It turns out that I have 2 children sitting at each computer, I think this is problematic.

> Usually, I prepare a lesson as a PowerPoint presentation. Today, I have four lessons, and they are all in different rooms. I know that I won't be able to give the presentation to everyone because many classrooms do not have projectors, and some of them might be out of order.

Access to high-speed internet was another issue in rural schools, as the teachers pointed out. According to the teachers, there are distant rural areas that do not have an internet connection, though teachers of those schools have to fill out online forms as teachers of any other school in the country. One of the teachers stated:

> Well, we had a school in a district where there was no internet at all. They went up the mountain to catch the Internet. This is in the age of

digitalization! The so-called and well-known Kundelik should be filled. How to fill it in such schools?

Besides the scarcity of equipment, rural teachers experience a shortage of stationery and other teaching aids on a daily basis. Some interviewed teachers mentioned that they often spend their resources to buy stationeries or materials necessary for the lessons. *"Any material that needs to be printed or prepared, we all do at our own expense. All consumables, at our own expense,"* said one of the teachers during the interview. A similar view was provided by another teacher:

> when we have a shortage of money, we buy papers ourselves. Our department is not given any paper. No one gives us paper, all of which we buy at our own expense. So much work. For instance, if we have weekly events, we need to buy posters and paper, and so on.

4.5 Poor Infrastructure

The data showed that most rural schools lack appropriate buildings, play areas, and washrooms. The participants described their school buildings as old and insufficient, lacking adequate classrooms, a library, a computer lab, and a playground. For example, a school outside Almaty city was built for about 600 students, but it was being used by over 2,000 students in different shifts. The participants also mentioned that most schools in far-flung villages lack spaces and facilities, such as clean drinking water or proper functional sewage systems.

In the Oskemen region, students mentioned during a focus-group interview that they were unable to conduct practical science experiments because of the absence of labs and consumables. The research team, while visiting rural schools for data collection, observed that access to and conditions of washrooms in schools with newly constructed buildings were good with an uninterrupted supply of water and proper maintenance. However, washrooms in some of the older school buildings were found to be almost unusable. They also observed that some schools did not have a supply of hot water during winter. The school principals and vice principals mentioned that schools in far-flung villages lacked appropriate amenities and resources. However, they also mentioned that most rural schools undergo renovation, depending on the state of the school buildings.

5 Discussion

The importance of rural schools in Kazakhstan cannot be overstated, with teachers in these contexts playing a particularly crucial role in providing education to disadvantaged communities. This study explores the opportunities and challenges faced by rural teachers in Kazakhstan's educational landscape. The findings indicate that while opportunities exist in the form of professional development, financial incentives, and the chance to make a positive impact on students and local communities, teachers also grapple with challenges stemming from inadequate infrastructure, limited resources, and increased workload.

Echazarra and Radinger (2019) suggest that providing ongoing training in remote areas, such as rural villages, is costly, leading to fewer professional development opportunities for rural teachers. However, this study revealed that Kazakhstan's rural teachers are satisfied with the available professional development courses, particularly valuing workshops at the school and regional levels where they can share experiences and learn from peers. These teachers also appreciate training offered by institutions such as Nazarbayev Intellectual Schools (NIS) and Nazarbayev University (NU). Nonetheless, they note that these sessions often prioritize theory over practice, and therefore, teachers find it difficult to apply the knowledge they gained from the courses to their classroom teaching, a typical example of gaps between theory and practice.

Financial incentives were identified as another opportunity for rural teachers. Additional payments for higher qualifications and student achievements also serve as motivating factors for rural teachers. This finding resonates with studies conducted in other countries that found a positive correlation between teacher bonuses and retention rates in rural schools (Castro & Espasito, 2021), especially for teachers working with students from disadvantaged socio-economic backgrounds (Springer et al., 2016). However, participants in the current study reported inconsistent implementation of financial incentives across different rural schools, signalling the need for more uniform policies across regions and schools.

Echazarra and Radinger (2019) claim that rural teachers should be trained to work with underrepresented groups in rural areas, including families from disadvantaged backgrounds and ethnic minority students. Similarly, the participants in the current study also displayed a strong dedication to enhancing not only the academic but personal development of their students. They often go beyond their formal teaching duties and conduct extra classes as required, nurture the distinct talents of students, assist them with university applications, and prepare for competitions without additional pay. Many teachers also provide financial assistance from their own pockets to students in need, purchasing essential resources such as clothing, stationery, and even heating coal. Several teachers mentioned that they spend a significant portion of their salaries each month to purchase teaching aids and stationery due to insufficient budgets provided to their schools.

Despite their dedication and hard work, rural teachers encounter substantial challenges. One major challenge is the excessive workload resulting from additional teaching hours, administrative paperwork, and classroom supervision responsibilities without additional compensation. This finding is congruent with that of previous studies conducted in Kazakhstan (Irsaliyev et al., 2009) and other countries (Öztürk & Yildirim, 2013), which found heavy workload as a key challenge that can lead to teacher attrition and burnout.

As discussed earlier, limited resources and poor infrastructure also pose challenges, with shortages of classrooms, computers, stationery, and limited internet access, hindering effective teaching and learning in rural schools. Teachers often have to use their own money to purchase necessary materials, adding to their financial burden. This finding is consistent with the results of another study conducted in Kazakhstan by Smanova (2021), who argues that principals in rural schools were significantly more likely than their counterparts in city schools to report that their school's capacity to provide instruction was challenged by limited educational materials and poor physical infrastructure. City schools have more computers and better internet connectivity as compared to rural schools where one computer is shared by 10–15 students. Similar results are reported by Nurbayev (2021), who found outdated computers and lack of high-speed internet as "the most urgent issue" in Kazakhstani rural schools. These challenges, if not addressed timely, can impact teachers' job satisfaction, effectiveness in the classroom, and overall well-being. These may also contribute to high turnover rates in rural schools as teachers may seek employment in schools with better resources and infrastructure.

6   Conclusion

The study delved into the opportunities and challenges experienced by teachers in Kazakhstani rural schools.

While these teachers benefit from professional development opportunities, financial incentives, and recognition of their hard work, they also struggle with the increasing workload, poor infrastructure, and limited resources that impede effective teaching.

To address or at least mitigate these issues, the government should develop practice-oriented training courses tailored to the needs of rural teachers. Additionally, organizing more events where rural teachers can exchange experiences and knowledge would foster a supportive learning environment in rural schools, leading rural teachers to become communities of practice.

Reducing the workload of rural teachers and providing additional payment for extra work could improve the working conditions in rural schools. Other incentives, such as locality allowances, additional vacation, and transfer entitlements could also help motivate rural teachers.

Investing in infrastructure and addressing the shortages of classrooms, computers, and other essential resources is also crucial for quality teaching. Priority should be given to schools with the greatest need based on student number and geographical location.

Special attention needs to be paid to the issue of insufficient computers and high-speed internet. Despite the government's policies on digitalization and improving broadband internet access, rural schools continue to face challenges in this area. This issue requires urgent attention, as the quality of teaching is closely linked to the provision of quality materials and technical resources, such as high-speed internet and well-equipped computer labs in schools (Nurbayev, 2021).

By comprehensively addressing these challenges, policymakers can significantly improve the quality of rural schools, benefiting teachers, students, and the communities at large.

Acknowledgement

The authors greatly appreciate the valuable contributions made by the research team members and all research participants from Kazakhstani rural schools. We also acknowledge with gratitude that this research study was supported by *Nazarbayev University's Collaborative Research Grant (Grant # 021220CRP1322)*.

References

Bell, J. (2005). *Doing your research project: A guide for first-time researchers.* John Wiley & Sons.

Bureau of National Statistics of Agency for Strategic Planning and Reforms of the Republic of Kazakhstan. (2024). *Statistics.* https://stat.gov.kz/en/

Biddle, C., & Azano, A. P. (2016). Constructing and reconstructing the "rural school problem": A century of rural education research. *Review of Research in Education, 40*(1), 298–325. https://doi.org/10.3102/0091732X16667700

Bridges, D., & Sagintayeva, A. (2014). Introduction. In D. Bridges (Ed.), *Educational reform and internationalization: The case of school reform in Kazakhstan* (pp. XXII–1). Cambridge University Press.

Burrola, A., Rohde-Collins, D., & Anglum, J. (2023). Conceptualizing rurality in education policy: Comparative evidence from Missouri. *The Rural Educator, 44*(3), 17–33. https://doi.org/10.55533/2643-9662.1389

Cohen, L., Manion, L., & Morrison, K. (2007). *Research methods in education* (6th ed.). Routledge Falmer.

Castro, J. F., & Esposito, B. (2021). The effect of bonuses on teacher retention and student learning in rural schools: A story of spillovers. *Education Finance and Policy, 17*(4), 693–718.

Darling-Hammond, L. (2000). Teacher quality and students' achievement: A review of state policy evidence. *Education Policy Analysis Archives, 8*(1). http://dx.doi.org/10.14507/epaa.v8n1.2000

Echazarra, A., & Radinger, T. (2019). Learning in rural schools: Insights from PISA, TALIS, and the literature. OECD. https://doi.org/10.1787/19939019

Fimyar, O., Yakavets, N., & Bridges, D. (2014). Educational reforms in Kazakhstan: The contemporary policy agenda. In D. Bridges (Ed.), *Educational reform and internationalization: The case of school reform in Kazakhstan* (pp. 53–70). Cambridge University Press.

Frost, D., Fimyar, O., Yakavets, N., & Bilyalov, D. (2014). The role of the school director in educational reform in Kazakhstan. In D. Bridges (Ed.), *Educational reform and internationalization: The case of school reform in Kazakhstan* (pp. 217–238). Cambridge University Press.

Irsaliyev, S. A., Kamzoldayev, M. B., Tashibayeva, D. N., & Kopeyeva, A. T. (2019). Teachers of Kazakhstan: Why young people choose this profession and what motivates them to stay. *Beles.*

Malhoit, G. (2005). Providing rural students with a high-quality education: The rural perspective on the concept of educational adequacy. *Rural School and Community Trust.* https://www.ruraledu.org/user_uploads/file/Providing_Rural_Students.pdf

Mehisto, P., Kambatyrova, A., & Nurseitova, K. (2014). Trilingualism in educational policy and practice. In D. Bridges (Ed.), *Educational reform and internationalization: The case of school reform in Kazakhstan* (pp. 152–176). Cambridge University Press.

Merriam, S. B., & Tisdell, E. J. (2016). *Qualitative research: A guide to design and implementation* (4th ed.). Jossey-Bass.

Miller, K. (2010). Why definitions matter: Rural definitions and state poverty rankings. *Rural Policy Research Institute.* https://rupri.org/wp-content/uploads/Poverty-and-Definition-ofRural.pdf

Ministry of Education and Science. (2019). *State programme of education development in the Republic of Kazakhstan for 2020–2025.* Ministry of Education and Science.

Nurbayev, Z. (2021). Inequality between students of rural and urban schools in Kazakhstan: Causes and ways to address it. *Central Asia Program.* https://centralasiaprogram.org/inequality-students-rural-urban-schools-kazakhstan-ways-address

Öztürk, M., & Yildirim, A. (2013). Adaptation challenges of novice teachers. *Hacettepe Üniversitesi Eğitim Fakültesi Dergisi, 28*(1), 294–307.

Semke, C. A., & Sheridan, S. M. (2012). Family–school connections in rural educational settings: A systematic review of the empirical literature. *The School Community Journal, 22*(1), 21–48.

Smanova, N. K. (2021). Can we overcome the achievement gap between urban and rural students in Kazakhstan through school resources: Evidence from PISA 2018. *Proceedings of the 5th International Conference on Education and Multimedia Technology.* https://doi.org/10.1145/3481056.3481064

Springer, M. G., Swain, W. A., & Rodriguez, L. A. (2015). Effective teacher retention bonuses: Evidence from Tennessee. *Educational Evaluation and Policy Analysis, 38*(2), 199–221.

Tajik, M., Shamatov, D., & Fillipova, L. (2021). Stakeholders' perceptions of the quality of education in rural schools in Kazakhstan. *Improving Schools, 25*(2), 187–204. https://doi.org/10.1177/13654802211031088

Tajik, M., Shamatov, D., & Fillipova, L. (2022). Teachers' quality in Kazakhstani rural schools. *Bulletin of Kazakh National Women's Teacher Training University, 3*(91), 6–16.

Tastanbekova, K. (2020). Professional prestige, status, and esteem of teaching in Kazakhstan: Temporal, regional, and gender analysis of payroll data. *Journal of Eastern European and Central Asian Research, 7*(2), 175–190.

United Nations. (2007). *Millennium development goals in Kazakhstan.* https://www.undp.org/sites/g/files/zskgke326/files/publications/Kazakhstan_MDGReport_2007.pdf

Welsh, R. O. (2024). Does rural mean not urban? Reconsidering the conceptualization and operationalization of rural school districts. *Urban Education,* 0(0). https://doi.org/10.1177/00420859241227929

Winter, L., Rimini, C., Soltanbekova, A., & Tynybayeva, M. (2014). The culture and practices of assessment in Kazakhstan: The Unified National Test, past and present. In D. Bridges (Ed.), *Educational reform and internationalization: The case of school reform in Kazakhstan* (pp. 106–132). Cambridge University Press.

Yakavets, N., & Dzhadrina, M. (2014). Educational reforms in Kazakhstan: Entering the world arena. In D. Bridges (Ed.), *Educational reform and internationalization: The case of school reform in Kazakhstan* (pp. 28–52). Cambridge University Press

CHAPTER 15

Exploring Assessment in Kazakhstani Pre-Service Teacher Education

Insights and Experiences

Zhadyra Makhmetova

Abstract

The double role of pre-service teachers (PTS) as future teachers and as students challenge the findings of many studies on PTS' understanding of assessment. Only a few studies consider PTS to be both students and teachers at the same time. More research is needed in this field, and more specifically in the context of Kazakhstan, where there are limited studies examining primary PTS' education. This chapter presents the key findings and implications of the PhD dissertation, which explored how Kazakhstani PTS learn about and develop their understanding of educational assessment during their initial teacher training in Kazakhstani universities. The results of this study revealed that Kazakhstani primary PTS' experiences—as pupils at schools, as students at universities, and as student-teachers during practicum—contributed to their perception of multiple understandings of assessment with a dominant view on control, accountability, accuracy, and teaching values. The study suggests several implications for theory, policy and practice, and for teacher education programs.

Keywords

experience of assessment – understanding of assessment – pre-service teachers – initial assessment training – assessment education – teacher education – mixed-methods

1 Introduction

Assessment in teacher education has multiple contributions towards becoming a teacher. In the teacher education context, assessment has complex and multiple dimensions, such as understanding and conceptions of assessment, experiences of assessment, assessment literacy, assessment competencies, and assessment identity explained using various theories and contexts (Coombs & DeLuca, 2022

© ZHADYRA MAKHMETOVA, 2025 | DOI:10.1163/9789004726345_016

DeLuca et al., 2024). Gavin Brown's research (2002) has been very influential in the field of study, and significantly contributed to the field of studies on teachers' understanding and conceptions of assessment with the development of his inventory on Teachers' Conceptions of Assessment. The inventory measures conceptions of assessment through purposes of assessment with identified four assessment conceptions: improvement, teacher and school accountability, student accountability, and irrelevance. The inventory was validated and adapted in different contexts (e.g. Brown et al., 2011; Gebril, 2016). Daniels and Poth (2017) used Brown's inventory to explore the relationship between the pre-service teachers' conceptions of assessment and their intended instruction and assessment practices, revealing that pre-service teachers who believed in improving teaching conceptions tended to practice competence-oriented assessment.

Studies after the pandemic re-envisioned assessment education towards innovative teaching and learning, authentic assessment or meaningful assessment, real-world assessment practices and the importance of feelings of pre-service teachers about it, attitudes, and reflections (Al-Haddad et al., 2023; Coleman et al., 2023; Doyle et al., 2024; Ketonen et al., 2023; Young et al., 2024). Gungor et al. (2024) emphasise assessment practices' dynamic and interactive nature and their impact on pre-service teachers' learning. Other studies emphasised assessment literacy in digital environments (Estaji et al., 2021). More studies appeared around the effects of experiences of assessment and educational contexts in shaping pre-service teachers' understanding of assessment (e.g. Crawford et al., 2023; DeLuca et al., 2021; Lin et al., 2024; Magaji & Ade-Ojo, 2023), and therefore calling for holistic approaches in assessment education (Coombs & DeLuca, 2022).

Holistic approaches in assessment education address the issue of the complex nature of initial assessment education, wherein learners have the dual role of student and teacher at the same time (e.g. Brunker et al., 2019; Hill et al., 2017). They advocate for integrating innovative and experiential assessment methods into teacher education programs to enhance teaching competencies and prepare future educators (Atojen et al., 2024; Canadas, 2023; Coombs & DeLuca, 2022). Studies highlight the need for experiential learning projects, reflective practices, digital literacy, and authentic assignments to enhance pre-service teachers' assessment literacy and overall teaching competencies (Crawford et al., 2023; DeLuca et al., 2021; DeLuca et al., 2019; DeLuca et al., 2024; Gotwals & Cisterna, 2022; Gungor & Gungor, 2024). Other studies in this perspective provide key strategies, including practical training, integration of formative assessment practices, and the active involvement of teacher educators in navigating and shaping assessment policies (Brunker et al., 2019; Startk et al., 2023; Van Orman et al., 2024; Young et al., 2024). By addressing these areas, teacher education programs can better prepare future educators to assess and support student learning effectively.

However, it should be noted that all these studies mentioned above are emerging in the Global North context. Limited studies about initial assessment education exist in Kazakhstan. A recent study on in-service teachers' assessment literacy discusses the role of assessment literacy as a crucial component of professional competence for teachers in Kazakhstan amidst educational reforms. It highlights the importance of developing assessment literacy in initial teacher training institutions (Shmigirilova et al., 2021). Burkhalter and Shegebayev (2012) examined the development of higher-order and critical thinking skills in Kazakhstani teacher education, focusing on Soviet pedagogical legacies. They found that mainly training had surface learning, emphasis on memorisation, lecturing, text adherence and oral exams hindered student-centred and active learning, and lack of holistic grading. Yakavets, Bridges, and Shamatov (2017) found that in Kazakhstan, compared to in-service training, pre-service training obtained "in the Pedagogic Institutes still followed a traditional Soviet pattern that tended to emphasise subject knowledge teaching over the development of teaching skills" (p. 597). The study underscores the importance of developing assessment literacy to adapt to changes in the evaluation system and improve teaching practices.

Research on Kazakhstani teacher education reveals a persistent influence of Soviet education, which emphasises control, correction, memorisation, and surface learning and lacks reflective and critical thinking skills. There is a notable gap in research on pre-service teachers' assessment skills, with no studies specifically focusing on assessment education. This study addresses this gap by exploring pre-service teachers' experiences of assessment and their understanding of assessment. The experiences of assessment are shaped by per-service teachers' environment and educational contexts, and below, the Kazakhstani teacher education context is described.

2 Teacher Education in Kazakhstan

During the Soviet era, teacher training in Kazakhstan had a robust foundation, maintaining three tracks: vocational education, higher education, and in-service training (Tastanbekova, 2018). However, during the economic crisis of 1991–2000, the teaching profession experienced a decline in prestige due to factors like burnout, low pay, and privatization. This led to a lack of motivation among high-performing applicants, resulting in mainly low-achieving students enrolling in teacher education programs (Tastanbekova, 2018).

To address these issues, Kazakhstan initiated radical educational changes after 2010, focusing on modernizing teacher training institutions and improving the prestige of the teaching profession. The Ministry of Education and Science (MoES, 2015) prioritised the modernisation of teacher education programs, introducing special examinations for applicant dispositions, increasing stipends, and developing new enrollment guidelines.

The third stage of radical educational changes (after 2010) is curriculum reform and assessment reform, shifting from norm-based to criterion-based assessment (Winter et al., 2020). This led to massive professional development for in-service teachers (Tastanbekova, 2018). Modernisation of pre-service teacher training institutions supported by MoES took place a bit later, which included the development of teachers' professional standards (Atameken, 2017) and the introduction of a course titled "Technology of Criterion-Based Assessment" into the curriculum (NTC, 2016). Despite the recent introduction of this course, according to Teaching and Learning International Survey, 84.8% of Kazakhstani teachers reported that "monitoring students' development and a learning" components were included in the content of ITE (OECD, 2019). Those are the responses from the teachers who did not have a separate course on assessment. OECD (2019) collected data from in-service Kazakhstani teachers during the period when an explicit mandatory course on assessment had just been introduced in ITE training. It means that although there was no explicit mandatory assessment course in ITE training, pre-service teachers still learned about assessment. It follows that the state of assessment education in ITE programs in Kazakhstan requires a deeper look and exploration.

However, after conducting this doctoral study, several changes took place. First, universities started to develop their own educational programs as before. Teacher education programs needed to be developed using standardised educational programs. However, curriculum development or design is a relatively new concept for post-Soviet countries. Pantic and Wubbles (2012), exploring teacher education curriculum reform in Serbia, oppose two approaches: the German pedagogical culture of Didaktik and the Anglo-Saxon Curriculum culture, and highlight the importance of understanding these two cultures in curriculum reform. This is especially true for Central Asian countries, the secular education of which were mainly recipients of Russian (European) education, and later of Soviet education, characterised as state-controlled, centralised, and focused on theoretical knowledge, and then shifted to outcome-based education, which is about on pre-defined program outcomes (Pantic & Wubbles, 2012). Outcome-based education requires alignment and measurable outcomes, and pre-defined program outcomes need to be aligned with the education program aim, learning outcomes, subject learning outcomes, and aligned with assessment approaches. However, working as the Head of the academic quality enhancement team at the regional university during the 2023–2024 academic year, I can highlight that university teachers still struggle with curriculum development and course syllabi design. Another change that is taking place is the World Bank project on enhancing teacher education in Kazakhstan, within which Kazakhstan HEIS, in collaboration with the Ministry of Higher Education and Science, Nazarbayev University, and HAMK and JAMK universities in Finland, designed 30 new teacher education programs. The project started in 2022 and aims to shift to an outcome-based, student-oriented curriculum. Starting the next academic year, it is planned to disseminate developed teacher education programs and modernise other teacher education programs. Professional development courses for university tutors or teacher educators support establishing these teacher education programs. Like all other education programs, the program's content is publicly available in national databases of educational programs (Unified Platform of Higher Education, n.d.).

Initial teacher education training at universities has its peculiarities in its development challenged by reforms in higher education. One of the important changes is that State universities received the status of Joint-stock company status, having more autonomy, but still restricted as mainly one exclusive shareholder, which is the Ministry (European University Association, 2018). Another change, the Ministry of Education and Science is separated into the Ministry of Education and the Ministry of Science and Higher Education. This structural change might bring some discrepancies, particularly to teacher education programs, such as connections between schools and universities, school education reforms, and teacher preparation for these reforms. Furthermore, the Ministry of Science and Higher Education ordered to assess students using the normal curve distribution, according to which only 10% of students can receive A grades, and 10% of students receive F grades (Dzharasova, 2023), which is a bit contradictory to the philosophy of criterion-based assessment and formative assessment. The current study does not collect data during these changes. However, based on the existing findings and recent literature, the study will discuss the implications of these changes in initial assessment education at teacher training universities in Kazakhstan.

3   Theoretical Framework

The study integrates theories from Dewey (1938), Lortie (1975), Schön (1983), and Bullock (2011) to explore the development of pre-service teachers' understanding of assessment through their experiences as pupils, university students and during teaching practicum. Dewey's Experiential Learning (1938) refs to learning is a continuum where each experience influences future ones. High-quality assessment experiences in school shape a foundational understanding of assessment for pre-service teachers. These experiences are interconnected and influenced by external factors, emphasising the importance of providing valuable learning experiences. Lortie's Apprenticeship of Observation (1975) explains that pre-service teachers form educational beliefs through extensive classroom observation as school students, which can be difficult to change during initial teacher education training. These preconceived notions impact their professional socialisation and understanding of teaching and assessment. However, the apprenticeship of observation continues to take place throughout pre-service teachers' education. This is because pre-service teachers still experience teaching, learning, and assessment in higher education as students. For example, they develop an understanding of assessment by observing teacher educators' assessment practices, the assessment practices of mentor teachers during their field placements, and from being assessed by teacher educators at the university. Thus, the current learning experiences of pre-service teachers also have implications for the development of later experiences, which are the practices of teaching, learning, and assessment during their study in a teacher education program. Bullock's Propositional Knowledge (2011) is about the content of teacher education programs and is divided into substantive (subject matter) and syntactic (pedagogical) disciplines. Bullock criticizes the traditional focus on transmitting knowledge without considering how pre-service teachers learn to teach. Concerning this Schön's Knowing-in-Action and Reflecting-in-Action (1983) argue that knowledge is gained through practicum experiences (knowing-in-action) supported by reflection on these experiences (reflecting-in-action) is crucial for developing practical teaching skills. This approach turns propositional knowledge into experiential knowledge. Overall, the study emphasises the importance of integrating experiential learning, observation, practical knowledge, and reflection in developing pre-service teachers' understanding of assessment.

4 Research Design

The study employs exploratory sequential mixed methods. The exploratory sequential mixed method design uses "sequential timing" in three phases. It begins with a qualitative phase to explore a phenomenon (here, understanding of educational assessment) and collect and analyse data. Based on the findings of this qualitative exploration, "considering the resulting categories as variables," in Phase 2, the researcher develops or adapts a quantitative instrument (in the case of the present research, adaptation of Chinese Teachers

Conceptions of Assessment instrument Inventory (Brown, Hui, Yu, & Kennedy, 2011) and a 6-point Likert scale survey on Experiences of assessment). The researcher administers this survey in Phase 3 to a large number of participants "to assess the overall prevalence of these variables" (Creswell & Plano Clark, 2018, p. 67). The flowchart below describes each step in these three phases of the study. The research site of the study was former state universities which offer teacher education programs, particularly the *Pedagogy and Methodology of Primary Education Program*. The qualitative phase took place in one university. It involved the participation of 34 pre-service primary teachers in 6 focus group interviews, 5 teacher educators in one-to-one interviews, and document analysis. Analysis of these data led to the design of a culturally relevant survey of Chinese Teachers's Conceptions of Assessment Instrument Inventory (Brown et al., 2011) and the development of Kazakhstani. Phase 3 involved the participation of 10 universities and received responses from 210 primary pre-service teachers.

First, qualitative and quantitative data were separately analysed. Qualitative data were analysed in MaxQDA using conventional content analysis (Hsieh & Shannon, 2005). Quantitative data were analysed in emplying Exploratory Factor Analysis for 30 "understanding of assessment" and 15 "experiences of assessment" scales. EFA aims to explore the factor structure of the scale (Holmes Finch, 2020), or "to determine the minimum number of common factors" (Izquierdo et al., 2014, p. 395).

In the exploratory sequential mixed methods design, Creswell and Plano Clark (2018) view the integration of qualitative and quantitative phases as "a central feature of mixed methods" (pp. 297–298), its "centerpiece," its "signature," and it occurs on two levels (Berman, 2017a, p. 7): the design-level integration and the interpretation-level integration. The second stage of integration is at the "interpretation level" which transcends qualitative and quantitative findings and provides "new insights" through the joint display and joint interpretation of qualitative and quantitative findings (Fetters et al., 2013, p. 2143; in Berman, 2017a, p. 7). At this level, the "interpretation-level linking of data (Fetters et al., 2013, p. 2143; Creswell & Plano Clark, 2011) will allow the formulation of meta-inferences" (Berman, 2017b, p. 21). Meta-inferences are "an overall conclusion, explanation or understanding developed through and integration of the inferences obtained from the qualitative and quantitative strands of a mixed method study" (Teddlie & Tashakkori 2008, p. 300; in Berman, 2017b, p. 21; also see Creswell & Plano Clark, 2018, p. 218). According to Berman (2017b) "It is in these meta-inferences, [that] qualitative and quantitative data will be compared and contrasted and will ultimately address the purpose of the study" (p. 21), to better comprehend Kazakhstani primary pre-service teachers' understanding of educational assessment. Thus, the findings section of this chapter will first present Joint displays of qualitative and quantitative findings

EXPLORING ASSESSMENT IN KAZAKHSTANI PT EDUCATION   321

STEP 1 — Qualitative Phase 1

Qualitative Phase 1 – RQ 1

- Conducted a qualitative study to explore how Kazakhstani prirmary pre-service teachers learn about and develop their understanding of educational assessment.
- Obtained permission and access to Sary University.
- Identified documents to be analyzed.
- Identified qualitative purposeful samples: 34 Sary University PTs nrolled in *Methodology and Pedagogy of Primary Education Program,*and 5 of their TEs.
- Conducted interviews: focus group with PTs and one-on-one with TEs.
- Analyzed qualitative data with preliminary analysis and conventional content analysis using MaxQDA software, to answer the qualitative questions (RQ1: RQ1.I, RQ1.II, RQ1.III), and identify the information needed to develop a new quantitative instrument in Phase 2.

STEP 2 — Development Phase 2

Instrument Development Phase 2

- Designed, developed, and piloted a Likert scale survey grounded in Phase 1 qualitative findings.
- Created a 33 item pool on experiences of assessment built on qualitative survey findings.
- Based on qualitative findings on purposes of assessment, I selected the Chinese version of Teachers' Conceptions of Assessment inventory (C-TCoA) (Brown et al., 2011) from which I borrowed 31 items on "understanding of assessment."
- Translated the new survey in Kazakh and Russian, and applied procedures to verify the quality of the translations and of the new survey.
- Obtained permission and access to Alasha University to pilot the survey.
- Pilot tested new survey distributed via Qualtrics to all 80 Alasha University PTs enrolled in *Methodology and Pedagogy of Primary Education Program*; 59 responses (74% response rate).
- Analyzed results of pilot test using descriptive statistics and exploratory factor analysis.
- Refined survey based on the results of the pilot.

STEP 3 — Quantitative Phase 3

Quantitative Phase 3 – RQ 2

- Obtained permission and access to 10 HEIs (volunteer sample) across Kazakhstan which offered the *Methodology and Pedagogy of Primary Education Program*
- Selected quantitative sample: all 500 PTs enrolled in *Methodology and Pedagogy of Primary Education Program* in the 10 Kazakhstani participating HEIs.
- Administered new contextually and culturally sensitive Likert scale survey via Qualtrics to all 500 PTs; obtained 210 responses (42% response rate).
- Analyzed quantitative data using descriptive analysis and exploratory factor analysis to answer the quantitative question, RQ 2.

STEP 4 — Integration

Joint Interpretation, Integration

- Summarized and interpreted results for qualitative Phase 1 and for quantitative Phase 3.
- Conducted joint interpretation of the qualitative and quantitative findings on experiences and understanding of assessment of Kazakhstani primary PTs enrolled in the*Methodology and Pedagogy of Primary Education Program.*
- Identified and discussed dominant trends in integrated data from both strands, qualitative and quantitative, in current understanding and experiences of assessment among participating Kazakhstani primary PTs enrolled in the *Methodology and Pedagogy of Primary Education Program.*
- Discussed to what extent and in what ways qualitative findings helped better understand quantitative findings, while quantitative results projected PTs' understanding of assessment onto a larger sample of 210 PTs enrolled in *Methodology and Pedagogy of Primary Education Program* at 10 participating HEIs across Kazakhstan.

FIGURE 15.1   Flowchart of the basic procedures implementing the exploratory sequential mixed methods design in this study (after Creswell & Plano Clark, 2018, p. 88)

on experiences of assessment and understanding of assessment, followed by a discussion of meta-inferences.

5 Findings

5.1 Integration and Interpretation of Experiences of Assessment Findings

Phase 1 explored the perspectives and experiences of one university's primary pre-service teachers and their teacher educators and analysed supportive documents. In their interviews, PTs described their assessment experiences at their schools as pupils, at the university as students, and at teaching placements as student-teachers and described how they developed their understanding of assessment through their experiences. Quantitative Phase 3 captured the perspectives and experiences of assessment of 210 Kazakhstani primary PTs in their responses to the 15-item scale on experiences of assessment. The analysis results revealed a two-factor solution: PTs' experiences of assessment as students and teachers' experiences of assessment as teachers.

A joint display of qualitative Phase 1 and quantitative Phase 3 findings on assessment experiences (Table 15.1) connects the two data strands in two main themes: *experiences of assessment as students and experiences of assessment as teachers.*

Experiences of assessment as students. Interviews showed that PTs' experiences of assessment as students consisted of provision of theoretical knowledge on educational assessment (Key Findings 1–3), learning from teacher educators' strategies to teach assessment (Key Findings 4–6), experiences of assessment as pupils at their former schools, as students at the university, observation of their mentor teachers' assessment approaches at teaching placements (Key Findings 7–9), and learning from observing these assessment approaches (Key Finding 10). In particular, these experiences were: courses on the *Methods of Teaching Subjects*, theoretical knowledge about assessment, teacher educators' approaches to teach assessment, lesson planning, trial lessons, peer-assessment, memories of assessment approaches used by their schoolteachers, assessment approaches used by teacher educators, getting feedback from teacher educators, control of knowledge, and observation of experienced mentor teachers at school placements. The statistical analysis of the survey data revealed the sources named above as one factor for PTs' Experiences of Assessment as Students, which explained the largest proportion of variance (58.8%). Responses to the survey indicated that 210 primary PTs moderately agreed with these experiences of assessment helping them understand assessment.

EXPLORING ASSESSMENT IN KAZAKHSTANI PT EDUCATION 323

TABLE 15.1 Joint display of qualitative phase 1 and quantitative phase 3 findings on Kazakhstani primary pre-service teachers' experiences of assessment

Qualitative findings phase 1	Quantitative findings phase 3	Joint themes
13 Key findings	Factor structure	
The analysis of documents revealed a lack of integration in the assessment knowledge provided to Kazakhstani primary PTs Contextualized assessment knowledge was promoted in the Kazakhstani curriculum provided to primary PTs.	Pre-service teachers' experiences of assessment *as students*	– theoretical knowledge on assessment – strategies to teach assessment
Promoting teaching values in the Kazakhstani primary curriculum is relevant to educational assessment. TEs mainly use a task-based approach to teach assessment Peer-assessment was the improvement-oriented assessment approach most frequently used by TEs to teach assessment. Some primary PTs believed that they did not study assessment during their university courses.	Items on learning from theoretical knowledge on assessment: 3.1–3.3 Items on learning from strategies to teach assessment: 3.4–3.7	– observing teachers' assessment practices – observing and experienc-ing former schoolteachers' assessment practices
Primary PTs mainly experienced and observed traditional assessment at their schools, universities, and teaching placements Primary PTs mainly experienced and observed subjectivity and imprecision in assessment Most of primary PTs' experiences of assessment revealed the high value attributed to grades Some primary PTs learned about assessment mostly from observing their teachers	Items on learning from observation of assessment, and experiencing assessment: 3.8–3.13	– observing and experiencing TEs' assess-ment practices – observing men-tor teachers assessment practices

(cont.)

TABLE 15.1 Joint display of qualitative phase 1 and quantitative phase 3 findings on Kazakhstani primary pre-service teachers' experiences of assessment (*cont.*)

Qualitative findings phase 1	Quantitative findings phase 3	Joint themes
13 Key findings	**Factor structure**	
Primary PTs reflected mostly on the differentiation aspect of assessment in Kazakhstan, as observed during their teaching practicum Some primary PTs explained gaining some understanding of assessment from their active involvement as teachers assessing their own pupils during their practicum A few primary PTs reported some problematic issues between theoretical and practical knowledge of assessment when they had to assess their own pupils	Pre-service teachers' experiences of assessment *as teachers* during their teaching practicum Items on learning from reflection on application of assessment knowledge into practice: 3.14 -3.15	– PTs' perceived their university knowledge as "outdated" and "not suitable for pupils." – PTs' first experiences of assessment acting as teachers during their practicum – assessment of children at teaching placements challenged PTs' understanding of assessment – PTs questioned the fairness of assessment in schools – PTs perceived a disconnection between knowledge provided at the university and assessment practices in real classroom settings

Jointly, experiences of assessment as students refer to theoretical knowledge on assessment, strategies to teach assessment, observation of assessment, and experiencing assessment.

Experiences of assessment as teachers. Interview data revealed that as teachers, PTs reflected on the differentiation aspect of assessment (Key Finding 11), gained a better understanding of assessment from their active involvement as teachers assessing their own students (Key Finding 12), and reflected on some problematic issues between theoretical and practical knowledge of assessment (Key Finding 13). In the responses to the survey, the factor "PTs' Experiences of Assessment as Teachers" explained the smallest proportion of variance (9.3%), consisting of only two items. Compared to the first factor ("as students"), this factor captures the challenge of PTs' application of their knowledge which showed that it was "outdated" and "not suitable for pupils." Items of this factor show some degree of reflection, and relate to the realization, the understanding that comes when knowledge is applied. Qualitative and quantitative data on experiences of assessment as teachers are about their "reflection-in-action," which is challenged by a lack of theoretical knowledge and of its alignment throughout the curriculum, and by a weak fostering of PTs' reflection skills.

5.2   Integration and Interpretation of Understanding of Assessment Findings

A joint display of qualitative Phase 1 purposes and quantitative Phase 3 findings on understanding of assessment (Table 15.2) revealed five main themes emerging from this study. Assessment:
-   can control learning, and hold learners and teachers accountable
-   may be irrelevant, or ignored
-   can help improve learning and teaching
-   carries risks of imprecision and measurement error
-   can support development, motivation and values

Jointly, both strands of data suggest that assessment can monitor and control students' learning and hold both learners and teachers accountable. Kazakhstani primary PTs understood assessment as accountability from the double perspective of learners (pupils and students), and teachers. In both research strands, PTs agreed about teacher accountability, which suggests that PTs saw the assessment of students' results as an indicator of the quality of teachers' work. For participating Kazakhstani primary PTs, accountability in assessment was essentially about holding both learners and teachers accountable for learning results, which needed to be trusted.

The next joint theme is the improvement purpose. Kazakhstani primary PTs believed that final grades or learning results held them as learners accountable for their own improvement in learning. In other words, improvement

TABLE 15.2 Joint display of qualitative phase 1 and quantitative phase 3 findings on Kazakhstani primary pre-service teachers' understanding of assessment

Qualitative findings phase 1		Quantitative findings phase 3		Joint themes
Assessment purposes	Description	Factors	Factor structure	
To control pupils' learning and hold pupils accountable To hold teachers accountable	Emphasis is placed – on controlling students' learning – on quality of teachers' work and performance	Understanding of Assessment as Accountability	Includes: – items on students' and teachers' accountability – one item on accuracy	Assessment is to control learning, and hold learners and teachers accountable
To improve learning and teaching	Improvement of learning and teaching through multiple understandings of assessment and to be aware and responsible for one's own learning, and teaching	Understanding of Assessment as Improvement	Includes: – all items referring to improvement in learning and teaching – one item on students' accountability – one item on accuracy	Assessment can help improve learning and teaching
To determine level/ diagnostic assessment	Identifying pupils' level of development; determining pupils' level of preparedness for secondary school	Understanding of Assessment as Development	Includes: – all items referring to students' development – items on students' accountability and – items on accuracy	Assessment can support development, motivation and values

(cont.)

TABLE 15.2   joint display of qualitative phase 1 and quantitative phase 3 findings on Kazakhstani primary pre-service teachers' understanding of assessment (*cont.*)

Qualitative findings phase 1		Quantitative findings phase 3		Joint themes
Assessment purposes	**Description**	**Factors**	**Factor structure**	
To encourage studying	Developing willingness to study, work harder via means of grades, praise			
To teach values	Using assessment to teach values via means of grades; grades as means of reward and punishment			
To compare and compete	Comparing grades and works; emphasis on competition to make pupils, students to study, work harder and better			
Imprecise assessment	Concerns having no trust in assessment due to cases of subjectivity and imprecision.	Understanding of Assessment as Measurement Error	Includes: – all items referring to measurement error	Assessment carries risks of imprecision and measurement error
Subjective assessment	Concerns having no trust in assessment due to cases of subjectivity and imprecision.	Understanding of Assessment as Irrelevant	Includes: – all items referring to irrelevance in assessment	Assessment may be irrelevant, or ignored

was associated with the accountability purpose of assessment. Furthermore, participating Kazakhstani primary PTs understood that assessment could help improve learning and teaching, that is if those results are indeed accurate and used to control learning and teaching. Both strands of data revealed a connection between assessment promoting development and the accountability purposes of assessment and accuracy. For the participating Kazakhstani primary PTs, assessment promoting development was about potential support for learners' personal development, keeping them motivated to learn by means of grades and teaching them values.

The joint interpretation of qualitative and quantitative data revealed that participating Kazakhstani primary PTs were cautious about assessment results and understood the importance of considering the risk of measurement error in assessment. Measurement error in learning results or final grades might lead to disgrace (*masqara, uyat* in Kazakh; *pozor* in Russian), and demotivation to study and to improve learning. In general, data from both strands suggest that participating Kazakhstani primary PTs could anticipate that irrelevance in assessment might have a negative impact on learning since they were students. However, they were less inclined to recognize and understand that irrelevance in assessment might have some impact on teaching, or interfere with teaching, probably due to the fact that they were not "teachers" yet, but only pre-service teachers as students, with no or very little teaching experience.

Qualitative and quantitative data on Kazakhstani primary PTs' understanding of assessment supported each other concerning emphasis on control of learning, accuracy in assessment and being aware of the risks of measurement error, imprecision, subjectivity, and teaching values.

5.3 Summary to Joint Interpretation of Qualitative and Quantitative Strands of Data

Joint display, integration and interpretation of qualitative Phase 1 and quantitative Phase 3 findings allowed more depth and breadth on Kazakhstani primary PTs' experiences and understanding of assessment. Joint data revealed that they are distinct from pre-service and in-service teachers' understanding and pre-service teachers' experiences of assessment in other countries. The integration of both strands of data indicated that the participating PTs believed that the specific experiences they encountered throughout their *Pedagogy and Methodology of Primary Education Program* had some strong influence on the development of their understanding of assessment. Those were recollections from their former schoolteachers, from their university courses and teacher educators, and from their field experiences and mentor teachers.

6 Discussion

Joint themes revealed in the integration of qualitative and quantitative findings revealed trends identified in Kazakhstani primary PTs' understanding and experiences of assessment (Table 15.3). These themes contribute to the development of meta-inferences, or joint conclusions. In this study, meta-inferences are dominant trends in control, accuracy, teaching values, and multiple understandings of assessment.

6.1 *Control*

The predominant understanding of assessment as a tool for accountability or controlling learning is widespread among primary teachers in Kazakhstan. This understanding is shaped by the educational culture's emphasis on monitoring, checking, and grading. assessment. Primary teachers' experiences in Kazakhstan have been moulded by this dominant culture of control, which is specific to the post-Soviet context, Kazakhstan, and communist countries (Brown et al., 2011), and in the high-stake examination contexts (Gebril, 2016). The deeply ingrained culture of control presents challenges in implementing assessment reforms in secondary education, as seen in the resistance to shifting from traditional daily grades to formative assessments

TABLE 15.3   Dominant trends in Kazakhstani primary pre-service teachers understanding of assessment identified from joint themes

Trends identified in joint themes	Meta-inferences dominant trends
Student accountability, teacher accountability. control of learning, traditional assessment, monitoring, checking, grading	Control
Subjectivity, imprecision, accuracy, bias, unjust assessment, cases of subjectivity and imprecision in assessment, irrelevance in assessment	Accuracy
Development, teaching values, motivation, differentiation, diagnostic assessment	Teaching Values as Assessment Purpose
Student and teacher accountability, improvement and accountability, development and accountability, motivation and grades, accuracy in assessment, assessment of academic performance and behavior	Multiple Understandings of Assessment

using narrative comments. Concerning control, Bukhgalter and Shegebayev (2012) problematised assessment used for the purpose of controling over a classroom as it did not facilitate independent, critical, and creative thinking but led to the fear of non-conformity. The centralised control inherited from the Soviet era continues to exert a strong influence on the education system in Kazakhstan, impacting the curriculum in teacher education programs and hindering the adoption of new teaching and assessment methods. As Yakavets et al. (2017) pointed out, "the courses at the universities were still taught in a traditional style, and changing mindsets takes time and is not straightforward" (p. 611). This is the biggest challenge for teacher education institutions as assessment education requires adaption to the flux contexts, digital environments, and dynamic nature of assessment (DeLuca et al., 2024). From my personal experience of working at regional universities, it can be said that changes in teacher education programs are still bureaucratic procedures and require approval from the unified national database of educational programs.

6.2   *Accuracy*

The next predominant understanding of assessment among participating PTs is accuracy. Insights on accuracy from the interviews and the responses to the survey showed that PTs observed and experienced subjectivity and imprecision in assessment over a long period of time, as pupils at their former schools, as students at the university, as learners and observers throughout their teacher education program, and as teachers during their teaching practicum. This might be connected to teachers' feelings about assessment, contributing to their understanding of it (Doyle et al., 2024). They may have strong feelings about accuracy because of the public grace of assessment, as in the context of the high-stakes examination culture in China (Brown et al., 2011). This also relates to the comparative nature of assessment in which students are publically compared to each other. Despite the shift to criterion-based assessment reform at the secondary school level, assessment criteria are rarely used. In their interviews, PTs explained that their schoolteachers and teacher educators assessed them by comparing them to their peers. This is about norm-referenced assessment, which prevailed in Kazakhstani education (Winter et al., 2020). Furthermore, the recent changes in the assessment policy of higher education universities towards assessing students using the normal curve (Dzharasova, 2023) might further contribute to strengthening this understanding of assessment. It also contradicts promoting authentic, formative assessment experiences as students during their teacher education study, which become, as the literature suggests, the crucial component of assessment education (e.g. Coleman et al., 2023).

6.3   *Teaching Values*

Another unique understanding of assessment, identified in this study, is using assessment to teach values (*tarbie*, тәрбие in Kazakh; *vospitanije*, воспитание in Russian). *Tarbie*, or teaching values referred to in this study, is about assessing learners. Interview insights showed that some PTs believed in assessing pupils' behaviour and academic performance. This was done to improve pupils' behaviour and foster compliance. This was also their experience of assessment as pupils at their former schools. The teacher education curriculum for Kazakhstani primary PTs also promotes teaching values. For example, the *Pedagogy* course offered a topic on "punishment," which was presented as a motivation tool. This understanding of assessment is unique to post-Soviet countries and China as a communist country. Brown et al. (2011) referred to teaching values as the developmental purpose of assessment, which "cultivates positive moral and ethical qualities and values in students" (p. 317). As a final point, *vospitanie*, or teaching values, integrated in the curriculum in the Soviet education still has a strong influence on the current Kazakhstani context, shaping pre-service teachers' experiences of assessment, and contributing to their understanding of assessment. In this regard, Bogachenko and Perry (2015) found that *vospitanie* persisted in many post-Soviet countries, but was changed to teaching values of the country's patriotism and a "moral code rooted in the local culture" (p. 550).

6.4   *Multiple Understandings of Assessment*

The joint integration and interpretation of findings suggest that Kazakhstani primary PTs hold multiple or multifaceted understandings of assessment. Kazakhstani primary PTs' multiple understanding of accountability in assessment indicates that they understood assessment from both perspectives, i.e., as students and as teachers. This tendency of Kazakhstani primary PTs to hold multiple understandings of assessment, both as students and as teachers, can be explained by the Kazakhstani context, wherein assessment tends to be similar at all levels of education (Key Finding 7; Key Finding 8). This study supports findings on the dual role of pre-service teachers and its implications on having a multifaceted understanding of assessment (Brunker et al., 2019). Promoting teaching values in the Kazakhstani primary curriculum through educational assessment might also contribute to understanding the multiple purposes of assessment. As teachers, they faced the clash of theory and practice when they applied their university assessment knowledge in the classroom at their teaching placements. These first experiences as teachers during their practicum involved "reflection-in-action," which challenged their understanding of assessment acquired at the university. In this regard, Lin et al.(2024) advocate for developing teachers' ability to harmonise multiple assessment purposes with educational contexts and their own experiences.

7 Implications and Recommendations

7.1 Implications for Teacher Educators

The study indicates that pre-service teachers learn significantly about assessment through observing their teacher educators' strategies. This highlights the importance of using improvement-oriented assessment methods to shift pre-service teachers' focus from traditional control-based assessment to formative, improvement-oriented practices. Young et al. (2024) suggest that active engagement with real-world assessment practices helps pre-service teachers connect theory with practice, thereby enhancing their assessment skills and confidence. Crawford et al., (2023) argue that experiential learning projects provide pre-service teachers with practical, hands-on experiences that are essential for their professional development. These projects enable pre-service teachers to apply theoretical knowledge in real-world contexts, facilitating deeper learning and better preparation for classroom challenges. Furthermore, teacher educators should consider pre-service teachers' previous assessment experiences as pupils and during their practicum. Understanding these backgrounds can help educators tailor their teaching strategies effectively.

7.2 Implications for an Integrated Teacher Education Program

The findings support an integrative and ecological approach to pre-service teacher education. Despite alignment between assessment policy, theory, and practice, pre-service teachers may still experience a disconnect, which can serve as a learning opportunity through critical reflection. An integrated program must incorporate reflective and analytical approaches at university and practicum levels, continually interacting with pre-service teachers' personal experiences.

7.3 Implications for Policy Makers and Leaders of Teacher Education Programs

Pre-service teachers' understanding of assessment is influenced by their own assessment experiences as students. Current summative and norm-based assessment approaches in the curriculum conflict with the goals of new assessment reforms like the Technology of Criterion-Based Assessment course. Introducing improvement-oriented and learning-oriented assessment methods at universities can help pre-service teachers appreciate these approaches' value. Advocating for holistic grading can foster creativity and critical thinking skills, moving away from control-focused assessments. For having an improvement-oriented assessment policy, universities offering teacher education programs should have academic freedom to employ it.

7.4 Implications for Theory

This exploratory sequential mixed methods study provides a holistic and integrative framework to explore the development of Kazakhstani pre-service teachers' understanding of assessment in their dual role as students and as teachers while enrolled in the *Pedagogy and Methodology of Primary Education Program*. This integrative framework considers learning theories and includes Dewey's (1938) theory of "experiential learning" and "experiential knowledge," Lortie's (1975) "apprenticeship of observation," Schön's (1983) "reflection-in-action," and "theory-in-action," and Bullock's (2011) "propositional and content knowledge," In combination, these theories helped to develop interview questions and items for the survey, and interpret qualitative and quantitative findings on Kazakhstani pre-service teachers' understanding of assessment and the development of their understanding. Even though these theories date as far back as Dewey's 1938 theory of "experiential learning" and "experiential knowledge," the current study suggests that, in combination, these theories are still most relevant and helpful in teacher education. For example, applying Dewey's (1938) experiential learning helped understand pre-service teachers' experiences of assessment as sources of development of their understanding, and Lortie's (1975) apprenticeship of observation revealed its continued impact on pre-service teachers' understanding of assessment throughout the teacher education program and beyond.

8 Conclusion

Kazakhstani primary PTs' experiences—as pupils at schools, as students at universities, and as student-teachers during practicum—contributed to their perception of multiple understandings of assessment with a dominant view on control, accountability, accuracy, and teaching values. This study explored Kazakhstani primary pre-service teachers' understanding of assessment based on their experiences as students throughout their schooling, their teacher education program, and as teachers in their teaching practicum. Similar to previous research, this study suggests the importance of practice-based learning. However, in contrast with several previous studies, PTs' learning about assessment in the *Pedagogy and Methodology of Primary Education Program* in Kazakhstan lacked well-aligned theoretical assessment knowledge, improvement-oriented assessment (LOA), and systematic reflection on their learning and experiences of assessment. As teachers, they faced the clash of theory and practice when they applied their university assessment knowledge in the classroom at their teaching placements. These first experiences as teachers during their practicum involved "reflection-in-action," which challenged their understanding of assessment acquired at the university.

Kazakhstani primary pre-service teachers' experiences of assessment contributed to their perceptions of assessment as control, accuracy, teaching values, and multiple understandings of assessment, as indicated by the result of a joint integration and interpretation of the joint qualitative and quantitative data strands. Based on their experiences as students through their schooling and teacher education program and as teachers through their teaching practicum, this study allows a deeper appreciation of the Kazakhstani primary PTs' experiences and understanding of assessment.

Acknowledgement

I would like to express my heartfelt gratitude to my Ph.D. committee: Dr. Denise Egéa, Dr. Rita Kasa, Dr. Liz Winter, and external examiner Dr. Theo Wubbles. From the bottom of my heart, I am eternally grateful to my main adviser, Professor Emeritus Denise Egéa. Her unwavering support, invaluable guidance, and insightful feedback have been instrumental throughout my Ph.D. journey. Her thoughtful questions and encouragement have challenged and inspired me, shaping both my research and academic growth. I am truly grateful for her mentorship and generosity.

References

Al-Haddad, S. S., Afari, E., Khine, M. S., & Eksail, F. A. A. (2023). Self-regulation, self-confidence, and academic achievement on assessment conceptions: An investigation study of pre-service teachers. *Journal of Applied Research in Higher Education, 15*(3), 813–826. https://doi.org/10.1108/JARHE-09-2021-0343

Atameken. (2017). *Professional standard of the teacher* [Professional'nyy standart «Pedagog»]. National Chamber of Entrepreneurs of the Republic of Kazakhstan.

Atjonen, P., Kontkanen, S., Ruotsalainen, P., & Pöntinen, S. (2024). Pre-service teachers as learners of formative assessment in teaching practice. *European Journal of Teacher Education*, 1–18. https://doi.org/10.1080/02619768.2024.2338840

Berman, E. (2017a). An exploratory sequential mixed methods approach to understanding researchers' data management practices at UVM: Integrated findings to develop research data services. *Journal of eScience Librarianship, 6*(1).

Berman, E. (2017b). An exploratory sequential mixed methods approach to understanding researchers' data management practices at UVM: Findings from the quantitative phase. *Journal of eScience Librarianship, 6*(1).

Bogachenko, T., & Perry, L. (2015). Vospitanie and regime change: Teacher-education textbooks in Soviet and post-Soviet Ukraine. *PROSPECTS, 45*(4), 549–562.

Brown, G. T. L. (2002). *Teachers' conceptions of assessment* [Doctoral thesis, University of Auckland]. https://repositorio.minedu.gob.pe/bitstream/handle/20.500.12799/2866/Teachers%20%20Conceptions%20of%20Assesment.pdf?sequence=1

Brown, G. T. L., Hui, S. K. F., Yu, F. W. M., & Kennedy, K. J. (2011). Teachers' conceptions of assessment in Chinese contexts: A tripartite model of accountability, improvement, and irrelevance. *International Journal of Educational Research, 50*(5–6), 307–320. https://doi.org/10.1016/j.ijer.2011.10.003

Brunker, N., Spandagou, I., & Grice, C. (2019). Assessment for Learning while Learning to Assess: Assessment in Initial Teacher Education Through the Eyes of Pre-Service Teachers and Teacher Educators. *Australian Journal of Teacher Education, 44*(9), 89–109. https://doi.org/10.14221/ajte.2019v44n9.6

Bullock, S. M. (2011). *Inside teacher education: Challenging prior views of teaching and learning.* Sense Publishers.

Burkhalter, N., & Shegebayev, M. R. (2012). Critical thinking as culture: Teaching post-Soviet teachers in Kazakhstan. *International Review of Education, 58*(1), 55–72. https://doi.org/10.1007/s11159-012-9285-5

Cañadas, L. (2023). Contribution of formative assessment for developing teaching competences in teacher education. *European Journal of Teacher Education, 46*(3), 516–532. https://doi.org/10.1080/02619768.2021.1950684

Coleman, K., Uzhegova, D., Blaher, B., & Arkoudis, S. (Eds.). (2023). *The educational turn: Rethinking the scholarship of teaching and learning in higher education.* Springer Nature Singapore. https://doi.org/10.1007/978-981-19-8951-3

Coombs, A., & DeLuca, C. (2022). Mapping the constellation of assessment discourses: A scoping review study on assessment competence, literacy, capability, and identity. *Educational Assessment, Evaluation and Accountability, 34,* 279–301. https://doi.org/10.1007/s11092-022-09389-9

Crawford, R., Jenkins, L. E., & Wan, L. (2023). Experiential learning projects as assessment in initial teacher education. *Australian Journal of Teacher Education, 48*(1). https://doi.org/10.14221/1835-517X.5787

Creswell, J. W., & Plano Clark, V. L. (2018). *Designing and conducting mixed methods research* (3rd ed.). SAGE Publications.

Daniels, L. M., & Poth, C. A. (2017). Relationships between pre-service teachers' conceptions of assessment, approaches to instruction, and assessment: An achievement goal theory perspective. *Educational Psychology, 37*(7), 835–853. https://doi.org/10.1080/01443410.2017.1293800

DeLuca, C., Searle, M., Carbone, K., Ge, J., & LaPointe-McEwan, D. (2021). Toward a pedagogy for slow and significant learning about assessment in teacher education. *Teaching and Teacher Education, 101,* 103316. https://doi.org/10.1016/j.tate.2021.103316

DeLuca, C., Willis, J., Cowie, B., Harrison, C., & Coombs, A. (2024). The landscape of assessment education. In *Learning to assess. Teacher education, learning innovation and accountability.* Springer. https://doi.org/10.1007/978-981-99-6199-3_2

DeLuca, C., Willis, J., Cowie, B., Harrison, C., Coombs, A., Gibson, A., & Trask, S. (2019). Policies, programs, and practices: Exploring the complex dynamics of assessment education in teacher education across four countries. *Frontiers in Education, 4,* 132. https://doi.org/10.3389/feduc.2019.00132

Dewey, J. (1938). *Experience and education.* (Reprinted in 1997). TOUCHSTONE.

Doyle, A., Donlon, E., Conroy Johnson, M., McDonald, E., & Sexton, P. (2024). Re-envisioning pre-service teachers' beliefs and feelings about assessment: The important space of authentic assignments. *European Journal of Teacher Education,* 1–21. https://doi.org/10.1080/02619768.2024.2338854

Dzharasova, G. (2023). *Control of knowledge and assessment of learning results.* https://enic-kazakhstan.edu.kz/files/1677493043/6-dzharasova-kontrol-znaniy.pdf

Estaji, M., Banitalebi, Z., & Brown, G. T. L. (2024). The key competencies and components of teacher assessment literacy in digital environments: A scoping review. *Teaching and Teacher Education, 141,* 104497. https://doi.org/10.1016/j.tate.2024.104497

Fetters, M. D., Curry, L. A., & Creswell, J. W. (2013). Achieving integration in mixed methods designs—Principles and practices. *Health Research and Educational Trust, 48*(3), 2134–2156.

European University Association. (2018). *Transition to university autonomy in Kazakhstan.* https://eua.eu/downloads/publications/trunak%20eua%20report%20wp1_final.pdf

Gebril, A. (2016). Language teachers' conceptions of assessment: An Egyptian perspective. *Teacher Development, 21*(1), 81–100. https://doi.org/10.1080/13664530.2016.1218364

Gotwals, A. W., & Cisterna, D. (2022). Formative assessment practice progressions for teacher preparation: A framework and illustrative case. *Teaching and Teacher Education, 110,* 103601. https://doi.org/10.1016/j.tate.2021.103601

Güngör, M. A., & Güngör, M. N. (2024). Relocating assessment in pre-service teacher education: An emerging model from activity theory lens. *European Journal of Teacher Education,* 1–21. https://doi.org/10.1080/02619768.2024.2339522

Hill, M. F., Ell, F. R., & Eyers, G. (2017). Assessment capability and student self-regulation: The challenge of preparing teachers. *Frontiers in Education, 2,* 1–15. https://doi.org/10.3389/feduc.2017.00021

Holmes Finch, W. (2020). *Exploratory factor analysis.* SAGE Publications.

Hsieh, H.-F., & Shannon, S. E. (2005). Three approaches to qualitative content analysis. *Qualitative Health Research, 15*(9), 1277–1288.

Izquierdo, I., Olea, J., & José Abad, F. (2014). Exploratory factor analysis in validation studies: Uses and recommendations. *Psicothema, 26*(3), 395–400.

Ketonen, L., Körkkö, M., & Pöysä, S. (2023). Authentic assessment as a support for student teachers' reflection. *European Journal of Teacher Education,* 1–22. https://doi.org/10.1080/02619768.2023.2229004

Lortie, D. C. (1975). *Schoolteacher: A sociological study.* University of Chicago Press.

Lin, L., Li, G. Y., & Guo, X. (2024). Pre-service Chinese language teachers' conceptions of assessment: A person-centered perspective. *Language Teaching Research, 28*(1), 273–295. https://doi.org/10.1177/1362168821996529

Magaji, A., & Ade-Ojo, G. (2023). Trainee teachers' classroom assessment practices: Towards evaluating trainee teachers' learning experience in a teacher education program. *Social Sciences & Humanities Open, 7*(1), 100467. https://doi.org/10.1016/j.ssaho.2023.100467

Ministry of Education and Science of the Republic of Kazakhstan (MoES). (2015). *State program on educational and science development of the Republic of Kazakhstan for 2016–2019*. Ministry of Education and Science of the Republic of Kazakhstan. https://www.akorda.kz/upload/SPED.doc

National Testing Center (NTC). (2016, September 29). *The second international pedagogic scientific conference on assessment.* http://testcenter.kz/en/press/events/2nd-international-scientific-practical-conference-pedagogical-measurements-experience-and-prospects.html

Organisation for Economic Co-operation and Development (OECD). (2019). *TALIS 2018 Results (Volume I).* https://www.oecd-ilibrary.org/content/publication/1d0bc92a-en

Pantić, N., & Wubbels, T. (2012). Competence-based teacher education: A change from Didaktik to curriculum culture? *Journal of Curriculum Studies, 44*(1), 61–87. https://doi.org/10.1080/00220272.2011.620633

Schön, D. A. (1983). *The reflective practitioner: How professionals think in action.* Basic Books.

Shmigirilova, I., Rvanova, A., Tadzhigitov, A., & Kopnova, O. (2021). Assessment literacy as a component of the professional competence of a teacher in the conditions of reforming the evaluation system in Kazakhstani schools. *Journal of Educational Sciences, 68*(3). https://doi.org/10.26577/JES.2021.v68.i3.10

Starck, J. R., O'Neil, K. M., & Richards, K. A. (2023). Preservice teachers' perceptions of and intentions to utilize assessment. *Curriculum Studies in Health and Physical Education*, 1–16. https://doi.org/10.1080/25742981.2023.2240300

Tastanbekova, K. (2018). Teacher education reforms in Kazakhstan: Trends and issues. *Bulletin of Institute of Education, University of Tsukuba, 42*(2), 87–97.

Unified Platform of Higher Education. (n.d.). [*Dataset*]. https://epvo.kz/#/register/education_program

Van Orman, D. S. J., Gotch, C. M., & Carbonneau, K. J. (2024). Preparing teacher candidates to assess for learning: A systematic review. *Review of Educational Research, 00346543241233015*. https://doi.org/10.3102/00346543241233015

Winter, L., Makhmetova, Zh., & Kurakbayev, K. (2020). Low-hanging fruit – Flawed assessment and inaccurate textbooks as easy pickings in criticism of the renewed content of education. *Bilim – Obrazovaniye, 92*(1), 2–26.

Yakavets, N., Bridges, D., & Shamatov, D. (2017). On constructs and the construction of teachers' professional knowledge in a post-Soviet context. *Journal of Education for Teaching, 43*(5), 594–615. https://doi.org/10.1080/02607476.2017.1355086

Young, A.-M., MacPhail, A., & Tannehill, D. (2024). Teacher educators' engagement with school-based assessments across Irish teacher education programmes. *Irish Educational Studies, 43*(2), 189–206. https://doi.org/10.1080/03323315.2022.2061562

CHAPTER 16

Teachers and Teaching during the Times of Crisis
Reflections of the COVID-19 Pandemic

Tsediso Makoelle

Abstract

The advent of the COVID-19 Pandemic has seen a transformation in how teachers deal with teaching and learning during this time of crisis. The introduction of technology and distance learning has impacted how well teachers go about their duties. This chapter reflects on how teachers' role was transformed due to the period of the pandemic. The chapter discusses the opportunities and challenges brought by this process and makes some recommendations about the way forward regarding teachers' skills and competencies during times of crisis.

Keywords

COVID 19 – learning – pandemic – teaching – teachers

1 Introduction

COVID-19 started in 2019 when the coronavirus was identified and spread worldwide. The virus was first identified in the Wuhan Province of China and made public by the Chinese Department of Health in December 2019. It spread so rapidly that by 11 March 2020, the World Health Organization (WHO) declared it a pandemic.

The pandemic presented many challenges to different education systems. For instance, La Velle et al. (2020) states that disparities in terms of resources, assessment, and student's learning needs, the digital divide, and digital poverty all began to emerge as challenges, raising the need for online pedagogy (Pokhrel & Chhetri, 2021). On the other hand, Mseleku (2020) postulates that the pandemic has brought challenges for students living in rural areas and those from low-income families. Students experienced stress, depression and anxiety.

Most countries, including Kazakhstan, began considering alternative forms of schooling as contact between students meant more infections. Kazakhstan,

© TSEDISO MAKOELLE, 2025 | DOI:10.1163/9789004726345_017

like most countries, switched its mode of teaching and learning from face-to-face to online. According to the Eurasian Research Institute (no date), Kazakhstan registered its first two patients on March 13th, and on March 16th, by order of the state president, school children were officially sent home.

This was the beginning of online teaching and learning. It has been nearly four years since the start of the pandemic. Therefore, it is important to reflect on the impact the pandemic had on teaching and learning and on teachers' skills, knowledge, values, and attitudes toward their teaching practice. This chapter aims to make recommendations about teachers and teaching and learning in times of crises going forward.

2 Method of Review

This review was aimed at exploring teachers and teaching during times of crisis and reflections on the COVID-19 pandemic. The review was mapped to achieving the following objectives:

- To explore the impact of the pandemic on teachers and teaching;
- To make recommendations about teachers and teaching and learning in times of crises going forward;
- To suggest measures of sustaining teaching and learning post-pandemic.

The criteria used to select the literature were guided by the availability of supportive empirical evidence. Speculative literatures were deliberately excluded. While the literature was reviewed for a study focused on teachers and their teaching during COVID 19 pandemic, some of the reviewed work had inclined towards education as closely related disciplines such as educational psychology and sociology of education were considered.

I consulted several databases such as Eric, Scopus, and Google Scholar. Further sources of relevant information were internationally accredited journals, among others, the International Journal of Inclusive Education. The Nazarbayev University library was consulted, and books, articles, theses, and electronic sources were perused to find relevant, up-to-date literature on the topic.

3 Conceptual Framework

In this chapter, the conceptual framework of Makoelle and Burmistrova (2023) on the sustainability of teaching and learning post-pandemic is adopted. Makoelle and Burmistrova (2023) use five cardinal pillars to assess the sustainability of teaching and learning. Although this model was used to assess the

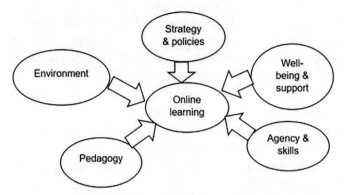

FIGURE 16.1 Five cardinal pillars for sustainable teaching and learning (Adapted from Makoelle & Burmistrova, 2023)

higher education context, the five cardinal pillars are borrowed and used to assess the role of teachers and their teaching in sustaining teaching and learning post-pandemic in schools. The cardinal pillars are strategy and policies, well-being and support, agency and skills, and pedagogy and environment, as shown in the Figure 16.1.

Strategy and policies: Educational institutions have the responsibility to ensure that their institutional policies and strategies provide guidance and direction on teaching and learning, even in times of crisis or emergency.

Well-being and support: it is prudent that educational institutions put in place well-being and support measures for both teachers and students.

Agency and skills: when students and teachers are free to apply their agency, they may be able to influence or help transform the nature of teaching and learning structures.

Pedagogy: It is also important that teachers are able to apply transformative, enabling, and empowering pedagogies that promote interactivity and connectivity between role players in the educative process.

Environment: collaboration is crucial component of sustainable learning environment because it may help build communities of practice on part of teachers and communities of learning on part of the students thus creating an ecosystem of sustainable teaching and learning.

4   An International Perspectives

The change from face-to-face to online teaching and learning has resulted in several changes, opportunities, and challenges. Although not planned, most teachers in schools were presented with the opportunity to incorporate technology in their teaching, perhaps not as a matter of choice but obligation and absence of alternatives. According to Carrrilo and Flores (2020), the fact that teachers were compelled to use technology for teaching presented them with the opportunity to develop their online teaching practices. Hassan, Mirza and Hussain (2020) cautioned that the opportunity to teach online in developing and developed countries was not the same. They state that the effect of teachers and teaching in developing and developed countries showed that the developed countries had the infrastructure for online teaching already, but in developing countries, there was first a need to set up structures but also conduct training for teachers who might not have been able to use technology before.

Although online platforms were hailed as an alternative to face-to-face teaching and learning, challenges were experienced. Yao (2020) states that the fact that using online technological platforms was new, some teachers felt the platforms were not interactive enough, and students were unable to form collaborative learning groups. There was also the challenge of reaching students in remote places with low internet connections. Shelton et al. (2020) talk about how they altered the assessment during the pandemic, but most importantly, how they incorporated the voices of students in the process.

Teachers lamented difficulty with teaching subjects that required abstract thinking, e.g., those that needed to understand numbers and theoretical formulae. Then, during the process, it became apparent that virtual communities were needed to foster collaboration by teachers and students. Noor et al. (2020) state that although there were challenges with technology, the success of teachers was influenced by their ability to work together as a community rather than as individuals. This indicates the need for virtual communities of practice (Makoelle, 2024).

The pandemic affected the well-being of teachers and students. According to Alves, Lopes and Precioso (2021), although teachers indeed had concerns about teaching online and their skills, it seems as though more concerns were about professional well-being, which related to the future of the teaching profession. Anderson et al. (2021) postulate that the COVID-19 pandemic affected teachers' creativity due to prolonged airy and stress. As a result, more support was needed to lower the effect. Walter and Fox (2021) identified factors that affected teachers' well-being during the pandemic. They classify them as 1) individual factors: lack of boundaries between home and work; disconnection with students, low self-efficacy, emotions due to stress; 2) Contextual Factors: a lot of paperwork, unrealistic expectations, limited teaching input and lack of autonomy and flexibility. Although the pandemic impacted the well-being of teachers, Stang-Rabrig et al. (2022) found that availing the much-needed resources to teachers during the crisis alleviated their stress and anxiety.

The fact that most teachers worked under stressful conditions affected their efficacy. According to Dolighan and Owen (2021), online teaching efficacy was higher in teachers who got professional development and support. However, Pressley and Ha (2021) state that the online efficacy is still significantly lower than face-to-face teaching. There are those who contend that the pandemic not only affected teachers' work in schools but also presented an opportunity to reimagine the preparation of teachers in order to ensure that future teachers would deal with the crisis better when it presented itself. For instance, Sepulveda-Escobar and Morrison (2020) argue that dealing with crises should be part of the teacher preparation curriculum to enable them to deal with this as and when it happens. Similarly, La Velle et al. (2020) suggest a framework for Knowledge enhancement framework for blended teaching in the post-COVID for the pre-service teacher practicum, which is based on what they call a "virtual learning environment" based on the following components: generation, acquisition, mediation and utilisation.

According to this framework (*La Velle et al, 2020: 605*)

Generation	"New knowledge is generated by research (e.g. online publication)"
Acquisition	"The knowledge is acquired by teachers and trainees (e.g. www, social media, conferencing platforms)"
Mediation	"This knowledge is transformed into pedagogic content knowledge (simulation software, multimedia; cloud-based collaboration)"
Utilisation	"The knowledge is used in the classroom or online within a planned lesson, task or activity or sequence of these, during which the teacher/trainee evaluates its effectiveness, assessing what is being learned and after which s/he reflects, coming to an enhanced level of pedagogical understanding (communications media, presentation software, poll-ing/voting software; word processing software, etc.)"

The framework creates a systematic process of virtual preparation and engagement of pre-service teachers during their practicum. In so doing, pre-service teachers are also socialized digitally on how to engage in digital pedagogy.

5   The Kazakhstani Context

The pandemic affected Kazakhstani education negatively. According to Burakanove, Orazgaliyeva and Pinaev (2021), Kazakhstan's education system was not ready to move to an online teaching mode. Schools and teachers were not ready, but preparations were done afterwards, and digital equipment was distributed to schoolchildren, although teachers began to teach online. Abaidylda (2020) found that moving to online teaching by teachers in Kazakhstan was affected by the length of their teaching experience. This meant that more senior teachers who might not have been trained to use digital platforms used traditional teaching methods. At the same time, their relatively newly recruited counterparts seemed familiar with using digital platforms for their teaching.

There were also teacher well-being issues in Kazakhstan. For instance, Kenebayeva et al. (2022) found that women in urban areas experienced more anxiety and depression during the pandemic than their rural counterparts.

Not only were teachers affected, but students also found themselves in a difficult situation. For instance, Hajar and Manan (2020) aver that there were complications with giving more homework to students during the pandemic. Because of the high volume of homework, students were overwhelmed, and there was a lack of collaboration between students due to low chances of interactivity.

Parents were also in disarray; for instance, Bokayev et al. (2021) postulate that Kazakhstani parents thought some teachers were not ready for online learning. They valued the competency of teachers as a critical factor in their ability to teach students online.

The pandemic affected both the education process and the profession. According to Kozhabayeva and Boivin (2022), the uncertainty caused by the pandemic deprofessionalized teachers' identities due to blurred boundaries between home and work. Reflecting on achieving sustainable development goal 4—equitable quality education, Durrani et al. (2023) lament that inequalities between elite public schools and public mainstream schools widened the inequality gap even more.

6 Sustainability in the Future

The post-pandemic period has been characterized by educational institutions planning to sustain digital online teachers, albeit in a blended mode. The pandemic seems to have provided schools with an alternative way of complementing the face-to-face mode of curriculum delivery. Various ways have been suggested for teaching and learning to be sustained post-pandemic period. Zhao & Waterson (2021) argue that a more developmental, personalized, evolving, student-centred, inquiry-based, authentic, and purposeful curriculum is needed to sustain post-pandemic teaching. On the same point, Kaur & Bhatt (2020) suggest that post-pandemic virtual teaching medium has to be maintained parallel to face-to-face mode.

Ossiannilsson (2021) states that the sustainability of teaching and learning may be achieved when effective strategies, agile and flexible leadership, digital platforms, partnerships, and the ability to respond quickly to change and encourage flexible learning and support are critical aspects of education. Sa (2021) postulate that to sustain teaching and learning, educational institutions need to ensure that all stakeholders are digitally literate and competent. Similarly, Larsari et al. (3023) suggest the incorporation of digital education, mobile learning, redesign of national policies and curricula, improvement of infrastructure, development of educational resources and the improvement of student-teacher digital technology skills as important if teaching and learning were to be sustained.

While most studies focus on technical aspects such as skills, Megahed and Ghoneim (2022), postulate that developing a holistic e-learning ecosystem would ensure the restructuring of teaching and learning with all related aspects. This could be achieved by engaging in enquiry, classification, design, and evaluation of the teaching and learning processes.

On the other hand, Iyengar (2021) states that teaching and learning will thrive with the involvement of parents. It is suggested that parents could play a critical role in student learning projects or experiential learning.

In Kazakhstan, Yelubayeva, Tashkyn, and Berkinbayeva (2023) argue that online teaching and learning should be sustainable with inclusivity principles in mind. On the other hand, Amantaev et al. (2022) contend that the move to sustain digital teaching and learning should occur within the realm of the transforming digital environment in all sectors in order to tap into resources and support.

7 Lesson from the Review

Using Makoelle and Burmistrova's (2023) cardinal pillars, the impact of the pandemic on Kazakhstan is analysed, and recommendations are made about the sustainability of teaching and learning post-pandemic.

Strategy and policies: The review shows that Kazakhstan, like many other countries, was unprepared for the COVID-19 pandemic. Although contingency measures were taken to contain the disruptive nature of the pandemic by providing resources and pursuing online teaching and learning, a sustainable plan needs to be developed as we advance. Kazakhstan will have to move rapidly to digital education, provide the resources needed to most schools in rural places, and ensure that the curriculum delivery is blended. According to the World Bank (2020), proper planning based on lessons learned from the pandemic is necessary to sustain the gains of the digital and online learning endeavours practised during this period. This is consistent with Rogers & Sabarwal (2020), who state that proper planning for the future is a significant strategic move.

Well-being and support: The ways the pandemic affected teachers and students were catastrophic. It would be prudent to develop a comprehensive well-being strategy to ensure sustainable learning environments even during times of crisis or emergency. Most teachers and students were left alone to deal with the stressful situation with minimum intervention. Teachers and students need to be capacited about coping measures for stress, anxiety and depression. Cabezas et al. (2022) postulate that future planning and procurement of sufficient resources for online and digital teaching and learning would reduce the stress related to this and thus ensure the proper well-being of teachers.

Agency and skills: Teacher and student agencies seem to have been affected by the restrictive measures that schools adopted during the pandemic. Teachers and students were hardly engaged about their expectations for effective teaching and learning and could not apply their agency. As Thumvichit (2021) posits, the enablement of teacher and student agency hovers over dialogue, communication, autonomy, continuity and goal-directedness processes. Although teachers and students developed resilience during this period, creating an enabling and supportive environment wherein they could act as agents of change could have been helpful. Gudmundsdottir & Hathaway (2020) enable teachers agency during times of crisis, ensuring their resilience and the ability to navigate the challenges of the crisis.

Pedagogy: Schools' restrictive measures negatively impact teachers' ability to apply transformative and emancipatory pedagogies. Ng & Renshaw (2020:1) postulate that "transformative pedagogy should build a purposeful connection between school curriculum, cultural knowledge and family practices". In Kazakhstan, establishing virtual communities of practice and learning was sometimes challenging because there were fewer interactions and connections between stakeholders (schools, communities and homes). Establishing virtual communities of practice and learning could go a long way in ensuring mutual collaboration and equitable teaching and learning that fosters teacher and student empowerment. Wardoyo & Firmansyah (2020) state that teachers' pedagogical competency is critical in applying transformative and emancipatory pedagogies. As such, teaching professional learning in collaboration with others is crucial. La Velle et al. (2020) posit that forming virtual learning environments (VLEs) is crucial in ensuring student and teacher connectivity and interactivity for support and mutual learning. According to La Velle, teachers' actions must be based on research-based knowledge (evidence-based).

Environment: it seemed as though it was difficult for teachers and students to form communities of practice and communities of learning, respectively.

The challenge of developing collaborative communities was impacted by incompetency with digital platforms and a general lack of proper planning. According to Kurbakova, Volkova & Kurbakov (2020), creating a supportive virtual environment enhances the student learning process. As such, the teacher's skills in applying digital platforms to create virtual learning communities are essential. According to Ehren et al. (2021), the virtual community should enable teachers and students to exercise their individual and collective agency, which enhances mutual support and learning.

8 Conclusion

This chapter provided a detailed review of the effects of the COVID-19 pandemic on teachers, teacher preparation and teaching internationally and in Kazakhstan. The main lessons drawn from the review is that teachers and teaching were affected in ways that impacted policies, teachers' well-being, teachers' agency, their pedagogy and the educational environment. This chapter contributes some insights into how teachers, teacher preparation and teaching may be sustainable post the pandemic. Although this paper might form the basis for future discussion on the creation of virtual learning and teaching environments by teachers in Kazakhstan, it must be kept in mind that the process that started during the pandemic to digitise the education process is continuous and may be influenced by the availability of resources for teachers as well as their skills and competencies. Kazakhstan's education system is rapidly changing as a result of educational reforms, and as such, the findings in this chapter might not be conclusive. However, the chapter may form the basis for further discussion as Kazakhstan and other countries grapple with the challenges posed by the pandemic and the quest to achieve sustainability given the sustainable development goals espoused in the UN Agenda 2030.

References

Alves, R., Lopes, T., & Precioso, J. (2021). Teachers' well-being in times of COVID-19 pandemic: Factors that explain professional well-being. *International Journal of Educational Research and Innovation, 15,* 203–217.

Abaidylda, Y. (2022). Comparing the experience of Kazakhstani teachers before and during COVID-19 pandemic. Astana: Nazarbayev University.

Amantaev, Y., Dyussembekova, M., Nechaeva, Y., Baishan, G., & Issayev, N. (2022). State policy of sustainable digitalization of Kazakhstan education in the experience of transformation during the pandemic period. *Rivista di Studi sulla Sostenibilita,* (2022/1).

Anderson, R. C., Bousselot, T., Katz-Buoincontro, J., & Todd, J. (2021). Generating buoyancy in a sea of uncertainty: Teachers' creativity and well-being during the COVID-19 pandemic. *Frontiers in Psychology, 11,* 614774.

Bokayev, B., Torebekova, Z., Davletbayeva, Z., & Zhakypova, F. (2021). Distance learning in Kazakhstan: Estimating parents' satisfaction with educational quality during the coronavirus. *Technology, Pedagogy and Education, 30*(1), 27–39.

Burakanova, G. M., Orazgaliyeva, A. G., & Pinaev, S. M. (2021). Psychological, pedagogical, and digital aspects of distance learning in Kazakhstan in the context of the COVID-19 pandemic. In *SHS Web of Conferences* (Vol. 113, p. 00021). EDP Sciences.

Burmistrova, V., & Makoelle, T. M. (2023). Change from face-to-face teaching and learning to online learning: A case of a cross-sectional study in a Kazakhstani medical university. *Cogent Education, 10*(2), 2282800.

Cabezas, V., Narea, M., Irribarra, D. T., Icaza, M., Escalona, G., & Reyes, A. (2022). Teacher well-being during the COVID-19 pandemic in Chile: Demands and resources for tackling psychological distress. *Psykhe: Revista de la Escuela de Psicología, 1*–24.

Carrillo, C., & Flores, M. A. (2020). COVID-19 and teacher education: A literature review of online teaching and learning practices. *European Journal of Teacher Education, 43*(4), 466–487. https://doi.org/10.1080/02619768.2020.1821184

Dolighan, T., & Owen, M. (2021). Teacher efficacy for online teaching during the COVID-19 pandemic. *Brock Education Journal, 30*(1), 95. https://doi.org/10.26522/brocked.v30i1.851

Durrani, N., Qanay, G., Mir, G., Helmer, J., Polat, F., Karimova, N., & Temirbekova, A. (2023). Achieving SDG 4, equitable quality education after COVID-19: Global evidence and a case study of Kazakhstan. *Sustainability, 15*(20), 14725.

Ehren, M. C. M., Madrid, R., Romiti, S., Armstrong, P. W., Fisher, P., & McWhorter, D. L. (2021). Teaching in the COVID-19 era: Understanding the opportunities and barriers for teacher agency. *Perspectives in Education, 39*(1), 61–76.

Ferdig, R. E., Baumgartner, E., Hartshorne, R., Kaplan-Rakowski, R., & Mouza, C. (Eds.). (2020). *Teaching, technology, and teacher education during the COVID-19 pandemic: Stories from the field.* Waynesville, NC: Association for the Advancement of Computing in Education.

Gudmundsdottir, G. B., & Hathaway, D. M. (2020). "We always make it work": Teachers' agency in the time of crisis. *Journal of Technology and Teacher Education, 28*(2), 239–250.

Gurung, S. (2021). Challenges faced by teachers in online teaching during the COVID-19 pandemic. *The Online Journal of Distance Education and E-Learning, 9*(1), 8–18.

Hassan, M. M., Mirza, T., & Hussain, M. W. (2020). A critical review by teachers on the online teaching-learning during COVID-19. *I.J. Education and Management Engineering, 5,* 17–27. https://doi.org/10.5815/ijeme.2020.05.03

Hajar, A., & Manan, S. A. (2022). Emergency remote English language teaching and learning: Voices of primary school students and teachers in Kazakhstan. *Review of Education, 10*(2), e3358.

Iyengar, R. (2021). Rethinking community participation in education post-COVID-19. *Prospects, 51*(1), 437–447.

Kaur, N. (2020). The face of education and the faceless teacher post-COVID-19. *Horizon, 2,* 39–48.

Kenebayeva, A., Nam, A., Tabaeva, A., Altinay, F., & Altinay, Z. (2022). COVID-19 and Kazakhstani women teachers: An empirical study of factors affecting mental health. *European Education, 54*(1–2), 3–20.

Kozhabayeva, K., & Boivin, N. (2022). Emergency remote teaching in the Kazakhstan context: Deprofessionalization of teacher identity. In *Emergency Remote Teaching and Beyond: Voices from World Language Teachers and Researchers* (pp. 113–132). Cham: Springer International Publishing.

Kurbakova, S., Volkova, Z., & Kurbakov, A. (2020). Virtual learning and educational environment: New opportunities and challenges under the COVID-19 pandemic. In *2020 The 4th International Conference on Education and Multimedia Technology* (pp. 167–171).

Larsari, V. N., Wildová, R., Dhuli, R., Chenari, H., Reyes-Chua, E., Galas, E. M., ... & Lanuza, M. H. (2023). Digitalizing teaching and learning in light of sustainability in times of the post-COVID-19 period: Challenges, issues, and opportunities. In *International Conference on Digital Technologies and Applications* (pp. 366–375). Cham: Springer Nature Switzerland.

La Velle, L., Newman, S., Montgomery, C., & Hyatt, D. (2020). Initial teacher education in England and the COVID-19 pandemic: Challenges and opportunities. *Journal of Education for Teaching, 46*(4), 596–608.

Megahed, N. A., & Ghoneim, E. M. (2022). E-learning ecosystem metaphor: Building sustainable education for the post-COVID-19 era. *International Journal of Learning Technology, 17*(2), 133–153.

Mseleku, Z. (2020). A literature review of e-learning and e-teaching in the era of COVID-19 pandemic. *International Journal of Innovative Science and Research Technology, 5*(10), 588–597.

Ng, C., & Renshaw, P. (2020). Transforming pedagogies in Australian schools amid the COVID-19 pandemic: An activity theoretic reflection. *Best Evidence in Chinese Education, 5*(2), 635–648.

Noor, S., Isa, F. M., & Mazhar, F. F. (2020). Online teaching practices during the COVID-19 pandemic. *Educational Process: International Journal, 9*(3), 169–184.

Ossiannilsson, E. (2021). The new normal: Post-COVID-19 is about change and sustainability. *Near East University Online Journal of Education, 4*(1), 72–77.

Pokhrel, S., & Chhetri, R. (2021). A literature review on the impact of the COVID-19 pandemic on teaching and learning. *Higher Education for the Future, 8*(1), 133–141.

Pressley, T., & Ha, C. (2021). Teaching during a pandemic: United States teachers' self-efficacy during COVID-19. *Teaching and Teacher Education, 106,* 103465.

Rogers, F. H., & Sabarwal, S. (2020). COVID-19 pandemic: Shocks to education and policy responses. *World Bank.* https://doi.org/10.1596/33696

Sá, M. J., Santos, A. I., Serpa, S., & Ferreira, C. M. (2021). Digitainability—Digital competences post-COVID-19 for a sustainable society. *Sustainability, 13*(17), 9564.

Sepulveda-Escobar, P., & Morrison, A. (2020). Online teaching placement during the COVID-19 pandemic in Chile: Challenges and opportunities. *European Journal of Teacher Education, 43*(4), 587–607.

Stang-Rabrig, J., Brüggemann, T., Lorenz, R., & McElvany, N. (2022). Teachers' occupational well-being during the COVID-19 pandemic: The role of resources and demands. *Teaching and Teacher Education, 117,* 103803.

Thumvichit, A. (2021). English language teaching in times of crisis: Teacher agency in response to the pandemic-forced online education. *Teaching English with Technology, 21*(2), 14–37.

Walter, H. L., & Fox, H. B. (2021). Understanding teacher well-being during the COVID-19 pandemic over time: A qualitative longitudinal study. *Journal of Organizational Psychology, 21*(5).

Wardoyo, C., & Firmansyah, R. (2020). Contribution of teacher competence (pedagogy and personality) in teaching practice during the COVID-19 pandemic and 4.0 era. *Technium Social Sciences Journal, 14,* 66.

World Bank. (2020). The COVID-19 pandemic: Shocks to education and policy responses. *World Bank.* https://doi.org/10.1596/33696

Yao, J., Rao, J., Jiang, T., & Xiong, C. (2020). What role should teachers play in online teaching during the COVID-19 pandemic? Evidence from China. *Scientific Insight Education Front, 5*(2), 517–524.

Yelubayeva, P., Tashkyn, E., & Berkinbayeva, G. (2023). Addressing challenges in Kazakh education for sustainable development. *Sustainability, 15*(19), 14311.

Zhao, Y., & Watterston, J. (2021). The changes we need: Education post-COVID-19. *Journal of Educational Change, 22*(1), 3–12.

CONCLUSION

Teacher Education in Kazakhstan

Past, Present and Future

Tsediso Michael Makoelle and Kairat Kurakbayev

Abstract

This concluding chapter draws crucial insights from the previous chapters, offering a deep understanding of the historical development of Kazakhstani teacher education. Placing Kazakhstan in a comparative perspective with other post-Soviet and Central Asian states and systems of teacher education, these insights explore the key factors that have historically shaped Kazakhstan's teacher education. In light of the findings presented in earlier chapters, this chapter also examines the current state of teacher education within the context of ongoing educational reforms and provides forward-looking recommendations for the future of teacher education in Kazakhstan.

Keywords

teacher – teacher education – professional teacher development – post-socialist transformations – Central Asia

1 Nature and Evolution of Teacher Education in Kazakhstan

The evolution of teacher education in Kazakhstan shows that the Kazakh traditions were initially influential in how teaching and the role of teachers were configured. Mynbayeva and Anarbek (this volume) contend that while much research has focused on the Soviet and post-Soviet periods, as well as the current globalization of teacher education, it is equally important to examine the pre-Soviet era of schooling and teacher education in Central Asia, particularly in Kazakhstan. This search for national traits, characteristics, and historical foundations has led to a deeper investigation into the development of Kazakh education during the pre-Soviet period (see Mynbayeva & Anarbek in this volume).

© TSEDISO MICHAEL MAKOELLE AND KAIRAT KURAKBAYEV, 2025
DOI:10.1163/9789004726345_018

The role of the teacher emulated that of knowledge holder who was entrusted with the education of the young. However, teaching and teacher education began to change due to Sovietization, which prioritized Soviet values (Menter, 2024). While it seemed as though the regions within the USSR had powers to determine their teacher education, the Soviet approach through the centralisation of educational administration began to set principles that must be followed (Fimyar & Kurakbayev, 2016). It was not until the collapse of the Soviet Union that Kazakhstan began the process of redressing the Soviet legacy of education (Kalimullin & Valeeva, 2022). The de-Sovietization of Kazakh teacher education reflected the process of educational modernization and internationalization of school reforms (Bridges, 2014). Indeed, the national government's efforts to introduce and scale up global education policies, such as learner-centered pedagogy, outcomes-based curricula, and the Western concept of the teacher as researcher, could not bypass reforms in the systems of initial teacher education and continuing professional development.

Among the hundred steps proposed by the former president of Kazakhstan, Mr Nursultan Nazarbayev, was the introduction of a Western form of education, which required teachers to be trained and prepared differently. As a result, the establishment of the NIS schools and Nazarbayev University were to contribute to schooling transformation and change. However, teacher education in Kazakhstan has not fully benefited from such reforms. Still, two streams of teacher education preparation have been established, i.e., the international NIS system with different sets of educational values and the broader mainstream and ungraded schools with others. Teacher preparation has not bridged the gap between traditional and modern teaching approaches currently in existence in schools. As Nurkesheva (2015) postulates, the translation of the NIS experience into the broader mainstream schools will require time and effort as the training of teachers in the mainstream still bears the hallmarks of the Soviet teacher education practices. Although there have been concerted efforts to change the teacher education policy, there is a gap between policy and practice (Sarmurzin, 2024).

2 Change and Content

It is evident that modern Kazakhstan teacher education is transforming the teacher's role from knowledge transmitter to the facilitator of teaching and learning. However, many changes have occurred in the NIS teacher preparation system compared to the broader mainstream and ungraded schools. Although there is a concerted effort to democratize teaching and learning and provide teachers with some responsibility through processes such as teacher professional learning (Ayubayeva, 2018), action research (Berikkhanova et al., 2023) and other approaches, it seems as though much still needs to be done. There have been efforts to use action research as a tool for teacher development (Rizakhojayeva, 2020; Ayubayeva & McLaughlin, 2023). However, Nagibova (2019) cautions that teachers in Kazakhstan often lack action research skills and are not accustomed to being critical and reflective about their work.

On the other hand, teachers in NIS embark on lesson study and embrace notions such as teacher leadership (Qanay et al., 2019). According to Khokhotva and Elexpuru Albizuri (2020), this enables teachers to self-critique and reflect on one's practice, which is vital for improving their teaching practices. However, the centralized control by the Ministry of Education has not benefited other categories of schools. While adopting inclusive education policy has taken off, teacher preparation has not transformed teacher training institutions to enable equitable and equal teacher education curricula (Makoelle & Burmistrova, 2021). It is apparent that the new curriculum reforms have placed more demands on teachers; as such, a different teacher preparation model is needed to ensure teachers can implement new changes (Gimranova, 2018). According to Azhmukhambetov (2020, p. 1), although some teachers are enthusiastic about implementing new curriculum reforms, there is also resentment because of aspects such as big class sizes, insufficient technical facilities and resources, and a lack of continuous support from reform officers.

3 Challenges

While much effort has been made to improve teachers' status through legislative processes on teachers' working conditions, including salaries and other benefits, challenges such as teacher well-being, recruitment, retention, teacher turnover, and attrition remain persistent (Harris-Van Keuren, 2011; Sarmurzin, 2024). According to the study by Nurmukhamed et al. (2025), which draws on Teaching and Learning International Survey 2018 (TALIS) data, educational policies and reforms that influence teachers' stress levels play a role in the turnover rates among Kazakhstani teachers. It seems there are still challenges, such as workloads, lack of skills and competencies, and teacher professional development (Meirkulova & Gelişli, 2022). There have also been efforts to balance gender in STEM education and school leadership. In STEM education, various factors have affected STEM education negatively, i.e., the gender gap between males and females (Kusayinkyzy & Doskeeva, 2020: Syzdykbayeva,

2020) and a general lack of interest among the student population (Ibrayeva & Shaushekova, 2022). However, Kazakhstan teacher education remains one of Central Asia's most gendered (Silova & Magno, 2004; CohenMiller et al., 2021), with female teachers dominant (Tastanbekova, 2020). According to Baishemirov (2024), teacher education in Kazakhstan should align with the principles of Education for Sustainable Development (ESD). To achieve this, it must prioritize inclusivity, enhance the quality of teacher training, and promote widespread awareness and support for ESD initiatives. According to Shamatov, Ablaeva, and Tajik (2023), the conditions in rural schools have not significantly improved; as such, more efforts are needed to improve the conditions of rural teaching. On the other hand, regarding pre-service teacher preparation, there are challenges in preparing teachers for all levels of schooling, but more challenge is experienced in the preparation of teachers for early childhood education and care (Amirova et al., 2015). While the pre-service teacher practicum is run between schools and teacher training institutions, it seems as though more needs to be done to strengthen the mentoring program for pre-service teachers. For instance, one of the challenges of effective teacher mentoring is the different teaching ideologies between local teachers and their international mentors (Schulleri, 2020). It is also evident that a more decentralized teacher education model (Imangaliyev, 2019) and a distributive leadership model are necessary to ensure teacher agency.

4 Kazakhstan's Teacher Education Compared with other Fourteen Post-Soviet Countries

Kalimullin and Valeeva (2022) postulate that while Central Asian countries, Ukraine, and Belarus have transformed their teacher education, they seem to have preserved some features of the Soviet model, demonstrating the post-Soviet identity in teacher education as compared to others such as Latvia, Lithuania, Estonia, and Moldova. In this work, reference is made to Kazakhstan as one of the countries that have retained largely its Soviet teacher education identity.

Teacher education in Kazakhstan, albeit transforming, has remained the same way teachers conceptualize excellent or effective teaching. Burkhalter and Shegebayev (2012) observed that Kazakhstan's teacher education system, like other former Soviet teacher education systems, retained a teacher-centered approach shaping the teaching and learning process. However, with the current emphasis on teacher quality and continuing professional development in national school reforms, this approach is likely evolving toward more student-centered and progressive practices. Despite these efforts, the legacy of Soviet teacher education continues to shape educators' perceptions and practices. In support of this, Fimyar and Kurakbayev (2016) found that memories of Soviet teacher education continue to linger, suggesting that a fundamental paradigm shift is still needed to fully transform teaching practices. In his latest edited volume of comparative analysis, Menter (2024) of the fifteen post-Soviet countries' teacher education systems regards the current period as a period of rebuilding teacher education and de-socialization of teacher education. Menter (2024) avers that the analysis of teacher education in post-Soviet educational systems is premised on two dimensions, i.e. the Soviet past was characterized by centralisation and the attempt of the education systems to adopt the more decentralized approach borrowed from the West. However, Menter (2024) asserts that borrowing Western policy, has not yielded desirable results as teacher education still mirrors the centalized and bureaucratic nature of governance in post-Soviet countries. Menter's (2024) analysis of teacher education in post-soviet countries confirmed the same assertions that emerged in this volume, focusing on Kazakhstan. For instance, although there are efforts to globalize teacher education, the legacy of Soviet education persists. There is also a lack of a coherent articulation of education reforms in other educational sectors, creating a disjuncture among others with teacher education. It is also evident that teacher education is increasingly playing a pivotal role in nation-building and shaping national identity. However, this will require a total overhaul of the initial teacher education.

While post-Soviet countries, especially Kazakhstan, are trying to improve the status of teachers, the conditions have mostly stayed the same. For instance, according to Chernobay and Tashibaeva (2020), Russia and Kazakhstan should be more engaged in monitoring or assessing young and beginning teachers. It has also been established that teacher induction and mentoring should have been prioritized.

Professional learning is a promising platform for teacher professional development. While professional learning is viewed positively, Kurakbayev (2009) postulates that it may be promoted by building a culture of reflective teaching. However, their agency must be enabled for teachers to be reflective practitioners. In support of this, Yakavets et al. (2023) posit that enabled teacher agency might foster a collective conscience that fosters teacher collaboration. Yakavets, Bridges and Shamatov (2017) posit that while teacher professional knowledge in Kazakhstan is changing as a result of the programs of the Centre of Excellence, it will require a change of teacher beliefs in order to shift from the Soviet legacy of pedagogical practice. Kutsyuruba (2011) echoes this view in his analysis of Ukraine's transformation of teacher education, highlighting the tension between remnants of Soviet pedagogical traditions and the neo-liberal changes introduced through internationalization, which often clash. This is also evident in the context of Kazakhstani teacher education.

Introducing English as a medium of instruction (EMI) has presented teachers in post-Soviet countries with many challenges (Belyaeva, & Kuznetsova,

2019; Tajik et al., 2023). For instance, according to Isaacs & Polese (2018), the notion of the teacher multilingualism approach is "imagined" rather than "real" as post-Soviet, mainly central Asian countries, aim to develop their languages although claiming to be multilingual in policies. For instance, Kazakhstan's trilingual policy has faced many challenges, yet curriculum developers, schools, and teachers have made significant efforts to develop high-quality Kazakh-medium teaching and learning resources.

It is also evident from this volume that most post-Soviet countries decided to restructure their teacher education curriculum. For instance, while the Russian initial teacher education curriculum is premised on a competency-based curriculum model (Valeeva & Gufurov, 2019), the Kazakhstani model of initial teacher education curriculum leans towards an outcomes-based curriculum model. According to Smolentseva, Huisman and Froumin (2018), the transformation of higher education (including teacher education) in post-Soviet countries is tied to the country's economic prospects. As such, the improvement of teacher education could be impacted by general education funding. The funding may impact on the provision of resources. This is evident in the rural-urban distribution of education resources. For instance, teachers in the rural schools of Kyrgyzstan continue to lament the shortage of teachers and adequate resources to provide quality education (Shamatov, 2013). This is also the case in Tajikistan (Niyozov, 2001). Although Kazakhstan has a bigger economy and budget for education, the problems of rural teachers and schools still need to be fully resolved (Tajik, Shamatov, & Fillipova, 2022).

It is interesting to note that in all fifteen post-Soviet countries, teachers continue to understand the notion of inclusive education. Still, the influence of *defectology* (the science of special education during the USSR) continues to cloud teachers' memories (McGagg & Siegelbaum, 2017). In the recent study by Prisiazhniuk, Makoelle and Zangieva (2024) of Kazakhstan, Kyrgyzstan, Tajikistan, and Uzbekistan, teachers' attitudes towards the new policy of inclusive education were similar to those influenced by past Soviet special education practices. Still, in each context, teachers responded differently according to the demands of the education system. Similarly, teaching in early childhood education has been compounded by low attendance. According to Habibov (2012), early childhood education in Central Asian countries is influenced by factors such as poverty, the rural-urban divide, parents' educational status, and a shortage of adequately trained teachers.

5   Way Forward

It seems as though Kazakhstan's teacher education will have to strike a balance between the post-Soviet values that worked in that context and those that emerged as a result of the modernisation process. There is a view that adopting Western forms of teacher education without adapting them to local socio-cultural contexts could be regarded as another form of colonialization (Hwami, 2024). More efforts seem to be needed to equalize the quality of teacher preparation for both the NIS system and the broader mainstream and ungraded schools. The teacher preparation must ensure that teachers are capacitated to make decisions about curriculum and other teaching and learning-related matters. A well-coordinated pre-service teacher practicum and qualified mentors are needed to prepare pre-service teachers for quality teaching. According to Yakavets et al. (2023), enabling teacher agency was necessary for teachers' understanding and implementation of educational and curriculum reforms. To ensure gender equity in teacher education, other mechanisms and incentives are required to attract underrepresented groups in teacher education. While the law on the status of teachers is the first step in raising the standard of the teaching profession, implementing such a law is equally important. More attractive benefits for the teaching profession might assist in enhancing its status. Through the transfer of NIS experience, building a culture of action research to boost teachers' critical and reflexive skills would be prudent, which is vital for professional learning and improving their practices. Special programs for STEM teachers might help develop pre-service teachers but also enhance the skills of the in-service STEM teachers. Lessons from the COVID-19 pandemic could be helpful in developing a digital ecosystem that can support blended teaching and learning.

6   Conclusion

While this book makes an invaluable contribution to teacher education development in Kazakhstan, the authors are mindful that teacher education in Kazakhstan is changing rapidly and that some of the findings presented in this volume could be inconclusive. However, the volume serves as a critical resource and lays the foundation for further discussion and research in Kazakhstan and the Central Asian post-Soviet contexts.

References

Amirova, A. S., Muhamedinova, K. A., Erkebaeva, S. Z., & Makshieva, G. K. (2015). Preparing teachers in preschool education in the Republic of Kazakhstan. *Procedia - Social and Behavioral Sciences, 185*, 267–270.

Ayubayeva, N., & McLaughlin, C. (2023). Developing teachers as researchers: Action research as a school development approach. In C. McLaughlin, L. Winter, & N. Yakavets (Eds.), *Mapping educational change in Kazakhstan* (pp. 189–202). Cambridge University Press.

Ayubayeva, N. (2018). *Teacher collaboration for professional learning: Case studies of three schools in Kazakhstan* (Doctoral dissertation). University of Cambridge.

Azhmukhambetov, A. (2020). Teachers' experiences of the updated pedagogy within the scope of the curriculum reform: A case study of two mainstream schools in Kazakhstan (Master's thesis). Nazarbayev University.

Baishemirov, Z. (2024). Issues and perspectives on teacher education for education for sustainable development in Kazakhstan. In *Science education for sustainable development in Asia* (pp. 325–338). Springer Nature Singapore.

Berikkhanova, A., Sapargaliyeva, B., Ibraimova, Z., Sarsenbayeva, L., Assilbayeva, F., Baidildinova, D., & Wilson, E. (2023). Conceptualizing the integration of action research into the practice of teacher education universities in Kazakhstan. *Education Sciences, 13*(10), 1034.

Belyaeva, E., & Kuznetsova, L. (2019). Implementing EMI at a Russian university: A study of content lecturers' perspectives. *Journal of Teaching English for Specific and Academic Purposes*, 425–439.

Burkhalter, N., & Shegebayev, M. R. (2012). Critical thinking as culture: Teaching post-Soviet teachers in Kazakhstan. *International Review of Education, 58*, 55–72.

CohenMiller, A., Saniyazova, A., Sandygulova, A., & Izekenova, Z. (2021). Gender equity in STEM higher education in Kazakhstan. In *Gender equity in STEM in higher education* (pp. 140–157). Routledge.

Chernobay, E., & Tashibaeva, D. (2020). Teacher professional development in Russia and Kazakhstan: Evidence from TALIS 2018. *Voprosy obrazovaniya/Educational Studies Moscow*, (4), 141–164.

Fimyar, O., & Kurakbayev, K. (2016). 'Soviet' in teachers' memories and professional beliefs in Kazakhstan: Points for reflection for reformers, international consultants, and practitioners. *International Journal of Qualitative Studies in Education, 29*(1), 86–103.

Gimranova, A. (2018). *Implementation of new curriculum reform in secondary education of Kazakhstan: Study of teachers' perspectives* (Master's thesis). Nazarbayev University Graduate School of Education.

Habibov, N. (2012). Early childhood care and education attendance in Central Asia. *Children and Youth Services Review, 34*(4), 798–806.

Harris-Van Keuren, C. (2011). Influencing the status of teaching in Central Asia. In *Globalization on the margins: Education and postsocialist transformations in Central Asia* (pp. 173–201).

Hwami, M. (2024). A geopolitics of knowledge analysis of higher education internationalization in Kazakhstan. *British Educational Research Journal, 50*(2), 676–693.

Ibrayeva, E. S., & Shaushekova, B. K. (2022). Raising awareness for the lack of interest in STEM of primary school learners in Kazakhstan: Experiences and perspectives.

Imangaliyev, N. (2019). Kazakhstani teachers' perceptions of teacher autonomy (Master's thesis). Nazarbayev University Graduate School of Education.

Isaacs, R., & Polese, A. (2015). Between "imagined" and "real" nation-building: Identities and nationhood in post-Soviet Central Asia. *Nationalities Papers, 43*(3), 371–382.

Kalimullin, A. M., & Valeeva, R. A. (2022). Teacher education in post-Soviet states: Transformation trends. In I. Menter (Ed.), *The Palgrave handbook of teacher education research* (pp. 1–20). Springer International Publishing.

Khokhotva, O., & Elexpuru Albizuri, I. (2020). Student voice in lesson study as a space for EFL teachers' learning: A case study in Kazakhstan. *International Journal for Lesson and Learning Studies, 9*(2), 153–166.

Kurakbayev, K. S. (2009). The role of reflection in initial teacher education of Kazakhstan. In V. E. Lepsky (Ed.), *Reflective processes and management: Conference proceedings of the 7th International Symposium* (pp. 127–130). Kogito Center.

Kusayinkyzy, A., & Doskeeva, G. J. (2020). Gender gap in STEM studies and ways to overcome them: A Kazakhstan case. *Central Asian Economic Review*, (3), 91–105.

Kutsyuruba, B. (2011). Potential for teacher collaboration in post-Soviet Ukraine. *International Journal of Educational Development, 31*(5), 547–557.

Makoelle, T. M., & Burmistrova, V. (2021). Teacher education and inclusive education in Kazakhstan. *International Journal of Inclusive Education*, 1–17.

McCagg, W. O., & Siegelbaum, L. (Eds.). (2017). *The disabled in the Soviet Union: Past and present, theory and practice* (Vol. 233). University of Pittsburgh Press.

Meirkulova, A., & Gelişli, Y. (2022). The social status of the teaching profession: Teachers' views in Turkey and Kazakhstan. *Hacettepe University Journal of Education, 37*(2), 175–190.

Nagibova, G. (2019). Professional development: The challenges of action research implementation in Kazakhstan. *International Academy Journal Web of Scholar, 2*(9 (39)), 17–24.

Niyozov, S. (2001). *Understanding teaching in post-Soviet, rural, mountainous Tajikistan: Case studies of teachers' life and work* (Doctoral dissertation). University of Toronto.

Nurmukhamed, D., Chegenbayeva, A., Nurumov, K., & Hernández-Torrano, D. (2025). Stress stemming from educational reforms as a key determinant of teacher's turnover intentions: Evidence from TALIS 2018. *Quality & Quantity*, 1–20.

Prisiazhniuk, D., Makoelle, T. M., & Zangieva, I. (2024). Teachers' attitudes towards inclusive education of children with special educational needs and disabilities in Central Asia. *Children and Youth Services Review, 160*, 107535.

Qanay, G., Anderson-Payne, E., Ball, S., Barnett, P., Kurmankulova, K., Mussarova, V., ... & Tanayeva, A. (2019). Developing teacher leadership in Kazakhstan. *International Journal of Teacher Leadership, 10*(1), 53–64.

Rizakhojayeva, G. A. (2020). Educational action research as a powerful vehicle for transformation. *Bulletin of the Karaganda University Pedagogy Series, 98*(2), 71–79.

Sarmurzin, Y. (2024). Enhancing teacher status in Kazakhstan: The role of school leaders and policy support. *International Journal of Educational Development, 110,* 103142.

Schulleri, P. (2020). Teacher mentoring: Experiences from international teacher mentors in Kazakhstan. *Asian Journal of Education and Training, 6*(2), 320–329.

Shamatov, D. A. (2013). Everyday realities of a young teacher in post-Soviet Kyrgyzstan: The case of a history teacher from a rural school. In *Politics, identity and education in Central Asia* (pp. 133–157). Routledge.

Shamatov, D., Ablaeva, M., & Tajik, M. A. (2023). Professional capabilities of rural schoolteachers in Kazakhstan. *Scientific and pedagogical journal "Bilim" of the National Academy of Education named after Y. Altynsarin, 106*(3), 55–65.

Silova, I., & Magno, C. (2004). Gender equity unmasked: Democracy, gender, and education in Central/Southeastern Europe and the Former Soviet Union. *Comparative Education Review, 48*(4), 417–442.

Smolentseva, A., Huisman, J., & Froumin, I. (2018). Transformation of higher education institutional landscape in post-Soviet countries: From Soviet model to where? In *25 years of transformations of higher education systems in post-Soviet countries: Reform and continuity* (pp. 1–43).

Syzdykbayeva, R. (2020). Exploring gender equality in STEM education and careers in Kazakhstan. *STEM Education for Girls and Women,* 189.

Tajik, M. A., Namyssova, G., Shamatov, D., Manan, S. A., Zhunussova, G., & Antwi, S. K. (2023). Navigating the potentials and barriers to EMI in the post-Soviet region: Insights from Kazakhstani university students and instructors. *International Journal of Multilingualism,* 1–21.

Tajik, M. A., Shamatov, D. A., & Fillipova, L. N. (2022). Teachers' quality in Kazakhstani rural schools. *Bulletin of the Kazakh National Women's Pedagogical University,* (3), 6–16.

Tastanbekova, K. (2020). Professional prestige, status, and esteem of educational occupation in Kazakhstan: Temporal, regional, and gender analysis of payroll data. *Journal of Eastern European and Central Asian Research (JEECAR), 7*(2), 175–190.

Valeeva, R. A., & Gafurov, I. R. (2017). Initial teacher education in Russia: Connecting theory, practice, and research. *European Journal of Teacher Education, 40*(3), 342–360.

Yakavets, N., Winter, L., Malone, K., Zhontayeva, Z., & Khamidulina, Z. (2023). Educational reform and teachers' agency in reconstructing pedagogical practices in Kazakhstan. *Journal of Educational Change, 24*(4), 727–757.

Yakavets, N., Bridges, D., & Shamatov, D. (2017). On constructs and the construction of teachers' professional knowledge in a post-Soviet context. *Journal of Education for Teaching, 43*(5), 594–615.

Index

access 3, 49, 69, 78, 80, 81, 122–125, 131–134, 143–146, 150, 159, 181, 188, 224, 270, 271, 274, 275, 284, 285, 288, 296, 298, 300, 305, 307, 308, 310, 311, 321
agency 3, 69, 74, 75, 78, 79, 85, 87, 88, 90, 124, 125, 131, 132, 164, 165, 195, 196, 199, 204, 256, 260, 270, 340, 345, 346, 353, 354, 356
assessment 6, 36–39, 47, 69–73, 76, 80, 82, 87, 88, 91, 102, 109, 112, 126, 131, 138, 140, 142, 143, 241, 244, 253, 258–260, 277–279, 282, 298, 314–334, 338
assessment education 6, 315–318, 330

Bologna 36, 48, 240

challenges 2–6, 20, 25, 33, 34, 56, 63, 68, 74, 82, 85, 88, 90, 91, 99–101, 115, 123, 128–130, 133, 137, 138, 141, 144, 145, 149, 150, 154, 156, 162, 175–177, 181, 187, 188, 192, 200, 206, 241, 242, 246, 248, 250, 254, 256, 259, 271–273, 275, 277, 280, 281, 283, 285, 287, 288, 295–300, 302, 304–307, 309–311, 325, 329–333, 338, 340, 341, 345, 346, 352–355
classroom practices 46, 57
collaborative action research 4, 173–175, 179, 180, 182–188
collaborative culture 59, 166, 195, 196, 200
COVID 19 6, 338, 339, 341, 344, 346
curriculum XI, 1–2, 4, 27, 36, 39, 60–63, 67–72, 74–90, 110, 112, 114, 116, 127–129, 138, 140–143, 147, 148, 155, 156, 163, 164, 191, 198, 200, 206–211, 241, 258, 270, 280, 285–287, 296, 297, 305, 306, 317, 318, 323, 325, 330–332, 342–345, 352, 355, 356
curriculum reform XI, 1, 2, 4, 60, 67–72, 74–77, 79–82, 84, 85, 87–90, 200, 317, 352, 356

depersonalization 218
distributed leadership 195, 196, 199

Early Childhood Education and Care 5, 6, 270, 272, 275, 279, 281–283, 288, 353, 355
ECEC Curriculum 279, 280, 286, 287
emotional exhaustion 218, 221
equity 3, 4, 122–125, 131–134, 197, 203–211, 356
experience of assessment 314, 331

feminism 206, 208, 210

gender 4, 5, 26, 33, 76, 105, 125, 146, 150, 203–211, 217, 352, 356
gender equality 150, 203–208, 210
gender equity 4, 203–211, 356
gender parity 204, 205

higher pedagogical education 8–14, 17–19, 22–24, 27–37, 39–42, 48, 49

inclusion 3, 11, 44, 48, 106, 122–134, 138, 176, 178, 183, 188, 245
inclusive education 3, 37, 43, 47, 56, 59, 122–132, 134, 178, 183, 185, 205, 282, 284, 285, 287, 288, 339, 352, 355
initial assessment training 315, 316, 318, 319
initial teacher education 5, 34, 37, 60, 61, 104, 105, 108, 109, 114, 115, 149, 150, 154, 238–243, 245, 247–250, 253, 254, 256–260, 287, 317–319, 351, 354, 355
innovation 4, 9, 62, 68, 73–75, 77, 80, 83, 88–90, 139, 155, 158, 195–198

Kazakhstan IX, XI, XII, 1–6, 9–29, 31–40, 43, 44, 46–49, 55, 56, 60–62, 64, 67–73, 76, 88, 90, 91, 98–100, 104–107, 109, 112–116, 122, 123, 125, 130–134, 137–150, 155, 159, 160–162, 164, 173, 177, 178, 180, 188, 191, 192, 197–200, 203, 204, 206, 209–211, 215, 216, 219, 233, 238–244, 247, 250, 255, 260, 270–285, 287–289, 295–300, 302, 304–306, 308–310, 314, 316–318, 320–331, 333, 334, 338–346, 350–356

362   INDEX

learning IX, 1–4, 6, 9, 24, 32, 36, 38, 39, 45–47, 49, 57, 63, 69, 70, 72, 77, 79, 80, 83, 84, 87–89, 103, 108, 109, 114, 122–129, 132–134, 139, 142, 143, 145, 147, 153–160, 162–166, 174–177, 180, 181, 184, 187, 188, 192, 194, 195, 197–200, 240, 242, 252–254, 257, 277, 278, 280, 287, 288, 296, 303, 306, 310, 315–319, 322–326, 328, 329, 332, 333, 338–346, 351, 352, 354, 356

mentor 5, 59, 114, 128, 132, 210, 239–245, 247–260, 303, 319, 322, 323, 328, 353, 356

mentoring 5, 59, 61, 63, 160, 200, 210, 238–240, 242–251, 253–260, 353, 354

mixed-methods 75, 77, 161, 299, 319, 320, 321, 333

modernization 198, 317, 356

novice teachers 2, 5, 57, 59, 63, 98–100, 103, 104, 107, 109, 110, 112–116, 239, 243, 303

organization 3, 4, 174–177, 193, 194, 245, 254

organisational 163, 174, 177, 193, 197, 243, 250

pandemic XI, 6, 106, 158, 315, 338–346, 356

pedagogy 9, 11, 20, 22–25, 27, 30, 31, 36, 38, 46, 47, 69, 83, 107, 109, 134, 143, 195, 197, 199, 206, 207, 210, 211, 320, 321, 328, 331, 333, 338, 340, 342, 345, 346, 351

practicum 5, 57, 124, 126–129, 131, 132, 238–243, 245–251, 253–260, 318, 319, 324, 330–334, 342, 353, 356

pre-school education 273, 285

pre-service teacher 5, 6, 55, 57, 59, 61, 108, 124, 126–128, 131–134, 188, 207, 208, 239, 314–324, 326–329, 331–334, 342, 353, 356

professional development 1, 3, 4, 37, 55, 61, 62, 77, 90, 98, 101, 124, 126–128, 130, 133, 150, 155–160, 162–164, 175–177, 192, 196, 197, 200, 270–272, 282–284, 287, 299, 303, 309, 310, 317, 318, 332, 342, 351, 352, 354

professional networks 3, 153, 155, 157–159, 161, 163, 164, 166, 251

quality IX, 6, 45, 46, 49, 58, 60, 62, 71, 75, 79, 81, 88, 91, 98, 122, 130, 138–141, 143, 144, 153, 154, 175, 194, 203, 208, 215, 218–220, 239, 246, 256, 257, 270, 271, 275–278, 282, 284, 285, 296, 298, 299, 303, 311, 318, 321, 325, 326, 343, 353, 355, 356

quality education 46, 79, 91, 122, 141, 144, 153, 203, 208, 284, 296, 298, 343, 355

reforms IX, XI, 1, 2, 4, 9, 12, 13, 15, 32, 33, 37–39, 43, 45, 47, 60, 61, 67–72, 74, 75, 76–85, 87–91, 99, 124, 137, 140, 147, 150, 159, 160, 191, 196, 198–200, 204, 209, 211, 246, 247, 250, 260, 270–275, 285, 288, 316, 317, 329, 330, 332, 346, 351, 352, 354, 356

rural education 6, 297, 298

rural school 2, 6, 60, 76, 80, 83–87, 91, 99, 145, 150, 159, 161, 296–300, 302–311, 353, 355

school leadership 59, 60, 191, 193, 194, 198, 260, 352

school management 163, 193, 194

self-efficacy 220, 228, 255, 341

social media 3, 153, 155, 157, 158, 161, 162, 164, 165, 256, 342

Sovietization 351

STEM education 3, 137–140, 143–146, 148, 150, 210, 352

STEM education curriculum 2, 70–72, 74–80, 206, 207,

STEM teaching 3, 89, 141, 149

teacher IX–XII, 1–6, 8–14, 18, 22, 23, 25, 29, 30, 32, 34, 35, 37, 39–46, 49, 55, 56, 59–62, 64, 104, 108, 115, 116, 122, 123, 126–134, 137, 138, 146–150, 154, 192, 200, 203–211, 239, 240, 250, 283, 287, 314–320, 330–334, 350–356

teacher agency 69, 74, 75, 78, 79, 85, 88, 124, 131, 132, 164, 165, 353, 354, 356

teacher attrition 5, 57, 60, 61, 63, 218, 310

teacher autonomy 85, 86, 102, 109, 198, 218

teacher burnout 5, 215–220, 226, 228, 229

teacher development 3, 4, 9, 63, 188, 197, 257, 352

teacher education IX–XII, 1–6, 8–14, 18, 22, 23, 25, 29, 30, 32, 34, 35, 37, 39–46, 49, 55, 56, 59–62, 64, 104, 108, 115, 116, 122, 123, 126–134, 137, 138, 146–150, 154, 192, 200, 203–211, 239, 240, 250, 283, 287, 314–320, 330–334, 350–356

INDEX

teacher knowledge 101, 107

teacher leadership 1, 4, 56, 191–200, 352

teacher preparation 1, 5, 6, 55, 57–59, 104, 114, 127, 128, 131, 132, 155, 188, 208, 209, 271, 272, 287, 288, 318, 342, 346, 351–353, 356

teacher professional learning 3, 9, 63, 153–156, 158, 192, 352

teacher professionalism 2, 89, 98–103, 107, 112–116, 157, 196

teacher recruitment 1, 2, 6, 55–60, 62–64, 149, 208

teacher retention 3, 57–63

teacher responsibility 102, 103, 108, 110–116, 129, 158, 164, 165, 175, 194, 199, 207, 246, 248, 249, 256, 305, 306, 310, 340, 352

teacher well–being 1, 5, 59–63, 343, 346, 352

teaching IX, XI, XII, 1–6, 9, 12–14, 16–23, 25, 27, 28, 30–31, 34, 36–39, 41–43, 46–48, 55–59, 61–63, 71, 76, 77, 80, 81, 84–87, 89, 98–105, 107–115, 122–124, 126–134, 139, 141–144, 148, 149, 153, 156–158, 166, 174–188, 192, 194, 195, 197, 200, 208, 217, 219–221, 239–242, 244, 247, 249–260, 282, 287, 304, 305, 309, 310, 315, 316–319, 322–334, 338–346, 353–356

technical and vocational education 4, 22, 173, 276, 281, 283, 316

understanding of assessment 6, 315, 316, 318–322, 324–334

values X, 2, 9, 39, 49, 72, 75, 79, 87, 89, 103, 110–113, 115, 116, 128, 132, 154, 158, 160, 164, 175, 178, 207, 240, 246, 250, 256, 257, 272, 280, 323, 325, 326–329, 331–334, 339, 351, 355